Man in Africa

Contributors

J. A. BARNES *Professor of Anthropology, Australian National University*

R. E. BRADBURY *Senior Lecturer in Anthropology, Centre of West African Studies, University of Birmingham*

ROBERT BRAIN *Lecturer in Social Anthropology, University College London*

DON R. BROTHWELL *Senior Scientific Officer, Sub-Department of Anthropology, British Museum (Natural History)*

MARY DOUGLAS *Reader in Social Anthropology, University College London*

ROSEMARY HARRIS *Lecturer in Social Anthropology, Sussex University*

ROBIN HORTON *Lecturer in Social Anthropology, Institute of African Studies, University of Ibadan, Nigeria*

CLIFFORD J. JOLLY *Assistant Professor of Physical Anthropology, New York University*

PHYLLIS M. KABERRY *Reader in Anthropology, University College London*

I. M. LEWIS *Reader in Anthropology, University College London*

JACQUES MAQUET *Director of Studies, l'École Pratique des Hautes Études, Paris*

JOHN MIDDLETON *Professor of Anthropology, New York University*

PETER MORTON-WILLIAMS *Lecturer in Social Anthropology, University College London*

CLARA ODUGBESAN *Acting Curator, Nigerian Museum, Lagos*

MICHAEL ONWUEJEOGWU *Research Associate, Institute of African Studies, University of Ibadan*

FARNHAM REHFISCH *Professor of Anthropology, University of Khartoum*

M. G. SMITH *Professor of Anthropology, African Studies Program, University of California, Los Angeles*

VICTOR W. TURNER *Professor of Anthropology, Cornell University*

PETER J. UCKO *Lecturer in Anthropology, University College London*

JAN VANSINA *Professor of Anthropology, University of Wisconsin*

DARYLL FORDE

Man in Africa

EDITED BY

Mary Douglas and
Phyllis M. Kaberry

TAVISTOCK PUBLICATIONS

London · New York · Sydney · Toronto · Wellington

First published in 1969
By Tavistock Publications Limited
11 New Fetter Lane, London E.C. 4
Printed in Great Britain
in 11 pt Bell, 1 pt. leaded
by T. & A. Constable, Ltd.
Edinburgh

SBN 422 71900 5

Distributed in the U.S.A.
by Barnes & Noble, Inc.

Essays affectionately dedicated
to DARYLL FORDE in gratitude for
all he has given us

Contents

Contents

Illustrations

2 A 'sphingia' on the Palestrina mosaic of the second century A.D.

3-5 Photographs and drawings of gelada baboons (*Theropithecus gelada*), showing typical sexual skin of the female, upstanding nose, conspicuous maxillary fossae, and stance with tail carried in line with the body

Africa's Contribution to Palaeopathology (Plates I-II, Figure 1) *following page* 340

I Basal view of an early Nubian skull, showing massive bone destruction resulting from a malignant neoplasm. Changes at the bone margin show clearly that the process was certainly *pre-mortem*. British Museum (Natural History)

IIa Lateral aspect of part of the upper dental arch of the Upper Pleistocene Rhodesian skull. Caries and apical abscesses (arrowed) can be seen, as well as alveolar recession

IIb Part of the jaw of *Telanthropus capensis*, showing a caries cavity on the mesial surface of the lower right second molar. Photograph by courtesy of Dr A. J. Clement

FIGURE

I Lateral and frontal views of part of the mummy of a priest of Ammon. Spinal curvature and psoas abscess are indicated by arrows. Drawings by Rosemary Powers

339

Preface

A twenty-first anniversary is a time for celebration. Thus, when we realized that Daryll Forde had been head of the Department of Anthropology at University College London for that period, we decided to mark it by a collection of essays. We chose to limit the theme to Africa because there he has most actively developed research. The contributors have been former students and also past and present members of staff in this department.

First of all we should like to thank Katharine Attwood, who resigned in July 1966 after twenty-one years as Daryll Forde's Departmental Assistant. She compiled the bibliography of his publications. We are indebted to Olga Wolfe, Secretary of the International African Institute, who kindly provided us with details of his work at the Institute. We also thank Patricia Blair, who took Katharine Attwood's place as secretary and has most devotedly re-typed the manuscripts, and Patricia Aylott, departmental technician, who has made so many maps for members of staff and who has produced the map of Africa. In the preparation of the manuscripts for publication we are grateful for the assistance given by the members of the editorial committee: Professor Barnicot, Dr Ucko, Dr Morton-Williams, and Dr Lewis, who suggested the title of the book.

The contributors were invited to choose their own topics and we thank them for their cordial co-operation. We particularly appreciate the originality of the approaches they have chosen. Some have offered new themes, for instance, Robert Brain on friendship, and Farnham Rehfisch on dreams as instruments of change. Others have opened up old issues with new insight. Inevitably there is a bias towards West Africa, the area in which Daryll Forde has worked longest, but other regions are well represented, as the map shows (see p. xxvii).

The convenient headings under which the essays have been grouped do not quite show their range. In the *Political Economy* section, Robert Bradbury gives an analysis of the Benin political system in terms of Weber's ideal types – gerontocracy and patrimonialism. The gerontocratic principle derives from the archaic village social order, the patrimonial from the kingship. Three other essays in this section are all novel exercises in the analysis of social change. Robin Horton asks what kind of community New Calabar was before it embarked on the Atlantic Trade. Why did it make its particular response, rather than develop like Old Calabar or Bonny? Assuming that New Calabar started out with the same organization and culture as now exist among its village neighbours, he proceeds to consider what the study of these villages can tell us about the hidden origins of New Calabar. Here follows a subtle analysis of social process. Peter Morton-Williams's essay illustrates another meeting of history and anthropology. He asks how much the development of West African kingdoms was stimulated by trade along the east-west routes as well as by the more usually emphasized north-south routes and Atlantic Trade. His strongly ecological approach is matched by Ioan Lewis's analysis of differences in the Somali political scene. When the Somali migrated to fertile lands in the south and gave up nomadism for agriculture, their social structure changed definably. Other essays also deal with change: for example, in the *Kinship* section, Mary Douglas asks whether matrilineal descent will survive in modern Africa – and answers, yes.

Anthropologists rarely try to derive insights from African society to apply to Europe's problems, but the study of law in action in African communities can throw light on the difficulties that beset the English legal system. John Barnes tries to correct the tendency to see law as a specialized autonomous system insulated from the pressures of daily life. He uses African experience to show that law is always embedded in the political process.

There are other ways in which knowledge of Africa helps to solve peculiarly European puzzles – in medicine, in palaeopathology, and in the classics, for example. There is great interest now in discovering what were the diseases that afflicted our ancient forebears. Don Brothwell describes how new African archaeological material throws light on palaeopathology. The sphinx-monkey is mentioned in the works of the Greek and Roman authors; sometimes it is associated with the Sphinx of myth and art, but it has not been identified. Clifford Jolly and

Peter Ucko, in a highly compressed work of detection, re-examine the evidence. They suggest that the mysterious animal may have been none other than the gelada baboon and that the same species could well have given rise to the mythology of the Sphinx.

Several of the essays take up problems of classification. Jacques Maquet considers how African cultures can be classified. Phyllis Kaberry asks whether anthropologists' categories for studying incest should not be revised. Rosemary Harris poses the problem whether a unilineal descent system should be classed as such when it is only implicitly, and not overtly, recognized by the people themselves as a principle of organization. Michael Smith refines the analysis of segmentary lineage systems.

The feminine principle in culture comes in for attention from several angles. Clara Odugbesan discusses femininity in art; John Middleton writes of the role of post-menopausal women as diviners; and Michael Onwuejeogwu of *Bori* spirits which possess women more readily than men and throw them into a state of trance.

An entirely new approach to poison ordeal for convicting witches is offered by Jan Vansina. This widespread institution, which disappeared before it could be studied and fully described, he presents as a central act of Bushong religion, a *rite de passage*, an affirmation of religious truth. There is a vast area of Central Africa in which religious worship does not take the form of sacrifice. Jan Vansina sees in the ritual of the Bushong poison ordeal something analogous to a sacrificial act, a suggestion with radical implications for other religious studies. In Victor Turner's essay, there is a cross-cultural comparison of religion. He finds that the exegetical approach which was so richly revealing for Ndembu symbolism can also be used in distant Gisu rituals.

Our choice of Michael Smith to write the Foreword needs no justification. Of all Daryll Forde's students from this College he is one of the most distinguished, and we thank him for the sensitive picture he has given us of Daryll Forde, both as a teacher and as a scholar.

M. D. and P. M. K.

M. G. Smith

Foreword

This volume of essays is dedicated to Professor Daryll Forde by some of his colleagues and former students of the Department of Anthropology, University College London, which he has led and developed since 1945. The editors and contributors represent a far larger body of anthropologists and Africanists who have benefited in many different ways during this period from Professor Forde's generous encouragement, assistance, and advice, and who have drawn inspiration from his friendship, teaching, and work. To limit the size and range of this votive offering it was necessary therefore to restrict its scope to anthropological studies of African materials, since these represent the major focus of his activities over the past three decades.

To anyone interested in African affairs, Professor Forde will be known as the Administrative Director of the International African Institute (IAI) and the editor of its quarterly journal, *Africa*. To human geographers, economists, and archaeologists[1] his name will probably recall different contributions. (His first degree was a B.A. Honours in Geography in 1922.) However, for about forty years he has practised social anthropology with a range of interests and activities that is quite unusual. His comprehensive conceptions of the role of social anthropology and of its relations to other disciplines and to processes of social development are shown by his activities as Director of IAI and by his anthropological work, both before and after moving to London. Perhaps we may best illustrate this broad and creative approach to social anthropology by a brief review of his career at the IAI and as a social anthropologist.

When Daryll Forde succeeded Sir Reginald Coupland in 1944 as Director of the IAI, and editor of *Africa*, the future of both was in jeopardy. Under pressure of war, the Institute and its journal had been forced to curtail their activities. The Institute's international character had been virtually destroyed by the alignments of war, and its survival as an independent agency for international communication and study of African problems was extremely uncertain; routine decisions were often confounded by uncertainties of the changing situation. For the new Director, on whose vision and energies the future of the entire operation depended, these early days must often have ended in nightmare. Now, after two decades of unparalleled achievement and growth in its services, despite the recent establishment of several specialized agencies and journals, the Institute remains the major international body concerned equally with all dimensions of African affairs and with the integrated development of African studies in documentation, teaching, and research. This remarkable record of sustained expansion and diversification in the Institute's services since 1944 is largely due to its Director's vision, judgement, and energy. While recent developments in African studies owe a great deal to the leadership of the IAI, the Institute itself owes much to him, especially for identifying emergent needs and organizing apppropriate academic responses in this rapidly changing field of study. Such developments as *African Abstracts*, the *Handbook of African Languages*, the *Ethnographic Survey of Africa*, the series of international seminars on African topics, the Institute's bibliographical work, the recruitment of distinguished Africans to its executive, and the restoration of links with European scholars and organizations, are merely obvious indices of the Institute's remarkable revival and growth. In addition, it has continued to support African field researches in several disciplines. Recently, for the first time, the Institute has also been able to make modest contributions from its own funds towards African field researches.

From this record it might seem that the administrative direction of the Institute, coupled with editorial responsibilities for *Africa*, would keep an active man busy; however, immediately on arriving at the Institute, Forde began to undertake new tasks. In 1944 he revived a plan prepared in 1937 for an Ethnographic Survey of indigenous African societies. In 1945, having secured support for the first five years of this scheme from the Colonial Social Science Research Council, he initiated the programme as its Director and general organizer. Two years later, just before the first volume of this Ethnographic Survey was due to appear, the Institute could expect financial support from French and Belgian sources. Since 1950 some 57 volumes of this Survey have been published and several have been reprinted. The work continues. In assessing this *Survey* programme, its Director's responsibilities for securing appropriate financial and scholarly support were perhaps more onerous than his strictly editorial tasks; however, he was not content to leave entirely to others the tedious tasks of sifting and collating the scattered ethnographic materials, but characteristically undertook these himself for those Nigerian peoples with whom he was familiar. Thus in 1950, with Mr G. I. Jones of Cambridge, he prepared the Survey volume on the Ibo and Ibibio; in 1951 he summarized the Yoruba ethnography and in 1955 he did likewise for Nupe. By these contributions he helped to set the standards of presentation and documentation which the Survey has maintained under his editorship.

In 1945 Forde also prepared plans for a classified card catalogue of publications in African ethnology, sociology, linguistics, and related subjects, to be included in the Institute's routine programme under a full-time librarian paid from the Institute's funds. This important innovation made it possible to prepare quarterly summaries of articles on African subjects, a development which gave rise to *African Abstracts*, first published in 1950 under his editorship with support from UNESCO. This quarterly has proved of such value to Africanists that recently it has been necessary to arrange publication of separate French and English versions, beginning in 1967. Other fruits of these early bibliographical arrangements include the Institute's various published bibliographies on African topics and regions, based on its classified catalogue. In 1966 also, the 'current bibliography' contained in each issue of *Africa* was further developed and refined. These bibliographical services now rank among the Institute's most important routine contributions to African studies.

Between 1947 and 1950, with UNESCO support, the late Professor A. R. Radcliffe-Brown and Daryll Forde together edited the celebrated symposium on *African Systems of Kinship and Marriage*. To complement this comparative sociological treatment of African kinship systems, on behalf of the Institute, and in association with the International Missionary Council,

B   xvii

Forde initiated a documentary survey of the legal, sociological, and mission literature on African marriage and family life, with support from the Carnegie Foundation. At this period, following the report of an IAI Committee on African linguistics and with financial support from the British Government, he organized the Institute's programme of linguistic field research in the Northern Bantu borderland from the Cameroons to Kenya. These field researches were incorporated in the *Handbook of African Languages*, a series of which the first volumes appeared in 1952, the last in 1966. In scope and quality this linguistic survey worthily matches the Ethnographic Survey.

In 1951, with UNESCO support, Forde also undertook to assemble and edit the collection of studies of traditional African cosmologies and value systems published in 1954 as *African Worlds*. With *African Political Systems* and *African Systems of Kinship and Marriage*, this symposium has been reprinted several times in various languages. Together these three collections rank as classics in modern social anthropology and as essential readings for Africanists of any discipline.

In 1951 Forde secured UNESCO's financial support for an interdisciplinary study of African urbanization and industrialization under the aegis of the IAI. Following preliminary researches, an intensive interdisciplinary field study of Stanleyville was conducted in 1951-3, the preliminary results being discussed at a working conference in Abidjan, Ivory Coast, in the following year. The volume of reports and studies yielded by this project was published by UNESCO in French and English in 1956, with an introductory survey of the relevant literature by Forde. During these years, on behalf of the Institute, he was also responsible for coordinating support for a study of pastoral Fulani in former French and British territories of the Central and Western Sudan.

His experience of the working conference at Abidjan in 1954 convinced Forde of the great advantages of periodic meetings between scholars engaged in analysis or field studies of related problems in different African milieux. In 1956 the Institute accordingly sought funds to support such a series of working seminars: and, with a grant from the Ford Foundation in 1957, renewed in 1962, eight international seminars were held at various African university towns, beginning at Kampala in

January 1959. Six volumes of these seminar proceedings have already appeared; their cumulative importance is largely due to their concentration on central features of the changing African situation and important issues of African development, as their titles indicate (Southall 1961; Biebuyck 1963; Vansina, Mauny & Thomas 1964; Fortes & Dieterlen 1965; Lewis 1966; Lloyd 1966; Baeta 1968; Gluckman, in press). These volumes afford excellent evidence of the phenomenal growth of African studies in range, specificity, and variety of research problems and approaches since the first IAI symposia on African politics, kinship, and cosmologies appeared.

Again, in April 1964 with support from the Ford Foundation, Forde organized a major international meeting of Africanists of all disciplines and many countries, on behalf of the Institute, to review current programmes of teaching and research on African subjects, to coordinate programmes, to identify current and foreseeable needs, and to devise the appropriate responses to them. This meeting, held at Ibadan and reported fully in *Africa* (1965, Vol. 35, No. 1), expresses Forde's interest in the unsatisfied or emergent needs of African scholarship and his concern to stimulate the appropriate international action to meet them. These activities of Daryll Forde as Director of the IAI illustrate his conception of the scope and role of social anthropology and its contributions to the study and development of African societies.

Despite this record of creative scholarship and administration at the IAI, throughout these years Forde was primarily engaged in creating and directing a vigorous new Department of Anthropology at University College London. Few of us who then attended the Department could have guessed how smoothly and thoroughly he had transformed its orientation on assuming its Chair of Anthropology in 1945. As a teacher, Forde presented us with the full range of contemporary approaches in social and cultural anthropology, combining with Malinowski's functionalism the comparative approach and analytic concepts of Radcliffe-Brown, Robert Lowie's critical temper and historical perspective, and Kroeber's imaginative breadth, erudition, and devotion to detail. Setting all these perspectives in their appropriate intellectual contexts, he showed us their strengths and limitations, and emphasized the relevance of ecology, technology, demography, and history to social and cultural analyses.

He taught also the interconnection of these dimensions of social life and inquiry, the central significance of the negative case, the scientific value of measurement and carefully controlled comparison, the virtues and limitations of hypotheses and models, the primacy of objective data and criteria of relevance, the salience of cultural assumptions and values in ordered social life, and the dependence of social and cultural studies on new perspectives, methods, and problems for continued vitality. He taught these and many other lessons of equal value by example as well as exposition, and presented us with a personal model of enthusiastic and disinterested devotion to social anthropology, encouraging us by his modesty, integrity, exuberance, and warmth. In discussion, his tolerance and interest assured lively exchanges to which even retiring students contributed freely. Though he discouraged discipleship, we all recognized the erudition and analytic powers to which Maurice Freedman (1963: 16) alludes, in noting how 'we are all characteristically astonished when, as is outstandingly the case with Professor Forde, we find a man with encyclopaedic knowledge and the mental stamina to contain the subject as a whole under one skull'. This comprehensive view of anthropology and commitment towards it Daryll Forde may have owed to his great teachers at Berkeley, Robert Lowie and Alfred Kroeber; for some of his students, this conception, which is illustrated by his academic work and at the IAI, represented a major focus of his teaching. To trace the development of this perspective, we need briefly to review his anthropological career.

On completing his doctorate in prehistoric archaeology, Daryll Forde was awarded a Commonwealth Fellowship in Anthropology for 1928-30, tenable at the University of California, Berkeley, where Kroeber and Lowie then taught. While holding this Fellowship, he studied the Hopi and Yuma of the south-western United States. Despite earlier interests in human geography, it was probably the contrasting societies and cultures of these peoples that directed his interests to the general problem of relations between human ecology and society. On completing his Hopi and Yuma ethnographies, he undertook an extensive comparative analysis of the relations between environment, ecology, and social organization based on systematic reviews of relevant literature on societies selected to represent all the major ethnographic and ethnological zones. This work, *Habitat, Economy and Society* (1934), ranks high as a classic demonstration of comparative method in social anthropology, and as a basic treatise on human geography. Considering its range and quality, the study was completed with remarkable speed, following on Daryll Forde's return to Britain in 1930 on appointment as Gregynog Professor of Geography and Anthropology at the University College of Wales, Aberystwyth, in his twenty-eighth year.

Shortly after completing this fundamental work, Forde visited the Yakö of South-eastern Nigeria in 1935 on a Leverhulme Fellowship for six months. There he carried out pioneer quantitative field studies of relations between ecological, demographic, and institutional conditions of a traditional society in processes of change. This inquiry demonstrated the importance and feasibility of combining statistical and geographical techniques in field studies of social ecology and economy (Forde 1937a, 1946). Though primarily concerned on this visit with population dynamics and ecology, he also studied Yakö patterns of trading and local government, their double unilineal descent, corporate associations, and moral and ritual life.

Returning to Aberystwyth, he analysed these data for publication (Forde 1937b, 1938, 1939a, 1939b); and revisited Umor in 1939 on another Leverhulme Fellowship for three months to investigate Yakö systems of family and marriage. On this occasion also he employed statistical procedures to quantify, support, and refine his analysis of institutional conditions. On his return to Britain he received the Wellcome Medal for anthropological research from the Royal Anthropological Institute. In the following year, despite emergencies of war and increased duties, he published the monograph on Yakö family life which perhaps best illustrates his emphasis on the need for quantitative methods in social anthropology 'to determine the actual behaviour involved . . . and the relation of such behaviour to native ideals' (Forde 1941: 2). His earlier studies of social ecology had demonstrated the value of measurement applied to well-defined features and conditions of the social milieu. Besides demography, land use, crop yields, and other economic data, he had already used quantitative data to study lineage organization. In his analysis of Yakö marriage and family life, he showed also how meaningful indices of bridewealth, divorce, widowhood, marital ages, and individual case histories could illuminate and enrich qualitative analyses of structural norms and procedures, their variations and correlates.

From these two brief visits, Forde also developed the first detailed account of double unilineal descent in an African society, and the first systematic analysis of a traditional polity as complex as the Yakö. Even before the development of formal models of segmentary lineage systems, his examination of Yakö patrilineages furnished the first specific study of lineage segmentation, accretion, and organization. This work remains a model of its kind.

As these investigations of Yakö ecological, demographic, and structural conditions indicate, by 1943 Forde had developed his own distinctive approach to social anthropological field studies of traditional societies. This differed from the then dominant methods of Malinowski and Radcliffe-Brown primarily in emphasizing the quantitative investigation of institutional variability and material conditions of social organization, and in the demand that analyses should relate social systems firmly to their specific ecological, historical, and demographic contexts. These new directions represented a systematic development of perspectives latent in his earlier studies of the Yuma and Hopi, and explicit in his comparative work on *Habitat, Economy and Society*.

In Nigeria, among the Yakö, Forde had also found his final calling in the service of African studies, a task which could only be pursued at the personal cost of further opportunities for fieldwork or theoretical study of the ecological aspects of social organization. Though briefly delayed by a term at Oxford (1943-4), the move to London was inevitable on his appointment as Director of the IAI.

On arriving at University College London in 1945, Professor Forde was already engaged on his comparative study of indigenous Nigerian economies in their traditional and changing contexts (Forde & Scott 1946). He somehow also managed a brief spell of fieldwork in Senegal and Gambia that year; and from 1947 to 1949, in addition to his duties at University College and the IAI, he served as President of the Royal Anthropological Institute. In 1947 also he acted as President of

Section H of the British Association for the Advancement of Science. Characteristically, Daryll Forde devoted his Presidential addresses to Section H of the British Association in 1947 and to the Royal Anthropological Institute in 1948 to the unity of anthropological studies and the multi-determinate character of social and cultural facts (1947, 1948). In essence, he then appealed for systematic comparative studies of structural similarities and uniformities which gave appropriate attention to their multi-dimensional qualities and requisites. Social anthropologists have yet to recognize fully the wisdom of these recommendations. At that date the currents of opinion and interest ran in other directions.

As his various duties allowed or required, Daryll Forde visited Europe, Africa, and the United States. In 1949 he rejoined his friends and teachers at Berkeley. In 1953 he visited Yale. On both occasions he advised these anthropological departments on their programmes of African studies. In 1956 he returned once more to Berkeley. In 1963 he visited Harvard, Philadelphia, and other universities in the USA. These longer visits and several shorter ones have enabled him to maintain his contacts with American anthropologists and Africanists, and thus to keep in direct touch with the changing currents and interests of American intellectual life. Such visits were among the chief means by which senior British anthropologists improved their working relations with American colleagues during this period; and their value to the Department of Anthropology at University College and to the IAI is evident.

Meanwhile, Forde's academic obligations continued to grow. In 1956 he received the Rivers Memorial Medal of the Royal Anthropological Institute, and he edited the diary of Antera Duke of Calabar (Forde 1956). In 1958 he analysed Yakö cosmological beliefs in his Frazer lecture. Since then he has written mainly on Yakö religion and ritual, although periodically employing other data to examine general questions of lineage or political theory, as for example in his Simon and Munro Lectures at Manchester and Edinburgh in 1960 and 1961 (Forde 1961, 1962), and in his contribution to the volume dedicated to the late Mrs Brenda Seligman by the Royal Anthropological Institute (Forde 1963).

In 1964, after repeated requests from many colleagues, including the present writer, Forde published an integrated collection of his essays on the Yakö. This book (*Yakö Studies*) is a testimony to his unrivalled gifts as a fieldworker, and indicates the regrettable loss to field studies in social anthropology occasioned by his devotion to the promotion and organization of African studies. These disciplinary losses, however, have in large measure been compensated for by his brilliant editorial and organizing activities. In 1966, with Phyllis Kaberry, he edited another collection of studies on *West African Kingdoms in the Nineteenth Century* (1967); and in that year he was elected a Fellow of the British Academy.

Such a remarkable record of creative work in so many different branches of anthropology and in the service of African studies needs no encomium. In this volume we simply wish to honour a man who has employed his varied talents selflessly and without pause for many years in the service both of scholarship and humanity; one who has never failed to give generously of his ideas, experience, energy, and time to all who have had the fortune to work with him in any capacity.

EDITORIAL NOTE

1. It is worth recording that Professor Forde's very early published works on megaliths (1929, 1930) presented a new view of the archaeological evidence that has become classic, and remains the basis of current archaeological interpretations (see Daniel 1963: 76-9).

REFERENCES

BAETA, C. G. 1968. *Christianity in Tropical Africa.* London: Oxford University Press for the International African Institute.

BIEBUYCK, D. (ed.) 1963. *African Agrarian Systems.* London: Oxford University Press for the International African Institute.

DANIEL, G. 1963. *The Megalithic Builders of Western Europe.* London: Hutchinson.

FORDE, D. 1929. The Megalithic Culture Sequence in Iberia. *Annals of Archaeology and Anthropology,* 16 (3-4).

— 1930. The Early Cultures of Atlantic Europe. *American Anthropologist,* 32: 19-100.

— 1934. *Habitat, Economy and Society*. London: Methuen.

— 1937a. Land and Labour in a Cross River Village, Southern Nigeria. *Geographical Journal*, **90**.

— 1937b. Social Change in a West African Village Community. *Man*, **37**: 8.

— 1938. Fission and Accretion in the Patrilineal Clans of a Semi-Bantu Community in Southern Nigeria. *Journal of the Royal Anthropological Institute*, **68**: 311-88.

— 1939a. Government in Umor. *Africa*, **12** (2): 126-62.

— 1939b. Kinship in Umor: Double Unilateral Organization in a Semi-Bantu Society. *American Anthropologist*, **41**: 4.

— 1941. *Marriage and the Family among the Yakö in South-Eastern Nigeria*. London School of Economics Monographs on Social Anthropology, No. 5. (Second Edition, London: Lund Humphries for the International African Institute, 1951.)

— & SCOTT, R. 1946. *The Native Economies of Nigeria*, pp. 44-64. London: Faber.

— 1947. The Anthropological Approach in Social Science. *Advancement of Science*, **4** (15): 213-24.

— 1948. The Integration of Anthropological Studies. *Journal of the Royal Anthropological Institute*, **78**.

— (ed.) 1956. *Efik Traders of Old Calabar*. London: Oxford University Press for the International African Institute.

— 1961. The Governmental Roles of Associations among the Yakö. *Africa*, **31** (4): 309-23.

— 1962. Death and Succession: An Analysis of Yakö Mortuary Ceremonial. In M. Gluckman (ed.), *Essays on the Ritual of Social Relations*. Manchester: Manchester University Press.

— 1963. Unilineal Fact or Fiction: An Analysis of the Composition of Kin Groups among the Yakö. In I. Schapera (ed.), *Studies in Kinship and Marriage, Dedicated to Brenda Z. Seligman on her 80th Birthday*. London: Royal Anthropological Institute, Occasional Paper No. 16.

— 1964. *Yakö Studies*. London: Oxford University Press for the International African Institute.

— & KABERRY, P. M. (eds.) 1967. *West African Kingdoms in the Nineteenth Century*. London: Oxford University Press for the International African Institute.

FORTES, M. & DIETERLEN, G. (eds.) 1965. *African Systems of Thought*. London: Oxford University Press for the International African Institute.

FREEDMAN, M. 1963. A Chinese Phase in Social Anthropology. *British Journal of Sociology*, **14** (1): 16.

GLUCKMAN, M. (ed.) in press. *Ideas and Procedures in African Customary Law*. London: Oxford University Press for the International African Institute.

LEWIS, I. M. (ed.) 1966. *Islam in Tropical Africa*. London: Oxford University Press for the International African Institute.

LLOYD, P. (ed.) 1966. *The New Elites of Tropical Africa*. London: Oxford University Press for the International African Institute.

SOUTHALL, A. (ed.) 1961. *Social Change in Modern Africa*. London: Oxford University Press for the International African Institute.

VANSINA, J., MAUNY, R. & THOMAS, L. V. (eds.) 1964. *The Historian in Tropical Africa*. London: Oxford University Press for the International African Institute.

Africa: Location of Peoples

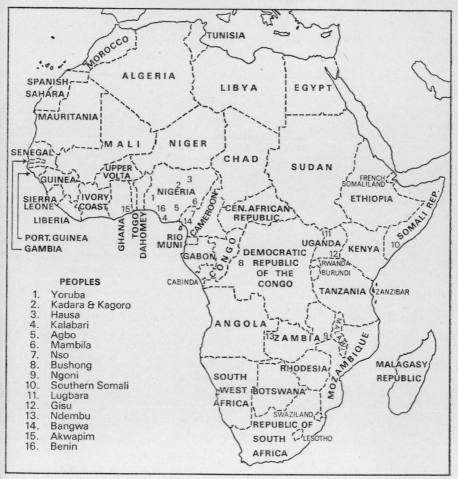

PEOPLES

1. Yoruba
2. Kadara & Kagoro
3. Hausa
4. Kalabari
5. Agbo
6. Mambila
7. Nso
8. Bushong
9. Ngoni
10. Southern Somali
11. Lugbara
12. Gisu
13. Ndembu
14. Bangwa
15. Akwapim
16. Benin

PART I

General

Jacques Maquet

The Cultural Units of Africa

A Classificatory Problem

Among Daryll Forde's contributions to the advancement of anthropological knowledge, the publication of the *Ethnographic Survey of Africa* under his initiative and editorial responsibility is an outstanding achievement. Undertaken shortly after the second world war, the first volumes appeared in 1950; about fifteen years later, the series was not far from its sixtieth volume. Africanists know that any anthropological research begins with the *Survey* (when, of course, there is a book available on the people they wish to study): it is needless to insist further on the utility of that remarkable tool which is in process of completion.

I

When, back in the late forties, Daryll Forde and his collaborators decided to make a survey of all ethnographic information 'based on original field studies, as well as on published sources', and concerning social and cultural phenomena of traditional Africa, they were confronted with the preliminary problem of the units of division and classification of these phenomena. Previous anthropologists had studied the African socio-cultural reality by using different frames of reference: some were exclusively interested in a certain aspect (e.g. religious beliefs, matrimonial institutions, crafts); others considered Africa as a whole (Frobenius, for instance); others attempted to reconstruct the cultural history of the continent (such as Baumann and Westermann); others had presented a division of the continent into several culture areas (Herskovits, for instance); but most of

3

them restricted their research to a region, a society, or a linguistic area. The ethnographic literature on Africa was mainly made up of monographs devoted to such particular subjects.

The main unit studied by anthropologists was, in fact, a society, in the sense of a global society (to use Georges Gurvitch's expression), identified by a name, and whose social heritage constitutes a culture, usually well integrated. Since 1922, the year Malinowski's *Argonauts of the Western Pacific* and Radcliffe-Brown's *Andaman Islanders* were published, the success of functionalism had been so complete that a decade later it was taken for granted that an ethnographic research had to study the culture of a global society.

Two other factors contributed to that trend. Ethnography more than any other social science has been made by nonprofessionals: missionaries, officers of the colonial administrations, settlers. These amateurs, because of their main activities, usually spent several years in the same place and came to know a single society very well. It is the case for Roscoe who, in spite of the fact that he became in his middle age a trained anthropologist, remained a one-kingdom ethnographer. What he has written on the Baganda is definitely better than his books on other interlacustrine societies. There are many publications devoted to a single society because it was the only one known by the person who happened to be there and to be interested in it. Another factor was the importance accorded by the colonial authorities to the traditional chiefs, and consequently to the groups they represented. During the colonial period, Africans had no alternative to identification with their former traditional societies, though the latter were denied essential characteristics of a global society: political autonomy and self-government. The only possible alternative was identification with the colonial territory, and obviously Africans did not feel, and were not encouraged to feel, that a colony was theirs.

For any reason whatever, most of African ethnographic literature, and the best of it, has taken as its frame of study the culture of a group of men whose complementary activities are organized in such a way as to make possible individual and collective survival and development. The members of such groups are conscious of what is common among them and makes them different from others.

4

The Cultural Units of Africa

Global societies were numerous in traditional Africa. In his
Africa: Its Peoples and Their Culture History (1959), Murdock
enumerates about eight hundred and fifty of them. If the *Survey*
had to devote one separate study to each of them, the enterprise
would have been hopeless.

II

Considering the impressive series of the *Survey*, we may infer
that the editorial policy was to keep global societies as separate
units but to gather several of them together and to deal with
them as a whole. In the titles, the term *society* and the term
culture are not used: the groups considered are referred to as
peoples (in French, *populations*, and in the monographs written
by Belgians, *peuplades*), as *tribes* and as *kingdoms*, but, whenever
possible, the proper name was chosen: the Tiv, the Wolof, les
Dogon, les Senoufo, les Bira, etc.

Criteria according to which several peoples are assembled in a
single monograph are varied. A common origin has been considered the crucial factor of classification in a few cases (for
instance, *The Akan and Ga-Adangme Peoples*, by Madeline
Manoukian; *Le Groupe dit Pahouin: Fang, Boulou, Beti*, by
Pierre Alexandre and J. Binet; *The Western Lacustrine Bantu* by
Brian Taylor). In many more cases, a common language has been
considered the principle of relatedness (*The Yoruba-speaking
Peoples of South-Western Nigeria*, by Daryll Forde; *The Swahili-
speaking Peoples of Zanzibar and the East African Coast*, by
A. H. J. Prins). Geographical proximity on a same territory is
another principle often used (*The Peoples of the Plateau Area of
Northern Nigeria*, by Harold D. Gunn; *Les Populations du Nord-
Togo*, by J.-C. Froehlich, P. Alexandre, and R. Cornevin). Other
terms are used which refer to racial groupings (*The Nilotes*, by
Audrey Butt), to religion (*Pagan Peoples of the Central Area of
Northern Nigeria*, by Harold D. Gunn); *Les Populations paiennes
du Nord Cameroun et de l'Adamaoua*, by B. Lembezat), to a
system of descent (*The Matrilineal Peoples of Eastern Tanzania*,
by T. O. Beidelman). The latter terms cannot be said to be
criteria; obviously they have been chosen only because they
commonly designate a certain group of peoples considered by
the editor as related.

Volumes are distributed into seven broad categories which are definitely geographical: Western Africa, North-Eastern Africa, East Central Africa, West Central Africa, Congo, Southern Africa, Madagascar. That division bears witness to the colonial times: Central Africa refers to the region the Colonial Office designated by that term; Congo has a place of its own because Belgian anthropologists are responsible for the writing of the monographs devoted to the peoples of the former Belgian Congo.

The aim of the *Survey* is to offer an easily accessible summary of what is known on traditional African societies. As several of them had to be treated together, the simple criteria of common historical origin, common language, and common habitat have been used whenever possible, to found the unity of a monograph. When it was imposssible, the *Survey* has just followed the clues of the ordinary language: for example, the neighbouring peoples of the Cameroons, Fali and other groups are designated by the blanket name of *Kirdi*, which means *pagan*; the *Survey* has simply picked up the unit drawn by the local linguistic customs. The classification of the *Survey* is a pragmatic device, very well adapted to its purpose; it does not pretend to be based on theoretical foundations.

The same may be said about the relationship existing between the peoples treated together: they have something in common but what it is remains vague or rather is not identical in each case. It is very well expressed by the words *and related peoples* and *et les peuplades apparentées* which appear sometimes in the titles (e.g. *Bemba and Related Peoples, The Azande and Related Peoples, Les Bali et les peuplades apparentées*). A certain relatedness is asserted, nothing more.

III

This is not a criticism of the solution given by the editor of the *Survey* to the problem of the cultural units larger than global cultures. We just want to point out the inevitability of a problem so often overlooked because of the implicit functionalist assumption that the culture of a society is an integrated whole to be studied as if it were an autonomous unit. When theories of evolutionism and diffusionism prevailed in the second half of the nineteenth century and the first two decades of the twentieth, anthropological researches were rarely limited to a single society: cultural phenomena were considered across wide areas, continents or even the whole primitive world. Let us remember Frazer and Lévy-Bruhl. A comparative point of view was at that time taken for granted by every anthropologist. Comparisons were sometimes superficial, and cultural similarities based on them questionable. To avoid these misuses of the comparative method, it was certainly healthy to encourage for a time the deep study of a single global society. And indeed the procedure has been rewarding, particularly in the African field: we now possess a great number of excellent monographs on particular tribes and kingdoms of traditional Africa. But to restrict anthropological studies to the global-society frame of reference entails drawbacks and impoverishments.

The most obvious difficulty arising from the lack of large cultural units has been made clear in our examination of the *Survey*. When attempting to describe the cultural and societal reality of Africa south of the Sahara, global societies and global cultures are not useful tools. They are too numerous to be manageable. But there is more than a problem of setting forth varied facts in a form fit for a book or a series of volumes: even if it were feasible to devote a monograph to each of the eight or nine hundred African societies, it would not be an ideal procedure: cultural identities would be concealed by societal diversity.

Let us take the case of the kingdoms of the Lacustrine area. Each of them was a societal unit particularly well defined as it was embodied in a single system of political relations focused on the monarchic institution. The culture of each of them may be described and analysed separately – and this has been done to a large extent in the last two decades thanks to the East African Institute of Social Research (Makerere University College, Uganda) and the Institut pour la Recherche Scientifique en Afrique Centrale and its successor, the Institut National de Recherche Scientifique (Butare, Rwanda) – as if each kingdom had been an autonomous going-concern. Now, when reading the monographs, one cannot fail to notice that some chapters are very similar, almost identical. The kingdoms situated on the western shores of Lake Victoria were using the same techniques

7

to cultivate similar crops; all the Lacustrine groups followed the same basic rules to count descent, to organize marriage; several of them had established about the same specific institutions (feudal ties existed in Ankole, Burundi, Rwanda); some myths and cults were widely spread in the area, for instance the ones centred on Ryangombe; social stratification and political systems were organized along the same patterns. There are thus cultural phenomena that seem to cross societal boundaries; to ignore that aspect of them is to distort the cultural picture of the region.

Another important set of problems that cannot be solved by the exclusive study of global cultures concerns relations between different aspects and different levels of a culture. We find that, in a particular society, the sculptures manifest a tradition of form that we call a style; what are the relations between that artistic aspect and the other ones (political, economic, familial, etc.) of the same culture? Integration is easily said, but to measure the degree of autonomy of a style, one has to know if it is not common to several societies which differ politically, economically, or in their kinship system.

The study of large units in Africa would be no mean contribution to anthropological theory, which is rather impoverished on the conceptual elaboration of cultural realities. The concept of culture as the collective heritage of a global society permits us to delineate easily the contours of a particular culture: one assumes that society-members and culture-bearers are the same individuals. As the members of a society are conscious of their membership, they may be identified without much difficulty; and as they are also the exclusive bearers of a culture, the limits of the latter are clear-cut. But the perfect correspondence between global society and global culture does not exhaust the richness of cultural phenomena. Non-figurative art is a cultural reality whose borders do not coincide with the boundaries of any contemporary national society (a national society being the global society of our industrial era); the same may be said of an economic system such as capitalism, or of a political régime such as parliamentary government. Now, what is the logical status of these cultural entities which do not have a societal basis or whose bearers do not form a global society, not even a society (non-figurative artists of London, Paris, Prague, New York and their publics do not constitute any kind of societal organization)? Another theoretical problem on which the study of large African cultural units could throw some light is the question of possible integrated cultures founded on – or corresponding to – social units other than global societies such as castes or classes, religious bodies or political associations, age-sets or economic situations (what has been recently termed 'culture of the youth' and 'culture of poverty'), marginal groups and minorities. An empirical study of traditional Africa could furnish new ideas on that part of theoretical anthropology which pertains to the nature of culture and society, that is to say to the logical and real status of the two fundamental concepts of our discipline.

IV

In the search for large cultural units, two different approaches may prove to be fruitful. They are not exclusive but complementary. The first starts from the assumption that the African cultural phenomena are a continuum geographically (from the Sahara to the Cape, from the Atlantic to the Indian Ocean) and 'categorically' (from techniques of production and acquisition to beliefs, myths, and world-views). Of course, this is not peculiar to Africa. Everywhere, it is the anthropologist who projects on the continuous cultural fabric his conceptual frames and divisions. In the 'facts', there is no political system, no economic network, no magical belief, and no religious representation: there are behavioural and verbal patterns that we classify under different headings, economic or political, magic or religious. In the 'facts', there is no culture of the savanna peoples opposed to another of the forest peoples but ways of life of populations unevenly distributed on the surface of the continent, which gradually differ in language, customs, and institutions. Again, it is the anthropologist who decides where the dividing line should be drawn. To assume the seamless continuity of cultural phenomena is not an original view but it helps us to remember that evidence may be helpful here.

Fully aware that he is projecting his own categories, the anthropologist may attempt to divide the African continuumt 'horizontally', that is to say to consider the usual aspects or compartments of a culture separately without taking into account the 'vertical' division of global cultures. He may take up, for instance, the visual arts and study the whole of African sculpture without considering its societal origins as relevant; he will classify them according to the criteria used when dealing with works of art (e.g. figurative and non-figurative, symbolic and imitative, convex and concave face features, etc.); he will obtain finally an Africa-wide picture of the art category. Similar research may be made in other cultural compartments: religious beliefs may be differentiated as animism, ancestor worship, cults honouring high gods, etc.; systems of descent which are patrilineal, matrilineal or present different intermediate forms; political organizations with the now widely known distinction between states and stateless systems.

In this perspective, the work of Daryll Forde is, again, to be mentioned and praised. He edited with an introduction such a 'horizontal' study of cosmological ideas and social values of African peoples, *African Worlds* (1954); he is the co-editor, with Radcliffe-Brown, of *African Systems of Kinship and Marriage* (1950). As Director of the International African Institute, he promoted other studies of the same kind, from the celebrated *African Political Systems* edited by Fortes and Evans-Pritchard (1940), to *African Systems of Thought* edited by Fortes and Germaine Dieterlen (1965).

Such researches provide us with the materials necessary to draw several cultural pictures of Africa. From their comparison, we could discover significant correlations between the different cultural aspects which, in that connection, may be considered as variables. We could also learn something about the conditioning of one aspect by another. Finally, by plotting on a map the localizations of, say, styles, economic systems, types of government, etc., large cultural units could be spotted where several maps would indicate, by superposition, areas of coincidence.

V

The second approach in our quest for large cultural units finds its starting-point in the global societies. The culture of a few specific societies, as described in monographs, are analysed in order to build cultural models. Of course, this is done along some theoretical lines indicating to the anthropologist what to look for, what to consider as important, what to judge essential. It is exactly what we expect from the theory we choose. For instance, a cultural model of a hunters' society may be built from what we know of the Bambuti pygmies of the Ituri forest and of the !Kung Bushmen of the Kalahari. By the same methods, we have constructed in *Les Civilisations noires* (1962) several other cultural models: of the forest cultivators, of the savanna peasants, of the pastoral warriors, of the urban craftsmen and merchants.

The utility of a model is in helping to determine significant similarities between concrete global cultures. There are many common features among different cultures; what are the features that allow us to group different cultures in the same category? The ones essential to the model. This may seem arbitrary: if one had built other models, other features would appear significant. The answer to that objection lies in the explanatory value of the theory basic to the models: if it accounts for the facts better than other theories, let us keep it until an alternative of higher value is found.

A large cultural unit is thus made of a collection of concrete global cultures whose internal organization corresponds to the same model. Such units are not based on similarities in one aspect (government, style, or kinship), but on a structural identity: in each concrete society belonging to the same large unit, the relations between the compartments or levels (which are universal) delineate the same configuration.

The division of the African continuum into units, each of them embodying a distinct model, may be said to be 'vertical' in the sense that it cuts across the different cultural compartments which may be visualized as layers or levels superimposed on each other, from the technical basis which allows different kinds of goods to be obtained from the environment through the different networks of human relations (economics, kinship, political organization, family, associations, etc.), up to collective representations (cosmological ideas, philosophy, art, language, etc.).

If horizontal and vertical classifications agree, broad cultural units reached by both approaches have their validity reinforced. It is by convergence and by indirect checks that the measure of objectivity of large units may be assessed and strengthened. The units are not arbitrary but their objectivity is not a simple yes-or-no relationship between a classification and a 'reality' standing in its genuineness and autonomy. The only cultural reality is a continuum: all our categories are observer's mental creations which establish order and intelligibility. If they succeed in that, they are objective.

To present a comprehensive view of the whole of traditional Africa has of course been attempted more than once. In the historical perspective, there are the impressive works of Baumann and Westermann (c. 1940) and Murdock (1959); in a purely anthropological perspective, there is the short but illuminating study of Denise Paulme (1953), and Herskovits's researches on African culture areas which have resulted in several publications presenting revised versions of his classification (the last is dated 1962). But knowledge is never definitive, particularly in its syntheses. New attempts are justified.

The rich material gathered in the *Ethnographic Survey of Africa*, in the books encompassing a cultural aspect of the whole of Africa published by the International African Institute have not yet been fully exploited. The immense work achieved by Daryll Forde, or under his direct impulse, should be pursued. Research oriented towards cultural units of traditional Africa is certainly one among many possible lines of development, and a most promising one.

REFERENCES

ALEXANDRE, P. & BINET, J. 1958. *Le Groupe dit pahouin: Fang, Boulou, Beti.* London.

BAUMANN, H. & WESTERMANN, D. 1948. *Les Peuples et les civilisations de l'Afrique.* Paris (German original edition c. 1940).

BAXTER, P. T. W. & BUTT, A. J. 1954. *The Azande and Related Peoples of the Anglo-Egyptian Sudan and Belgian Congo.* London: International African Institute.

BEIDELMAN, T. D. 1967. *The Matrilineal Peoples of Eastern Tanzania.* London: International African Institute.

BUTT, A. J. 1952. *The Nilotes.* London: International African Institute.

FORDE, DARYLL 1951. *The Yoruba-speaking Peoples of South-western Nigeria.* London: International African Institute.

The Cultural Units of Africa

FORDE, DARYLL (ed.) 1954. *African Worlds*. London: Oxford University Press.

FORTES, M. & EVANS-PRITCHARD, E. (eds.) 1940. *African Political Systems*. London: Oxford University Press.

— & DIETERLEN, GERMAINE (eds.) 1960. *African Systems of Thought*. London: Oxford University Press.

FROEHLICH, J.-C., ALEXANDRE, P. & CORNEVIN, R. 1963. *Les Populations du Nord-Togo*. Paris: Presses Universitaires de France.

GUNN, HAROLD D. 1953. *The Peoples of the Plateau Area of Northern Nigeria*. London: International African Institute.

— 1956. *Pagan Peoples of the Central Area of Northern Nigeria*. London: International African Institute.

HERSKOVITS, MELVILLE, J. 1962. *The Human Factor in Changing Africa*. New York: Knopf.

LEMBEZAT, B. 1962. *Les Populations païennes du Nord-Cameroun et de l'Adamaoua*. Paris: Presses Universitaires de France.

MALINOWSKI, B. 1922. *Argonauts of the Western Pacific*. London: Routledge & Kegan Paul.

MANOUKIAN, MADELINE 1950. *The Akan and Ga-Adangme Peoples*. London: International African Institute.

MAQUET, JACQUES 1962. *Afrique, les civilisations noires*. Paris: Horizons de France.

MURDOCK, GEORGE P. 1959. *Africa: Its Peoples and Their Culture History*. New York: McGraw-Hill.

PAULME, DENISE 1953. *Les Civilisations africaines*. Paris.

PRINS, A. H. J. 1961. *The Swahili-speaking Peoples of Zanzibar and the East African Coast*. London: International African Institute.

RADCLIFFE-BROWN, A. R. 1922. *The Andaman Islanders*. London: Cambridge University Press.

— & FORDE, DARYLL (eds.) 1950. *African Systems of Kinship and Marriage*. London: Oxford University Press.

TAYLOR, BRIAN 1962. *The Western Lacustrine Bantu*. London: International African Institute.

VAN GELUWE, H. 1960. *Les Bali et les peuplades apparentées*. Tervuren, Brussels.

WHITELEY, W. & SLASKI, J. 1951. *Bemba and Related Peoples of Northern Rhodesia (including Ambo) and Peoples of the Lower Luapula Valley*. London: International African Institute.

PART II

Political Economy

R. E. Bradbury

Patrimonialism and Gerontocracy in Benin Political Culture

ELDERHOOD AND KINGSHIP

In the late fifteenth century, when the first Portuguese explorers reached the area of the Niger Delta, Benin City (*Edo*) was already the capital of a powerful kingdom and an expanding military empire. If tradition be relied upon, a dozen or more kings of the Oranmiyan dynasty, which is said to have continued unbroken up to the present day, had by that time succeeded each other. According to its mythical charter, this dynasty had originated in a request by the elders (*edion*) of the Edo to the *Oghene n' Uhe* (Oni of Ife) that he should send them a king. The Oghene sent his son Oranmiyan, but the latter found the language and manners of the Edo uncongenial to him. He therefore contented himself with begetting a son by the daughter of an Edo village chief and departed for home. Trained for the kingship by some of his father's followers who had been left behind for the purpose, Oranmiyan's son, Eweka, was accepted by the Edo as their first Oba (king).

There is little reason to doubt that this dynastic myth incorporates a folk memory of the advent of alien rulers, but, I have suggested elsewhere (Bradbury 1967: 1-3), the particular form which it took served to epitomize the relationship between the Oba and the Edo on which the social order of the kingdom was founded. As a scion of a stock which provided the rulers of other kingdoms, the Oba was a being set apart from his subjects and had an intrinsic right to be obeyed. Yet, as the myth asserts, the kingship came into being by the will of the elders of the Edo community. The first Oba was himself born into that community and he and his successors were therefore bound to respect its norms and institutions.

17

Thus interpreted, the myth gives expression to two opposed yet complementary conceptions of authority which pervade Benin political culture: the authority of kings and the authority of elders. These two conceptions of authority conform, in many respects, to Weber's ideal types 'patrimonialism' and 'geronto-cracy' (Weber 1947: 346 ff.), and I shall therefore make use of these terms. The crucial point of difference between patrimonialism and gerontocracy lies, as Weber observed, in the basis of the relationship between the holders of authority and those who are bound to obey it. Where gerontocracy obtains, governors and governed share equal membership rights in the corporate group whose boundaries define the area over which authority is exercised. Their reciprocal role-expectations are defined first in terms of common membership rights, and secondly in terms of relative seniority. The elder's authority is in no sense a private possession but is exercised, transmitted, and devolved according to gerontocratic rules. We may add that – presuming male authority and excluding women – the governed are the potential successors to the governors.

By contrast, patrimonialist conceptions place primary emphasis on qualitative differences between the governors and the governed. The ruler's uniqueness, which may be justified in various ways, allows him to 'own' his subjects in a sense in which elders do not own their juniors. Since it belongs to him as a private possession, the patrimonial ruler can devolve his authority as he wishes. In the extreme case he alone has the right to choose his successor.

In the nineteenth-century Benin kingdom, gerontocratic principles were most explicitly manifested in the structures and processes of village government. Ideally, the whole male population of the village was ranked according to order of birth, and it was in this order that men passed through the youth (*iroghae*), adult (*ighele*), and elder (*edion*) age-grades. The *edion* (literally 'those who (are) senior') were the repository of the land, laws, rights, and reputation of the village, which they held in trust back through the generations of their predecessors to the first nameless elders who had founded the community. The shrine of the dead *edion* was the village council hall. Here the living elders assembled to judge disputes and conduct village business. They were presided over by the oldest man (*odionwere*) who, by virtue

18

of his closeness to them, was the priest of the dead *edion* as well as of the village earth (*oto*) in which they were buried. Except in a minority of villages which had hereditary chiefs (*enigie*), the *odionwere* was the village head. In most villages the next four elders (*edion nene*), but in some the next seven (*edion nihiron*), were accorded special respect.

It would be wrong to say that the elders had no legislative functions. From time to time they purposefully modified the rules which governed intra-village relationships. Nevertheless the emphasis, in their authority, was on the conservation of that code as it had been handed down to them from the original elders. In consultation with his fellow-elders, the *odionwere* regulated the performance by the two lower age-grades of their customary community roles. The *ighele* had policing functions and carried out the more skilled communal tasks. It was from their ranks that troops were recruited into the Oba's army, on the basis of a nationally organized seven-point cycle of age-companies. The *ighele* were explicitly regarded as the collective heirs to the collective authority of the elders, and relations between the two grades displayed the characteristic ambiguities of the holder-heir relationship (cf. Bradbury 1966: 144-52). To the *iroghae* (youths) fell the more menial community tasks and it was they who carried the village's annual tribute to the Oba in the capital.

Strict age-ranking was subject to various qualifications. In some villages the *odionwere* was the oldest man of the oldest ward. In villages that had hereditary chiefs, the position was sometimes reserved for the oldest man of the chief's ward. There were also various kinds of adjustment between the authority structure of the family and that of the village community (see Bradbury 1957: 31-34), but, though it was regarded as desirable that each family should be represented among the *edion*, they were not primarily conceived of as a body of lineage representatives. Order of birth into the village community *per se* was the dominant criterion for the ascription of authority. The norms and structures of village government served as a model for the government of territorial and associational groups of all kinds, including, as I shall suggest, the kingdom as a whole and its central administrative organs.

Patrimonial authority inhered (by definition) in the kingship, though certain hereditary chiefs also possessed patrimonial rights within their own limited domains and subject to the Oba's overriding jurisdiction. Conceptually, each Oba conferred the right to rule on his successor when he designated him as his legitimate senior son. Ultimately, as we have suggested, this right derived from outside the Edo community. It was justified by the unique capacity, transmitted from king to king, to prosper and revitalize the community. The fertility, health, and longevity of the Edo depended on the Oba's capacity to use his own person to transform natural vitality into social value. Annually, in the complex *Igue* rite, his body was brought into contact with the life-giving products of the forest. His vitalizing energy was thereby regenerated. Then, under conditions of ritual control, the Edo people were exposed to its creative force.

Dynamism was the essence of the kingship in its political as well as in its mystical dimensions. Whereas the gerontocratic social order of the village was a cyclical ahistorical order, the political order of the kingdom was in constant flux. At his death, the individuality of the elder was assimilated to the undifferentiated collectivity of his predecessors in that status (Bradbury 1966: 132). The past kings, as depicted in legend and anecdote, were lively individual personalities, each of whom had left his imprint on the political culture. Every change in the fortunes of the state and the configuration of its institutions was attributed to their creative genius and political strivings. As they strove to impose their will on 'the Edo', order was repeatedly reduced to chaos and a transformed order re-emerged. In the annual cycles of festivals in honour of the past kings, the multi-dimensional structural-historical relationship between the Oba and the Edo was continuously re-created. Ritual enactments of 'events' in the reigns of past kings, and the myths and legends which interpreted them, provided the rationale for the structural position of each state office and institution. They also furnished the ideological idiom of political dispute. According to patrimonialist representations, rank, competences, and prerogatives were shown to be privileges granted by one king and therefore liable to be redefined or withdrawn by another. Opposition to these claims took the form of denying the Oba the right to alter the dispensations that were demonstrated to have been made by his predecessors. Rank was equated with antiquity. Administrative segments and individual office-holders laid claim to their various capacities as age-sanctified rights. In these and other ceremonials both the political tensions between the Oba and the various segments of the political elite and the institutionalized compromises that regulated them were ritually objectified. The refusal of individuals or groups to perform their customary roles was a sign of disaffection.

According to Weber, in a gerontocracy 'administrative functions are performed "on behalf" of the corporate group', whereas 'appropriation by the chief personally is a phenomenon of patrimonialism. It may vary enormously in degree to the extreme cases of a claim to full proprietorship of the land and to the status of master over subjects treated as slaves' (Weber 1947: 349). These criteria of extreme patrimonialism were fully realized in the Benin ideology of kingship, but each was countered by an opposite principle. 'The Oba owns the land' (*Oba nya oto*) was no shibboleth; he appointed an official to regulate its distribution and also a band of 'surveyors' to show people their boundaries. Yet the land belonged to ward and village communities and was administered by their elders (Bradbury 1957: 76). As Dapper rightly reported in 1668, 'all the Benin people, high and low, are bound to acknowledge themselves to be the slaves of the king' (cited in Ling Roth 1903: 91); but Nyendael was no less accurate when, in 1701, he wrote: 'All male slaves here are foreigners; for the natives cannot be sold for slaves, but all are free, and alone bear the name of the king's slaves' (Bosman 1967: 402). In fact only freeborn Edo had the right to be branded with the facial and body markings which distinguished 'the Oba's slaves' (*evien-Oba*) from 'real slaves', that is the slaves of (ordinary) 'people' (*evien-onbhan*) and the private slaves of the reigning incumbent (*evien-Omo*). Finally, all administrative titles and capacities were held to be privileges conferred by the king; but, as I hope to show, those who held and exercised them did so as 'elders' either of the corporate political associations to which they belonged, or of the Edo community as a whole.

THE KINGDOM AS AN EXTENSION OF THE OBA'S HOUSEHOLD

A primary characteristic of patrimonialism is that 'governmental offices originate in the household administration of the ruler'

(Bendix 1960: 334). In this respect the pre-colonial Benin régime had a markedly patrimonialist flavour. The Oba's palace retainers were divided into three major segments among which were distributed the menial, craft, administrative, and ceremonial functions necessary to maintain his household and his royal dignity. Briefly, the *Iwebo* had charge of royal regalia, the *Iweguae* supplied the king's servants and attendants, and the *Ibiwe-Eruerie* were responsible for the discipline and welfare of his wives and children. These retainer associations were also the main instrument for the recruitment and training of governmental personnel and for the execution of the Oba's civil and ritual authority throughout his domains. Their senior titled officials, the *Eghaebho n'Ogbe* or Palace Chiefs, were great officers of state whose range of governmental functions excluded only that of military command. As a corporate group the *Eghaebho n'Ogbe* were formally ranked below two other groups of chiefs: the *Uzama*, whose titles were hereditary, and the *Eghaebho n'Ore* or Town Chiefs who, like the Palace Chiefs, were appointed by the king; but in terms of power and prestige they were by no means their inferior.

Iwebo, Iweguae, and *Ibiwe* were constituted as corporate associations. Each was made up of a number of grades of untitled retainers and two tiers of titled offices, *Ekhaenbhen* and *Eghaebho n'Ogbe*, within each of which titles were ranked in lineal sequence. To each association as a corporate group and to their component subdivisions and individual offices specific administrative competences were assigned.

Recruitment into retainer service was open to all male freeborn commoners. Indeed, in principle, every *ovien-Oba* was by paternal filiation a member of one of the retainer divisions. However, unless he was formally initiated into his association ('entered the palace') his membership of it remained purely nominal, affording him no access to its apartments in the palace or to its revenue or deliberations. Since Benin villages were made up of a number of patrilineal groupings of disparate origins, each village contained members of all the palace associations. There is, however, no evidence that members of the same associations constituted structural units at the local level. Nominal palace affiliation was mainly significant as a mechanism of political socialization. Symbolically, it afforded the individual a sense of direct participation in the central institutions of the patrimonial régime. As he grew up every young Edo became aware of a direct bond between himself and the king, bypassing the distance-maintaining chains of official communication whose links were village headmen, chiefs, and the agents of territorial administrators based in the capital. These symbolic functions were the more effective in that they were linked to practical opportunities for advancement. For the ambitious young villager initiation into the lowest grade of a retainer association was the first step on a ladder whose highest rungs were the great Town and Palace titles. His prospects of reaching the top were slight, for he had to compete for promotion against the sons and grandsons of chiefs who, in terms of family wealth, influence, and opportunities for acquiring political and administrative expertise, enjoyed great initial advantages. Nevertheless, there was no formal status barrier to upward mobility and it was by no means unknown for talented men of humble origins to achieve high office.

It seems probable that the systematic recruitment of retainers on a universalistic basis dates back to a period at which the Benin kings were seeking to create a centralized régime and to mobilize popular support for it among the freeborn Edo population. Indeed it is possible that in the sixteenth and seventeenth centuries, when the Benin state was at its apogee, periods of service in the palace were obligatory. In the nineteenth century the bulk of initiated retainers were drawn from patrician families resident in the capital, that is families with an established tradition of court and government service. Even so, the proportion of villagers who entered the palace was considerable. A new initiate into the lowest grade of his association spent a week or two in the palace, during which time he paid fees to existing members, took oaths of loyalty and received instructions in his duties and obligations. Villagers who secured the patronage of the Oba or Palace Chiefs remained at the capital to compete for administrative assignments and promotion. However, a court career, though it was prestigious and could be materially rewarding, was also precarious. Many retainers of village origin returned sooner or later to a life of subsistence farming. Thus in any village there were men who had some direct experience of retainer service and who, on their visits to the capital, had entry into the palace. This was one of the more important ways in which direct communication between the court and the villages took place. Thus retainerdom, apart from its overt administrative functions, was an important mechanism for maintaining a high level of commitment among the general population to the ideology and values of the patrimonial régime. The presence of erstwhile retainers in the villages also helped to temper relations with active retainers who visited them on a variety of extractive missions.

It was not only at the individual level that the political community was conceived of as the king's household writ large. The population of each of the numerous wards into which the capital was divided was constituted as a corporate group of craftsmen or ritual or ceremonial functionaries. Each of these groups, whose internal affairs were regulated through a system of appointive or hereditary offices combined with graded structures derived from the village age-grades, claimed to have been founded by one of the past kings to perform some special service for himself and his successors. For purposes of administrative coordination, each group of special functionaries was affiliated to one of the palace associations. However, the more important groups, such as the *Ewaise* (the king's doctors and diviners) and the *Ihogbe* (the priests of the kings' divinity), whose functions were continuous, claimed equality of status with the palace associations and conducted their business with the Oba in person.

Many villages were similarly incorporated as bodies of special functionaries charged with specific duties relating to the upkeep of the royal household, the administration of the king's estate, and the fulfilment of his ritual and secular functions. These, too, carried out their tasks under the surveillance of Palace Chiefs. Villages lacking specific retainer functions had no corporate association with the palace. They were assigned for purposes of tribute collection, military recruitment, and their own support to individual title-holders of all the chieftaincy orders. Tribute was rendered collectively in the forms of yams and other foodstuffs. For the village youths, the annual tribute-carrying expeditions to the capital were the event of the year. When they had delivered their loads to the Oba they could test their strength in wrestling contests with the Oba's pages. The most popular rags-to-riches stories are those which recount how a youth's wrestling prowess caught the eye of the king, who took him into his service and set him on the road to high office. The founders of some of the most patrician families are said to have started their careers in this way.

HEREDITARY ELDERHOOD AND PATRIMONIAL PREFERMENT

The dominant positions in the government of the nineteenth-century Benin kingdom were occupied by the Oba and his appointed officials of the *Eghaebho n'Ore* and *Eghaebho n'Ogbe* orders. It was the kingship and the Town and Palace titles, together with their associated competences and prerogatives, that constituted the main arena of political competition and conflict. According to dynastic traditions this had not always been the case. Many legends recount the struggles of the early kings to escape from the domination of the *Uzama*, a group of hereditary nobles whose first five members are identified as the descendants of the elders who had invited the *Oghene n' Uhe* to send them a king. The fourth Oba, Ewedo, is said to have moved the palace from its original site, which was surrounded by the settlements of the *Uzama*, to its present location a mile or two away; and to have begun to confer titles on Edo commoners in order to enlist their support against the nobles. But it is the fifteenth Oba, Esigie, who is credited with finally disposing of the threat which the *Uzama* presented to the king's personal authority. Esigie is attributed to the early sixteenth century and tradition has it that European visitors, armed with guns, assisted him in quelling the powerful nobles. When the *Uzama* showed their disaffection by refusing to play their part in the king's rituals, Esigie is said to have nominated a new set of *Uzama* to replace them. Eventually, however, the real *Uzama* submitted to the king's superior power. Their rank and ritual competences were restored, but from Esigie's time onwards traditions no longer portray them as a serious threat to the Oba's authority.

These myths and the rites which enacted them provided the charter for the ambiguous, but important, position which the *Uzama* occupied in the nineteenth-century Benin régime. In so far as their relationship with the king perpetuated that between the first elders and the first king, the *Uzama* were conceptually

25

located outside the boundaries of patrimonial authority. Unlike the Town and Palace Chiefs, they held their offices by hereditary right. Spatially, too, they were set apart. Whereas the appointed officials were bound to reside within the wall and ditch which surrounded the capital, the villages of the *Uzama* lay beyond it, and the fact that they had to cross the ditch to reach the Oba's palace was a potent symbol of their detachment. Within their own villages the individual *Uzama* were virtually autonomous rulers. While accepting that they could not inflict the death penalty without the Oba's consent, they otherwise claimed complete jurisdiction over their own subjects, who were *evien-Uzama* rather than *evien-Oba*. Although on a much smaller scale, their households were organized along the same lines as the royal court and staffed by retainers on whom they conferred titles. By a curious twist of the gerontocratic/patrimonial dichotomy, these hereditary palatine privileges reinforced the role of the *Uzama* as the elders who 'owned' the kingship. Being semi-independent rulers and having themselves some of the attributes of kingship, they were able, at least in symbolic terms, to treat with the Oba on a basis of near equality, and thus to act as the guarantors of the compact between the Oba and the Edo which gave the patrimonial régime its legitimacy. This compact was ritually renewed each year at the Festival of the Oba's Father, when the Oba stepped down from his throne to sacrifice a goat to the earth in which the dead elders of the nation were buried; the *Uzama*, as *edion*, made reciprocal contributions to the offerings to the king's predecessors. But the most important of the system-maintaining functions performed by the *Uzama* as elders related to their role as 'kingmakers'. To these I shall return later.

These gerontocratic conceptions of the status of the *Uzama* were countered by other representations which placed them within the purview of the king's patrimonial prerogatives. The latter position was justified by the legends and rites which recounted Esigie's victory over their ancestors, but also by myths which indicated that their individual titles had been conferred on the primeval elders by the first Oba. On this basis the Oba claimed ultimate jurisdiction over succession to these titles; hereditary succession could be held to be a privilege that might be withdrawn rather than a perpetual right. In the absence of an independent judiciary and formal law, where such a conflict of principles coincided with a conflict of interests, the issue could only be settled by political action. Where no conflict of interest was at stake, the conflict of principles was dealt with by a series of symbolic compromises. The Oba normally respected the principle of hereditary succession and, in return, the *Uzama* acknowledged themselves, though not their subjects, to be *evien-Oba*. As such, they were eligible as individuals to receive patrimonial preferment to administrative competences. The benefices and prerogatives assigned to them tended to be appropriated as hereditary rights, though from the king's point of view they were only privileges that had to be renewed when each title-holder was succeeded by his son. The succession procedures are of particular interest. In principle the holder of an *Uzama* title, like the king, designated his senior son as his heir. Before the latter could be inducted into office, however, he had to pay accession fees both to the king and to his fellow-*Uzama*. Furthermore he had to be initiated into one of the Oba's palace associations, a procedure which involved not only swearing oaths of loyalty but also the implication that he had served, however nominally, as a retainer in the king's household. Finally, he received his title from the Oba through the medium of the latter's senior appointed official, the *Iyase*. There was one exception to this procedure: *Oliha*, the senior member of the order, was inducted by the Oba himself. The significance of these succession procedures will, I think, become clear as this essay proceeds.

THE KING AND HIS PATRIMONIAL STAFF

The subversion of the power of the hereditary *Uzama* is linked in tradition with the growing power of officials directly appointed by the king. The establishment of the *Eghaebho n'Ore* and *Eghaebho n'Ogbe* as contraposed rank orders is attributed to the twelfth Oba, Ewuare, though some of the titles he incorporated in them are said to have been created by earlier kings. Ewuare was the grandfather of Esigie, the Oba who is credited with having got the upper hand over the *Uzama*. Tradition-derived chronologies locate him in the fifteenth century, just beyond the range of the earliest Portuguese descriptions of

Benin, so there is no contemporary documentation of his existence or his achievements. Nevertheless, so many of the characteristic features of the pre-colonial polity are attributed to his
creative genius that it is difficult to avoid associating the name
Ewuare with an important phase in its evolution.

The innovations ascribed to Ewuare hang together with remarkable consistency. As well as founding the *Eghaebho n'Ore*
and *Eghaebho n'Ogbe* orders, he is said to have been the first
Oba to persuade his freeborn subjects to let their sons take up
retainer service in the palace, It was he, too, who first decreed
that all his freeborn Edo subjects should be marked with the
common pattern of scarifications which distinguished *evien-Oba*
from royals, slaves, and foreigners, all of whom were excluded
from the palace. Another of his accomplishments was to
organize the population of the capital into corporate wards, each
characterized by the particular craft or ritual service which it
owed to the king. The majority of these groups, together with
similar ones located outside the capital, trace their foundation to
Ewuare and his immediate successors, Ozolua and Esigie.
Ewuare is also said to have been the first Oba to confer the heir-
apparent's title, *Edaiken*, on his senior son. This attribution
coincides with an apparent shift in the pattern of succession to
the throne indicated in oral king-lists. Before Ewuare's time the
kingship was transmitted collaterally. From the reign of his son,
Ozolua, it passed lineally, except for a period in the seventeenth
century following a failure in the direct line. Ewuare, Ozolua,
and Esigie are also credited with the creation of the extensive
empire whose existence is confirmed in the earliest Portuguese
accounts of Benin.

With the later and better-documented examples of Buganda
(Southwold 1961) and Ashanti (Wilks 1967) in mind, it is at
least a useful heuristic hypothesis that these traditions represent
a phase of political centralization and administrative differentiation in which the kings were able to subvert descent-group-
based claims to authority, and appropriate to themselves a large
measure of control over the means of administration. Wilks has
convincingly related what he calls the 'Kwadwoan revolution' of
late eighteenth- and early nineteenth-century Ashanti to the
demand for a more differentiated and professional administrative
organization posed by military expansion over extensive and

culturally heterogeneous territories (Wilks 1967: 211 ff.). This paper proceeds on the hypothesis that the main structural outlines of the nineteenth-century Benin polity were established as the result of broadly similar developments taking place in broadly similar circumstances as far back as the fifteenth and early sixteenth centuries. The detailed structural and procedural configurations of the nineteenth-century régime I take to be the product of conflicts and compromises between subsequent generations of kings and officials pursuing their individual and group interests in an environment of historical contingencies.

ELDERHOOD AND THE PATRIMONIAL RÉGIME

The tiered hierarchies of offices in each retainer association were founded on a series of 'untitled' grades which the Edo themselves saw as being analagous to the village age-grades. The *edion* grade of *Ibiwe-Eruerie* and the *edafen* grades of *Iwebo* and *Iweguae* were equated with the *edion* grade of the village to the extent that a man who achieved *odion* (*odafen*) status in the palace was automatically recognized as an *odion* of his village. His rank in the village order of birth might not be materially affected: he could not become *odionwere* before those who were born before him; but he was exempted from the prestations to existing elders and the rites of passage which marked promotion to village elderhood, and he was no longer obliged to participate in the activities of the *ighele*. Palace elders were easily distinguishable in the village by their hair style, which was like that of state chiefs and a simpler version of the Oba's own coiffure. Their appearance alone served to remind villagers of their allegiance to the Oba and the fact that they had the right of entry into the palace afforded their opinions special respect in village councils. Thus the concept of equivalence between palace and village elderhood was of some importance as mediating between the political cultures of the village and the state.

The fact that the Edo established continuities between village and palace grades should not be allowed to obscure the differences that existed between these institutions. Progress through the palace grades was a function not of age but of achievement. Advancement depended on wealth and on ability to secure the patronage of the king and palace chiefs. Furthermore, the grades within each palace association were internally differentiated, as the village grades were not, into groups of specialized functionaries, trained in particular skills and charged with specific duties relating to the fulfilment of the Oba's ritual and governmental functions, both in the palace and in his wider domains. Nevertheless promotional procedures and role-relationships within and between the grades of the associations were informed by gerontocratic norms. As in the village, promotion involved prestations to existing members. It is true that, in the village, the cost of promotion was so low as to exclude only the most wretched individuals, whereas wealth was an important differential in competition for promotion through the palace hierarchies; but underlying this difference was the common principle that status within the group was conferred by the group as a corporate body. Preferment by the Oba had to be matched by acceptance by the elders. Seniority within the untitled grades was reckoned, if not by age, then by the analagous principle of date of entry. Tasks and perquisites were apportioned to individuals and groups by the Oba or his titled agents, but benefits also accrued to the grades as collectivities and these were shared according to seniority. At a palace feast, as at a village feast, the grades received and ate their portions separately.

Within each association the elders, like the village elders, were the repository and defenders of the group's rights, traditions, and rules of behaviour, which they held in trust from the dead *edion*. Each association had its shrine to the spirits of past elders, and service at this shrine was led, as in the village, by the living elder nearest to them in seniority (cf. Bradbury 1966: 139 ff.). When a palace elder died his senior son was obliged to perform the rite of *izakhwe*, whereby the deceased was assimilated to the company of palace elders in the spirit world, precisely in the same way as he was bound to assimilate his father to the dead elders of his village, kin group, and any other association in which he had achieved elderhood. In the palace, as in all these other groups, completion of *izakhwe* was a prerequisite for the recognition of the senior son himself as an elder (Bradbury 1964: 108-9; 1966: 140).

Having established the presence of gerontocratic norms in the infrastructure of the patrimonial régime, we may follow them upwards into its superstructure. This consisted, as has been indicated, of the Palace and Town hierarchies of chieftaincy, which together made up a single promotional field. A system of individual titles conferred arbitrarily by a king who had the right to alter their rank order and to redistribute competences between them, smacks of that extreme form of patrimonialism which Weber (1947: 347) called 'sultanism'. This view of the title system existed (and still exists) at the level of a conscious model, and argument and action predicated upon it are readily distinguishable ingredients of political conflict in both the colonial and pre-colonial periods (Bradbury 1968). But it co-existed with equally explicit and quite contrary principles. One of these was the notion that once a man had 'completed' his title, it was his for life. The only 'constitutional' means whereby the Oba could render it vacant was by making out a charge of treason against the holder, that is, a charge meriting the death penalty.

A clear distinction must be made between the conferment of a title and its 'completion' (*orefo*), which could take place soon after conferment, or much later, or never. Conferment was the king's private prerogative, exercised by the dispatch, by night, of a personal emissary (*ukonyenbhen*, the messenger of joy) to the successful applicant's home, to tell him of the honour bestowed upon him. In making his choice, the Oba could seek advice and he himself might be subjected to much political pressure, but there was no constitutional impediment to the exercise of his free will. However, before the new title-holder could take up his office he had to be approved by his fellow chiefs. This meant that he not only had to pay fees to the Town and Palace orders as corporate bodies, and to the king himself, but also that he had to visit each chief who had completed his own title, pay him a fee, and kneel down before him to seek his blessing. Only when he had done this could he complete his title, that is, undergo a public ceremony of induction performed, in the Oba's presence, by the senior Town Chief (*Iyase*) acting explicitly in his role as the Oba's chief spokesman but also, by implication, in his role as the leader of the people (*okao evien Oba*). Any chief who had not received his fees could attend this ceremony and halt the proceedings, at least until an apology and reparations had been made. It was at the completion ceremony that the Oba informed the new chief, through the *Iyase*, what benefices and prerogatives he was conferring upon him. Finally,

31

the chief took oaths of loyalty to the king and to his order or sub-order.

It will be apparent that the conferment and completion ceremonies demarcated an arena in which bargaining and conflict over the distribution of offices and competences took place between the Oba and his chiefs. Indeed the title-making procedures as a whole (which are far more complex than can be indicated here) represent a compromise between 'sultanic' arbitrariness and the rights which the chiefly orders were able to appropriate as corporate groups. Before completion there was nothing to stop the Oba revoking the title. Once the chiefs had sanctioned the completion rites, he was no longer free to do so.

There was, of course, an immense gap between the ascriptive context of promotion to village elderhood and the highly competitive context of recruitment to state titles, but parallels between village elders and state chiefs were quite overt. The manner in which the chiefs sanctioned the induction of a designated title-holder was regarded as homologous to the procedure whereby a villager, seeking promotion to the *edion* grade, had to kneel before each elder in his house to present him with yams and seek his blessing. Thus, according to contrary but equally explicit principles, the chiefs' authority derived from both the Oba and from the community. It was as elders of the Edo that the Town and Palace chiefs accepted the Oba's appointees into their ranks.

The interplay of patrimonial and gerontocratic ideas is particularly explicit in a final phase of the title-taking procedure, of which two phases have already been distinguished. When a man accepted an *eghaebho* title from the Oba he thereby mortgaged to him his whole personal estate. In order to redeem it he had to perform a most elaborate and costly rite known as *inyahien*, which by no means all chiefs succeeded in accomplishing before they died. *Inyahien* involved the chief in a further round of prestations to the king and his fellow-chiefs. At the culmination of this rite the chief wore on his head a block of white chalk, over which was sprinkled the blood of a cow sacrificed to his head by the Oba's own priests. This chalk was known as *ede*, meaning, literally, 'grey hair'. The late *Osuma*, who was one of the few chiefs to have performed *inyahien* in the twentieth century, explained that the *ede* signified the Edo belief that no man was worthy of a voice in public affairs until he had the experience and wisdom that comes with age. The central meaning of *inyahien* is, I think, plain. It effected a symbolic resolution of the contradiction between the patrimonial and gerontocratic components of chiefly authority. By empowering his own priests to bless the head of the chief and thereby relinquishing his claim to death dues, the Oba recognized the complementarity of the kingship and the community as sources of authority.

It was more particularly the Town Chiefs who assumed the mantle of elders of the Edo community. The paradox noted elsewhere (Bradbury 1967: 25-28) that, although they were appointed by the king, they were yet regarded as the proper defenders of the Edo against Palace tyranny, becomes intelligible in these terms; as do the contradictory elements in the role expectations of their leader, the *Iyase*, who was both the Oba's first subject (*okao-evien-Oba*) and his most likely worst enemy. According to the Edo model of political conflict, the *Oba* and *Iyase* occupied polar positions around which opposing factions were always likely to crystallize (Bradbury 1968).

The first four Town Chiefs, *Iyase*, *Esogban*, *Eson*, and *Osuma* were known as The Four *Eghaebho* (*Eghaebho n'Ene*) or The Four Pillars of Edo (*Ikadel 'Ene Edo*), the latter term – which refers to the four poles supporting the roof of a farm shelter or market stall – being also applied to the *Edion n'Ene* – that is, the four oldest men of a village. Moreover, the *Esogban* was – figuratively but functionally – the 'oldest man' of the Edo community, the *Odionwere-Edo*. In his official house he kept the altar of the *Edion-Edo*, on which was placed the *Ukhurhe-Edo*, the carved staff which symbolized the authority of the dead elders of the nation. Across the broad avenue which divided the palace from the rest of the capital, the shrine of the *Edion-Edo* confronted the row of walled quadrangles which housed the altars of the past kings. This symbolic confrontation had great political significance. In times of political crisis, when there was serious dissension between the king and his chiefs, a request by the Oba to the *Odionwere-Edo* that he should sacrifice to the *Edion-Edo* was a clear indication of the king's desire to restore peace. By renewing the compact between himself and his predecessors and the people and their dead, he indicated his willingness to negotiate a settlement of the issues at stake.

The Oba's inability to dismiss officials who had completed their titles – whether in his own reign or his predecessor's – was an important restraint upon his personal power. Another such restraint was afforded by the popular conviction that the rank order of the uppermost titles in each hierarchy was unalterable. Opposition to the king's claim to the right to promote, demote, and abolish titles at will was expressed in the gerontocratic formula that titles should rank in order of their antiquity; that is, by reference to the position in the king-list of the Oba who had created them. The king's ability to put his 'sultanic' claims into effect depended upon the efficacy of the political support that chiefs adversely affected could secure from other chiefs and from the public. As far as lesser titles were concerned, the cross-cutting of interests that I have described elsewhere (1968: 198-9) gave him considerable manipulative scope. But the senior titles in each group appear, from both tradition and such contemporary documents as bear upon this matter, to have remained undisturbed over a period of centuries. Indeed, the senior titles in each order or sub-order are said to be those which were given to the founding members when it was first established – in many cases by Oba Ewuare.

The sacrosanct quality of these senior titles rested, in part, on the fact that they were associated with ritual functions indispensable to the fulfilment of the Oba's mystical obligations to the Edo. The king's mystical powers were ineffective unless they were complemented by mystical powers inherent in the community itself. At the level of the kingdom these powers were concentrated in the senior chiefs – especially the Town Chiefs – just as at the village level they were concentrated in the elders. The precise order of rank among the village *edion* was not of crucial importance until it became necessary to fill a vacancy among the *Edion n'Ene*. These first four positions had the character of offices, and seniority resided in the office rather than in the age of the incumbent – though ideally the two should coincide. This latter requirement was absent with respect to state titles but, in Edo eyes, the titles *Iyase, Esogban, Eson,* and *Osuma* were the oldest in their order and therefore equivalent to the *Edion n'Ene*. Their rank order was as immutable as that of the four days of the Edo week with which they were ritually associated (cf. Bradbury 1967).

CONCLUSION – THE PRINCIPLES DRAMATIZED IN THE CEREMONIAL OF SUCCESSION

Nowhere are patrimonial and gerontocratic principles more intricately opposed than in the formal and ceremonial procedures by which the kingship was transmitted. In order to become an elder of the nation, an Edo commoner had first to receive a patrimonial appointment. Again, as we have noted, before the successor to an *Uzama* title could be inducted into office he had to be initiated into one of the palace associations. This involved not only taking an oath of loyalty to the king but also serving, if only nominally, as a retainer in the royal household. With one exception, the *Uzama* were inducted into office by the *Iyase*, the senior title-holder of the Town order. The exception was the most senior of the *Uzama*, the *Oliha*. A new *Oliha* had to be invested by the Oba personally. This was not a device to avoid questions of seniority between *Oliha* and *Iyase*: the Edo were asserting the complementary relationship between the king and the elders of the kingdom, just as they did in the creation of a new king.

According to the patrimonial ideology, the king himself chose his successor. He made his will known by causing the child whom he regarded as his senior son to undergo a series of rites of passage which culminated in the bestowal upon him of the title of *Edaiken*. Like all other patrimonial appointees, the heir-apparent, however, had to make prestations to the chiefs and be inducted into office by the *Iyase*, acting in his dual role as spokesman for the Oba and for the Edo. Thereupon he took his place as the most junior member of the *Uzama* order.

When these nobles ate together, the *Edaiken's* task, as the most junior of them, was to share out the food, just as the most junior *odion* in the village served food to the village elders. When the senior *Uzama*, *Oliha*, broke kola nuts the *Edaiken* was the last to receive his portion. It will be recalled that the *Uzama* were identified as the elders whose request to the Oni of Ife led to the founding of the dynasty. In the rituals of kingship they, rather than the Town Chiefs, were explicitly cast in the role of *edion* (elders). Thus it was by admission to the *Uzama* order that the future Oba achieved elderhood. Through the elderhood of the *Uzama*, the Edo asserted their claim that, in the final reckoning, the Oba ruled by the will of the community. In their capacity as *edion* they owned the kingship. They received the fees that the heir paid on his accession, and a new reign began when the *Edaiken* knelt before them to be pronounced Oba by the *Oliha*.

The Edo say '*Oba* makes *Oliha* and *Oliha* makes *Oba!*' The ceremonies thus characterized show dramatically the dialectic of patrimonialism and gerontocracy in the Benin polity.

REFERENCES

BENDIX, R. 1960. *Max Weber: An Intellectual Portrait.* London: Methuen.

BOSMAN, W. 1967. *A New and Accurate Description of the Coast of Guinea.* (New edition). London: Cass.

BRADBURY, R. E. 1957. *The Benin Kingdom and the Edo-speaking Peoples of South-Western Nigeria.* Ethnographic Survey of Africa, Western Africa, Pt. XIII. London: International African Institute.

— 1964. The Historical Uses of Comparative Ethnography with special reference to Benin and the Yoruba. In J. Vansina, R. Mauny & L. Thomas (eds.), *The Historian in Tropical Africa.* London: Oxford University Press.

— 1966. Fathers, Elders, and Ghosts in Edo Religion. In M. Banton (ed.), *Anthropological Approaches to the Study of Religion.* Association of Social Anthropologists Monographs, 3. London: Tavistock.

— 1967. The Kingdom of Benin. In D. Forde and P. Kaberry (eds.), *West African Kingdoms in the Nineteenth Century.* London: Oxford University Press for the International African Institute.

—1968. Continuities and Discontinuities in Pre-Colonial and Colonial Benin Politics (1897-1951). In I. M. Lewis (ed.), *History and Social Anthropology.* A.S.A. Monographs, 7. London: Tavistock.

ROTH, H. LING 1903. *Great Benin: its Customs, Art and Horrors.* Halifax: F. King & Sons.

SOUTHWOLD, M. 1961. *Bureaucracy and Chiefship in Buganda.* East African Studies, No. 14.

WEBER, M. 1947. *The Theory of Social and Economic Organization.* London: Hodge.

WILKS, I. 1967. Ashanti Government. In D. Forde and P. Kaberry (eds.), *West African Kingdoms in the Nineteenth Century.* London: Oxford University Press for the International African Institute.

Robin Horton

From Fishing Village to City-state
A Social History of New Calabar

This essay is an interim report on work towards a social history of the Niger Delta trading state of Owame or New Calabar.[1] Any such work must, of course, take into account Dike's pioneering book on the external relations of the Delta states and Jones's follow-up on the internal structure and development of these states (1965). From my fairly extended stay in New Calabar, indeed, I have come to feel that Jones's masterly account of its structure and development in the seventeenth to the nineteenth century cannot be substantially improved upon (ibid. esp. chs. 9-12). None the less, Jones leaves several fascinating questions open for further research, and it is here that I come in.

One of the outstanding questions is: what kind of a community was New Calabar before it embarked upon the Atlantic Trade? Another is: why did New Calabar make the particular response it did to the challenge of this trade – a response which was very different from that of Old Calabar and rather different even from that of its Ijo neighbour Bonny? These two questions are almost certainly connected. For, if the various states developed in different ways under the same external stimulus, this must have been because there were important differences between them at the outset.

Now, in trying to answer these questions, one is clearly on ground much more slippery than that trod by Dike and Jones. Thus Jones was able to make an impressive reconstruction of seventeenth-to-nineteenth-century history by cross-checking copious oral traditions with numerous contemporary European documents. But for the earlier, formative period of New Calabar history, say the fourteenth to the sixteenth century, one is faced with very scanty traditions and a complete absence of European documents. Here, then, less orthodox methods must be found.

My approach to this difficult task has been influenced from the first by the observation that New Calabar shares its language and large areas of its culture with twenty neighbouring villages – the whole population being known as Kalabari. The culture and social organization of New Calabar does, it is true, differ in certain respects from that of its village neighbours. But then it was the only one of these communities to abandon fishing and enter fully into the Atlantic Trade. Now, since one can reasonably suppose that these last two facts are connected, I have set out by assuming that New Calabar started out with roughly the same culture and social organization as we see among its contemporary village neighbours, but later underwent certain changes as a consequence of entering into the Trade. On such an assumption, a study of the villages can provide important clues as to the pre-Trade characteristics of the state.

There are of course difficulties. As its power grew with the success of the Trade, New Calabar came to exercise suzerainty over many of its neighbours; and it has been argued that those of its cultural features which the latter share may simply have been imposed on them during this period of suzerainty. If this were true, it would invalidate the initial assumption and make the programme based on it fruitless. Fortunately, however, I think we can discount this argument. If its premiss were true, one would expect to find that the degree of a neighbour's cultural affinity with New Calabar was proportional to the degree of suzerainty the latter had been exercising over it. In fact, however, we find no such correlation. On the one hand, several neighbouring villages that retain a blatantly foreign linguistic and cultural flavour came very strongly under New Calabar influence. On the other hand, several villages that show very close cultural affinities with New Calabar were on the fringes of this influence.

Another difficulty besetting our attempts at reconstruction comes from the implied assumption that, while the culture of New Calabar has departed markedly from its fifteenth-century baseline, the culture of its neighbours has not done so. Since a period of at least 450 years is involved, this assumption may well seem dubious. One way out here is to invoke the well-tried sociological generalization that, in pre-industrial societies, spontaneous change tends to be far less spectacular than change induced by gross external pressures. So far as we know anything about the course of the last 450 years in this area, it seems unlikely that the villages have been subjected to any gross external pressure comparable with that represented in New Calabar by the Atlantic Trade. Hence we can say fairly that they are likely to be far closer to the fifteenth-century baseline than is New Calabar itself. Again, as I hope to show presently, the salient features of village organization are consistent with an environmental background which, so far as we know, has remained constant for several hundred years – another reason for thinking that they have not diverged in any spectacular way from the pre-Trade baseline.

In any case, what we have here is a hypothesis. As such, its value does not depend on the possibility of direct confirmation of each of its several assumptions. If these assumptions, taken jointly, prove to have high explanatory power, then the hypothesis can be treated as a likely one. In fact, it does account very fully for the pattern of similarity and difference between New Calabar and its neighbours. It also accounts for the particular pattern of New Calabar response to the Slave Trade, and suggests plausible reasons why this pattern differed from those that emerged in Old Calabar and Bonny. It is in this light that the whole enterprise must be judged.

THE FISHING VILLAGE

In building up a model of the baseline socio-cultural patterns of the area, I have instituted a sort of double-check. On the one hand, I have worked intensively in the village of Soku. This village is particularly relevant in the present context. It is one of the communities which, while showing marked cultural affinities with New Calabar, has been on the very fringe of the latter's domination. Its affinities are thus more readily explained as dating from the pre-Trade era than as products of such domination. On the other hand, I have done less intensive survey work in a representative sample of the rest of the fishing villages.[2] As the basis of my model, I have made a list of salient features which are (*a*) characteristic of Soku, and (*b*) common to most of the other fishing villages. That they are characteristic of Soku rules out the possibility of their having been borrowed from New Calabar. And that they are common to most of the other villages excludes, of course, the possibility of their being peculiar to Soku.

In presenting my picture of the 'typical' Kalabari fishing village, I shall use the past tense. This seems advisable because, although many of the traditional institutions are still functioning smoothly, some have been heavily modified or put out of action by the changes of the last fifty years.[3]

The typical village was a compact settlement of some 200-1000 people. Most of the men were engaged in fishing, for which they used fence-traps, lines of hooks, and spears. They sold their surplus fish in the hinterland markets, whence they brought down foodstuffs. The Kalabari fisherman had great freedom in the choice of a working partner, who might come from anywhere in the village, and in the choice of fishing ground, which might be anywhere in village waters.[4]

Although the fisherman enjoyed unrestricted rights to the productive resources of the village, his rights to settlement land came to him through membership of a descent group known as a 'house', *wari*. Each *wari* was organized on the basis of a dual system of marriage. In *iya* marriage, payment of high bride-wealth incorporated the offspring into the father's *wari*. In *igwa* marriage, payment of low bridewealth left them in the mother's *wari*. This meant that a person traced descent from the founder of his or her *wari* through a line of mixed male and female links, a line whose exact composition depended on the kinds of marriage made by the person's forebears. Of the two kinds of marriage, *iya* was the most prestigious, but the cost made it rare. Hence the links through which *wari* membership was traced were predominantly uterine.

A number of descent groups commonly formed a larger unit, also known as *wari* or as *polo*. Following Jones, I shall refer to this larger unit as a ward (Jones 1965: 55 and 159). The descent groups making up the ward were often of unequal size. They were not usually thought of as genealogically related. Rather, they were thought of as united by ties of common origin from a particular earlier settlement.

Like the descent group, the ward was predominantly concerned with the allocation of land and of heritable wealth generally. In both units, deliberations on such matters took place under the presidency of a man who had been appointed head of the group on consideration of mature age and wisdom.

Descent group and ward had very partial claims to the allegiance of their members. Indeed, there were many other kinds of ties which competed with and diminished the force of these claims. Most important of these, perhaps, were kinship ties outside the *wari*. There was a feeling that close relatives should always support one another, no matter what the line through which relationship was traced. *Inter alia,* this feeling gave many people a second line of claim to settlement land.[5] This strong bilateral emphasis, I suggest, was connected with a tendency to marriage within the village. A consequence of this tendency was that one's kinsmen outside the *wari* were as much one's neighbours as one's kinsmen within it; hence they came to be considered as equally important. As a result, allegiance to the *wari* was weakened by a thick web of interpersonal ties binding the villagers to one another in every conceivable direction.

Another focus of loyalty outside the *wari* was membership of an age-set, *biri*. The foundations of the age-set were laid down in childhood when a gang of young boys, of roughly the same age and drawn from all parts of the village, ran loose together in play. When they reached adulthood, members of the gang came to be recognized as members of one *biri*. The *biri* provided an important setting for conviviality and recreation. Members were obliged to come to each other's aid on all occasions, and especially at funerals of parents and other close relatives. To preserve solidarity, they were pledged to avoid interfering with one another's wives. The number of *biri* formally recognized varied from village to village. Typically, it fell between seven and fifteen.

Let us turn now to the organization of the village as a functioning whole. People thought of their village in terms very different from those in which they thought of their descent group. In the first place, village origin myths made no use of the idea of descent from a common ancestor. On the contrary, they tended to stress diversity of origins. In positive terms, people defined their village by its territorial isolation from other communities, by its political autonomy under a distinctive body of village laws, and above all by its possession of a distinctive culture or way of life – its *amangangabara*.

So far as village origin myths took account of the various descent groups and wards, they laid stress not on their equivalence and potential opposition but on their complementarity. In some villages, each ward was said to have 'brought something' from its original settlement, and these supposed contributions were the basis for allocating ritual offices.

Most important of the various village institutions was the assembly, *ama kobiri*, which had both policy-making and judicial functions, and dealt with all village affairs other than minor matters arising within particular descent groups or age-sets. The assembly was made up of the entire adult male population, which in this context sat in two age-grades – elders (*umungiapu*) and young men (*asawo*). Presiding over it was the village head (*amanyanabo*), who was typically appointed from a descent group in the ward that claimed discovery of the village site. Reasons for meeting and the substance of decisions were announced by a spokesman (*amaso*), who also was usually appointed from a particular ward. More coveted than either of these offices, however, was the informal leadership of the assembly. Such leadership was open to anyone of a mature age and depended on sheer political and rhetorical ability. It could be lost to another leader as readily as it had been gained. In building up a following in the assembly, the would-be leader made use of a variety of claims – membership of the same *wari*, membership of the same *biri*, friendship, etc. Hence conflict in the village tended to be between temporary and shifting personal followings rather than between permanent groups such as the *wari*.

Two major concerns of the assembly were ensuring the smooth performance of the communal rituals that maintained the strength of the village, and directing warfare. Ritual offices were distributed among the various wards; and the assembly made sure that, whenever one of these offices fell vacant, the appropriate ward produced a replacement. In arranging a military expedition against some other village, the assembly often packed all its young men, under the leadership of one of their number, into a single large war canoe. In larger villages, there might be two canoes, with the village wards divided into two groups for the purpose of filling them. The individual ward, however, was not a fighting unit.

Two other important village institutions functioned alongside but independently of the assembly. First of these was the *ekine* society. *Ekine* was an association devoted to the performance of masquerades representing the water-spirits. Entry was open to any adult male who could convince an established member that his dancing ability warranted the latter's sponsorship. The fee was a small payment of trade gin. The association had a junior and a senior grade, and promotion from one to the other was also largely determined by dancing ability.

In *ekine*, a series of religious rituals had been developed into something that was virtually an art practised for its own sake (Horton 1963). At the same time, *ekine* served as an instrument for education in the finer nuances of village culture – this through its insistence on learning the drum language as a central skill involved in the masquerade, and on learning to 'point' in response to calls from the drums. First of all, since the drum language consisted essentially of tone patterns abstracted from speech, one had to acquire a complete fluency in the ordinary language in order to learn it. Secondly, the 'pointing' ceremonial of the masquerade, in so far as it involved pointing to the shrines of hero-gods and ancestors in response to their drum names, involved the acquisition of a fund of the community's myth and history. Thirdly, since many of these drum names took the form of proverb or metaphor, learning them plunged one deep into traditional imagery and attitudes. Finally, the drum language was a vital means of communication, used in many contexts of village life. In short, a member of the senior grade of *ekine*, having mastered the drum language and the pointing ceremonial, was a cultured member of the community in the deepest sense. Understandably, then, Kalabari villagers felt that being a senior member of the association was almost a *sine qua non* of full citizenship.

The last village institution I shall mention is the headhunters' association, *periapu ogbo*. This was an association of all those who had successfully caught a man alive and brought him back to the village to kill. Whenever such a killing took place, the society foregathered for a feast and for a demonstration of its collective powers. Though head-hunting was an inevitable by-product of war, it also took the form of individual expeditions to waylay travellers in times of peace. The head-hunting expedition typified the enterprising, dashing, aggressive style of life expected of the Kalabari villager. It was, indeed, the sign and seal of his manhood.

The salient features which emerge from this brief account of Kalabari fishing village society are the encouragement of individual choice, enterprise, and achievement in all spheres of life, the relatively limited importance of descent groups, the compactness, self-sufficiency, and hostility to outsiders of the community as a whole, and the concurrent insistence on the 'open' criteria of culture and residence as the bases of communal identity.

These features, it seems to me, are highly consistent with the characteristics of the Eastern Delta environment, and with the prevailing techniques used to wrest a living from it.

First of all, unlike farming, fishing can be carried on without long, continuous attachment of a particular person or people to a particular site. Hence it does not demand a clearly defined set of rules for allocating territorial rights. Secondly, if we consider the creeks and their fish as the community's main productive resources, it is evident that compared with land they are none too amenable to subdivision. Fish tend to congregate in different parts of the community's waters at different seasons. Then, even at a given season, they are not always to be found moving in the same way from year to year. Areas of land can usually be fairly divided because they behave with relative constancy. Areas of creek behave inconstantly enough to make any scheme for their division difficult. And this perhaps is why the majority of Kalabari villages left their waters undivided.

This lack of subdivision of the productive territory left maximum scope for the exercise of individual initiative in choice of fishing grounds and planning of fishing operations. Further, it meant that the owner of a canoe and tackle was not bound to partners of his *wari* or of any other sub-group, and was able, within the limits of the village, to get help from anyone he liked. It also meant that no partnership need be more than ephemeral. All this, once again, favoured individual choice and enterprise.

Because the descent group and the ward held rights in settlement land but not in productive resources, their importance in village life was correspondingly limited. The weakness of these units contributed in turn to the fostering of individual choice and initiative in village affairs.

Producing fish but not other foodstuffs, Kalabari villagers traded their surplus product upstream. Economic interchange with neighbouring Delta communities was low. This led to a high degree of social isolation of the individual village. One symptom of such isolation was village endogamy which, as I have already suggested, contributed to the weakening of descent group ties. Another symptom was the head-hunting and raiding which seem to have been such prominent features of life in this area.

Now in a situation dominated by absence of strong inter-village ties, by head-hunting raids, and by punitive counter-raids, there would have been strong pressure on the community to adopt citizenship criteria suited to absorbing newcomers and hence to building up defence potential. The criteria of culture and residence, referring to achieved rather than ascribed characteristics, were well suited to these ends.[6] Such criteria, in turn, gave further encouragement to the prevailing individualism.

The features of the ecological situation that I have just outlined have almost certainly been operative since before the days of the Atlantic Trade. The fact that the salient features of Kalabari village organization are highly consistent with them gives one a good reason for thinking that the latter are of equal antiquity. It also gives one confidence in the usefulness of this model of village organization as a basis for understanding the New Calabar response to the Atlantic Trade.[7]

THE CITY-STATE

Owame, or New Calabar as the European traders called it, was the first Kalabari community to turn from fishing to the Atlantic Trade. Though members of two or three other communities came in later, they did so under the aegis of New Calabar.

New Calabar was sited a few miles from the mouth of one of the larger and more navigable Delta estuaries – well placed for contact both with the European merchants and with the hinterland markets. Its first contacts with the merchants probably took place at the end of the fifteenth century. And the first written accounts giving any details of its social organization, those of Dapper (1686) and Barbot (1746), suggest a community whose organization was already markedly different from that of the fishing villages.

One of the most striking consequences of entry into the Atlantic Trade was the eclipse of the rather modest descent groups of the fishing village by other institutions which, though they too took on the name *wari*, exercised an altogether more dominant influence on the lives of their members. Following Jones, I shall refer to these newer institutions as canoe houses (Jones 1965: 55).

Though we shall never know exactly how the canoe house came to replace the older type of descent group, what probably happened was something like this. The European merchants made contact with enterprising individuals in the community, gave them advances of trade goods, and asked them to go up to the hinterland markets to bring back cargoes of slaves. With profits from the trade, these enterprising people started to buy slaves not only for sale at the mouth of the river, but also for incorporation into their own households. As the trading households grew larger, their heads gave promising slaves advances of goods to start trade on their own account. These minor traders, however, could only carry on their deals with the merchants by permission of their household-heads. Moreover, they paid a tax of trade goods to their household-heads in return for this permission.

The system of putting ultimate control of the trade in the hands of a few known and reputable operators made minor traders dependent on the big men, and the big men responsible to the merchants for the minor traders' honesty. We cannot now tell how far this was a European-inspired arrangement, but it was adopted at several points along the coast; and one imagines that, from the point of view of securing a smooth flow of trade, it made good sense to both sides. It was this big trader's household, with its minor traders operating only with their head's permission and on payment of a tax to him, that crystallized into the New Calabar canoe house.

The canoe house was not only a trading corporation under the control of an independent trader, it was also a military unit manning a thirty-man war canoe. On the one hand, the war canoe was an essential piece of trading equipment, for slave cargoes often had to be convoyed down from the markets to avoid ambush by members of rival trading communities such as Okrika, Bonny, and Nembe. On the other hand, it was a weapon of offence or defence which the house-head was expected to bring to the service of the community. For both the merchants and the people of New Calabar, then, the ability to man a war canoe would have been a sign of substance and responsibility. So when the houses came to be formally recognized by the community, it became the criterion both of fitness to establish a new house and of fitness to continue as the head of an old one.

As I have said, the first canoe houses were almost certainly founded by wealthy traders, and the qualifications for succession to their headship continued to lay great emphasis on commercial ability and drive. Although it was considered preferable for one of a man's sons to succeed him in the headship of a canoe house, a slave-born person who by character and ability was more fitted to the position than any of the sons had a good chance of succeeding in their stead.

Although succession was a matter for determination by all male members of the canoe house, the new head, once installed, enjoyed a measure of real power quite unknown to the head of the village descent group or ward. The sources of this power were several. First of all, he was the only member of the house with whom the merchants would negotiate on matters of trade, and in this capacity he determined who of his members could trade on their own account and who could not. Secondly, as well as being the custodian of house funds generally, he was the recipient of a tax from all those to whom he granted permission to trade. And these resources he used not only to maintain the war canoe and its ammunition, but also to give a start to such of his house people as enjoyed his favour. Thirdly, he was an important source of wives. Not only did he tie his favourite traders to him by giving them his daughters in marriage, he also used his wealth to buy female slaves who were, again, distributed to his favourites as wives.

Whereas the village descent group had a relatively stable population and did not segment, the successful canoe house was constantly enlarged through the activities of the head and his traders in buying slaves for recruitment into the group. When an able trader had bought a sufficient number of slaves to enable him to carry on independent commercial operations as well as man a war canoe, he usually pressed his house-head to let him establish his own independent canoe house. In practice, the house-head seldom refused this since, by giving his permission, he gained a new ally in the state council, whereas had he withheld permission he would have landed himself with a chronically disgruntled section within the house. In any case, the whole process leading up to the budding off of a new house was to a considerable extent under the house-head's control, for it was he who could advance or retard the ambitious man's career by giving or withholding slaves and loans of trade goods.

You will notice that I have been treating the canoe houses as the successors of the village descent groups. They were, in fact, the successors of these groups in two senses. First of all, they grew up alongside them, eclipsed them in importance, and finally absorbed what was left of them by offering their members protection. Secondly, however, they took over the kinship idiom of the descent groups. For, in buying slaves for integration into his household, the buyer not only bought them very young, he also gave them fictional kinship ties to himself, to the wife who looked after them, and to his children by this wife. He was 'father' to them, his wife was 'mother' to them; and his own children were 'brother' and 'sister' to them. These fictions were far from empty ones. When the newly bought slave arrived in the community, the breaking-off of all his previous kinship ties and the assumption of a whole series of new ties was brought home to him by means of a dramatic *rite de passage* in which his new 'mother' shaved his head clean and then gave him a ritual meal. From then on, the 'mother' was supposed to live up to her title in the fullest possible sense. One of the reasons for the large number of wives taken by canoe house-heads seems to have been the provision of enough women to do an adequate job of 'mothering' all the young slaves they bought. There were severe penalties for referring publicly to the fictional nature either of a man's kinship ties to his fellow house-members or of his descent from his house-founder. Publicly calling a slave a slave was a heinous crime. The use of kinship idiom, then, did a great deal to ensure that the slave was assimilated into the house on the same footing as the free-born, and to instil in him the same loyalties.

48

This device, of course, did not work perfectly. Though one might never allude openly to the fact that somebody was not the real son of his 'mother' or the real brother of her children, a clear distinction remained in people's minds and did influence their behaviour. But although this distinction operated to the disadvantage of the slave-born in some circumstances, it operated to their advantage in others. For the slave who grew up stupid and unadaptable, life seems to have been hard and insecure. True, the law of the land gave the man who had been bought into the community a right to life and livelihood which was theoretically the same as that enjoyed by the son of the soil; but in practice things were a bit different. When the stupid, unadaptable slave got himself into trouble, 'mother' and 'brothers' tended to remember that they were not really of the same flesh and blood, and seldom insisted very strongly on the unfortunate man's rights. In consequence he was often mercilessly punished or deprived of his life, where a free-born would have been let off lightly. For the intelligent and adaptable slave, on the other hand, this very lack of real mothers and brothers was his greatest asset. Such a man often enjoyed more of his master's confidence than did the latter's own sons. For whereas he was entirely dependent on his master's favour, the real sons were always protected by their mothers' families, and were apt to be influenced by them in ways beyond their father's control. In other words, though the unadaptable or lazy slave got short shrift, the adaptable and ambitious slave had chances of rising to eminence which were sometimes as good as or better than those of the free-born son. In this respect, the canoe house was a relentless sorting machine, crushing the ill endowed but propelling the more dynamic, intelligent personalities to the top of the social scale.[8]

This sketch of the canoe house brings out the overwhelmingly important part that it came to play in everybody's life. Whereas in the village the individual's economic fortunes were in no way controlled by the descent group, in New Calabar such fortunes were intimately linked to those of the house. Again, whereas in the village a man's political advancement scarcely depended on his descent group, in New Calabar it was absolutely dependent on his house. Yet again, while the villager turned for mutual aid and conviviality to his age-set, the man of

New Calabar found these within his house. Finally, while the villager took his wives from descent groups other than his own, this was not true of the average member of the New Calabar house. For although the head of the house and some of the most influential members married widely from other houses, the average member mostly took or was given his wives from within the house. On the one hand, then, the individual became dependent on his house for nearly everything he needed in life; and, on the other, group memberships and individual relationships that might have weakened loyalty to the house largely withered away.

Added to all this was the radically changed manner in which these segments of the community were seen to be related to each other. In the village, descent groups and wards were seen as standing in a complementary relation to one another. One descent group or ward had brought one thing to the community, while another had brought something else. In New Calabar, the canoe houses stood to each other in no such complementary relationship. They were seen as fully comparable and equivalent, and always as potentially opposed.

The overwhelming importance of the houses in the lives of their members, the withering away of cross-cutting ties, the absence of any idea of complementary relationship – all these left the new institutions standing starkly opposed and ready for conflict. And conflict there was in plenty.

Let us now turn to the community as a whole. Basic ideas about the nature of the community remained the same as in the villages. Ideas of descent from a single founder played no part. Rather, the diversity of origin was stressed. In positive terms, the identity of New Calabar was seen in terms of the possession of a distinct, isolated settlement area, of autonomy under a distinctive body of laws, and of the possession of a distinctive culture. As in the villages, this definition of identity was essentially open in its implications. Anyone who could acquire the culture and pull his weight could become a citizen. As the drum name of the earth of New Calabar put it: 'If a dog walks on him, he does not spurn the leg; if a goat walks on him, he does not spurn the leg.' Although this open definition of the community was part of the pre-Slave-Trade inheritance of New Calabar, it clearly had important implications for the slaving era. Indeed,

it can be seen as forming the background to the whole programme of assimilating slaves into the canoe houses.

As in the villages, the public assembly was the most important
communal institution and the principal organ of government in
both policy-making and judicial spheres. But although the
assembly owed something to earlier traditions of village government, its organization was really rather different. In the first
place, participation in it was far more restricted. Instead of the
entire adult male population, only the house-heads and the
amanyanabo (see below) were now permitted to take part.
Secondly, there was no longer any sign of the division into two
age-grades. Instead, there was a division into 'big chiefs'
(those who in addition to heading their own houses exercised
an influence over whole groups of related houses) and 'small
chiefs' (those who merely headed their own houses). Thirdly,
whereas in the villages representation in the assembly was not
on a segment-by-segment basis, in New Calabar it was. One
house provided one chief. These various changes reflected certain
general consequences of the switch from a fishing to a slave-
trading economy: the concentration of power in the hands of the
limited number of people who controlled the Trade, the decline
in the importance of age as a status criterion, and the emergence
of the house system as a way of subdividing the population
which overrode and overwhelmed all others.

As in the villages, the New Calabar assembly was headed by
the *amanyanabo*. By the time of the earliest written accounts,
however, the latter had come to exercise very much more real
power than his village counterpart and could be described as a
paramount chief or king. Although he was still appointed from a
particular descent group, and had to be able to claim real descent
from its founder, he had also to be a man of substance in his own
right, with wealth and a large following of slaves. At his most
powerful, he was a constant initiator and enforcer of policies;
and even at his least powerful, he was an important holder of
the balance between factions in the assembly. Like the power of
the house-heads, that of the *amanyanabo* was buttressed to an
important extent by his position *vis-à-vis* the European merchants. As we saw earlier, the merchants held the house-heads
responsible for the honesty of all minor traders. In turn, they
held the *amanyanabo* responsible for the safety of themselves and

their properties at the hands of the house-heads and of his people generally. In return for the discharge of this responsibility, he was entitled to receive from every merchant about to open trade a standard but handsome sum of protection money known as 'comey'. Since he was already a substantial trader, this second source of income did much to keep him in a dominant position.

As the principal organ of government, the assembly of house-heads and *amanyanabo* was not particularly successful in maintaining order and regulating conflict. Indeed, throughout most of its career as a trading state, New Calabar remained in a condition of chronic instability. Rivalry between powerful groups of houses actually blew it apart on two occasions: once in the late seventeenth century, when the *amanyanabo* Oweri Daba and his followers fled and scattered over the Eastern Delta; and once during the late nineteenth century, when the state finally broke up to form the three towns of Buguma, Abonemma, and Bakana. For long periods in between these explosions, there was an ever-present threat of civil strife.[9]

As I said earlier, the canoe houses, by their very nature, were in a state of constant potential opposition. Much of their actual strife stemmed from competition between their heads for the position of prime influence of the *amanyanabo*. Some of the bitterest strife arose from competition for the office of *amanyanabo* itself – vastly attractive compared with its village prototype. Such competition took two forms. First, two candidates from within an established chiefly descent group tended to recruit rival house-heads to help them dispute their claims. Secondly, from time to time, one house or group of houses tried to replace another as the chiefly descent group.

The assembly was able to do very little to regulate these types of competition. If anything, indeed, it was so constituted as to encourage them. Thus house-by-house representation dramatized the prevailing lines of cleavage instead of blurring them. Again, though the ordinary public no longer took active part, they were by all accounts enthusiastic spectators. Every house-head, then, was on display before his house-members; and, since it was to the latter alone that he was responsible for his conduct, there was continual pressure on him to put sectional interests before those of the community.

Given the obvious inadequacies of the New Calabar assembly, one may well ask why some wise and powerful *amanyanabo* did not encourage the *ekine* society to take a more active governmental role. *Ekine*, with its exclusion of the public from its meetings, with its abhorrence of sectional rivalries, and with its immense prestige, could well have provided a forum for government more conducive to the spirit of compromise and communal interest. Such an assignment of governmental roles to secret cult associations has been a common feature of West African political development: think for instance of the Yoruba *Ogboni*, and, nearer the area we are talking about, the Efik *Ekpe*. Perhaps the reason why neither *ekine* nor any other institution was allowed to usurp the authority of the assembly of house-heads was that, as the Atlantic Trade developed, the power of these men over their respective segments developed *pari passu* with the power of the *amanyanabo* over the state as a whole. At no time would the house-heads have agreed willingly to give up part of their collective authority to an institution in which they rubbed shoulders with commoners; and at no time was any *amanyanabo* powerful enough to force them into doing so.

But, although *ekine* was never adapted to resolving the problem of stable government which so plagued New Calabar, it proved of great value in relation to that other preoccupation of the trading state – the assimilation of slaves.

In the state, as in the villages, *ekine* masquerades continued to be executed and attended to as works of art in their own right. As regards the more general educative function of *ekine*, this was insisted upon if anything more strongly than in the villages. Thus in the bigger masquerades, one of which a man had to perform before being promoted from the junior to the senior grade of *ekine*, a good deal of understanding of the drum language had always been involved. But in New Calabar, this knowledge of drum language was made the subject of a rigorous ordeal, whereby the masquerader had to point to thirty-three shrines of state heroes and royal ancestors when their names were called on the drum. If he failed on one call, he was publicly demasked and ridiculed – a fate which people say was once enough to provoke suicide.

The implications of *ekine* activities for a state trying to conduct a massive integration of aliens were profound. On the one hand, anyone who amassed wealth and some power without becoming an accomplished member of *ekine* could only be regarded as a ridiculous *parvenu*, so that the pressure to join the society and get on in it was immense. On the other hand, the only prerequisite for getting on in *ekine* was ability to learn the various skills involved in the masquerade – something a slave was as likely to be endowed with as a free-born. Not surprisingly then, most intelligent, ambitious slaves employed a great deal of their energy in becoming accomplished members of *ekine*. And, given the nature of *ekine* activities, they could hardly help but come to the top of the social ladder as deeply acculturated people.[10]

The last of the three key communal institutions of the village was, it will be remembered, the association of head-hunters. Like *ekine*, it survived in the New Calabar state – though again with certain changes of emphasis which seem significantly related to the nature of the state. The main object of the association remained the catching and killing of men. Once again, the emphasis was on individual enterprise and on spectacular execution. An aspect of the association which seems to have been unique to New Calabar was an inner group known as *koronogbo* – lit., the strong club. It is difficult to be sure what the aims of this group really were, but older informants say that its members came out on certain appointed nights and challenged everyone they met. If those challenged gave their names with a good Kalabari accent, they were allowed to go their way. But, if they gave their names with an accent betraying Ibo or Ibibio origin, they were promptly seized and killed. My own feeling is that *koronogbo* was probably more important in threat than in execution. It may well have been an instrument for terrorizing the poorly acculturated, and for encouraging them to hurry up and learn the Kalabari language. If this interpretation is correct, *ekine* and *koronogbo* must have functioned together like the proverbial carrot and stick – *ekine* offering the reward of high social status to the intelligent and adaptable, and *koronogbo* threatening the ultimate punishment to the lazy and inept.

As instruments of assimilation, *ekine* and *koronogbo* must be seen as working in concert with the canoe house, whose functions in this context I have already described. The joint efficacy of these various institutions can be gathered from two things.

First from the fact that in all the history of New Calabar, there was never a conflict in which slave-born formed up *en bloc* against free-born. Secondly, from the fact that, despite one hundred years or more during which a slave was being brought in from the Ibo hinterland for every person born in the community, the people of New Calabar were remarkably little affected by the language and culture of the immigrants. In both language and culture, they remained almost as thoroughly Kalabari as the fishing villagers.

If New Calabar was chronically unable to solve the problem of containing those conflicts inherent in the nature of the canoe house system, it showed genius in solving the problems of assimilation. Perhaps failure in the first respect was part of the price of success in the second.

If we assume that New Calabar developed from a fishing village baseline, we are likely to be impressed first and foremost by the enormous changes resulting from its entry into the Atlantic Trade. There was the enormous increase in the importance of the segmentary system, and the concomitant atrophy of the various social ties that formerly cut across segmental boundaries. There was the radical change in the pattern of politics. While the village political scene was dominated by shifting personal followings in which descent group membership was only one among many possible bases of recruitment, the New Calabar scene was dominated by oppositions between houses and groups of houses which frequently outlasted the lives of several generations of their individual heads. Finally, there was the great concentration of power in the hands of a small number of people – a concentration reflected in the change from the mass assembly of the village to the chiefly council of the state.

Yet if it is radical change that first impresses us, there was certainly continuity as well. Take, for example, the New Calabar segmentary system. The patterns of canoe-house segmentation were quite unlike those found in the lineage-based societies of the hinterland. Thus an able young man could bud off from his parent house when he had bought and integrated enough slaves to man a war canoe. To begin with, the head of this parent house would sit in the assembly as a big chief – i.e. one who was head of his own house and in addition had a protective influence over one or more 'buds'; the young man would sit as a small chief. But if the young man built up his bud as a powerful and wealthy house, he might well end up by sitting as a big chief, while the head of his parent house was relegated to the rank of a small chief. Not only could an able leader reverse the rank order of himself and his segment in this way, he could, just conceivably, become king and make his house into the royal house. In normal circumstances, succession to the paramount chieftainship was from among the true descendants of the founder of the ruling house. But legends speak of at least one case where, in an era of crisis, a man of exceptional ability came from outside a failing ruling house to found a new dynasty of his own. Nor was this all. The position of house-head was, as we have seen, open to a foreigner or even to a slave who had managed to build a retinue of the required size. And finally, it is worth remembering something many New Calabar people still secretly believe, that the greatest king in their history was a man of foreign birth. We shall never know whether this legend is true or false, but it is said to have inspired ambitious dreams in the mind of at least one ambitious and able slave. All of this is most uncharacteristic of the lineage systems of the hinterland. But its unique character becomes less puzzling when we see it as a product of the individualistic, achievement-oriented values carried over from the village society.

The second point of continuity is, of course, the retention of those open criteria of citizenship (culture and residence) which we found to be such a prominent feature of village organization. These criteria, indeed, were almost certainly the key to the fantastic success of slave integration in New Calabar. Only where they were constantly insisted upon could the idiom of kinship have been used so effectively to make the slave feel as much at home as the free-born, rather than to remind him constantly of his separateness. Only where they dominated social thinking could high political office have been opened to men of foreign birth. Only with their help could slave-versus-free-born alignments have been so completely avoided. And, finally, only with their help could the flood of those who were bought rather than born into the community have been turned so completely into good Kalabari culture-bearers.

This line of thought not only makes good sense of the New Calabar response to the Atlantic Trade. It also suggests why certain other communities, notably Old Calabar, should have responded so differently to the same stimulus. In some ways, Old Calabar is New Calabar turned upside down. Where New Calabar was constantly plagued by rivalries between houses and groups of houses, such rivalries worried Old Calabar much less. But where New Calabar succeeded so brilliantly in the integration of slaves, Old Calabar became increasingly troubled by its inability to integrate them, and eventually suffered from a series of revolts in which they played an important part.[11]

So far as we know anything about the origins of Old Calabar, most things point to an Ibibio community formerly living in the hinterland. Now both Ibibio and Ibo communities typically contrast with the Eastern Delta villages in the following respects: lineages, which control productive resources as well as settlement land, are consequently stronger, a diminished scope for individual enterprise and achievement going with stronger lineages, and finally an emphasis on the closed criterion of descent as the basic qualifier for full citizenship. Following up my earlier suggestion, we can see these points of contrast in the baseline societies as rooted in differences of habitat and economy. They do much to explain why Old Calabar failed where New Calabar succeeded, and vice versa.

NOTES

1. This work was started in 1958 and 1959-60, with the aid of funds supplied by the Horniman Foundation and by the Department of Anthropology, University College London. It has been continued since 1964 as part of an interdisciplinary research project on the Social History of the Niger Delta, sponsored by the Institute of African Studies, University of Ibadan.

2. So far, I have completed survey work on ten out of the twenty 'true' Kalabari villages. I hope to have completed work on all of them by the end of next year.

3. In fishing, the throwing-net is rapidly replacing traditional techniques. And whereas people formerly spent most of their time based at home or very close to it, many now spend most of the year following the fish shoals in cosmopolitan camps far from home. Warfare and headhunting have also, of course, died out.

4. So far in my village survey, two out of ten villages have claimed to have some sort of division of their creeks on a descent-group or ward basis, but in both cases the division seems to be a very partial one.

5. The existence of this second line of claim would appear to account for the scattering of particular descent groups through a number of wards which is found in several Kalabari villages.

6. I am indebted to Professor Daryll Forde for this point.

7. It is here that my analysis differs considerably from that of G. I. Jones. Jones, who did not have the opportunity to do fieldwork in the Kalabari villages, assumes that the baseline New Calabar community was a segmentary system similar to those of the Ibo and Ibibio Hinterland (1965: 5). My own contention, based on acquaintance with a fair sample of the Kalabari villages, is that the latter differ quite considerably from the typical Ibo or Ibibio community. Further, I believe this difference enables us to account for the fact that New Calabar responded to the Atlantic Trade very differently from, say, Old Calabar.

8. For an extended account of the Eastern Delta canoe house, see Jones, (1965: chs. 4 and 10).

9. For a sketch of the history of these conflicts, see Jones (1965: ch. 9).

10. For an analysis of the masquerade as an instrument of acculturation, see the writer's 'Igbo: an Ordeal for Aristocrats' (1966).

11. For a vivid sketch of Old Calabar political development, see the essay by G. I. Jones (1956).

REFERENCES

BARBOT, J. 1746. *A Description of the Coasts of North and South Guinea.* London.

DAPPER, C. 1686. *Description de l'Afrique.* Amsterdam.

DIKE, K. O. 1956. *Trade and Politics in the Niger Delta 1830-1855.* Oxford: Clarendon Press.

HORTON, R. 1963. Kalabari Ekine Society: A Borderland of Religion and Art. *Africa, 33.*

— 1966. Igbo: An Ordeal for Aristocrats. *Nigeria Magazine,* September.

JONES, G. I. 1956. The Political Organization of Old Calabar. In D. Forde (ed.), *Efik Traders of Old Calabar.* London: Oxford University Press.

— 1965. *Trading States of the Oil Rivers.* London: Oxford University Press.

I. M. Lewis

From Nomadism to Cultivation

The Expansion of Political Solidarity in Southern Somalia

THE PROBLEM AND ITS SETTING

The southern cultivating Somali, with whose social structure this paper is concerned, derive to a very considerable extent from immigrant waves of northern nomadic pastoral Somali who have settled on the land and adopted cultivation in the most fertile region of southern Somalia. As well as adopting many new elements of culture, in the process these northern settlers have become absorbed in the distinctive social structure of the south, which differs in a number of important respects from that characteristic of the northern pastoralists. These differences, I shall argue, follow from the contrasting economic and historical circumstances of these two great fractions of the Somali nation. The particular southern structural features for which I shall thus try to account are: the formation of large, stable politico-legal groups in the south; the associated development of a hierarchical, though far from strongly centralized, authority system; and the widespread adoption of foreign clients in group formation. These are all characteristics that are either rare or absent in northern pastoral Somali social structure (cf. Lewis 1961a), and which seem to be closely interrelated in southern Somali social organization.[1]

Although the influence of some of the factors which I discuss can already be seen among neighbouring northern Somali who have recently adopted some cultivation in the vicinity of the Shebelle River (e.g. some Hawiye clans), I shall confine my argument here to the southern cultivating Somali proper. By this useful but arbitrary designation I mean those tribes of the

Rahanwin and Digil clan-families[2] which inhabit the vast wedge of fertile land, almost 200,000 square kilometres in extent, running from the Juba River in the south to the Shebelle in the north-west and bounded to the east by the Indian Ocean. This region, which contains the principal agricultural resources of the Somali Republic and includes the plantation banana-farming industry along the rivers, provides two forms of traditional cultivation: dry-farming on the upland soils of the hinterland (known as *adableh*), and wet-farming in the irrigated rich alluvial soils (*doobay* and *doollo*) of the river basins. The principal traditional crop in the former areas is sorghum millets, while in the better-watered conditions of the latter maize takes precedence. At the same time, there are large wide areas of plain with a lighter red soil (*doi*) which though unfit for cultivation supply excellent pasturage.

These conditions give rise to striking variations in modes of livelihood and degrees of settlement and encourage a degree of economic diversity which is fully paralleled in the ethnic and tribal heterogeneity of the region. The present Digil and Rahanwin populations are in large measure the outcome of a long, disjointed series of migrations and expansionary movements by Somali nomads from the north and north-west, their conflicts and agreements with earlier Galla and Bantu communities, and the blending of these elements in a variety of patterns of mutual accommodation (cf. Colucci 1924: 55). In no other part of the Somali culture area is there evidence of such admixture and diversity.

SOUTHERN SOMALI SOCIAL ORGANIZATION

In this historical setting which spans some three or four centuries in time (cf. Lewis 1960), the Digil and Rahanwin clans are largely but not exclusively cultivators. Some groups live in sedentary cultivating villages and though often keeping cattle and small stock have no nomadic patrimony, while others participate in both the cultivating and nomadic economies. Others again are solely pastoralists, although most of the nomads who move through this area, pasturing their herds of camels and cattle on the stubble in harvested fields as well as in the grassy plains, are not actually of Digil and Rahanwin affiliation. These are described as visiting graziers (*daaqsita*) and have merely a relationship of economic interdependence with the settled cultivators. They exchange milk and dung, and sometimes also money, for rights of access to stubble grazing and wells and water-ponds in the dry seasons.

Within the Somali Republic as a whole, the Digil and Rahanwin who speak a separate dialect of Somali constitute a distinct subculture, but in this paper we shall only be concerned with particular aspects of this in so far as they relate to the structural distinctions associated with the southern practice of cultivation. Those Digil and Rahanwin who live as nomads move similarly to their northern nomadic kinsmen in small groups of close kin with their nomadic hut, or tent, loaded on burden camels, their flocks of sheep and goats and herds of cattle, settling temporarily wherever grazing conditions and water resources are suitable. The camels on the other hand, again as in the north, form a separate herding unit in the charge of young men, although wherever possible some milch camels are attached to the other less widely moving domestic unit based on the husbandry of sheep, goats, and cattle.

No single Digil or Rahanwin clan is wholly devoted to nomadism, however, and throughout this area where people of these groups do practise pastoralism it is ancillary to their fundamental concern with cultivation. Thus here, in contrast to the north, the primary focus of Digil and Rahanwin social organization is the maintenance of territorial solidarity in relation to arable land, water-ponds, and wells. The basic local unit is the village community consisting of several, and sometimes as many as a few hundred, nuclear families living in round mud-and-wattle huts (sg. *mundille*) surrounded by a patchwork of fields and gardens. Unlike the situation among those northern nomads who have recently adopted cultivation in the north-west (see Lewis 1961a: 114) each village here has a distinct local name, and some of the larger villages have a history going back several generations. Although some villages are in their male population based essentially on a small patrilineal segment of the clan to which they belong, more typically villages contain men of several different lineages and are therefore heterogeneous in agnatic composition. Their inhabitants, moreover, are well aware of this scattering of kinsmen and state explicitly that it serves to promote overall clan unity (cf. Colucci 1924: 57). Thus, although, as will presently be shown, lineages are the foci of social and political identity and of heritable rights in land and water, they seldom appear as distinct territorial divisions within a clan. Unlike the position among such peoples as the Nuer (Evans-Pritchard 1940) or the Bedouin of Cyrenaica (Peters 1960), territorial divisions within the clan do not generally mirror the clan's lineage segmentation.

Villages are based on artificially excavated water-ponds in the dry-farming areas, and on stretches of river with associated irrigation canal systems among the wet-farmers. Every village has of necessity rights of access to at least one such source of water both for domestic use and for the watering of sheep and goats and cattle. Camels are watered along the rivers and at deep wells especially constructed for this purpose. Whatever their lineage affiliation, all the members of a village are regularly associated in the construction and maintenance of water-ponds, the actual watering of stock, and similarly in any aspect of cultivation which requires collective endeavour. There is thus a distinct sense of village unity and autonomy, although this may be cut across by the various lineage and other external ties of village members. Notwithstanding the identity of the village, however, and unlike the position in so many other African cultivating societies, there is no office of village headman as such. Village affairs are organized by the elders of the various lineage fractions living together, and collective work in cultivation, water-management, hunting, recreation, and ceremonial are assigned to parties of young men under the leadership of a youth of appropriate character dignified with the title of 'head of the youngmen' (Aw barbar). Within the total territory claimed by the clan, constituent villages are not regularly grouped in an ever-widening series of territorial divisions. Indeed, between the clan in its role as a sovereign territorial entity and the village there is no intervening category of territorial unit. Except where contiguous villages share the same lineage segment affiliation, there is therefore little sense of any wider territorial solidarity outside the village until the clan as a totality of villages is reached.

In keeping with this lack of any clearly defined hierarchy of territorial divisions, the clan's internal politico-administrative system is not territorially defined but is based on lineage segments. The clan has a fixed skeletal structure of segments and each lineage has an office of headman (with usually several assistants) whose importance decreases with decreasing segment size. Thus, although as with the northern nomads, at every level of grouping all adult males have a right to speak in the group's council, there is here a definite and permanent administrative organization paralleling the internal segmention of the clan. Today, the largest primary segments of a clan each have at least one officially recognized and stipended headman, known traditionally as *Gob*, but in the Italian-inspired administrative jargon now generally styled 'Capo'; and a large clan with a strength of several tens of thousands of people may have half a dozen such offices vested in it. These segment leaders traditionally exercise informal judicial as well as political functions, but did not possess formal courts such as those presided over by chiefs in more centralized African societies. Overall clan policy is decided by meetings of the headmen of component segments acting as representatives for their kinsmen, and some clans have a final single titular head ('Capo *qabila*') representing the clan as a whole on a similar basis in its external relations.

As already indicated, segments within the clan vary in size and consequently in their political importance. Usually, however, one particular segment, often the smallest, has a special ritual status to be discussed presently. And there is regularly also a group of religious leaders who, as part of the clan structure, or external to it and then serving several clans, perform such specialist tasks as the ritual blessing of new villages and waterponds and the protection of the crops from the unwelcome attentions of bird pests. They also officiate at marriages, deaths, and other ritual occasions: their duties thus to some extent often overlap with those of the ritual segment of the clan referred to earlier.

THE STRUCTURE OF CORPORATE GROUPS

We are now in a position to examine the structure of corporate groups as this is expressed throughout the Somali culture area in terms of the payment and receipt of compensation for injuries and death. Among the Digil and Rahanwin, participation in these arrangements relates not merely to the maintenance of personal security and livestock interests, but also to land-holding and associated watering rights. For land titles are primarily vested in clans, and secondarily in their constituent segments. Each of the forty or so Digil and Rahanwin clans, with populations varying between 5,000 and 100,000, are thus essentially land-holding corporations. They also act as units in the payment and receipt of compensation and thus participate in the nation-wide systems of indemnification.

As with the northern pastoral nomads, here also there is a general correlation between the structural proximity (or remoteness) of groups and the amounts of blood-money which they customarily offer as compensation for a killing or lesser injuries. Thus, Digil or Rahanwin clans that are territorially and socially in close contact and consequently on friendly terms pay smaller amounts of damages than those which are more distant. For example, the Elai of Bur Hacaba, who are the largest single Rahanwin clan (some 100,000 strong), their smaller neighbours the Helleda, and the neighbouring and formerly subject Eyle clan, all occupy adjacent lands round the three hills of Hacaba, Jegis, and Heibe. These are striking granite outcrops in an otherwise level plain and the three clans are often referred to collectively, both by themselves and others, as the 'People of the Three Hills'. They jointly observe a single tariff of blood-compensation according to which any killing among them requires payment of blood-money at the rate of sixty camels (or £300) in the case of a man's death, and half that figure for a murdered woman. With more distant groups who stand outside this tripartite agreement rates are correspondingly higher. Similarly, among the Bay Hargan territorial cluster of six contiguous clans round the wells and religious centre of Saraman, forty camels (or £200) is the normal rate of compensation for the homicide of a man (and half that figure in the case of a woman). Again, externally a higher tariff applies.

Likewise, at a higher level of grouping, all those clans which fall within the Siyeed (or 'Eight') moiety of the Rahanwin confederacy exchange smaller rates of payment than those obtaining between members of this group and the other half of the clan-family, the Sagaal (or 'Nine'). And between the Rahanwin and the related but structurally more remote Digil clan-family, higher rates still are normally applied. Within the seven-clan-strong Digil group itself, there is a pronounced sense of overall unity and the usual tariff of indemnification is 2,500 shillings for the killing of a man.

Although these gradations are more systematized among these contiguous southern cultivators than they are among their northern counterparts, there is a much more striking and important difference to note. In the north, whole clans never act as single compensation-groups except temporarily in the short-lived circumstances of protracted inter-clan war. Here, however, most Digil and Rahanwin clans exhibit this characteristic as a permanent feature, and not as something which is only evoked fleetingly in special circumstances. Thus, the solidarity of these southern clans as land-holding units is paralleled in their unity as indemnification-groups; and their internal segments, although incipiently political and capable of splitting off, are more typically internal administrative divisions of a permanent political structure.

This is evident in the internal arrangements for paying and distributing compensation within a clan. While the clan is in almost all cases a single unit in external transactions, its internal segmentation determines the arrangements which obtain in the collection and distribution of dues in which it is involved. Among the Elai, for example, an incoming blood-wealth of 6,000 shillings is divided into two parts valued at 1,000 shillings each, and a third portion of 4,000 shillings. The first is allotted to the immediate kin of the deceased – brothers, a father, or sons – while the second is paid to agnatic cousins within the minimal lineage. The remaining sum of 4,000 shillings is divided into three equal parts and distributed among the three primary segments of the clan. In outgoing dues, the murderer and his immediate patrilineal kin are responsible for providing the expenses of the deceased's funeral, while the remainder is paid by the clan as a whole on the same principle as that applied in distributing incoming awards.

In cases of internal clan homicide, however, a much smaller rate of compensation is the rule. Where the murder occurs within one of its minimal segments only a few sheep are given, over and above the burial expenses. And between more remote segments this tariff is only slightly increased. This drastic reduction in the amounts paid and received reflects the high degree of unity which the clan exhibits as a single compensation-paying group. In the north, comparable features are only evinced at a much lower level of grouping, for among the nomads the most stable solidary units are not whole clans, but only small fragments of them.

THE ADOPTION OF CLIENTS

Politico-legal commitment in terms of payment and receipt of damages is, as I have said, intimately bound up with the distribution of rights to arable land and water among the Digil and Rahanwin. It is only by continuing to meet these legal responsibilities and liabilities that a person enjoys secure tenure of rights of access to these vital clan resources. If a stranger wishes to join a clan other than that of his birth he can only do so, and thus acquire rights to cultivable land and water, if he undertakes to make common cause with his hosts and to pay and receive compensation with them. This is graphically seen in the procedure for the adoption of clients, which is standard in form among all the Rahanwin and Digil clans.

Amongst the Hareyn clan of Molimud, for example, a would-be client approaches the clan elders and headmen with a gift of about 100 shillings and a camel, which is slaughtered for their benefit. In front of a formal assembly of elders, the client pledges his allegiance to the Hareyn as a whole and to the various internal segments of the clan to which he has been allocated. The formula runs as follows: 'I am now Hareyn, my segment is the Garaskunle lineage of the Warasile segment of the clan: my leader is Malak Alio. My blood is with Garaskunle. Whatever the Garaskunle undertake I shall participate in. If war breaks out I shall fight beside them; if they remain at peace I shall also be at peace as they are; if prosperity and plenty are their portion, I shall share these. But if drought and disaster overtake them, I shall endure these evils with them. Thus I renounce my birth place: my clan is now Hareyn and so it will be as long as I live.'

Having in this fashion undertaken to share the burdens as well as the joys of association with his patrons, the new client is allocated land for cultivation and his new holding is publicly demarcated by the elders of his segment. Such a newly installed client may not dispose of his land except to members of his patron group; nor can he immediately add to his holdings by buying further land. Should he leave his patrons, his rights automatically lapse; but if he stays on with them and dies among them, his heirs will inherit his fields. If, however, his heirs elect to leave their father's adopted group, they in turn will forfeit their inheritance, although they may claim compensation.

This institutionalized adoption of clients, which attaches strangers not to individual patrons but to groups and is extremely rare among the northern nomads (cf. Lewis 1961b) but very common among the southern cultivators, is crucial to any understanding of the differences in structure between the two Somali groups. Unlike their northern counterparts, the Digil and Rahanwin contain large numbers of adopted clients in various degrees of assimilation. Thus, in discussing the status of the members of their groups, both confederacies of clans draw a broad general distinction between those they call *deh*, or adventitious accretions, and those they call *dalad*, authentic lineal descendants. More specifically, three categories of local resident are usually recognized in terms of the formula: *dalad iyo duhun iyo shegaad*, authentic descendants, long-standing and assimilated clients, and recent client recruits. These last have less secure land rights than members of the other two categories, which in fact shade into each other to become virtually indistinguishable, save in a ritual context. The newest accretions are also often subject to such disabilities as not being considered fully eligible for appointment to the office of traditional battle leader or lineage headman; and, correspondingly, until their commitment with their protectors has ripened with the passage of years, they may not be treated as full members in terms of the payment and receipt of blood-compensation.

Thus, despite the formula for adoption quoted above, many new clients retain at least partial blood-compensation involvement with their own kin outside their hosts' group. Eventually, however, if a client wishes to identify himself completely with his hosts he must surrender his outside commitments. Only thus can he acquire full rights in his place of adoption and transmit these unfettered to his descendants. Most clients, consequently, go through a gradual process of assimilation which is fortified by endogamous marriage in the host clan, and which with the passage of years and ultimately of generations eventually fully absorbs new accretions in what were originally host groups. An access of further new clients, of course, intensifies this merging and enhances the assimilated status of those who preceded them.

Such processes of client adoption are not peripheral, but quite central to any proper understanding of the constitution of the Digil and Rahanwin clans in their present form. The vast majority of the members of these clans today are, in fact, of client origin. Although in the course of collecting and investigating hundreds of genealogies in this area, I encountered a few individuals and small groups that had become clients within the present generation, the great majority of the present Digil and Rahanwin peoples appear to be the descendants of much older foreign accretions, some certainly going back as far as ten generations. Many, indeed, are of such long standing that their present representatives have lost count of the number of generations that have elapsed since their original act of adoption and no longer retain precise knowledge of their former origins and provenance.

More than this, according to their own clan histories and other evidence, these southern Somali clans have in nearly every case developed from an original act of alliance (*balan*, promise) among disparate clusters of other clan fragments and fractions. They are thus essentially federative associations, although they have a genealogical structure, and I know of no single major Somali clan of whatever grouping or provenance that is not represented among them today and that has not in some measure participated in this federative and adoptive process. Indeed, so many layers of foreign settlement have been deposited by successive waves of immigrants that in a great many clans the original founding nucleus of authentic Digil and Rahanwin has not only been vastly outnumbered but has eventually withered away altogether. This situation of which they are well aware, although they try to conceal it from outsiders, the peoples of the region themselves compare to that of an old tree whose life has ultimately been sapped by an over-luxuriant parasitic creeper. This image is peculiarly appropriate. Not only is it couched in the common idiom of plant growth in which all Somali describe group formation and decay, but also the word used for such a climbing plant (*saar*) is in fact applied equally to designate adopted clients.

Thus, for example, of the large Elai clan with a total population of some 100,000 persons, none of the twenty-two official salaried headmen in 1962 were authentic descendants of the clan ancestor Elai. And if any genuine descendants of this ancestor survive today I did not meet them. Instead those who now call themselves Elai, own fields within the clan lands, and participate in its compensation-paying arrangements are in fact drawn from every conceivable Somali clan, and a large proportion are of nothern nomadic provenance. To varying extents these circumstances of heterogeneous clan composition are paralleled among all Digil and Rahanwin clans, although the Elai probably represent the extreme limit of this process of admixture, federation, and client adoption (cf. Colucci 1924; 51).

Yet despite the fact that the present population is largely descended from alien clients and includes such ethnically diverse elements as remnant Galla and Bantu communities in various stages of assimilation, it is the dialect and in large measure the culture of the original Digil and Rahanwin founding settlers that has survived. The culture of this original core community has, apparently, been accepted by all subsequent immigrants and thus perpetuated at the expense of the dialects and cultures of succeeding generations of northern clients. First-generation settlers who have come from the north usually speak both dialects of Somali, but their children born and reared among the Digil and Rahanwin speak the dialect of the latter. These features of Digil and Rahanwin history support the general evidence of tribal tradition to the effect that the process of clan formation in this area has been a gradual one extending over several centuries.

Hence the great majority of the Digil and Rahanwin tribesmen live today in clans which are not those of their original ancestors, and their contemporary functional genealogies are those of these new clans to which they are currently affiliated. These southern clans have typically much shorter genealogies than those of the northern nomads. A person normally counts some five or six named generations to the ancestor of his minimal segment, and another four or five supervene between this point and that of the name representing the clan as a whole. These latter names significantly correspond exactly to the internal segmentation of the clan. This is very different from the genealogical structure of northern Somali clans, where adoption and federation on this scale do not occur, and political mergers are not represented genealogically save in exceptional circumstances (cf. Lewis 1961a: 189 ff.).

Where in the south longer and more detailed genealogies do occur, as is sometimes the case, these are mainly of two types. People of authentic *dalad* founding stock, who form a minority in any clan, tend to possess longer and more diversified genealogies. Where, on the other hand, ordinary affiliates of a clan who cannot trace such connexion produce long genealogies of northern Somali type, these reveal their original clan identity and do not relate to their current, adoptive affiliation. This, frequently, they only know in terms of their attachment to the hierarchy of clan segments and associated headmen which represents their contemporary politico-legal identity. Hence, for the majority of the Digil and Rahanwin, clan pedigrees are at best 'genealogical charters' (cf. Bohannan 1952), rather than true genealogies of northern Somali type. And for many even this description exaggerates their genealogical character, which might be better described as little more than a schema of political divisions cast in the form of a genealogy (which will be discussed further in a forthcoming work).

Despite this high degree of clan heterogeneity and the absence of a widely ramifying genealogical structure recording the various proliferation of ancestors and descendants over the generations in northern Somali style, in each Digil and Rahanwin clan there is usually one segment which is especially singled out and given the term *urad* (first-born, in northern Somali), or more expressively *mindihay* (knife-bearer). This segment has traditionally the privilege of initiating all joint clan occasions, of, for example, entering battle first. But at the present time it is its ritual role that is most significant. Among the northern pastoralists the characteristic pattern of tribal ritual life within Islam is the annual commemoration of lineage ancestors, each order of lineage segmentation up to and including that of the clan celebrating its eponym's rites separately. Among the Digil and Rahanwin, however, where a precise and tightly drawn genealogical structure is lacking, this is generally replaced by an annual collective rain-making ceremony (*roobdoon*) performed

70

by the clan as a whole. On these occasions the ritual slaughtering of livestock in sacrifice to God is initiated by the 'knife-bearing' segment (cf. Lewis 1966: 260).

The segment that plays this important role is considered to represent the most authentic settler stock of the clan: indeed, it is often directly referred to as *dalad*, a term that, as we have seen, ideally designates authentic lineal descent from an ancestor. The implication is thus that in every Digil and Rahanwin clan there is normally at least one segment (often the smallest) which either in fact contains some true descendants of the original clan founder (or founders), or successfully maintains this pretension. The members of such ritually dominant segments are not typically scattered throughout the villages of a clan and do not therefore provide an articulating thread uniting the clan genealogically in the way that the members of dominant clans and segments do among the Nuer or the Lugbara. At the level of the clan, they are simply one, though a special one, of the various constituent segments. Nevertheless, in ritual contexts they represent the unity of the clan as a land-holding corporation, and thus symbolize the unity which Digil and Rahanwin clans exhibit despite their formal internal divisions and their extreme heterogeneity.

This unity, which rests fundamentally upon the defence of common land and water interests, is, as I have already suggested reinforced by the way in which village ties cut across those of segment membership. A further factor of importance here is the high degree of clan endogamy (indeed of classificatory patrilateral and matrilateral cousin marriage), which in direct contrast to northern Somali practice is the norm observed by both Digil and Rahanwin. When the patrilineal heterogeneity of these clans is taken into account, this form of marriage can be seen to have the effect of reinforcing weak or non-existent descent ties by a web of affinal and matrilateral links. It is also arguable that where people of the same original clan identity are scattered in different segments and villages of their adoptive clan, such ties as they continue to recognize on the basis of their true descent affiliation tend to provide further cross-cutting links making again for overall clan solidarity. For, despite the fact that all the members of these mixed clans have sworn solemnly to obliterate their former identity, in many cases this continues as an at least potential basis for social interaction. This potentiality, as the history of the Digil and Rahanwin shows, may, however, also threaten clan unity. This is particularly the case where the members of a given clan segment largely derive from the same former clan origin, such common identity often serving indeed as the basis for further recruitment from the original clan home.

CURRENT DIVISIVE TENDENCIES

Today we are presented by new circumstances with what is virtually an experimental situation for testing how effectively these various contrary pushes and pulls make for solidary Digil and Rahanwin clan units capable of withstanding external fissile forces pressing upon their heterogeneous structure. These pressures emanate from the modern political scene. In its drive to replace tribal particularism by national solidarity, the Somali government in 1960 passed legislation officially abolishing the status of client and upholding the right of every Somali citizen to live and farm where he should choose, irrespective of his particular clan or lineage affiliation (Law of 2 March 1960). In similar vein and partly directly aimed at the local Digil and Rahanwin political party, more recent legislation forbade the use by political parties of tribal names. The Digil and Rahanwin party adroitly met this difficulty by adopting a new title the initials of which still corresponded to those of the former tribal organization. But there is no doubt that in the six years since independence this local party has lost ground to the major national parties. At the same time, the fuller political involvement of all Somalis in the wider arena of national politics, which are dominated by fluctuating alliances between various clan power-blocs, has generally led to a quickening of lineage political awareness. The effect of these and other factors has undoubtedly been to stimulate particularistic movements within the Digil and Rahanwin and to encourage those former clients of proud northern clan origin particularly to assert their independent status. The consequent fluidity in imputed group affiliation among the Digil and Rahanwin which this has undoubtedly promoted has, however, been countered by the continuing need for individuals to belong to viable compensation-

groups which will effectively protect the security of their lives
and property and those of their dependants. Some conception of
the interplay of these rival forces in a situation where the final
outcome cannot yet be predicted can be seen in the following
case-history.

A man of Hadama origin came and settled among the Hareyn
about 1940 and was given land to cultivate and was allocated to a
segment of his protecting clan. Some years later, his son was
involved in a quarrel about a married woman in the course of
which he was killed by the husband. The husband belonged to
another segment of the Hareyn, and after the fight fled to a town
where he was arrested by the police and eventually sentenced to
fifteen years' imprisonment. The segment of which the dead man
was a client claimed blood-wealth, and eventually received a few
sheep and a camel from the lineage of the assailant. After all this
trouble, the father of the deceased decided to leave the Hareyn
and return home to his natal clan, the Hadama, to whom he
naturally related the circumstances of the affair. The Hadama
quickly sent a delegation to the Hareyn claiming 6,000 shillings
as blood-money for 'their deceased clansman' as they put it. The
Hareyn countered this claim, saying that the man in question
was one of their adopted clients and the matter had already been
settled internally. The Hadama retaliated by going to court.
After much litigation the high court ruled that the Hareyn
should pay blood-money to the Hadama and that in the circumstances this should be valued at 8,000 shillings. The Hareyn
responded to this judgement by declaring that in that case the
man would have to leave their land permanently and forfeit his
fields. The government, however, ruled, and this was given
local effect by the District Commissioner, that the man concerned need not do so. Since the Hareyn had given him land, the
status of client being no longer officially recognized, it did not
matter what his tribal affiliation was. The man is now apparently
back again with the Hareyn, but says he is Hadama. How long
he will be able to stay is doubtful, however, since it seems that
the local Hareyn are trying to send their unwelcome visitor to
Coventry and to deny him normal watering facilities and help in
cultivation.

I do not know the final outcome in this case. But as well as
indicating the interaction of the new separatist trends among

the Digil and Rahanwin, which government action tends to support, this brief history illustrates very clearly how rights to land, access to water, and personal security (expressed in terms of indemnification) are traditionally conceived of as three inseparable aspects of group affiliation.

CONCLUSIONS

In seeking to understand southern Somali social structure, we have been driven to refer repeatedly to their economic and historical circumstances; and, in underlining the effect of these factors, I have frequently invoked the northern pastoral nomads as a control in analysis. Northern Somali social structure here is all the more relevant, of course, since, as we have seen, a large proportion of those who today call themselves Digil and Rahanwin are in fact of northern nomadic provenance. So that in examining southern Somali structure we are also tracing, to an extent that would be difficult to measure exactly, the modification of the pastoral nomadic way of life in new ecological circumstances.

Let me now try to clinch my argument that without invoking the aid of these economic differences, in their particular historical settings, we could not properly understand the structural differences between these branches of the Somali nation. I refer again to the major distinguishing features of southern Somali structure with which we began: the expansion of politico-legal solidarity; the accompanying development of a more stable clan authority system; and the wholesale adoption of clients.

Consider first the circumstances of the northern nomads. With movable property as the focus of corporate interests, and in an environment where pasture and water, the two prime necessities of life, are in short supply and unequally and irregularly distributed in successive seasons, the pastoralists have developed a social system that permits the maximum deployment of the individual herder and his stock and militates against the formation of large stable corporate groups. There are few situations, save those of feud and war, when the security of the herder and his stock is threatened, which require sustained and intensive cooperation on any considerable scale. Authority likewise is minimal and fluid, for little is required of it. Underlying this essentially fluid arrangement of people and allegiances, the lineage system provides an enduring and unambiguous framework of grouping which is mobilized and given specific definition by contractual alliance as need arises. The security of the individual's person and mobile property is provided for by his membership, in every situation, of a specified blood-compensation group. This small association of agnatic equals only unites as an effective corporate entity when hostilities threaten or compensation has to be paid, or received. Wider alliances are evoked as occasion demands along the lines of agnatic connexion with the aid of contractual agreements of the same kind as those binding together the members of the minimal and most frequently mobilized compensation-paying group. Moreover, where disproportionate size forces groups to find security among distant allies, contrary to the theory of segmentary lineage opposition, such unions are not normally thought of as permanent and do not entail the sort of genealogical assimilation, and manipulation which is characteristic of Digil and Rahanwin clan structure.

In the south, on the other hand, the expansion of stable and effective, rather than merely *potential*, political solidarity, is facilitated by the advantages which population strength gives to groups in advancing claims to arable land and water-points and to maintaining their holdings against enemy incursion. For, traditionally, clan title to land is obtained and maintained only by effective occupancy, which in the past, if more rarely today, frequently entailed conquest and defence. Moreover, admittedly at a much lower level of association, cultivation requires a larger circle of sustained, regular cooperation – especially for water-pond excavation and maintenance – than is normally necessary in the nomadic economy. And since the units of land-holding are in principle here fixed and permanent, and not as in the north dispersed in a temporary and essentially transient pattern of distribution over pastureland and a multitude of different water-points, the incorporation of strangers implies a much more complete kind of social assimilation. The client, after all, acquires heritable rights to a fixed piece of land; and it is through this that he is strongly identified with the group that exercises traditional sovereignty over the land of which his holding is part. In contrast, among the northern nomads, temporary association for defence or aggression with remote agnates, or with those who are not patrilineal kinsmen, carries with it no fixed heritable patrimony.

The very different southern pattern of client adoption would seem itself to have been reinforced as a permanent associative device by the great admixture of peoples which the region has witnessed over a long period of time and by the remoteness of many client fractions from their original kin. For in those rare cases where something approaching the southern pattern of client adoption occurs in the north, the assimilated group are usually so remote from their own kin that they can no longer maintain effective ties with them and thus cannot count on their support when it is needed. The resulting heterogeneity of southern Somali clan structure, especially where clients of the same origin are allocated to different clan fractions, tends to foster a wider and more diversified solidarity, which is further encouraged by clan endogamy and the dispersal of clan segments in different areas of settlement within the clan territory. These, I believe, are the factors which encourage the expansion of southern political solidarity to the level of the clan, which give the clan as a territorial and politico-legal unit a notable degree of solidarity, and which promote the development of a more hierarchical and more stable authority system within it.

NOTES

1. This paper is based on field research in the south of the Somali Republic which began with a brief visit in 1957, and continued for three months in 1962 and a similar period in 1964. For these opportunities to study in this area I am indebted to the Colonial Social Science Research Council, the Carnegie Trust, and the Food and Agriculture Organization of the United Nations. I could not have carried out this research without the full and generous cooperation of the Somali Government.

2. The Somali nation as a whole is divided into six major agnatic divisions which I call 'clan-families'. These are the Dir, Isaq, Hawiye, Darod, and Digil and Rahanwin. The last two groups, which are the subject of this paper, are represented in the total national Somali genealogy as the children of Sab, while the others descend from an ultimate and opposed ancestor 'Samale', from whom the name of the Somali people may derive (cf. Lewis 1961a: 7 ff.).

REFERENCES

BOHANNAN, L. 1952. A Genealogical Charter. *Africa*, 22: 301-15.

COLUCCI, M. 1924. *Principi di Diritto Consuetudinario della Somalia Italiana Meridionale*. Florence.

EVANS-PRITCHARD, E. E. 1940. *The Nuer*. Oxford: Clarendon Press.

LEWIS, I. M. 1960. The Somali Conquest of the Horn of Africa. *Journal of African History*, 1: 213-30.

— 1961a. *A Pastoral Democracy*. London: Oxford University Press.

— 1961b. Force and Fission in Northern Somali Lineage Structure. *American Anthropologist*, 63: 94-112.

— 1966. Conformity and Contrast in Somali Islam. In I. M. Lewis (ed.), *Islam in Tropical Africa*. London: Oxford University Press, pp. 253-67.

PETERS, E. 1960. The Proliferation of Segments in the Lineage of the Bedouin in Cyrenaica. *Journal of the Royal Anthropological Institute*, 90: 29-53.

Peter Morton-Williams

The Influence of Habitat and Trade on the Polities of Oyo and Ashanti

Daryll Forde in a notable paper read to the New York Academy of Sciences in 1952 (see Forde 1953) discussed the interesting questions of how far and in what ways natural features of the environment in West Africa had influenced the emergence of societies of contrasting types. The opinion then current assumed that the savanna lands of the West African Sudan furnished a naturally favourable environment for societies with institutions of centralized government – the old kingdoms and paramountcies – and thus for the emergence of towns as centres of government and trade and for the conquest of large empires; while the Guinea Forest, primarily because of difficulties of communication, was a natural host for small-scale uncentralized 'tribal' societies. Such a view is explicit in E. W. Bovill's fine and influential historical study *Caravans of the Old Sahara* (1933); and it has been asserted in some recent histories, whose authors have, like Bovill, mainly concerned themselves with peoples of the northern grasslands. Frobenius was exceptional; his interest in the ancient Yoruba city of Ife, lying within the forest, freed him from the prejudice that such an environment was inimical to urbanization and to far-ranging movement; but his diffusionist ideas compelled him to seek external origins. Again he showed originality, in finding different origins for kingship and cities of the Western Sudan (overland from North Africa and Egypt) and of the forest (maritime immigrants from Greece).

Forde's discussion contributed a much more sensitive geographical and ecological analysis than Bovill's. The range of factors considered is reminiscent of the German and American

79

culture-historians and, surveying a longer period of time, he was able to show that the ecological values of geographical factors have changed enormously, for instance after the introduction of an exotic crop or iron tools. He observed that linguistic evidence indicated that from a very early period there had been a cultural separation of the northern, savanna-grassland peoples from the southern, forest-dwelling ones. Further evidence for such a separation was adduced from the exotic food plants found in each region, which he held implied different lines of diffusion into each of them. While agreeing that there is such a cultural separation, it is to be remarked that the zone of separation between the two cultural and ecological regions lies for the most part some distance to the north of the present forest margins and extends across the gap between the western area of forest (from the Volta into Sierra Leone) and the eastern (from Nigeria into the Congo); it corresponds more nearly to the highlands forming the watersheds of the northwards- and southwards-flowing rivers of West Africa. Rainfall and soil-moisture, for example, are often adequate over large areas of the southerly slopes to support yam cultivation.

Having established that broad contrast, Forde was able to discuss in better perspective the fact that both states and un-centralized societies were to be found in each environment. He posited that the main geographical controls over the siting of kingdoms and the location of uncentralized societies were the natural termini of the trans-Saharan routes (which Bovill had shown to lie, except for the markets on the Great Bend of the Niger, near latitude 12° North), and competition for control over the routes between them and over those to the centres of primary production of gold and forest products far to the south. Imperial expansion to the east and west, with its advantageous engrossing of markets and routes, was made easy by the terrain which favoured swift movement and cavalry warfare. While that particular technique of warfare inhibited expansion into the forest, the colonization or the diffusion of ideas of kingship gave rise to smaller and less powerful kingdoms there.

His analysis, nevertheless, like earlier studies, probably over-emphasized the homogeneity of the three vegetation zones of western Africa (desert, Sudan savanna, and coastal forest) as habitats within which characteristic zonal cultures have arisen.

In remarking that the ancient market-cities of the western Sudan were situated at the termini of the natural routes across the desert, Bovill, indeed, had implied not only that the grasslands had proved the most hospitable of the three zones to urban life, but also that the irregular distribution of water in the desert made it a less uniform region than the others. The location and histories of the savanna kingdoms and empires were envisaged as dominated by the struggle to control trade flowing northwards and southwards between the zones. Stateless societies survived only in residual areas, lying between trade channels and of no intrinsic economic or political significance. But stateless tribal societies were characteristic of the forest; they were the primary producers whose exchanges with the northern merchants took the form of dumb barter.

Contrasts in the ecological value of the two blocks of forest have escaped notice; most maps, moreover, ignore the break in forest cover where the grassland extends down to the coast between the Volta and the Ouémé rivers, and also the irregular reach of the northern forest boundaries. The presence of large concentrations of gold in some of the soils below the western forest, and of a particularly valuable strain of kola in its Ashanti sector, give it an economic importance different from that of the eastern block. The antiquity of some of the towns in the eastern forest, of Benin, and the Yoruba towns of Ife, Ijebu Ode, and Owu, for example, or the rapidity of the growth of Kumasi in the western, do not support the view that a forest environment has proved less congenial to the establishment of towns than has the savanna (or than the forests of Cambodia or Central America). With an iron-age technology, the forest appears at least as hospitable as the Sahel savanna.

A much fuller understanding of the political importance of the trade-routes has been growing during the last decade. Long-distance caravans in the western Sudan go east-west, not north-south; shorter routes branch from the great markets to north and south, important to the merchants because they bring local specialities to the markets, but not all travelled by them. It may be guessed that the far-ranging trading activities of the Yoruba and perhaps of the Hausa had their beginnings in bringing supplies to such markets; a large proportion of the numerous Yoruba traders in Ghana and the Ivory Coast, as well as throughout Nigeria itself, are today engaged in pan-buying and bulking local produce, and in bulk-breaking imports, rather than in the transport of goods over long distances. There are obvious advantages in keeping the movements of goods on these shorter routes in local hands.

The variety of goods produced as local specialities must be reckoned a determining factor in the growth of long-distance east-west trade. Kola from northern Ashanti distributed through the breadth of the Sudan, as well as to markets feeding trans-Saharan routes, or natron from Chad, are but two examples. Pilgrims supporting themselves by trade as they made their way north-eastwards are likely to have been important agents in the growth of the kola traffic. Further, it cannot be assumed that every desert caravan brought the same wares from North Africa. It is more probable that there were always differences in the items moving along each of the main routes: from Tunis, Venetian glass, Chinese silks re-exported from Genoa, Italian paper; from Morocco, Spanish metalware and manufactures from Western Europe. The long east-west routes were important for the redistribution of these goods within the region.

Two very important east-west trade-routes have been identified. In the north, one followed the great sweep of the Niger from Jenne past Timbuktu to Gao, and by the mid-fifteenth century it had been extended overland through Jega and Kano to Bornu (see map on p. 86). Local lines of distribution branched north and south from the markets along it. A more southerly one ran south-east from Mali to the southern Mande settlements round the markets of Begho, Bonduku, and Bole, and turned east to north of the Ashanti forest to Salaga and Yendi, to Old Oyo (on the same latitude as Bole, and midway between the latitudes of Salaga and Yendi) then bifurcated to cross the Niger at Jebba and Bussa. Through Jebba, a southern branch led through Nupe to the old kingdom of Idah, and up the Benue; and the route through Bussa went through Yauri to join the northern route to Bornu at Jega or Kano, with perhaps a loop through Zaria. (This more southerly route brought down from the north-east large quantities of the valuable culinary salt natron, for consumption, e.g. by the Hausa, Yoruba, and Dagomba.) But further research is needed before a thorough account of the traffic on this route can be given, though its importance is beyond question. These routes avoid the forest; but there are indications that there was an ancient route yet further south linking western savanna lands, perhaps through Ketu, to the forest kingdoms of Ife and Benin, and then leading eastwards beyond the lower Niger, perhaps towards sources of copper and salt.

Recent research has shown that, outside the urban centres of political power in the kingdoms of the western Sudan, the central governments were concerned to administer closely only the communities through which trade-routes passed and in which there were staging posts and markets to be protected. Large tracts of territory off these routes are better regarded as 'preserves' of rather variable extent from which tribute, whether in the form of goods or people, was extracted and the raiding of trade-routes or the establishing of alternative routes and markets, prevented. It is therefore a mistake to imagine the vast areas enclosed by encircling lines on the maps in most recent histories of the region as uniformly administered empires. The very term 'empire' is likely to be misleading unless qualified by reference to varieties of control within specific localities. Many small-scale acephalous societies survived centuries of life in the empires of the western Sudan.

Further, it is uncertain how far, in Mali and Songhai at least, Islam was the religion of more than the chiefly houses and the merchants. In the larger towns it may, nominally if not exclusively, have been the religion of the majority of the populace, but not in the country outside. Islam, nevertheless, even where it was the religion of a minority, was plainly another decisive factor, because of the nature of that minority. The Islamic ideal, however, did not make certain the identity of interests of all Muslims. For the traders, it provided guarantees. The ubiquitous Mande traders were privileged strangers wherever there were Muslim kings. But the Muslim priesthood and 'ulamā were a source of reformist movements as unsettling as the ambitions of rival states to kings, who had to balance against orthodoxy the stabilizing effects of pagan ritual and social patterns on their subjects and dependencies.

Inferences such as these about the forms of empires and the role of Islam, which could have been reached from Delafosse's early studies (1912), are clearly to be made from Mauny's broad survey of the historical and ethnographic sources (1961). They lead to certain methodological consequences.

The most direct conclusion to be drawn is that empires are unsatisfactory isolates in space and time for the definition of areas and periods of West African history. To present the history of West Africa under the headings 'The empire of Ghana, the empire of Mali, the empire of Songhai . . .' is to obscure beneath shifts in centres of power both important continuities and also important local social and cultural contrasts. States, because they make policies and attempt to execute them, remain important units; but – and this is especially evident in Africa, where states are not the only type of political organization – they do not provide the framework. Historians and prehistorians of the Mediterranean peoples or of ancient Mexico or Peru have encountered similar difficulties in choosing the framework within which to define topics and problems and have come to accept that reference must be made to heterogeneous limits, including geographical, political, technological, linguistic, sociological, and those set by value-systems; with the emphasis lying more on geography and technology for remoter periods, and on society and culture in the more recent.[1] Such a move away from the concept of empire as defining period and place facilitates discourse and collaboration between historians, archaeologists, geographers, and anthropologists.

Comparative discussion of the structures and histories of kingdoms of West Africa can now, for instance, take into quite detailed consideration, as a result of new advances in knowledge, not only relations with neighbouring peoples but also the complex influence of ecological factors on their development. The rest of this paper is an attempt to illustrate that briefly from a comparison of the parkland savanna state of Oyo and the forest state of Ashanti. They have in common their geographical position between the coast and the great inland traderoutes of the Mande.

MIGRATIONS OF THE MANDE

External trade was of decisive importance in the economic policies of Ashanti and Oyo. Near to both states were settlements of peoples speaking languages of the Mande group. That the trading interests of Mali were the stimulus to form colonies to the east of their homeland is a hypothesis put forward by Ivor Wilks in a short monograph (1961). More recent discussions by Jack Goody and Yves Person[2] have shown that the southeastwards movement of Mande was more complex than Wilks had supposed, colonization of the area below the Banda escarpment north-west of present-day Ashanti probably having taken place in four stages, speakers of different Mande languages arriving in each one. The two middle stages were those in which predominantly trading communities were formed. Wilks's argument seems nevertheless to be sound in essentials, and his dating of the arrival of Mande traders not unlikely.

Wilks's starting-point is the linguistic map of the distribution of the Mande languages (Westermann & Bryan 1952).[3] Isolated pockets of Mande-speakers are thought to reflect a movement of Mande traders to form settlements, and spread Muslim influence, 'along the "great trade route from the Niger down to Begho in the north-west corner of present-day Ashanti" '.[4]

Wilks sees as the impulse to that migration the growing commercial competition for the gold trade, along its central line of distribution from the gold-bearing regions of the forest and its savanna fringes to the Niger and the entrepôts for the North African caravans. The Mande penetration stopped short of the gold-fields, at the great market of Begho. Begho, situated at the northern edge of the high forest, and across a river gap in the Banda escarpment, was accessible to beasts of burden and to horsemen, and communicated through the gap in the escarpment with markets to the north-east as well as along the north-westerly route through Kong to Jenne.

Wilks tentatively dates this sector of the spread of Mande influence to early in the fifteenth century. The gold trade and the search for supplies increased in response to the quickly growing demand for gold in Europe during the fourteenth century. The Mande, however, did not attempt to mine the gold. The southern peoples, who did mine it, were not allowed beyond Begho. Thus the great Sudanic kingdoms retained their domination of the markets, and the producers of gold their local autonomy, protected from cavalry raids by the forests. The goods traded through Begho were, from the north, cloth, brassware, jewellery in stone and glass, and other manufactured

Distribution of the Mande Languages

Forest margins

Mande-speaking areas

MALI

SONGHAI

Timbuktu

Jenne

Segou

Bobo
Djoulasso

Kong

Salaga

Bonduku

Kumasi

ASHANTI

DAHOMEY

Accra

Cape
Coast

Takedda

Gao

Dendi

Kandi

Zugu

Nikki

Oyo

Kêtu

Ouidah

YORUBA

Ife

Bénin

Katsina

Illo

Jega

Bussa

Nupeko

Idah

HAUSA

Kano

Zaria

Gasrgamo

BORNU

0   100   200   300   400   500 Miles

18°   12°   6°   0°   6°   12°   16°

12°

6°

0°

12°

12°

8°

4°

16°

12°

8°

4°

12°

12°

goods; and from the south, gold and kola. Once the trade-routes had become established, warrior bands from other, mainly pagan, Mande groups came down them, some to found states, such as Gonja, in the southern savanna and fringes of the forest (Wilks 1961: 8; see also J. Goody 1967).

Leaving Wilks's analysis for the moment and returning to the map, it will be seen that Begho was not the most easterly of the Mande communities. Between latitudes 9° 40' N. and 12° N. there are four areas occupied by Mande-speakers lying along the routes that run from Jenne and Bobo Djoulasso southwards of Songhai (and of the patch of desert below the Niger bend) to cross the Niger lower down and lead to Kano, Nupe, and Yoruba. The four surround or adjoin several important centres. The most westerly lies between the Mossi town Tenkodogo and Fandangurma, the next had Zugu (Zogo) and Kandi, the third Illo on the Niger and the great market of Jega, and the fourth surrounds Bussa and the Niger rapids. A date, or *terminus ante quem*, near to that inferred for Begho, is suggested by a passage in the Kano Chronicle recounting events in the reign of the eleventh Sarkin Kano (A.H. 750-787, A.D. 1349-1385):

'In Yaji's time the Wongarawa [Mande] came from Mele, bringing the Muhammadan religion. The name of their leader was Abdurahaman Zaite. Others were . . . about forty in all' (H. R. Palmer's translation).

That dating may, however, be too early; a Kano manuscript discovered by M. A. Al-Hajj dates the arrival of the Wangara to A.D. 1435 (Last & Al-Hajj 1965: 231; Martin 1967: 57.) It is difficult on the evidence at present available to become convinced that this eastwards movement of the Mande on such a scale was part of their quest for gold, except consequentially as it stimulated trade in other goods. True, the geological map of Nigeria tempts surmise by showing gold areas both north and south of the Niger, and round Bussa itself, and also in the neighbourhood of Ife and Ilesha. All these gold-fields have produced tiny quantities of gold (though barely profitably) in this century; but the search for facts to show that any of these gold deposits were known to the Mande has so far proved a vain one, unless the geographically uncertain passage in Leo Africanus is to be taken as authoritative (Leo Africanus 1956 transl: 458-9; cf. Hallett 1964: 116n[1]). Although the ancient civilization of Ife must be presumed to antedate A.D. 1400, and there is evidence that here was an important centre of technical skills – in the production of iron, and for an early mastery of sculpture in brass and stone and the manufacture of glass and stone jewellery – nothing survives in material remains, or in tradition, or in accounts from elsewhere, to suggest that they utilized their rather thin resources in gold, even to exchange gold-dust for brass. Neither in Ife nor in the other gold-fields in Nigeria are there the great concentrations of gold found further west; and nowhere have any indications whatever been reported of the gold deposits having been worked in antiquity. If the Mande traded with the Ife Yoruba, it may have been because Ife (and Nupe, too) supplied iron implements and stone and glass beads.

Firmer grounds for speculation can be found in considering relations between Mali and Songhai; for the Mande colonies lie in a chain running to the south of Songhai. Gao and Timbuktu had been taken by Mali in A.D. 1324-5, but in 1333 the Mossi burnt Timbuktu, and Gao was independent of Mali from c. 1335 until 1351. In 1359 there was a short period of civil war in Mali, but after that Mali had garrisons in the Songhai markets and access to the Niger traffic until c. 1433. A first impetus to seek alternative east-west routes may be postulated in the disturbances of the second quarter of the fourteenth century. Much of the traffic that had previously moved down the Niger from Jenne could then have been transferred to the southerly routes; and their consolidation would then have continued during the general expansion of trade that followed. The evidence of the Kano Chronicle shows that 'Gonja' kola soon began to be transported eastwards to Hausa and Bornu, and that, as M. G. Smith has noted (1964), the Mande introduced the slave-trade to the Kano Hausa; while Arab travellers reported that natron was an important material carried westwards. During and after the heyday of Songhai, whose interests apparently were restricted to control of the Niger waterway and the markets along it (perhaps because the Mossi blocked their way to south), the overland routes continued to be travelled by the Mande. These routes remained important because of the communication they afforded with the southern lands, to which we now return.

OYO

The Yoruba kingdom of Oyo[5] was to the Arab geographers and historians of the western Sudan one of the pagan lands to the south of the civilized Muslim world. It was nevertheless not a forest kingdom. The capital of the kingdom, according to tradition, has occupied seven sites, some of them brief places of refuge: wherever the king has his court, there is Oyo. The capital of the kingdom, the kingdom itself, the people and their dialect, are all called Oyo. The present town of Oyo is situated in the southern limits of the savanna; but the earlier capitals had lain eighty miles and more to the north. Tradition places the first Oyo, the town of the founder of the royal lineage, furthest north of them all; north, perhaps of the area at present inhabited by Yoruba-speaking peoples. The king-list places this first king, or to use the Yoruba title *Alafin*, of Oyo, forty-one reigns behind the present Alafin of Oyo. The second king had his capital at a site some miles (between 20 and 30?) south-west of the Niger bend at Jebba, where the river changes its course from flowing south-wards to flowing eastwards.

By a rather hazardous procedure of extrapolation of dates along the king-list, the first Alafin may tentatively be supposed to have reigned *c.* 1400. This date suggests that there may be some connexion between the founding of Oyo and the movement of Mande-speakers into the region of Bussa, to the north of Jebba above the Niger rapids. What is less conjectural is that trade through Oyo to Bussa and beyond was an important factor in the policies of Oyo. As long as Oyo prevented other northern Yoruba kingdoms from engaging in warfare and raiding on their own initiative, trading caravans coming from the west through Bussa found the route through Oyo safer than the more direct one through the towns of Nikki and Kaiama, in the territory of the more turbulent Bariba people. When trade with European nations through ports on the Slave Coast began, Oyo again established a dominating position on the trade into the northern hinterland (see Morton-Williams 1967 for a detailed discussion of the political structure of Oyo and its control of trade, particularly in the eighteenth century).

The first kings of Oyo quickly subjugated a large number of

89

small Yoruba kingdoms in the parkland savanna region which extends from the watershed of the Okpara and Ogun river basins in the west to the rocky hills of Ekiti and Ijesha across the R. Oshun in the east. They thus controlled movement between the Niger and the forest.

No effective powers stood between Oyo and the coast to the SSW.; and trade to Ouidah came to have a decisive influence on the political fortunes of Oyo. Ouidah was made a port by the Dutch in the 1630s, and it was as a slaving port that it was important for more than two centuries. The Oyo were early on the scene; by 1660, shortly after the move back to Old Oyo, they had the reputation of being the most dreaded military power in the region and they were supplying a large proportion of the slaves sold there. It was customary for Oyo to launch military expeditions every second year; and they appear to have attacked not merely Yoruba and others beyond their dominions, but also subject towns that were alleged to have given offence in any way. With contingents levied from dependent kingdoms, they were able to put formidable numbers of troops, including a large cavalry force, into battle. By the late eighteenth century they had brought under their dominion the eastern Bariba and the old towns of Wawa and Bussa, thus controlling the approaches to the Niger. Further eastwards, they held the Nupe market town of Ogudu on the Niger. Thus both the trade from the coast to Nupe and Hausa and also the route from Gonja and Ashanti passed through territories under the control of Oyo.

The eighteenth century saw, too, the emergence of the kingdom of Dahomey. In 1727 Ouidah was taken by Dahomey; but, although the Dahomian army was equipped with firearms, in subsequent years the Oyo cavalry in dry season raids so harassed Dahomey that the kings of Dahomey in 1747 agreed to pay an annual tribute to Oyo. Dahomey, furthermore, was unable to prevent Oyo having direct commerce with the coast and giving protection to coastal kingdoms whose ports were in direct competition with Ouidah.

In spite of the concentration of power in Oyo, it was not the monopoly of the Alafin of Oyo. The political system placed the king in structural opposition to a Council of State recruited from several of the large and powerful non-royal patrilineages of Oyo. That structure was supported by impressive ritual sanctions.

Whether the Alafin or the Council of State in fact decided policy
at any moment depended apparently upon their command of real
power, including popular support for the king expressed through
ritual associations and his capability in exploiting rivalries
among the councillors. A king who failed to hold his own
against the Council of State was liable to be ordered by it to
commit suicide.

The main strength and reputation of the Oyo army lay in the
large numbers of mounted archers and lancers. The cavalry force
was maintained by a corps of seventy men of high rank and free
but non-royal status, the *esho*. It appears that each of the *esho*
supported his own band of cavalrymen and their mounts; in turn
the *esho* themselves were in the entourages of the state councillors.
Whenever the Alafin placed a palace man in command of an
army on the frontiers, that commander was never allowed into
the town of Oyo. The system also required the distribution of
much of the booty of war to the state councillors and the *esho*,
for the purchase of horses and the upkeep of their retinues; so
that wealth, like military power, was dispersed.

Late in the eighteenth century, the growing military strength
of Dahomey, which Oyo could not prevent, decided the Oyo to
establish a protected trade corridor to the coast through territories completely under their control. They colonized a depopu-
lated area lying just within the forest margin, setting up a chain
of tiny kingdoms nearly a hundred miles long from the south
of their ancient imperial territory to Ipokia, a town only a few
miles from the ports of Badagri and Porto Novo. These colonies
constitute much of the modern administrative unit, Egbado
Division. The Alafin kept the administration of this corridor to
himself, manning the frequent tollgates from his staff of eunuchs,
and stationing high-ranking slaves in charge of armed contingents and couriers at key points along it. He controlled the
traffic through it and kept the revenue from the tolls. Thus his
position was greatly enhanced both politically and economically,
while his dependence on the cavalry for protection of trade
diminished.

Unfortunately for Oyo, the new distribution of power did not
result in a stable, but more centralized, political structure. The
disturbances reached their height just after the Fulani conquest
of the old Hausa states; and the Fulani soon found ways to intrude

into the struggle, exploit the Yoruba rivalries, gain territory for themselves, and expedite the fall of Old Oyo, which was eventually abandoned c. 1837, the empire having collapsed during the previous years. The Alafin set up a new capital, the present town of Oyo.

By the early years of the nineteenth century some of the Oyo Yoruba had been converted to Islam. The Yoruba name for Muslims (adopted by Yoruba Muslims themselves) is *Imale* ('People of Mali') which implies that the Mande traders had introduced the Faith, probably in the first place to Yoruba traders and craftsmen. Although (according to tradition) the Alafin appointed an Imam, and heard his prayers, and Muslim magic was believed to be potent in war, Islam was a religion of the commoners (and slaves from the north) rather than of the king and state councillors; the importance of sanctions deriving from the indigenous religion in defining political powers and rights was an impediment to its becoming the state religion. During the years of turmoil before Old Oyo was abandoned, some at least of the Yoruba Muslims joined forces with the Fulani, hastening the collapse of the old kingdom.

The next stage in the history of the Oyo Yoruba is that of their regrouping as a people near to, and within, the northern edge of the forest. It was marked by their abandoning cavalry warfare for the musket. Coming when the kingship was already endangered, firearms did not become a royal monopoly outside Oyo itself, and so contributed nothing to restore royal power; instead, musketry enabled opportunists from the old free lineages of Oyo to set up as independent leaders who founded their own towns. Though they stopped the further advance of the Fulani, they also limited the role of the Alafin.

ASHANTI

The quest for gold that had brought the Mande to Begho also, as Wilks observes (1961: 6), brought the Portuguese to the Guinea Coast in the fifteenth century. They established maritime trading posts and changed conditions in the region. Routes were pushed down from the gold-fields near Begho, first to Elmina (discovered in 1471) and later to Cape Coast. Late in the seventeenth century a climax was reached in the struggle to control both the gold-fields and also access to the new markets between peoples of the Guinea hinterland, who were using new weapons, imported firearms. Denkyira for a time achieved domination over its Akan neighbours, until its power was broken in 1701, when an alliance of small chiefdoms thrusting towards the trade-routes between Begho and the coast won the ascendancy for the Ashanti at the battle of Feyiase.

The Ashanti embarked on a policy of military expansion, with two objectives: the control of the gold-fields and the control of the markets both in the north and on the coast. Their military techniques included increasingly efficient musketry and the formation of a small professional corps of musketeers attached to the court at Kumasi, and the raising of levies from newly conquered territories to fight for Ashanti under sanction of devastation of their homelands. Soon after Feyiase, the Ashanti fought through part of western Gonja to seize all the route to Begho and to Bonduku, its successor as a commercial centre. The northwards expansion of Ashanti swept through eastern Gonja soon afterwards, but was halted by Dagomba. A military stalemate between the Ashanti infantry and the Dagomba cavalry was settled by a treaty advantageous to the Ashanti, giving them effective control of the important market of Salaga in Gonja and privileged access to Yendi market in Dagomba. They were enabled thereby to exploit the trade route to Bussa and beyond, especially for the export of kola. Their hold on the ports was less sure, mainly because the European traders, wishing to avoid an Ashanti monopoly of the maritime trade, intrigued with, and aided, the coastal peoples.

In later papers Wilks (see especially 1966) has portrayed a most interesting feature of the political history of Ashanti: the building up of a centralized administration by successive Asantehene.

The first step was to restrict the external political initiative of the Kumasi chiefdom's former associates in the Ashanti Confederacy. The central government required their rulers to show their loyalty to the Asantehene in attending his annual Odwira festival in Kumasi, and by taking part in the Ashanti wars of expansion; but allowed them nearly complete internal autonomy. Passing them by, it extended its administrative and diplomatic network to remoter territories. It also controlled their access to the coast and to inland markets, and their acquisition through trade of firearms and gunpowder.

The second step was to remove high offices of state from the formerly powerful matrilineages of Kumasi and to replace the incumbents by an appointive bureaucracy. This procedure was not imposed on the other Ashanti states, which preserved the earlier structure of government. In Kumasi an elaboration of the bureaucracy followed (including the appointment of scribes to keep Chancery records in Arabic). Paths through the forest were well maintained to ensure the speedy movement of the many diplomatic envoys, messengers, and state traders. While its role increased, careful techniques were evolved to limit the initiative of the bureaucracy and prevent its becoming a threat to the king's personal control of government.

The emergence of a wealthy mercantile class of Ashanti was prevented by limitations on the access of free Ashanti to the markets of Bonduku and Salaga, and to the coast. Ashanti as members of a warrior nation had instead to seek advancement through military prowess or administrative ability. But Muslim Mande and Hausa merchants were allowed – as non-Muslim traders such as the Bariba were not[6] – to trade in Ashanti markets and they were encouraged to settle in Ashanti towns. The Islamization of Ashanti, which was repugnant to the remaining traditional chiefs as well as to the Asantehene, was prevented by such devices as the creation of the cult of the Golden Stool to symbolize the identity of the nation, and the barring of circumcised men of accession to chiefly office and to the shrines of lineage and national ancestors.

Another important characteristic of Ashanti was the ready assimilation of non-Ashanti. Men of talent from dependent territories could enter the service of the Asantehene as free men and rise to high office in Kumasi. The children of captives who had been made domestic slaves could look forward to absorption into the matrilineages of their owners, loss of the stigma of slave descent being hastened by an Ashanti law that made it a capital offence to name anyone's origin.

In the second half of the nineteenth century came conflict with the British, whose policies veered from control of the ports and the coastal peoples to extending protection over territories progressively further inland. Eventually they abetted other Ashanti states in their attempts to free themselves from the still-growing domination of Kumasi and the Asantehene's policy of greater centralization, which was now threatening their internal autonomy. The inevitable wars resulted in the breaking of the power of Ashanti (they lost the market of Salaga in Gonja after their defeat by the British in 1874) and the end of its sphere of political influence.

CONCLUSION

The kingdoms of Oyo and Ashanti both developed under the stimulus of external trade, owing much from their beginnings to their proximity to the Mande trade routes in the north, and later also to their fortunate positions in the hinterlands during the growth of the maritime markets on the coast. That stimulus can be seen to have overridden differences in habitat as a controlling factor in the emergence of these powerful states.

The influence of habitat was potent in less obvious ways. The forest had isolated the Ashanti area from potential northern invaders while a struggle to control the gold-fields took place between small chiefdoms of no great strength. Later, after the Ashanti Confederacy had emerged as a new and formidable power, the forest, while ensuring that the cavalry of their northern neighbours could not campaign effectively in Ashanti territory, had not prevented expansion or the growth of centralized government, because it was not an obstacle to the movement of troops equipped with firearms and the efficient Ashanti musketeers could vanquish Gonja and Dagomba cavalry on their own terrain.

The use of firearms rather than cavalry facilitated the centralization of government by the Asantehene. By making the importation of firearms and ammunition a royal prerogative, he made sure that in matters of military policy the power of decision was his; and, since the Kumasi chiefs had no large followings of armed retainers, he found he could disgrace them one by one and deprive their lineages of the right of succession to their offices. It is likely that the policy of centralization was made easier, too, by matrilineal descent, because matrilineage-groups cannot, even if they adopt slave children, increase their numbers like patrilineal groups practising polygyny on a grand scale. A rather similar process of the concentration of power can be seen in Dahomey, where, from the earliest days of the kingdom, the royal command of firearms and of the economy inhibited the emergence of large and wealthy patrilineages, so that as the state grew more powerful the monarchy became more absolute.

The gap between the eastern and western forest blocks provided Oyo with the opportunity to dominate the Atlantic commerce from a capital two hundred miles inland. But the ownership of war horses and the need for booty to buy them from the north ensured that the old aristocratic lineages of Oyo (like those in other savanna kingdoms such as Dagomba or Gonja, or, later, the Fulani aristocracies in the conquered Hausa states) could always frustrate attempts by Oyo kings to centralize power. When the Oyo kings achieved great power at the end of the eighteenth century as a result of their control of the administration of the new trade-route through the forest to the coast, they were nevertheless not strong enough to bring the holders of political and military offices under their authority; instead a struggle for power followed and prepared the way for the collapse of the kingdom.

NOTES

1. The problem of periodization in the history of cultures is discussed in several of the essays in A. L. Kroeber, *An Anthropologist Looks at History* (1963).

2. See bibliography of J. Goody (1953, 1959, 1964), and Y. Person (1964).

3. The division of the Mande languages by Westermann and Bryan (1952) into the two groups Mande Tan and Mande Fu is no longer accepted by the best linguistic opinion. Accordingly, it is not shown on the map.

4. Wilks (1961: I) quoting Goody (1959).

5. For the history of Oyo, see S. Johnson (1921); and also P. Morton-Williams (1964; 1967; and 1968).

6. See *Crowther's journal* for September 1857 in S. A. Crowther and J. C. Taylor, *The Gospel on the Banks of the Niger* (1859: 103).

REFERENCES

BOVILL, E. W. 1933. *Caravans of the Old Sahara.* London: Oxford University Press.

CROWTHER, S. A. & TAYLOR, J. C. 1859. *The Gospel on the Banks of the Niger.* London.

DELAFOSSE, H. 1912. *Haut-Sénégal-Niger.* 2 vols. Paris.

FORDE, D. 1953. The Cultural Map of West Africa. *Trans. New York Acad. Sci.* Series 2, **15**.

GOODY, J. R. 1953. A Note on the Penetration of Islam into the West of the Northern Territories of the Gold Coast. *Trans. Gold Coast and Togoland Hist. Soc.*, **1**.

— 1959. The Ethnohistory of the Akan of Ghana. *Africa*, **29**.

— 1964. The Mande and the Akan Hinterland. In J. Vansina, R. Mauny, and L. V. Thomas (eds.), *The Historian in Tropical Africa.* London: Oxford University Press.

— 1967. The Over-Kingdom of Gonja. In Daryll Forde and P. M. Kaberry (eds.), *West African Kingdoms in the Nineteenth Century.* London: Oxford University Press.

HALLETT, R. 1964. Records of the African Association. London.

JOHNSON, S. 1921. *The History of the Yorubas*, edited by O. Johnson. Lagos: Church Missionary Society.

KROEBER, A. L. 1963. *An Anthropologist Looks at History*, edited by T. Kroeber. Berkeley and Los Angeles: University of California Press.

LAST, D. M. & AL-HAJJ, M. A. 1965. Attempts at defining a Muslim in 19th century Hausaland and Bornu. *J. Hist. Soc. Nigeria*, **3**, 2.

'LEO AFRICANUS' 1956. *Description de l'Afrique.* Nouvelle édition traduit de l'Italien par A. Epaulard. Paris: Adrien-Maisonneuve.

MARTIN, B. G. 1967. Unbelief in the Western Sudan. *Middle Eastern Studies*, **4**, 1.

MAUNY, R. 1961. *Tableau géographique de l'ouest africain au moyen âge.* Mem. IFAN. No. 61. Dakar: IFAN.

MORTON-WILLIAMS, P. 1964. The Oyo Yoruba and the Atlantic Trade, 1670-1830. *J. Hist. Soc. Nigeria*, **3**.

— 1967. The Yoruba Kingdom of Oyo. In Daryll Forde & P. M. Kaberry (eds.), *West African Kingdoms in the Nineteenth Century.* London: Oxford University Press.

— 1968. The Fulani Penetration into Nupe and Yoruba in the Nineteenth Century. In I. M. Lewis (ed.), *History and Social Anthropology*, A.S.A. Monograph 7. London: Tavistock.

PERSON, Y. 1964. En quête d'une chronologie ivoirienne. In J. Vansina, R. Mauny, and L. V. Thomas (eds.), *The Historian in Tropical Africa*. London: Oxford University Press.

SMITH, M. G. 1964. The Beginnings of Hausa Society, A.D. 1000-1500. In J. Vansina, R. Mauny, and L. V. Thomas (eds.), *The Historian in Tropical Africa*. London: Oxford University Press.

WESTERMANN, D. & BRYAN, M. A. 1952. *Handbook of African Languages*: Part 2. Languages of West Africa. London: Oxford University Press.

WILKS, I. G. 1961. *The Northern Factor in Ashanti History*. Ghana: Institute of African Studies, University College of Ghana.

— 1966. Aspects of Bureaucratization in Ashanti in the Nineteenth Century. *J. African History*, 7.

— 1967. Ashanti Government. In Daryll Forde & P. M. Kaberry (eds.), *West African Kingdoms in the Nineteenth Century*. London: Oxford University Press.

J. A. Barnes

The Politics of Law

INTRODUCTION

My text is a remark made in 1950 by Sir Laurence Dunne, Chief Metropolitan Magistrate, at Bow Street, London, during the trial of ten men who were taking part in a strike which deprived north London of much of its gas supply for several days. The Magistrate remarked that his court 'was part of government but never part of the Government' (*The Times*, 6 October 1950).

In this remark, Dunne makes a distinction between the activities of the Government, the party in power for the time being, and the process of government, the maintenance of law and order and, among other things, the implementation of legislation. The distinction is important, but it is confusing to use the same term 'government' in two contrasted senses, and I shall therefore speak of a distinction between politics and administration. Politics is concerned with the struggle for power and with arguments about policy; administration is the process of organization and management of the affairs of a social unit (Smith 1956: 49; Barnes 1959). In this terminology Dunne would have said that his court was part of the administration but not part of politics. There are many people who support this view, either as an expression of fact or as a statement of what ought to be. The doctrine of the separation of powers, as well as the impediments against dismissing judges and the various conventions limiting their political activities, point to an acceptance among many Western nations of the point of view Dunne advances. Yet it may be worth while examining how far this notion is borne out in fact. Is it possible to keep entirely separate the pamphleteering, electioneering, lobbying, and disputation that characterize politics from the orderly operation of precise commands and

99

regulations that constitutes administration? When a Bill becomes an Act does it move from the disorderly and unpredictable world of competing interests into a quite separate orderly environment of balanced rights and duties where breach inevitably leads to remedy? Is legislation the alchemist's touchstone for transmuting the base metal of factional polemic into the pure gold of the sovereign will?

Put in this way, we may begin to doubt the validity of Dunne's model, even when applied to an idealized Western state, free from corruption and untroubled by revolutionary political parties. Our doubts will certainly increase if we try to apply the model to societies where a unitary autonomous legal sytem cannot be discerned. Some societies manage with comparatively little law; others are more than adequately supplied. On the one hand are those societies where legislation is not a well-established routine, or where the judiciary is not isolated from the political arena, or where there is no judiciary with power to enforce its judgments, or where administrative machinery is entirely lacking. On the other hand are those societies possessing a plurality of tribunals each claiming a monopoly to dispense justice. A glance at societies that in these various respects differ markedly from our own, or at least from the Utopian model of our own, may help us in determining to what extent in our own society the legal system is in fact insulated from political life. How far is Dunne's remark true, and how widely can it be extended to courts in other times and places?

In a single paper I cannot deal with all the issues relevant to the interconnexions of law and politics. Instead I shall present a study that bears particularly on how the legal apparatus is affected when politicians and administrators are mainly the same people; and what happens when there is more than one administrative machine each with its own specialized agencies for enforcing conformity.

LAW IN A PLURAL SOCIETY

In discussions about law in Western society, we usually assume there is a single nucleus of legitimate authority even though one part of the nucleus may act as a check on some other part. What happens if in a community there are two or more centres of authority, or at least of power, which do not form part of a single integrated system? We are familiar with conflicts between courts in our own legal history; between clerical and lay courts and between the courts of common law and of chancery. However, the conflicts I want to consider are of a different kind, at least in their early stage. In many plural societies, where peoples of differing ways of life and different expectations about what is right and wrong live alongside one another, one segment of the community is engaged in trying to assert its authority over the other. The conquerors try to claim for themselves a monopoly to dispense justice not only to their own people but also to those they have conquered. This situation was commonplace in colonies all over the world. The colonial power insisted that if one native killed another, the murderer should not be dealt with by his fellows but should be brought to trial in the colonial court. Even if the laws applied in the case were specific to natives, they were laws made by the colonial power and enforced in its courts. Yet in many native societies under colonial rule, indigenous tribunals of one kind or another existed and operated alongside the machinery of courts provided by the colonial Administration. The colonial courts looked legal; they operated according to accepted procedures and in British territories there was often the distant vision of the ultimate appeal to the Judicial Committee of the Privy Council to give them the stamp of orthodoxy. But if law is characterized, in Hoebel's phrase, by 'the application of physical force by an individual or group possessing the socially recognized privilege of so acting' (1954: 28), then in many colonial situations we would be forced to conclude that, in the eyes of the natives, their tribunals were legal and those of their conquerors were not. The indigenous people might recognize that colonial courts habitually used force, or the threat of force, but might yet regard this as unjustified and illegal. The habitual use of force was, to them, a clearly recognizable illegality; it was not a recognized privilege.

Similar situations prevailed in occupied countries during World War II. Actions that were legal in the eyes of the government in exile were illegal in the eyes of the occupying power and were punished in its courts; actions that were legal to the occupying power were illegal to the exiled government and in many cases were punished in its courts after the end of the war. In colonial societies, the two sets of legal apparatus existed simultaneously rather than in succession. In those colonies, notably British Africa after the 1930s, where the colonial Administration endeavoured to link indigenous tribunals and the Privy Council in a single system, the same individuals might function as judges in both systems. Thus Mitchell reports that, among the Yao of Nyasaland (now Malawi), chiefs, who in certain contexts acted as chairmen of Native Courts gazetted by the Administration and who there enforced regulations accepted as right and proper by the Administration, would, in other contexts, act as the leaders of tribunals that were not recognized by the colonial Administration. There they enforced rules, particularly in relation to accusations of sorcery, that were quite contrary to colonial policy (Mitchell 1949: 158). In this latter capacity, chiefs were acting illegally in the eyes of the Administration but legally in the eyes of their own people.

It would be possible to regard legality as merely a relative term and to argue that there is no contradiction involved in an action being legal in one system and illegal in another. If this view is taken, we can no longer speak of the legal system of a society, but only of the various legal systems that are possibly found within it. We have moreover then to drop any notion that legality depends ultimately on social recognition by the whole community, or upon a consensus of opinion. Each subculture provides its own set of legal norms, and within a plural society the norms of one segment may conflict with those of another. The important characteristic of plural societies is, however, not the mere diversity of legal norms and other aspects of culture. Characteristically, one segment imposes, or endeavours to impose, its norms on other segments that do not accept them but are coerced into partial conformity.

We do not need to go to the colonies to see diversity of norms, even though we may not readily accept some enforced norms as legal. There is, we say, honour among thieves, and Whyte has shown empirically that a fairly stable system of rights and obligations can be established among racketeers whose activities are, in terms of the law of the land, quite illegal (Whyte 1943). Hoebel's definition of law assumes that in a society some individual or group is recognized socially, that is by the society as a whole, as having the privilege of applying physical force. In many societies some individuals are so recognized only by one segment of the population and not by the rest, which may award a similar privilege to a rival group.

In this kind of situation, characterized by a struggle for legal power, it is clear that rival courts are instrumentalities used in the wider struggle for power of all kinds. Let us look at a primitive state which had its own courts before it came under white administration.

The Fort Jameson Ngoni live in eastern Zambia. I describe them as they were in 1946-9, when I worked among them in what was then the British protectorate of Northern Rhodesia. Before they were conquered by the British South Africa Company in 1898, they had a powerful chieftainship accompanied by a hierarchy of tribunals with appeals from lower to higher courts. The courts adjudicated in both public and private suits, and had power to enforce their judgments. These courts continued to operate in a modified form after 1898. They were not statutorily recognized by the British, but British administrative officers encouraged them to remain in operation. The British set up their own courts, and 'serious' offences, such as murder and failure to pay tax to the British Administration, were tried in the British courts. Cases equally 'serious' in Ngoni eyes, particularly those involving adultery or sorcery, were heard in Ngoni courts, but there was difficulty in enforcing judgments, and certain sanctions, such as the death penalty, could not be used except at the risk of offending the Administration. In 1929 some of the Ngoni courts were absorbed into the British legal system as officially recognized Native Courts. Their powers, membership, and jurisdiction were defined by the British, and their decisions became subject to review by Administrative officers. A chain of appeal led ultimately to the Judicial Committee of the Privy Council.

Despite this measure of legal assimilation, the actions of Ngoni Native Courts in 1946-9 can be understood only in terms of their historical roots in Ngoni society prior to 1929, and of the contemporary political scene, as well as in terms of the British legal system. The county chief who presided in the Native Court was the political leader of his people, and his actions as a judge were coloured by his political position. The

103

Ngoni Paramount Chief was political head of the tribe, and in addition presided over the Ngoni court of appeal. There was then no clear separation of the courts from politics. The chiefs appointed to posts in their courts followers whom they wished to reward; they were indeed few other posts that they had at their disposal. Any new aspirant to chieftainship phrased his ambition in terms of the right to hold a court. Conversely, a recognized chief might allow a trustworthy supporter to set up a court of his own, even though this had no standing in the eyes of the Administration. A court member whose intrigues against his chief were discovered was certain to lose his post.

For purposes of local government the chief was head of a body known as a Native Authority. The Native Court was used to implement the policy of the Native Authority. A chief anxious to gain favour with the British Administration saw that his court enforced with substantial penalties the various regulations in which the Administration was interested for the time being. A chief who wished to obstruct the Administration would neglect these regulations in his court. Thus for example there was at one time a regulation, passed as a Native Authority rule but inspired by the Administration, that once a child had begun a course in school he or she must remain at school to finish it. In one chiefdom this rule was interpreted much as the wording of the regulation indicated. In another, it was completely ignored despite the efforts of schoolteachers to get it enforced. In a third chiefdom it was interpreted to mean the every child must go to school. About a year later the Administration decided that as promulgated the rule was *ultra vires*, beyond the competence of the Native Authority, and that it must be cancelled. Nevertheless some chiefs continued to enforce it. This variation between chiefdoms was due not to capriciousness on the part of the chiefs concerned, nor to the energy or sloth of the court clerks who took the initiative in bringing actions of this kind. Some chiefs supported the Christian missions and the idea of Western education; others opposed them. Some were in alliance with the intelligentsia of their counties, others disliked them. These varying attitudes and alignments were reflected in the response to a new law. This was particularly noticeable where public delicts, such as absence from school, were concerned, for in general the court was its own law-enforcing agency. There was no professional police force. Public delicts came before the courts because of complaints by interested parties, schoolteachers in this instance, or because judges, clerks, and court messengers, on the days when they were not busy in court or about their own affairs might, if they were so inclined, wander through the villages on their bicycles looking for unlicensed dogs and unlicensed beer. The enforcement of the law relating to public delicts thus depended largely on the relationship between the chief and his supporters and the common people.

In the court the magnitude of the penalties imposed or damages awarded was influenced by political considerations, among others. Ngoni society was not egalitarian, and status differences were reflected in differences in penalties: for example adultery with a queen was more heavily punished than ordinary adultery, and certain foreigners were regularly discriminated against. These distinctions were, however, derived from the enduring structure of Ngoni society, and were not directly connected with the contemporary struggle for power. Political considerations of the moment showed themselves when a chief or other court member obstructed a suit brought by a litigant he disliked. The hearing might continually be postponed because some minor witness was absent, or it might be heard each time at the end of the day so that the litigants wasted time. A heavier penalty than usual might be meted out to a man who had been at enmity with members of the court. It is difficult to distinguish sharply between those occasions when the personal ties of a litigant or accused person with court members influenced their decision and those when they decided to treat him unexpectedly harshly or leniently as a matter of public policy. For example, a woman whose husband was away working in the copper mines sought divorce on grounds of desertion. The chief unexpectedly rejected her plea and told her to wait longer; he said that far too many women were being divorced from their absent husbands who, by working hard and earning money for the support of their families, were acting only in the best interests of the tribe. Was the chief implementing a new public policy or was he merely favouring his friend, the plaintiff's husband? Presumably both these notions were present in his mind.

The chief and his advisers tried to maintain their position as leaders of their people in the eyes of the Administration and, in turn, the Administration endeavoured to support the authority of those individuals it had recognized as chiefs, councillors, assessors, and the like. Although the Ordinance allowed a native to take his suit to the British District Commissioner's court in the first instance and thus to bypass the Native Courts, attempts to do this were usually rejected by Administrative officers on the ground that disputes should come to them only through the proper channel, the chief. Even after a suit had been heard in a Native Court and Native Appeal Court, a further appeal to the District Commissioner's Court, as provided for in the Ordinance, was sometimes regarded by the chiefs concerned as an attempt to undermine their authority and their monopoly of access to the Administration. Litigants and convicted persons in Native Courts were sometimes punished for stating that they intended to appeal to the Administration's courts. When a commoner brought an action against a chief in an Administration court, he was challenging the political pre-eminence of the chief. A commoner once successfully sued a chief in the District Commissioner's court for damages for adultery. His people came to the chief after the hearing to express their condolences, with the appropriate formality as after the funeral of a close relative, as an expression of loyalty in the face of this rebellious insult.

The chief was not the only person who tried to influence the findings of the courts. Missionaries endeavoured to persuade chiefs not to grant divorces to their converts; Indian traders sought to have their disputes with Africans heard in Native Courts rather than in those of the Administration, as was required by the Ordinance on Native Courts; white farmers instructed Native Courts to deal promptly with cases involving their labourers. Thus the Native Court did not operate inside a legal ivory tower; it was a part of the social machinery by which the political leader of the tribe, the chief, endeavoured to remain in power while subject to conflicting pressures from the Administration, missionaries, traders and farmers, his political supporters, and the mass of the people.

This situation is probably typical for most primitive states, where there is centralized authority without the presence of a professional administration, including specialized judges and police. However, these Native Courts were not only the successors of indigenous tribunals; they were also creatures of British legislation. Whatever the legal position, the British Administration would presumably have tried to influence the way in which cases were heard in native courts because of its interest in the maintenance of good government in the country as a whole and in the social and economic development of the population. It differed from the missionaries and other interested groups in that, in its own eyes, it could exert its influence *legally*. The indigenous tribunal was recognized as a Native Court and hence brought into the British legal system, but this was a matter primarily of interest to British administrators, and only of secondary interest to the Ngoni, who certainly did not seek this recognition.

The part played by the court in the essentially political relationship between the Administration and the Native Authority is made clear when we consider the sources of law administered in the courts. Native Courts were empowered to enforce both 'native law and custom' and certain regulations made by the then Northern Rhodesia central legislature and government. 'Native law and custom' was uncodified and largely unrecorded. In effect, the phrase related to a changing and not always consistent body of rules that courts saw fit to enforce from time to time, and which were regarded as ancient usage, or as specific to the Ngoni people, but which in fact were sometimes innovations. The court could also enforce Rules and Orders made by the Native Authority when these had been approved by the Administration.

When the Administration wished to change the behaviour of the people in some respect it could either make a regulation and then empower the Native Court to enforce it, or it could persuade the Native Authority to pass an order to the same effect, which would then be approved by the Administration and, as before, would come within the competence of the Native Court. The Administration usually sought to adopt the second alternative so that it might appear that the regulation represented the will of the people and not merely the dictates of the Administration (Barnes 1948: 102-4). This harmless legal fiction worried no one for, whatever the status of the regulation, its effective enforcement was at the discretion of the court.

New laws, however they originated, were enforced quite independently of their inclusion in or omission from the mimeographed list of statutory enactments issued from time to time by the Administration for the guidance of courts. Some courts had lost their lists. But it is significant that even this fiction could have political significance. On one occasion it was suggested that a soil erosion law, which had been first introduced by the Administration in the guise of a Native Authority Order, would be more accurately described as an Administrative rule which the Native Courts were empowered to enforce. Soil erosion was a great danger in the then Northern Rhodesia, and the Administration was quite prepared to admit that it had to take action to preserve the fertility of the land despite apathy and opposition from many conservative African peasants. However, the suggestion that the Native Authority Order should be cancelled in favour of an identically worded Administrative rule was rejected by a meeting of Ngoni chiefs. Chiefs preferred to appear as legislators enforcing their own laws rather than as the judicial servants of the Administration.

Chiefs and court members formed part of the elite in the Ngoni population. The vagueness of 'native law and custom' enabled them to make new law and discard old law much more readily than is possible for judges who have to respect a series of recorded enactments and whose discretion is limited. Quite apart from the fictional legislation described above, true legislation was a recognized process among the Ngoni and was performed at a series of meetings held under the chairmanship of chiefs and attended by any adult man who wished to do so. True legislation happened rarely, resulting in about one new law a decade. The conditions of life among the Ngoni had changed radically since 1898 and the courts had continually to deal with unprecedented situations and new claims. The new rulings were sometimes presented in the guise of good tribal customs of long standing that unfortunately had been neglected of late but should be revived. This fiction satisfied the Administration and it enabled the court members to make new laws without referring the matter to a tribal meeting at which anyone would have been free to speak his mind. Those who had achieved judicial power assumed for themselves the power to make laws as well.

Despite the difficulties of establishing what rules the courts actually enforced, there was on the whole regularity in the decisions arrived at, at least in a single court over a limited time. There was also justice, by which I mean popular acceptance of the correctness of court decisions. An aggrieved man who felt that the court had treated him harshly could appeal to the chief in his personal capacity, or to another court, or could try his luck with the Administration, his white employer, or his Mission, and the decision might be reversed, or more likely never enforced. Chiefs relied on their people for support against the Administration and against other chiefs. The group of persons around a chief was unstable and one favourite gave way to another. The fluidity of social life and the possibility of movement from one village to another, from one chiefdom to the next, and from rural to urban life, made prolonged exploitation of any group difficult.

Despite the use of the courts in the struggle for political power, Ngoni courts remained largely courts of conciliation rather than agencies for promoting social change or ensuring the domination of one group over another. The sanctions available to the court were limited, and the system worked because of the moral approval given to most of its decisions. There was general agreement about the rights and wrongs of the actions dealt with by the courts, and it is this that usually made a man in the end pay the damages or fines that had been awarded against him, rather than the threat of the Administration's force behind the Native Court. If a man was actually in court he could be handcuffed and taken off to the Administrative post. But if A had been told to bring £1 next Friday to hand over to B, A could either run away, or he could offer five shillings out of court and hope to hear no more of the matter, or he could persuade B that it would be wiser for him not to press his claim. If B wished to enforce his rights, he might have to wait months before he could persuade the court to send one of its messengers to bring A in by force, and by that time anything might have happened: even the court might have changed its mind about the case (Barnes 1954: 166). But A and B were likely to need each other's cooperation and assistance in many ways: if they had not been in social contact with one another, the dispute would not have arisen in the first place. Therefore they were likely to reach some solution whereby A admitted his fault but B did not press his advantage.

Prior to the British conquest, it was the custom among the

Ngoni, as with the Barotse (Gluckman 1955: 9), for chiefs not to hear cases themselves. Their councillors heard the parties, and referred their decision to the chief for confirmation. At the time of my study, since the chief was designated as head of the Native Court in his county, Administrative officers sometimes insisted that he should sit in court and hear cases along with his councillors and assessors. It was realized that the chief was head of the Native Authority and in a sense the chief executive officer of his section of the tribe. However, there was little administrative work to carry out other than the hearing of cases, and some Administrative officers considered that if the chief did not appear in court he was neglecting his duties and not earning his salary. There was only slight separation of powers between the judiciary and the executive among the Fort Jameson Ngoni prior to 1898 (Barnes 1954: 41-7), but the chief did stand to some extent above and apart from the administrative hierarchy. The colonial policy, whereby most of the day-to-day work of chiefs was hearing cases in court, prevented the development of an independent judiciary and promoted the direct utilization of the courts for political purposes.

Not only was the chief under the new dispensation both a judge and an executive officer; the court clerk, a new post without analogue in the indigenous system, was policeman and prosecutor as well as a minor executive official. Much of the Administrative pressure on Ngoni society was exerted in writing. The District Officer used to write to the chief to arrange a meeting or to give instruction or to seek information. Reports, including the record of cases heard in the Native Court, were sent in writing by Ngoni to the District Officer. In the 1930s, the court clerk was sometimes the only literate member of a court, and hence acted as secretary to the chief and to the Native Authority as well as performing his court duties. The clerk had control of the books of licences, passes and certificates of various kinds, and of the rubber stamps which more than anything else symbolized the delegated power of the Administration. The court became the centre of local administration, centred not on the chief but on the court clerk. The clerk was also postman, and might be able to intercept letters needed as evidence in cases before the court. He issued licences to brew beer for sale and was usually well informed of social life generally in the community. Thus the recognition of a Native Court and the payment of a semi-skilled man to record its judgments led to a new pattern of power and influence. The clerk was often fairly young and comparatively well educated and represented interests sometimes at variance with those of his conservative chief.

Unlike the Native Court, the Administration's courts were able to enforce their judgments effectively, and on occasion the Native Court might make use of the Administration's power, as when it sentenced a man to imprisonment. But punishment at the hands of the Administration was not regarded, either by Native Court members or by the common people, as a proper penalty for an offence. If a man was ordered by a Native Court to pay a fine or damages and refused to do so, or maintained that he had no money, the court usually ordered him to be imprisoned in the Administration's jail. When he came out again, he still had to pay. Imprisonment was regarded, as it were, as a special penalty for not cooperating with the Court, but not to be used for other offences.

There was, as is often the case in colonial societies, no stigma attached to imprisonment at the hands of the Administration. Prisoners were allowed a great deal of liberty, and at one time were allowed to go home on visits. Unskilled men were employed in the disposal of sewage in the township, and it was sometimes said that it was only this that kept people out of prison. Clerks and other white-collar workers who were in prison were sometimes seen visiting their friends in town. There was good technical training available for prisoners and many craftsmen owed their start in their profession to a stay in prison (Barnes 1954: 166). In other parts of the world, as in Palestine under the Turks and in Finland under the Tsars (Granqvist 1931: 104), it had been regarded as an honour to go to prison. This was not the case among the Ngoni (I refer to conditions as they were during 1946-9, before Federation became an active political issue); but the indifferent attitude of Africans in the then Northern Rhodesia towards imprisonment was shown in that, when Africans were first given seats on the Legislative Council of the Territory, one of the men elected had been in prison for what was regarded by Europeans as a serious offence. This attitude towards imprisonment had in part been adopted

111

by the resident whites who were able to make use of prison labour. Murderers were said by some to make good gardeners and it was argued that clerks who embezzled should be reinstated after serving their term of imprisonment, since they more than others would understand how Western financial institutions worked.

Litigation in the Native Court was comparatively cheap, predictable, and pleasant. There was usually plenty of gossip to be heard at court, and the journey there could be combined with other errands. The law that the courts administered, however vague it might be, was on the whole well understood by the litigants and their relatives and friends. On the other hand, the actions of the Administration, in legal affairs as in so many other matters, were unpredictable and likely to be dangerous and tedious. Hence people endeavoured to avoid becoming involved in a case pursued by the Administration whether they were principals or merely possible witnesses. The legal system operated by the Administration was not understood by the mass of the people. Indeed, it was assumed that the people did not need to know all its details. The Administration's courts operated in English, and it was the practice not to translate into the vernacular arguments between counsel when these were on points of law, although the principals often could not understand English. The terms 'guilty' and 'not guilty' could not be accurately translated into the Ngoni language without much circumlocution. Many verdicts and judgments appeared unexpected and inexplicable to the Ngoni. Hence even when a crime such as murder, reprobated alike by Ngoni and Administration, had been committed, the work of the Administration's police was often obstructed by villagers who might agree that the murderer should be brought to justice but who were anxious to keep clear of the Administration's legal process even in an innocent capacity.

POLITICIANS AND THE LAW

The Ngoni did not have a distinctive legal profession, and they formed part of a plural society. Both facts gave distinctive features to their legal system. The coexistence of Ngoni and British within the same social system entailed the coexistence of two legal systems, even though the Native Court in its colonial form played a part in both systems. The British system was a professional system and wielded great power, including the power to hang individuals and to suppress rebellion by force, but it lacked a consensus of approval among the Ngoni. The Ngoni system was run by men who were simultaneously politicians and executives as well as judges and police; it had limited power and could not readily enforce its judgments; it did not have a written body of law but was based on a changing body of orally transmitted tradition; yet it did enjoy general approval among the population it served. In this instance, therefore, we had the coexistence of two legal systems, even though they were unequal. We would expect conditions to be different from those among, say, the Plateau Tonga of Zambia where there were no indigenous courts, or among the peoples of the New Guinea Highlands, where not only were there no indigenous tribunals but also no Native Courts have been created by the Australian Administration. Conditions would be different again where the two coexistent legal systems are of the same type, both with professional practitioners and written bodies of law.

The lack of professional lawyers enables us to see clearly the interaction of law and politics among the Ngoni, for the connexion was close and direct. The virtual absence of legislation entailed law-making by the court, particularly in times of rapid social change. The judges were men of power and influence enjoying the patronage of their chief and hence were well qualified to sense the strength of public feeling and to carry through a ruling when once it had been made. Laws and precedents were not recorded, and the manner in which they were remembered and used was determined by present interests, principally by the interests of those in power who controlled the operation of the courts. Because the court members were not only judges, but also councillors and village headmen, they had an interest in good administration and in social development, in *order* as well as in *law*. Hence they tended to examine all the social implications of the specific dispute that was brought before the courts, ranging widely in their cross-questioning, and tried to find a solution which in many, though not all, cases reconciled the parties and at the same time upheld recognized rights (cf. Gluckman 1955: 21, 78; Krige & Krige

1943: 186). This tendency was reinforced by the comparative weakness of the sanctions at the disposal of the court.

In a society with a professional legal system, the utilization of the courts as part of the political processes is necessarily indirect. The very existence of legislation in many societies is a recognition that some control of the legal system is needed. The lawyers cannot be left alone, as it were; the law they are to administer must be decided by the politicians. But public delicts do not come before the courts automatically, and an autonomous judiciary does not go out into the highways and byways looking for malefactors. The police or their equivalent are part of the administration, and they act as professional enforcers of the law because they are paid to do so by a public or a government that in some measure must call the tune. Administrative direction in the process of law-enforcement is particularly necessary when laws are written down and preserved, for they do not then so readily fade away when they are no longer required. Lawyers as professional men concerned only with the law naturally tend to develop the law as a consistent intellectual and metaphysical system in its own right, but even they are not completely divorced from the contemporary climate of opinion. In Britain lay magistrates receive from the Home Secretary fairly specific instructions about how they are to administer the law and analogous instructions are sent to Chief Constables. Certain public suits may not be begun without the approval of the Director of Public Prosecutions. When a judge administers a new law, he is in a sense carrying out an instruction from his masters, the politicians. When he argues that the times have changed and that the precedents of a century ago are no longer applicable he is responding to the pressure of contemporary public opinion, or perhaps, since judges are slow to move, to public opinion of a decade or so ago.

Among the Ngoni, and among many other primitive peoples who have chiefs and courts but no professional lawyers, it is fairly easy to see judges and policemen responding in this way, for the judge is to some extent his own political master, and he, or his clerk, is also a part-time policeman. In Britain and similar countries the relevant information is concealed by the veil of official secrecy and by the reluctance of judges to make explicit the sectional interests that have brought about the accepted change in public opinion. Occasionally an administrator makes explicit his utilization of the legal apparatus when an old law is revived 'in the public interest'. The day after the trial of the ten strikers, to which I referred at the beginning of this paper, the then Attorney-General, Sir Hartley Shawcross, made an explanatory speech of which any Ngoni judge would, I am sure, have approved wholeheartedly. Sir Hartley used the word 'politics' with a fine distinction worthy of an experienced politician, but otherwise his meaning is quite straightforward. The report of his speech reads:

'. . . speaking of the enforcement of these laws (the Conspiracy and Protection of Property Act, 1875 and the Conditions of Employment and National Arbitration Order, 1940) the Attorney-General said he had to consider whether a prosecution would serve the general public interest. In some quarters he was being blamed for precipitate action and in others, because the proceedings had been successful, he was blamed because he had not taken them before. Precipitate action might produce exactly the opposite to the result desired. . . . One had to try to find the opportune moment when other factors, in addition to a successful prosecution, were likely to combine together to secure a return to work. . . .

'But while the law remained as it was, it was his clear duty to continue to enforce it in appropriate cases and at the appropriate time. . . .

'His duty (as Attorney-General) related to the criminal law. In the discharge of that duty he acted with complete independence, and there was no question of the Government or the Cabinet approving or disapproving of what he did. The constitutional position was that it was his duty, in deciding whether or not to authorize a particular prosecution, to acquaint himself with all relevant facts, including, for instance, the effect which a prosecution, successful or unsuccessful, would have upon public morale and order and with any other considerations affecting public policy. . . .

'. . . so long as he was Attorney-General, the duties of the office would be carried out in a quasi-judicial way without the intrusion of politics' (*The Times*, 7 October 1950).

In a parliamentary democracy with a fair measure of cultural homogeneity it is possible to talk thus of public policy as though it is something apart from politics. The law, and even the application of a specific law to a specific case, can be presented as the will of the people, of whom legislators and administrators

115

are only the specialized servants. In a plural society this pretence is impossible. On many issues there is no public interest, but only opposed interests. An Ngoni chief might tell his people that he was acting in the public interest in banishing an alleged sorcerer from his county on a trumped-up charge of failure to carry out the lawful orders of the chief, but even if his people accepted his action as right, the Administration, if it discovered the ruse, would quash the case and censure the chief. The Administration frequently told the Ngoni that it was acting only in the public interest in inducing them to pass laws against soil erosion, but nevertheless most Ngoni felt that many of the laws were irksome, unnecessary, and oppressive, and the courts did not enforce them.

The emphasis we sometimes put on the impartiality of the law would seem to be misplaced if we mean the legal system in action and not the law viewed as a timeless and consistent set of rules. The legal system is not a kind of calculating machine, with an input of wrongs and an output of remedies. It is part of the social process in which groups and individuals strive against one another and with one another for a variety of ends. The legal apparatus is used as part of this process. Legislation, where it is a recognized procedure, is one way by which the working of the legal system can be controlled despite its innate tendency towards intellectual autonomy in professional hands, but there are other control devices which may be as useful. Where there are no courts, as among the Plateau Tonga, jural institutions are not something separable from though influenced by political struggles but, in fact, provide the rules by which these struggles are carried on.

Yet we have to realize that, even in societies without lawyers, the law may nevertheless be regarded as an enduring consistent set of rules impartially applied. The Ngoni view that the chief should not sit in court indicates that he was thought of as an impartial umpire, somewhat removed from the political struggle and the administrative process, to whom there was an ultimate appeal. Ngoni recognized that, while the outcome of any particular case was never certain, the decisions of the courts were on the whole consistent, predictable, and equitable. If they were not, they could look to the chief for a remedy. Some measure of partiality in court members was to be expected. It is a sad commentary on the colonial scene that Ngoni said of a chief who acted arbitrarily and inequitably in court that he behaved like a European.

It has not been my intention in this paper to deny that a legal system may exist as an effectively autonomous and internally consistent social institution. We may choose to regard the law as given, an apparatus available for use by any politician who happens to gain power. Alternatively we can take the political struggle as given, as I have done, and can examine how in that struggle various institutions are made use of, including law. Both approaches stress the interconnexions of law and politics. Where there are lawyers we naturally pay more attention to the law as a separate system, but in the societies I have been mainly considering there were no professional lawyers. Gluckman (1955) has shown for the Barotse that, even without professional lawyers, a legal system based on oral communication may yet have an autonomy and internal consistency of its own. Ngoni jurisprudence was rough and ready compared with the elegance and nicety of Barotse legal reasoning. Hence in this paper I have stressed the dependency of law rather than its potential autonomy.

ACKNOWLEDGEMENT

An earlier version of this paper, under the title of 'Law as Politically Active: an Anthropological View', was contributed to *Studies in the Sociology of Law*, edited by Professor Geoffrey Sawer, Canberra, Australian National University, pp. 167-96 (mimeographed), 1961. I collected the field data used in this paper while working as a Research Officer of the Rhodes-Livingstone Institute. I am much indebted to the Trustees of the Institute for their generous support.

REFERENCES

BARNES, J. A. 1948. Some Aspects of Political Development among the Fort Jameson Ngoni. *African Studies*, 7.
— 1954. *Politics in a Changing Society*. London: Oxford University Press.
— 1959. Politics without Parties. *Man*, 59, art. 4.

GLUCKMAN, M. 1955. *The Judicial Process among the Barotse of Northern Rhodesia*. Manchester: Manchester University Press.

GRANQVIST, H. N. 1931. Marriage Conditions in a Palestine Village. Societas Scientiarum Fennica, *Commentationes Humanarum Litterarum* 3 (8) and 6 (8).

HOEBEL, E. A. 1954. *The Law of Primitive Man*. Cambridge, Mass.

KRIGE, E. & KRIGE J. 1943. *The Realm of a Rain Queen*. London: Oxford University Press.

MITCHELL, J. C. 1949. The Political Organization of the Yao of Southern Nyasaland. *African Studies*, 8.

SMITH, M. G. 1956. 'On Segmentary Lineage Systems'. *Journal of the Royal Anthropological Institute*, 86 (2).

The Times (London). 6 October 1950, p. 6: 'London gas strikers vote to return'.

— 7 October 1950, p. 6: 'Trade disputes and the law'.

WHYTE, W. F. 1943. *Street Corner Society*. Chicago: University of Chicago Press.

PART III

Problems in Kinship

Mary Douglas

Is Matriliny Doomed in Africa?

On many accounts matriliny appears to be a fragile institution and its future at risk. The scholarship that has been expended on analysing its nature tends to expose the internal strains and external pressures to which it is vulnerable. But, as far as I know, there has been no serious attempt to assess its prospects for survival in the modern world. Is it an accident of history that no matrilineal system of kinship is found among modern industrial nations? If so, can we expect to see new industrial nations emerge that reckon descent matrilineally? Or should we expect matriliny to give way to bilateral or patrilineal forms?

First to list some of the prophets of doom. David Aberle, using Murdock's *World Ethnographic Sample* (1957), tried to ask the question: 'Where do we find matrilineal kinship?' Matriliny turned out to be relatively rare in the representative sample of 565 cultures. It seems to flourish in a narrow ecological niche, mainly in economies with a horticultural base. It tends to be less commonly found with the plough, with animal husbandry or dominant pastoralism (Aberle 1961: 655 ff.). In general it is found where the agricultural yield is low. There are well-known exceptions that have hitherto obscured the correlation Aberle has revealed. I take it as my point of departure and ask what in the nature of matriliny tends thus to confine its distribution.

That matriliny is vulnerable to increasing wealth is independently asserted. According to Murdock, power, property, and prestige spell doom to the matrilocal principle (1949: 206-7) and for Murdock this implied doom also for matrilineal descent. Jack Goody has written also in this vein that a poor and egalitarian economy is compatible with matrilineal descent but increase of wealth, differentiation, and inequality are not.

'Among the Lodogaba the transfer of wealth outside the living-together group to distant uterine kin is based upon a recognition of reciprocity, so that what is lost in one transaction can be regained in the next. Large inequalities of fortune render such a mode of inheritance difficult to work, because they upset the operation of equal exchange; and nowadays people are more likely to hold on to wealth, since they can do more with it' (1962: 348).

Similarly, in *The Social Organization of the LoWiili*, he argues (1956: 110) that disparity of incomes weakens the principle of matrilineal descent. If this is so, matriliny is not compatible with economic advance, for the latter generally implies economic differentiation.

It has long been customary to draw attention to the difficulties of working a matrilineal system. It is true that Malinowski liked to show how conveniently matriliny resolved the conflict of emotion in father-son relations; Radcliffe-Brown remarked that 'There is no reason why a system of mother-right should present more difficulties for individual adjustment than a system of father-right' (1950: 80). But both took the provocative tone of the scholar whose insights go deeper than appearances. Others, who join Murdock in taking the elementary family as the basic and universal unit of society, frankly emphasize the conflict in the family created by matriliny. Kathleen Gough wrote in 1961 of the elementary family being ' 'torn" between two descent groups (649). Lévi-Strauss wrote, earlier, of the common case when matriliny goes with patrilocal residence:

'the husband is a stranger, an outsider, even an enemy, and yet the woman goes to live with him, in his village, to bear children which will never be his. The conjugal family finds itself broken up again and again, endlessly. How can such a situation have ever been conceived in the mind, invented and established? . . . Consider the artifices to which a matrilineal and matrilocal society must resort to create an order even approximately equivalent to that of a patrilineal and patrilocal society' (1949: 149-50).

Dr Richards used the expression 'the matrilineal puzzle' to describe the conflict of authority inherent in matrilineal kinship (1950: 246). And David Schneider lists several strains implicit in the matrilineal system:

'In matrilineal descent groups the emotional interest of the father in his own children constitutes a source of strain, which is not precisely replicated in patrilineal descent groups by the emotional tie between the mother and her children' (1961: 23).

'In matrilineal descent groups there is an element of potential strain in the fact that the sister is the tabooed sexual object for her brother, while at the same time her sexual and reproductive functions are a matter of interest to him' (ibid.: 13).

'Matrilineal descent groups have special problems in the organisation of in-marrying affines with respect to each other' (ibid.: 20).

The general impression of these analyses is that among kinship systems matriliny is a cumbersome dinosaur. Its survival seems to be a matter for wonder. Underlying them all is the implicit assumption that the elementary family is the basic, universal unit of society. If matriliny divides the elementary family, and if the latter is taken to be the most viable unit of kinship in the modern world, the outlook for matriliny may indeed be dim. Professor Arthur Lewis has called extended kinship ties 'almost certainly a drag on effort' (1955: 14) and Professor Bauer and Professor Yamey have echoed him in calling them 'a serious obstacle to economic progress' (1957: 66). Everything that has been said of the disadvantage of the extended family in the modern market economy must apply with full force to matriliny, for this, as I shall show, is essentially a system for wide extension of kinship ties.

Polly Hill remarks that 'outside observers of the matrilineal scene have never ceased forecasting its imminent collapse' (1963: 16). To support the prophets there are certainly well-attested cases in which the matrilineal principle has given way to inheritance by sons. Polly Hill cites two Gold Coast sources (Hill 1963: 123, fn. 4):

'Among the matrilineal peoples of the Gold Coast there is a distinct tendency nowadays for all forms of self-acquired property, including cocoa-estates, to be devised to sons rather than sisters' sons' (Meek 1957: 179).

'The tendency for the maker of a cocoa-plantation to leave his property to his son rather than his sister's son has almost brought a change from matrilineal to patrilineal descent' (Cardinall 1931: 84).

Elizabeth Colson, writing of modern tendencies among the Plateau Tonga, says:

'The importance of the matrilineal group wanes before the increasing demands of the household and the family for the loyalty of its members. New economic possibilities emphasize the importance of the house-hold working team, and give rise to clashes between the interests of its members and the interests derived from membership within a matrilineal group. The development of cash-crop farming, with the possibility of accumulating wealth either in the form of savings or in capital goods, is creating tensions in a system based on a male-centred household combined with matrilineal inheritance. More and more the Tonga are demanding, where a clash occurs between the interests of the two groups, that the matrilineal group should give way' (1958: 347).

V. Turner, writing of the cash-cropping farmers in Mwinilunga, said:

'Farm heads were disencumbering themselves of many of the obligations of kinship, and retaining for their own use and for the use of their elementary families money they earned as wages and by the sale of cash-crops or surplus subsistence crops' (1957: 113).

The formerly matrilineal Ehansu near Lake Eyasi in Tanzania made an overnight switch to patrilineal inheritance and succession (Virginia Adams who recorded this in the course of her fieldwork gave it to me in a personal communication). On the other hand, there are cases in which matriliny has triumphantly survived even in a modern differentiated economy. It is therefore worth asking what are the conditions in which matriliny offers advantages. The exercise is in the spirit of Daryll Forde's presidential address to the British Association (1947) in which he considered what thresholds must be reached for the effective organization of unilineal kin.

At this stage we must explore some of the logical implications of a matrilineal system. Many of them have been analysed clearly by David Schneider in his essay, 'The Distinctive Features of Matrilineal Descent Groups' (1961: 1-29). I accept all his results and shall draw upon certain of them. Some other implications of matriliny have been insufficiently noted hitherto. There are, on my reckoning, eight features of matrilineal kinship systems, features that inhere in the nature of a matrilineal tracing of descent, and are always therefore present in matriliny. This does not mean that they are not present in some patrilineal systems, but that they are never absent with matriliny.

1. Matrilineal descent groups are at a disadvantage for recruiting by birth compared with patrilineal descent groups. Given the

same hazards of disease and mortality in the population at large, matrilineal descent groups are likely to be more short-lived, more liable to dwindle and die out. This follows simply from the fact that a system in which descent is transmitted through males can offset the infertility of any particular woman by taking on more wives. A man's power to beget in patrilineal polygyny may be very great indeed. By legal fictions and adjustment of bridewealth there may be no limits to the increase of his progeny. By contrast, in a matrilineal descent group, if a woman dies or is barren the group suffers an irreplaceable loss of reproductive powers. Furthermore she cannot multiply her offspring indefinitely by multiplying the number of her husbands.

2. Except in chiefly lines, long genealogically articulated lineages are not found in matrilineal systems of descent. This can in part be attributed to the demographic factor above.

3. Matrilineal descent groups are organized to recruit members by other means additional to direct lineal descent. There is a tendency, well marked in Central Africa, for the matrilineal clan to be treated as a field for the recruitment of new members to local sub-units. Stefaniszyn records that the Ambo taught their marriageable girls to attract young men to the village (1964: 99). Turner has described the dynamism of Ndembu kinship largely in terms of the contrary pulls on a man's choice of residence exercised by his father's and mother's brother's groups (*op. cit.*). I have shown how important the successful canvassing of recruits from other villages is for the viability of matrilineal clan sections among the Lele (Douglas 1963: 94-9). Female pawns and slaves in this area were widely used to attract followers (Douglas 1964). Even among the Ashanti, where membership of a ruling lineage is an important claim to status, Fortes records that Ashanti try to forget close lineal links and to emphasize descent from a common womb. This lack of genealogical discrimination in recruitment to descent groups can also be attributed to the demographic difficulties implicit in matriliny. This recruitment factor makes its own contribution to another feature of matriliny, the lack of clear genealogical differentiation within descent groups (see point 7 below).

4. Matrilineal descent goes with a quality of openness in the texture of effective descent groups. This is a corollary of the above, but worth noting independently because it also relates to point 5 below.

5. With matriliny, it is men who straddle exogamous descent groups and who have dual residence and dual loyalty. In patri-

lineal systems connecting links are female. Jack Goody has pointed out that the 'male residual sibling' is in a stronger position to secure advantages for his offspring from his descent group than the 'female residual sibling' (1959). So when the end of a line is male he can expect to siphon off more privileges for his offspring.

6. This point would suggest that inter-group alliance is generally strong and group-exclusiveness weak in matrilineal systems. Here my interpretation differs from that offered by Schneider. He points out correctly that a matrilineal system is one in which descent groups retain control of both male and female members, in contrast with patrilineal groups in which some control over female members is relaxed (1961: 8-10). This important difference may explain the resilience and strength of matriliny. Where intermarriage takes the form of exchange of males, the cross-cutting ties which make for a criss-cross of reciprocal obligations are carried by the dominant sex. This implies more emphasis on intergroup alliance than in a system where the cross-cutting ties are carried by the weaker sex. Thus I would like to give a positive value to one difference between matriliny and patriliny, whereas Schneider's formulation gives it either a neutral or negative value. He implies that the matrilineal descent group is a more exclusive unit. But taking into account the intrusion of men from one unit into the residence and families of another (to which he also gives negative value as a 'source of strain') I would rate it as a less exclusive unit.

7. Within a matrilineal descent group, roles are not unambiguously ascribed by kinship. This has been very satisfactorily expressed by Schneider (1961: 24-7) thus:

'The processes of fission and segmentation in matrilineal descent groups do not precisely replicate those of patrilineal descent groups.'

As a result of the difficulties of precise genealogical segmentation he notes that

'Matrilineal descent groups would be more likely to merge lineal and collateral relatives terminologically than would patrilineal ones.'

He bases these conclusions entirely on the problems of distributing authority between males whose relations are mediated by females, a valid basis. But I would also point out that such problems would be accentuated by the open system of recruitment which matrilineal descent groups tend to adopt (see point 3 above).

8. Matriliny in itself does not provide a strong authority structure. There is a bias towards achievement of leadership roles in matrilineal descent groups which follows from the fuzzing of genealogical distinctions within them. For succession to leadership there may be resort to election of the most personally eligible man; this uses the matrilineal principle only to circumscribe the group within which leadership may be achieved. Or resort to the plain principle of seniority by age, regardless of genealogical or other status. This would make for weak leadership, as I have shown among the Lele where succession to village headmanship is based on straight seniority of age (1963: ch. IV). Fraternal succession in a wide range of collateral lines makes for confusion in the second generation and thus gives scope for manipulation of conflicting principles and achieved leadership, as Gluckman's analysis of Bemba succession shows (1954). All this contrasts with the clear devolution of authority possible in a patrilineal system.

But it is essential to note that weakly ascribed authority is not always a disadvantage. In so far as it gives scope for achievement, it can in certain circumstances have great adaptive value.

Surveying these features it should be possible to discern what aspects of matriliny make it apt for survival in the ecological niche which Aberle has revealed. We may ask what are the conditions in which the following features have a special value: open recruitment of talent and manpower, strong inter-group alliance, scope for achievement. The answer would seem to be – almost everywhere. But this is not so. There are circumstances in which a closed system of recruitment, weak inter-group relations, and strongly ascribed power would have high value. The kinship system with the most strictly closed pattern of recruitment by descent is the endogamous patrilineal lineage. This has an even narrower ecological niche than matriliny. It is found among pastoralists who fiercely contend proprietary rights in scarce pastures and water. Emrys Peters relates the closely controlled patterns of agnatic inmarrying of Bedouin in Cyrenaica to their need to be organized to resist encroachment on scarce fixed resources (1967: 279). A matrilineal system would be ill adapted for this social environment, and some light is shed on the incompatibility that Aberle has shown between matriliny with dominant pastoralism. In the present volume, Ioan Lewis describes how the Somali tend to contract their social ties when they settle down to cultivate, while the more fully nomadic northern Somali marry as widely as they can to extend their range of alliance. This suggests that among nomadic pastoralists the frequency of lineage endogamy would increase with the importance of exclusive claims to fixed resources.

The same applies to ascription of roles on a kinship basis. There are circumstances in which a close control on status claims is workable and advantageous: where it is desired to control internal competition for restricted resources, or where an unambiguous chain of command for defence purposes is called for, then it would be plausible to suppose that patriliny, because it is capable of providing these controls, has an advantage. To sum up the argument so far: matriliny provides the framework of a corporate descent group without making exclusive demands on the loyalties of males. It even forces men, whichever pattern of residence is adopted, to move from their natal village to another. It forces the local unit to accept newcomers within its bounds. It requires all males to accept conflicting responsibilities. In short it is a more dilute form of corporate grouping, less exacting than patrilineal descent. The latter merely permits weak female links between descent groups. Where residence harmonizes with descent it is at the cost of wider forms of allegiance. Matriliny is a form of kinship organization which creates in itself cross-cutting ties of a particularly effective kind. This is not to suggest that societies with patrilineal systems do not have such ties: they can produce them by means of cult or other associations, but matrilineal descent produces them by itself. This is in its nature. If there is any advantage in a descent system which overrides exclusive, local loyalties, matriliny has it. Furthermore, matriliny, by its ambiguities, gives scope to the enterprising individual to override ascribed roles.

Here I should draw attention to a theoretical implication in this discussion. As a descent system, matriliny, on this showing, has some of the wide-range, solidary effects which in alliance theory are attributed to matrilateral cross-cousin marriage (Needham 1960: 114–18). Matrilineal descent groups are equipped with counteractive arrangements which break down instead of developing and enhancing their exclusiveness. I venture to suggest that prescriptive marriage alliance of the first generation matrilateral type is not found in African matrilineal kinship systems because it is redundant.

Now to consider the appropriateness of such a system in the niche in which David Aberle has located it. The poorer an economy, the more primitive its technology, the more uncertain the yield of crops or game, the more should the pattern of distribution be wide enough to even out gluts and shortages. In some economies the unit of production is a cooperating group big enough to form an appropriate unit of consumption. A hunting band, for instance, or a herding unit is a productive team which provides a distributive unit bigger than the elementary family. Pastoralists may need to combine the men of several joint families to be able to give the different sections of their herds the specialized care they need. Transhumance encourages habits of wide-scale collaboration. Risk-spreading can be met without reference to descent either within the framework of the unit of production and residence, by milk-sharing and cow-lending arrangements, or by using a more wide-flung network of partnerships for dispersing a herd to restrict loss from disease.

However, hoe-culture does not produce the forms of collaboration discussed above. In economies based on rudimentary and unreliable forms of cultivation, the unit of production is much smaller than the ideal unit of distribution. As a cross-cutting device for this function, matrilineal descent is more easily related to the distribution of food than are age or cult associations. Here I am not arguing that matriliny always performs this function, but that it is well adapted to it. Meyer Fortes describes nightfall in an Ashanti village, where children with lanterns and plates of cooked food scurry from their mother's kitchens to their fathers' and mothers' brothers (1949: 63-4). Marguerite Robinson, summarizing Malinowski's and Powell's material on the transference of yams through 'patrifiliation', regards these transfers as meaningful in their own right and part of the total system of kinship (1962). It seems clear from the Trobriand material that the transfer of food from one conjugal work team to another conjugal eating and cooking unit allows everyone some choice between allocating their crops for prestige transfers and reserving them for subsistence needs. In a bad year the channel is there for directing crops into the neediest homes. It is obviously easier to divert crops to private subsistence needs in a system of general transfers than in a system where the norm is for each family to produce for itself and to make special calls on kinship ties only in an emergency. At a low level of agricultural technology individual risks loom large and threaten the community: risks from pests, from illness, and from differences in skill and diligence. It is for these low-yield agricultural economies that certain advantages are written in to the constitution of a matrilineal descent system.

This is a point which Goody clearly had in mind when he noted that the wide distributive pattern of matriliny is compatible with poor, egalitarian economies. But I suggest that his emphasis is not entirely right in implying that differential access to wealth puts a strain on the system. The examples of Plateau Tonga plough-owning maize-farmers and Ndembu cash-crop cultivators who are beginning to transfer their inheritance to sons could well support a slightly different emphasis. I would suggest that it is not differentiated wealth, in itself, that causes rich men to favour their sons so much as scarcity in the basic resources (fertile land in the two instances above). Competition in a restricted field causes men to draw in their horns and to concentrate their responsibilities on their nearest kin. As I see it, matriliny is fully compatible with competition in an expanding economy. Because of the open texture of its descent groups and its bias towards a wide-ranging recruitment of manpower, matriliny is well adapted to any situation in which competing demands for men are higher than demands for material resources. In poor agrarian systems, such as those in the traditional matrilineal regions across the centre of Africa, a man's labour is more valuable than any fixed capital: land is generally plentiful, labour is scarce. One of the problems a community in such a region must solve is how to recruit new blood and maintain its manpower at the necessary level of skills and energy. I have argued that matrilineal institutions serve this end. Flexibility of association is an advantage in communities most denuded of material wealth, where the value of material goods is much less than the value of persons. If it were always true that economic differentiation reversed this bias it would indeed tend to select against matriliny. But there is a circumstance in modern market conditions which is capable of reproducing the bias favourable to matriliny, that circumstance is economic expansion. Matriliny should be capable of flourishing in modern market economies wherever the demand for men is higher than the demand for things. Because of the scope it gives for personal, unascribed achievement of leadership, matrilineal kinship could have advantages in an expanding market economy. On my view the enemy of matriliny is not the cow as such, not wealth as such, not economic development as such, but economic restriction. Many societies changing from production for subsistence to production for exchange find themselves entering a very restricted field. Economic restriction lowers the relative value of humans. It produces a movement to close the ranks and resist encroachment by other people. The emphasis is less on finding men to exploit resources than on an equitable sharing of a fixed amount within a limited group. I am arguing that economic buoyancy, abundant opportunity, and steady expansion create the same favourable conditions for matriliny as a static, poor, undifferentiated economy.

To illustrate this I consider Polly Hill's account of the southern Ghanaian cocoa-farmers (1963). The great period of economic expansion for the Akwapim (both matrilineal and patrilineal groups) was from before the 1880s until the depression of 1929. During this period the principle of matrilineal descent was in no danger among the matrilineal Akwapim, as best exemplified by the Aburi. It is in the period of economic decline and failure following 1929 that we read of the narrowing of inheritance to direct lines, and neglect of wider collateral lines in favour of sons. Before 1886 the Akwapim had made plantations to produce and sell palm-oil, they collected wild vine-rubber and travelled extensively as rubber-traders. In this way they collected silver coin which financed their later land-buying when the price of palm produce fell and cocoa had become the most profitable enterprise. Education and travel made them alert to the possibilities of new crops. Empty lands belonging to the Akim on the other side of the Densu River were suitable for cocoa, and the enterprising and energetic Akwapim applied their funds to the purchase of lands and the farming and marketing of cocoa. The export of cocoa from Ghana was built up from scratch to the value of £2 millions by 1914. During this period of heavy capital investment and expansion there were two kinds of purchasing organization. The Aburi used their matrilineal clans, the members of which Polly Hill likens to shareholders. But the patrilineal Akwapim were unable to make the necessary financial outlay without combining lineages into purchasing 'companies' which had no descent basis whatever. The matrilineal farmers bought land by combining the funds of several members of a descent group; or two brothers would combine with their sisters' husbands. The profits of cocoa-farming were used to buy more land, and a nice balance was maintained between individual control of newly acquired property and its absorption sooner or later into the common property of the descent group. The enterprising were rewarded with scope for their abilities, wealth, and prestige; the weak and incompetent benefited, for they were allowed usufruct of a clansman's land. The population flowed in and out of any particular territory, and the rules of land transfer were as flexible as can only happen when the property has little value or is very abundant. There was nothing to prevent a matrilineal Aburi man from buying land for the use of his own sons. Such land could even become the land of the son's matrilineal lineage if a ceremony of transfer were performed. A man could persuade his sister's husband to help him on the grounds that in this way the latter could provide for his own sons. There was no residential segregation of lineages. Wide collateral lines were recognized in succession and inheritance. The whole emphasis of the documents concerning this period, which Polly Hill publishes as appendices to her chapters, is upon expansion. Then came the depression of the thirties and the disastrous drop in the price of cocoa. A gradual recovery in the forties and fifties led to the even worse disaster of the swollen-shoot disease which killed the cocoa trees.

To return to the observers quoted above, who noted the tendency to exclude matrilineal cousins from inheritance and to pass lands to sons rather than to sister's sons, Cardinall was writing in the period of depression and Meek in the period of swollen shoot. There is a strong case for supposing that the tendency they observed was an effect of economic restriction, not of economic differentiation as such. On the other hand, professional men, ministers, catechists, clerks (and Christian farmers who presumably felt they had opted out of the traditional inheritance system) were also concerned to provide for their own sons even as far back as 1900 (Hill: 81). Some of the men who tried to provide for both their sons and their true heirs in those early days seemed to have been abusing the old system, but the truth was that the new lands were so vast that the heirs did not know their limits (Hill: 134). Polly Hill suggests that men strive to provide for their sons when they fear that the matrilineal clans of the latter have inadequate resources.

'As most *abusua* now own much cocoa land, there is less reason today than there was in say, 1900, for an enterprising father to feel obliged for reasons of economic necessity to provide a land for his son' (ibid.: 136).

Polly Hill's study successfully makes the point that in certain conditions the extended kinship units are not a drag upon the economy but advantageous. The Aburi system, she says,

'grew from strength to strength because it accorded the individual enterprising farmer sufficient scope to operate as a commercially viable entity, while at the same time enabling him to benefit from the continued general support of his matrilineage. The less fortunate or less enterprising members of the matrilineage appreciated the need to allow their leaders to go on investing money, which might not strictly be regarded as their individual property, in the purchase of a succession of lands over which, at the outset at any rate, they had complete individual control, because they trusted in the strength of the matrilineal principle and knew that their own security would thus in the long run be enhanced' (ibid.: 82).

In modern industrial Europe, the extended family has been the core of support of many great business companies. It is not true that in all kinds of modern business the extended family basis has been a drag, not in merchant banking for instance, where the Lazards, Kleinworts, and Rothschilds, and many other great family names, have successfully developed expanding businesses over many generations. Matrilineal clanship on this showing would make a splendid basis for merchant banking. It would make a poor one, perhaps, for the less well-paid, learned professions where little property is accumulated. But there are undoubtedly niches in the new industrial Africa in which it will have a place to flourish. All it needs for its full creative contribution to the twentieth century are conditions for steady economic growth.

L   133

REFERENCES

ABERLE, DAVID 1961. Matrilineal Descent in Cross-Cultural Perspective. In Gough, K. & Schneider, D. (eds.), *Matrilineal Kinship*, pp. 655-727. Berkeley: University of California Press.

BAUER, P. & YAMEY, B. 1957. *The Economics of Underdeveloped Countries*. London (Cambridge Economic Handbook).

CARDINALL, A. W. 1931. *The Gold Coast*. Accra: Government Printer.

COLSON, ELIZABETH 1958. *Marriage and the Family among the Plateau Tonga*. Manchester: Manchester University Press.

DOUGLAS, MARY 1963. *The Lele of the Kasai*. London: Oxford University Press for IAI.

— 1964. Matriliny and Pawnship in Central Africa. *Africa*, 34 (4): 301-12.

FORDE, DARYLL 1947. The Anthropological Approach in Social Science. *Advancement of Science*, 4 (15).

FORTES, MEYER 1949. Time and Social Structure, an Ashanti Case-Study. In Fortes, M.(ed.), *Social Structure: Studies Presented to A. R. Radcliffe-Brown*. Oxford: Clarendon Press.

GOODY, JACK 1956. *The Social Organization of the LoWiili*. London: H.M.S.O.

— 1959. The Mother's Brother and the Sister's Son in West Africa. *Journal of the Royal Anthropological Institute*, 89 (1): 61-86.

— 1962. *Death, Property, and the Ancestors* London: Tavistock.

GLUCKMAN, M. G. 1954. Succession and Civil War among the Bemba: An Exercise in Anthropological Theory. *Rhodes-Livingstone Institute Journal*, 16: 6-25.

GOUGH, KATHLEEN 1961. *Matrilineal Kinship*, edited by Gough, K. & Schneider D. Berkeley: University of California Press.

HILL, POLLY 1963. *Migrant Cocoa-Farmers of Southern Ghana*. Cambridge: Cambridge University Press.

LÉVI-STRAUSS, C. 1949. *Les Structures élémentaires de la parenté*. Paris: Presses Universitaires de France.

LEWIS, I. M. 1969. From Nomadism to Cultivation: the Expansion of Political Solidarity in Southern Somalia (in present volume).

LEWIS, W. A. 1955. *Theory of Economic Growth*. Homewood, Ill.: Irwin; London: Allen.

MALINOWSKI, B. (no date). *The Father in Primitive Psychology*. London: Psyche Miniatures, Basic English Publishing Company.

MEEK, C. K. 1957. *Land Tenure and Land Administration in Nigeria and the Cameroons*. Colonial Research Studies No. 22. London: H.M.S.O.

Is Matriliny Doomed in Africa?

MURDOCK, G. P. 1949. *Social Structure*. New York: Macmillan.

— 1957. World Ethnographic Sample. *Amer. Anthropol.*, 59: 664-87.

NEEDHAM, RODNEY 1960. *Structure and Sentiment, A Test Case in Social Anthropology*. Chicago: University of Chicago Press.

PETERS, EMRYS 1967. Some Structural Aspects of the Feud among the Camel-herding Bedouin of Cyrenaica. *Africa*, 37 (3): 261.

RADCLIFFE-BROWN, A. R. & FORDE, D. 1950. (eds.). *African Systems of Kinship and Marriage*. London: Oxford University Press.

RICHARDS, A. I. 1950. Some Types of Family Structure amongst the Central Bantu. In A. R. Radcliffe-Brown and D. Forde (eds.), *African Systems of Kinship and Marriage*. London: Oxford University Press.

ROBINSON, MARGUERITE 1962. Complementary Filiation and Marriage in the Trobriands. In Fortes, M. (ed.) *Marriage in Tribal Societies*, Cambridge Papers in Anthropology. vol. 3. Cambridge: Cambridge University Press.

SCHNEIDER, DAVID 1961. The Distinctive Features of Matrilineal Descent Groups. In Gough & Schneider (eds.), *Matrilineal Kinship*. Berkeley: University of California Press.

STEFANISZYN, BRONISLAW 1964. *Social and Ritual Life of the Ambo of Northern Rhodesia*. London: Oxford University Press.

TURNER, V. W. 1957. *Schism and Continuity in an African Society*. Manchester: Manchester University Press.

Rosemary Harris

Unilineal Fact or Fiction

A Further Contribution

I

In a collection of essays dedicated to Professor Forde, it seems
appropriate to take up a theme he has discussed, the problem of
the significance of unilineal descent (Forde 1963). I shall examine it in the light of material I gathered at the village of
Adadama, a settlement of the Agbo people, whom it is especially
fitting to choose for this inquiry since they live only a few miles
away from the Yakö, on the opposite, northern bank of the
Cross River. Between the Yakö and the Agbo there is said to be
a strong linguistic tie,[1] and there are clearly very strong cultural
links as well.

The organization of Adadama village is in many respects
similar to that of Yakö villages, as depicted by Forde. Like these,
Adadama is divided into matrilineages and matriclans, and the
matriclan priests are ritually and politically important for the
whole settlement. Also, in Adadama, residence for men is
normally patrilocal, so that men who live as neighbours within
a compound are commonly paternally related; and compounds
are grouped together into wards. As well as these major similarities, there are also minor ones. For example, the age-
organization is similar to the Yakö pattern; diviners are grouped
into a kind of corporation closely associated with the matriclan
priests; and in Adadama, as in Umor, the *Ligwomi* association
has great significance. There is, however, a very considerable
difference between the organization of Adadama and that of the
Yakö (and also that of the neighbouring Mbembe). Both the
Yakö and Mbembe explicitly recognize the principle of patri-

137

lineal descent and possess groups formed on this basis, so that
'patrilineality' is part of the local 'home-made' model. The
people of Adadama, as we shall see, do not recognize such
groups, for they do not perceive their society to be organized in
terms of patrilineal descent at all. This is so despite the fact that
the outside observer finds it possible to distinguish *de facto*
patrilineal groups in the village. Material from Adadama has,
therefore, obvious relevance for Forde's contention that 'There
is need to consider how far in fact and in what sense any overall
distinctions between lineal and non-lineal groups are justifiable
ethnographically or adequate for the analysis of the factors involved in the composition and roles of descent groups' (1963:
38).

II

Physically Adadama looks very much like a small Yakö village.
It consists of a large, central village, Adadama proper, with a
population in 1953 of over 1,900, and four smaller, closely linked
hamlets which together bring the total population to over 3,100.
These settlements, like those of the Yakö and Mbembe, consist
of built-up areas which contain no farming land among the
houses. In Adadama itself there is a main market place, and
round this are grouped the three wards of Anati, Ekpon, and
Ivone, which make up the central settlement. As in Umor, so in
Adadama, each ward has its own central meeting-ground where
important shrines are located and where rites and ceremonies
are held. Moreover, just as in Umor the patriclans of a ward
tend to radiate out from the ward meeting-place (Forde 1964:
50), so in Adadama, on a smaller scale, the oldest and largest
of the compounds radiate outwards from the ward meeting-
place. In Ekpon ward, for example, there are five compounds
which border the meeting-place. These *gekuba* were traditionally
as physically distinct as any Yakö localized patriclan for,
until the recent advent of 'town planning' schemes, which involve
opening up wide streets, each compound was an almost fully enclosed complex of houses to which access could be gained only
through a single narrow opening. I was able to make a census of
three compounds and found that they contained respectively sixteen, twelve, and ten household heads and their wives and children.

Each compound possesses considerable unity, for not only is it physically distinct from its neighbours, but its male members also seem to spend much of their spare time together in the meeting-house which each compound possesses. In this respect again, the *gekuba* is comparable with the Yakö patriclan (Forde 1964: 53). Each compound has a recognized senior man, ideally the eldest member, who is called the *etulukpa gekuba* (lit. the compound elder) who is priest of the most important compound shrine, can settle internal disputes, and, to some extent, represent the group to outsiders – for example at ward rituals. The unity of the group is reflected in the fact that each compound possesses a separate name known to everyone in the settlement. Finally, as we shall see, all the members of the compound are bound by very strict rules designed to reduce the likelihood of sexual jealousy arising between the male members.

What is important for this discussion of the significance to be attached to the concept of unilineal descent is that, because of the residential rule of patrilocality for men, many compounds are, as has been said, *de facto* 'patrilineal' groups. Patrilocality is definitely the norm. The final stage in the process of marriage consists of the clitoridectomy ceremony for the woman; after this she goes to live with her husband and he usually builds a house in his father's compound if there is room, and the eldest son usually inherits the father's house. Moreover, if for some reason a man must leave his home compound it is explicitly recognized that, irrespective of his place of birth or rearing, he has the right to claim a building site in what he can show to have been the real home of his father or father's father; and he will seek to prove this by taking an elder to substantiate his claim in genealogical terms.

There is linguistic evidence that the men of a compound are commonly assumed to have some kind of paternal link, for I was told that the polite term used by a man to refer to other men in his compound is *wete gwomi leitei* (lit., my father's paternal half-brothers belonging to the place). Furthermore the term *levor* (pl. *gevor*), which means in a broad sense children of a man, occurred in at least one compound name. In Ekpon ward there is a compound called *Ekalevor*, and this name was said by the compound's senior elder to mean 'a good group of father's kin'.

The name chosen for this compound, *Ekalevor*, was clearly

appropriate, as I found when I got details of the people living in it. In all, I traced the histories of fourteen of the sixteen household heads. Of these, seven could claim direct 'patrilineal' descent back to the founder of the compound, who was said to be the father's father of the senior elder, my informant. Of the rest, three were related to this 'patrilineal' core in miscellaneous ways: one man was the compound elder's wife's son by a former marriage and had come as a child to the compound; a second man was a wife's brother's son of a deceased core member; and one was the sister's son of a man who was a kinsman of the compound's founder (the kin link being that the fathers of both had belonged to the same matrilineage). Of the four remaining men for whom I was able to obtain information and for whom no ultimate kinship link with the founder was forthcoming, all had longstanding 'patrilineal' connexions with the compound. Two of the men were brothers whose father and father's father had both lived in the compound; and of the two remaining men one had a three-generation, and the other a four-generation 'patrilineal' link with *Ekalevor*. It was an interesting indication of the reality of 'patrilineal' claims to house sites that three of the members of the core 'patrilineage' had been born elsewhere in the village: two were brothers born in a compound to which their father had moved as a young man, but as adults they had claimed their right to return to his natal home; the third man was a son of one of their brothers who had remained in their father's adopted compound. In this man's case the fact that he already had two of his father's brothers resident in *Ekalevor* influenced his decision to claim a site there; but that it was his patrilineal connexion to the place which gave him a right to do so was accepted as axiomatic by the compound elder.

There is thus no doubt that the people of Adadama acknowledge a close link, and the existence of important claims, between father and son. The son through his father claims rights to house sites, sometimes to houses, and, as we shall see, to a certain extent to land as well. The father has also claims over his son, from whom he expects help in farming and in other ways. The rights of the father over the son, and his rights as against those of the son's matrilineal kin, are symbolically expressed in the rules about the division of game killed by the son. Whenever a man kills a wild animal certain persons have claims over parts of it. Minor portions must be given to his age-mates and to his wives. The biggest claimants are, however, his father and the senior elder of his matrilineage; but it is the father who takes the bigger share (if the true father is dead it is the latter's matrilineal heir who receives the meat; in this, Adadama is like the Osopong Mbembe). The matrilineal elder should be given the right fore-leg, but to the father must be given the whole of the hind-quarters (and I saw this done). In practice, the father, having received the meat, cuts off the greater part of the left leg and returns it to his son; but the amount handed back is said to be at the father's discretion. His share is thus significantly greater than that of the matrilineal kin, and it is important to note that the giving of the meat to the father is an occasion for the formal expression of the son's submission to the father, since the son must accept thankfully whatever the father returns to him. It is also of interest that the son is explicitly said to make this gift of meat 'because he ought to be his father's right hand'.

III

The main point at issue here, however, is whether the stress laid on the father-son tie, and the claims which a man can make through his father and to some extent through his father's father, are in Adadama associated with an explicit notion of patrilineal descent. As I have already indicated, the answer to this question appears to be basically negative. Although the evidence just quoted was such as to make me think at first that patrilineality must be one of the explicit principles of this society, the more information I acquired the more definitely it seemed to be established that this was not the case. I thought at one point that I had obtained evidence for the recognized existence of patrilineal groups, and the entry in my notebook for that day begins: 'Success! I have at last been able to frame my questions as to get from Eni Icha (the compound elder of *Ekalevor*) evidence that something very like patrilineages did exist as perceived entities, at least in certain circumstances.' I wrote this after inquiring from this elder whether the descendants of Icha Evoli, the compound's founder, had any term by which they could distinguish themselves. Eni Icha said that they could do so by calling themselves 'children of Icha Evoli', *gevor Icha Evoli*. I asked if they customarily did so, but he said that only the old men ever used the term; indeed he admitted that the young men probably did not even know of their links with Icha Evoli and might even deny that they were descended from him. Nevertheless, when I asked if there had ever been occasions when the whole *gevor Icha Evoli* had gathered together for any purpose, he told me that they formerly did so for sacrifices at a shrine called *Iyayoga*. They had given up this shrine as their leaders had become Christians, but he thought that other groups still had such shrines and that groups of *gevor* would gather at them. It was only with considerable reluctance that I brought myself to realize that I had in part misunderstood what the elder was saying and that, despite all this, patrilineages existed only in my mind and not in those of the people themselves; in fact, the term *gevor* had a general bilateral and not a unilineal connotation.

I began to realize this almost immediately when I followed up the clue Eni Icha had given me that the shrine *Eyayogo* was in some way closely linked with groups of *gevor*, and I sought for a priest of a still active shrine of this cult. Few seemed to remain in Adadama, but I was able to question the priest of the shrine that is regarded as the most important in the village. This man, an elder, clearly saw the *gevor* not as any kind of patrilineal group but as consisting of *all* the descendants of a man; moreover, it seemed that he visualized the defining ancestor always in his role as the member of some matrilineal group. *Gevor*, as this priest described them, seemed to be primarily a man's own children, but he said they might include grandchildren, and indeed the children of his daughters as well as the children of his sons. The priest seemed prepared to argue also that ideally the link might carry on for further generations. For him the link to the ancestor was important in that it gave a man's descendants links with his matrilineal group.[2] He said that the cult (*Eyayogo*) assured the success of the yam harvest for members of matrilineal groups and for the offspring of their male members. These latter, the *gevor*, are particularly concerned because the priest of *Eyayogo* must be an elder who represents the *gevor*. This shrine, as the senior *Eyayogo* shrine of Adadama, had, as its core cult members, the priests of certain matriclans which are ritually senior to others in the village (these senior clans are known collectively as the '*Bikai*' clans). Each priest representing one of these clans at the *Eyayogo* rites represented not merely the clan members, but also that clan's *gevor*; and he himself as the priest represented not a matriclan but the whole *gevor* of all the *Bikai* clans.

This elder's conception of the *gevor* seemed quite consistent with the way in which he viewed his own paternal links, because when he described them he seemed all the time to be visualizing them as links between himself and matrilineal groups – a view which I realized was shared by my other informants. When I collected his genealogy and asked him to tell me whether his father had had any paternal half-siblings, he maintained that he did not know this. He said that he only knew that his father was the son of a man called Isang Eso who was a member of a matriclan called Iwiawia, and that his father had, therefore, been linked with others as *gevor* to this clan. In the same way he went on to explain to me that his own father was member of a matriclan called *Adz' Anong*, so that he and his paternally linked siblings were *gevor* to this clan. This same kind of thinking was followed on a different occasion by another elder when I gathered genealogical information from him. I soon realized that while he had detailed knowledge of kin on his mother's side his knowledge of his paternal kinsmen was somewhat sketchy and, realizing that I was questioning him about them without much success, I asked him simply to tell me the names of some people he knew to be related to his father's father. He immediately rattled off a list of four names, and I then began to ask him what kind of link these individuals had with his grandfather. It soon emerged that the names he had given me were those of the present priest and senior elders of the matriclan to which his father's father had belonged.

Further discussion with the *Eyayogo* priest showed that not merely were the *gevor* non-unilineal clusters of people linked by men to particular matriclans, but that for him, at least, it was scarcely possible to think of the *gevor* of particular individuals as opposed to the *gevor* of a matrilineal group as a whole. He said that there was not today, and he did not think there had been in the past, any ritual occasion for the offspring and descendants of his father to group themselves separately from the whole *gevor* of the matriclan *Adz' Anong*. He admitted that for such an event as the father's funeral a man's offspring might meet as a separate group. Such a group would, he said, be known as *bege wete gwomi* or *ge wete* for short (i.e. 'offspring of my father'), but he insisted that such a term must refer to *all* the descendants of a man, the children of his daughters as well as those of his sons. In his own case his father's only surviving daughter had died without children, and so he could not say that any of his father's daughter's children were included in his own *ge wete*; but he insisted that the term did include in his own case the children of two of his father's granddaughters. Moreover he maintained that there was no term at all by which he could refer separately to his father's sons and their descendants through males.

Once again, when I checked through my notes, I found that this statement was quite consistent with the information which had been given to me on another occasion by the elder, Eni Icha. I had asked him if there was any term by which it might be possible to refer exclusively to a man's full and paternal half-siblings and their descendants through males, and to his father's full and paternal half-siblings, etc., and he made it quite clear that there was not. A term *levon* (pl. *gevon*) could be used for a man's paternal half-siblings and their descendants; but this term specifically excluded full siblings of the father and a man's own full siblings. There was a slight difference in the accounts of these two elders, in that Eni Icha could not think of any term which included together both full and half-siblings, but he agreed in denying that there was any term which linked together full and paternal half-siblings and their patrilineal descendants.

It is also significant that Eni Icha's evidence concerning kinship terms was in other respects also consistent with the absence in Adadama of recognized patrilineal groups. He said for instance, that, when reference is made to the children of paternal half-siblings, the sex of the linking parent is not important – the children of a paternal half-brother and a paternal half-sister are equally *baba 'te gwomi*, i.e. 'offspring of my father'. This usage presents a contrast with that on the mother's side, for the children of females linked matrilineally are classified as 'full siblings', modified by terms meaning 'senior' or 'junior 'to mark differences of generation. On the other hand, the offspring of males linked matrilineally are classified formally as 'children';

and reciprocally members of the father's matrilineage are all classified as 'fathers', no matter what their sex or age. It is interesting that in these respects the Adadama terminology is exactly parallel to that of the Mbembe, *except* for the fact that the Mbembe do make a distinction on the father's side between the children of males, who are members of the patrilineage, and the children of females, who, of course, are not.[3]

IV

That patrilineal descent is not a local principle of organization, and indeed that apparently 'patrilineal' relationships are significant primarily because they provide links with particular *matriclans*, can be understood most clearly when we examine certain offices whose incumbents seem at first sight to have been selected because of some apparently 'patrilineal' link with a former office-holder. I am not concerned with the fact that, in practice, men who are titularly priests of particular matriclans may in reality be sons of men of the clan.[4] What is of interest here is the fact that there are certain offices which are apparently inherited in the same 'patrilineal' line generation after generation. Yet, instead of such descent lines being recognized for what the anthropologist thinks they are, these 'patrilineal' links are viewed as ties of a special type with some matrilineal group.

The first example of such offices relates to the *Ligwomi* association which here, as in Umor, played an important part in traditional village life; indeed it was said to have been the 'government' of former times, in the sense that it was responsible for issuing orders against certain offences and for punishing them. The central *Ligwomi* cult group is thought always to have consisted of seven core members of whom three are priests of leading matriclans who belong *ex officio*. The four others, however, hold seats which must be inherited in the male line. So strong in their case is this emphasis on 'patrilineal' inheritance in this cult that it is clearly expressed in belief and ceremonial. I was told that, if no paternal relative, preferably a son, comes to pay the fees to take up a dead member's seat (i.e. the stone allocated to a particular member as a seat in the central shrine), an offering is made to this stone and the members pray that a successor should be sent. Subsequently, any illness befalling a close 'patrilineal' kinsman of the former member is taken as a sign of punishment by *Ligwomi*. For example, my informant on this point said that although he himself was a Christian and had wished not to become a cult member, he had been forced to do so when his father, a member, died and, as the senior son, he himself had become ill as the result of *Ligwomi's* attack.

What is particularly striking about the succession to *Ligwomi* offices is that the *ex officio* matrilineal members of the group have to make special offerings at their installation which seem to suggest that the succession 'ought' to have gone in their cases too from father to son. I was told that at the ritual of installation of a new member all the other members stand round the stone seat which has been vacant and place offerings on it, principally the blood of a slaughtered goat. The senior elder then raises the stone, turns it over, replaces it, and the new man takes his seat. Now, the significant point is that a 'patrilineal' successor need offer only one goat, but a matrilineal successor must offer two goats, one of which is said to 'take away the father', i.e. to compensate the father for the fact that his son is not inheriting. In spite of all this, however, I could not even in this case get any evidence that the 'patrilineal' descent lines involved had any kind of conceptual identity as groups. Instead, it seemed that what were traced were merely individual ties through fathers between office-holders, each of whom was thought of as *wa wa wa*, child of child of child of some original man remembered in his role as the member of a matriclan.

As a final example of incipient patrilineages remaining unperceived as descent groups by the people themselves, the evidence of yet another elder may be quoted. This man is the holder of an office akin to that of *Okpebri* (the Village Speaker) of Umor. In Adadama the official is called *Okpobolo*. Like *Okpebri*, *Okpobolo* actually offers the sacrifices at those rituals where the senior matriclan priests officiate, and *Okpobolo* too publicly addresses and admonishes all the people at least once a year (this is on the occasion of the *Aji* rites, the main annual village festival, which takes place when the crops are planted). *Okpobolo* is particularly associated with sacrifices necessitated by great sins, especially homicide, which make it necessary for a man to placate the earth (*ekwo Leze*). And, partly I think because of the strength of the mystical forces he controls, *Okpobolo* is always credited with being the most powerful member of the sorcerers' association, *Njor*, in Adadama. To an outsider, succession to this important office would appear to be patrilineal. The priest gave me a list of four previous office-holders who had been respectively his father's brother's son, father's brother, father, and a paternal kinsman whose exact genealogical connexion was uncertain. Nevertheless, despite this pattern of inheritance and despite my quite deliberately leading questions, he did not explain the rule of succession in 'patrilineal' terms. Instead he maintained that succession depended in the first place on being a resident in a particular compound, called *Eduno*, in Evone ward; and, secondly, on being a 'son' of one of the *Bikai* matriclans.

If any further evidence is required for the non-recognition of patrilineal descent in Adadama, it can be found most clearly in the absence of rules proscribing marriage in the 'patrilineal' line. We know that, among the Yakö and the Mbembe, although compounds are not always rigidly patrilineal groups, there is a general assumption of patrilineal kinship among the majority of members, and those thought of as full members of the compound are bound by strict rules of exogamy which are phrased in patrilineal terms. In Adadama, on the other hand, the men of a compound are bound only by very strict rules against adultery with one another's wives.

It is an indication of the importance attached to avoiding adultery within the compound that it is impossible to speak of compounds at all without being reminded of its dangers. The very word for a compound, *gekuba*, is the word for a cult whose shrine is, or was, found at the entrance to every compound and whose sole *raison d'être* is to punish adulterers. Before compounds were opened up in recent years, each was almost completely enclosed except for a single narrow opening between two specially planted trees, and it is here that the *gekuba* shrine is found. In general, it is expected to attack any man, even one coming from outside, who commits adultery in the compound. But the punishment, which for outsiders might consist only of pains in the joints, is much more severe for offending members of the group and can result in death. The only hope lies in confession to the compound elders, who make a sacrifice at the shrine. Moreover, even if it is an outsider who actually commits adultery, punishment will fall on any man of the compound who assists him. Clearly, therefore, the need to protect the compound from strife caused by sexual jealousies is very strongly recognized, and it is the more significant that there are no rules of exogamy which explicitly bind the members. Marriage is in fact forbidden only with a member of a man's own matriclan, his father's matrilineage, and the daughter of a man of his own matrilineage. Unfortunately, I was unable in the time at my disposal to make any kind of census to discover how often marriage does take place within the compounds, but my informants made it quite clear that there was no rule against it.

In Adadama, therefore, we are presented with a somewhat surprising situation. The general rule of patrilocal residence for men gives rise in many cases to the existence of *de facto* patrilineages, some of which even appear to enjoy special rights and privileges. Yet their very existence and the general principle of patrilineal descent itself are totally unrecognized.

I am not seeking on the basis of this evidence from Adadama to argue that the existence or otherwise of the *concept* of unilineal descent is not in itself significant. Were more space available I could bring forward evidence to show that, if in fact the concept did exist, Adadama village organization would probably be rather different from what it actually is. For example, the rule of patrilocal residence is probably overridden even more frequently than it is in Umor, where it has been shown that it is often set aside in individual cases (Forde 1963: 41). In Adadama, not merely are there many instances in which individuals move out of their father's compounds for private reasons, but about a third of the compounds are very heterogeneous because they are the official residences of matriclan priests, who on appointment must go to live there no matter where they have been living earlier. Often they go accompanied by their sons, and these and children subsequently born to a priest frequently remain in the new compound throughout their lives. Censuses which I made of two such compounds (out of fifteen) showed them to be without any sort of 'patrilineal' core group. It is at least arguable that were the concept of loyalty to a patrilineage added to the normal rule of patrilocality, then these 'matrilineally' linked compounds would play a less important part in village structure.

More significantly it seems probable that the absence of any concept of patrilineal descent is one reason why, in Adadama, land which formerly passed from father to son is now inherited matrilineally. There is ample evidence to show that formerly rights to land use passed *de facto* from father to son, although ritual control over land was held by matriclans – a situation which, for example also formerly existed among the Okum Mbembe. There, in areas where land is now scarce, patrilineal groups have been recognized as legally exercising usufructuary rights over the land, but in Adadama such rights are now recognized by the courts as belonging to the matriclans. This extension of the rights of matrilineal groups, most unusual under modern conditions, seems undoubtedly connected with the fact that here there are no patrilineal groups to stand up, as it were, for the sons' rights to inherit from their fathers. Today men can in their lifetime allot some land to their sons, but, when the father dies, the sons' claims are gradually extinguished and they must look to their own matriclan heads for land.

Nevertheless, while there may be important differences between societies dependent upon whether they do or do not give explicit recognition to a concept of patrilineal descent, the Adadama material does serve to show that the distinctions are not nearly as clear cut as has sometimes been imagined. Professor Forde (1963: 38) has argued that 'the force of any principle of recruitment can itself be a matter of degree with reference both to the explicitness with which it is expressed and the frequency with which it is applied . . .', and he goes on to demonstrate that although the Yakö think in terms of an ideology of unilineal descent, patrilineal and matrilineal, recruitment to both types of group is affected by 'interests and ties extraneous to unilineal kinship' (1963: 56). Adadama obviously shows the other side of the picture, a society without an ideology of patrilineal descent where, nevertheless, practice in many contexts is such as to give rise to quasi-patrilineages. If we put the evidence of these two societies together, what better demonstration can we find of the argument that 'unilineal descent' is indeed a matter of degree?

NOTES

1. My thanks are due to the University of Sussex for granting me leave of absence and for a Hayter research grant, thus enabling me to re-visit the Cross River area from January to April 1966. Partly because of the unsettled political situation, I was able to spend only a mere three and a half weeks at Adadama, but I had already had considerable experience of this area and I was particularly fortunate in securing good informants, one of whom I had already known earlier elsewhere. Moreover the fact that I could show people my book on the Mbembe helped to allay their suspicions. My thanks are also due to a missionary couple, Klaus and Janice Spreda, who had been carrying out linguistic research in Adadama and whose description of it first made me realize that a study here might give interesting comparative material for understanding the Cross River region.

2. In this respect the Adadama *gevor* relationship is similar to the *akpan* relationship among the Mbembe (Harris 1965: 171), and to one aspect of the Yakö *yakpan* relationship (Forde 1964: 116-117).

3. It must be noted that this terminology is significant here, as elsewhere in the Cross River area, in formal situations and for reference. In address the individual's own name is used.

4. This is quite common and is indeed regarded as a fairly desirable situation: high fees cannot be demanded from the 'son' of a clan, because he is technically only a 'caretaker', but this means that the ceremonies are somewhat curtailed and their cost is comparatively low. Moreover, such a choice of leader is thought to preserve the clan from sorcery attacks for, in Adadama, as among the Yakö and Mbembe, sorcerers are thought to kill primarily matrilineal kin, and matriclan elders are particularly feared sorcerers. In Adadama a matriclan member chosen as clan priest is assumed to kill one or more of its junior members soon after his installation, but a 'son' of the clan chosen as leader is unable to do this.

REFERENCES

FORDE, D. 1963. Unilineal Fact or Fiction: an Analysis of the Composition of Kin Groups among the Yakö. In I. Schapera (ed.), *Studies in Kinship and Marriage*. London; Royal Anthropological Institute, Occasional Paper No. 16.

— 1964. *Yakö Studies*. London: Oxford University Press.

HARRIS, R. 1965. *The Political Organization of the Mbembe*. London: H.M.S.O.

M. G. Smith

Differentiation and the Segmentary Principle in Two Societies

This essay illustrates a neglected feature of Professor Daryll Forde's work which seems fundamental for the comparative analysis of segmentary relations and processes in acephalous societies based on unilineal descent groups. In such societies segmentary principles of organization are manifest in the situationally variable alignments of collateral descent groups to form contraposed blocks of elastic scale and roughly equivalent strength, span, and genealogical status. The structural relativity of these social units and their relations presupposes the primacy of genealogical and local principles of collective differentiation. Yet in his accounts of Yakö society Forde has repeatedly shown how these preconditions of segmentary lineage systems may be qualified or obstructed by other principles of structural differentiation and collective alignment, such as age-grouping, corporate associations, or double unilineal descent (1938, 1939, 1961, 1963).

Further, in considering the factors which determine the extent to which lineage organization is elaborated into larger groups of varying span and genealogical depth, Forde contrasted his field observations among the Yakö and Hopi with data from such societies as the Nuer, Tallensi, and Ibo in which relativity of lineage structure prevailed. For the Hopi, he observed that 'fission with continued inter-segmentary relationship is possible within clan and lineage inside the pueblo. But the continuance of wider group solidarity between segments, separated by migration to other pueblos, is inhibited because it conflicts with the economic, ritual, and political autonomy of the village unit' (1947: 221). Implicit in this discussion and in his analysis of Yakö society is the thesis that collective differentiations on non-

151

genealogical grounds may restrict or exclude segmentary relations, even in acephalous societies based on unilineal groupings.
To develop this thesis, it is merely necessary to show how
identical conditions of social differentiation exercise identical
effects on the lineage organizations of two or more distinct
societies, while differing modes of social differentiation promote
divergent effects. The following brief comparison of Kadara and
Kagoro societies seeks to illustrate this.

CONTEXTS AND HISTORY

The Kadara and Kagoro are two tribes settled about one hundred
miles apart, south-east of Kaduna in Northern Nigeria (Smith
1951a, 1951b; Gunn 1956). In 1950, when first visited, the
Northern Kadara of Kajuru District in Zaria Emirate numbered
about 9,000.[1] Another 8,000 Kadara in Kacia District due south-
west were also ruled by the Fulani Emir of Zaria. At that date
the independent Kagoro District in the extreme south-east of
Zaria Province contained 13,000 inhabitants, of whom 10,500
were Kagoro tribesmen, another 2,300 Kagoro being settled in
the Fulani Emirate of Jema'a, due south-west. Kagoro and
Kadara speak languages, provisionally classified as Nigerian
Semi-Bantu (Thomas 1925: 137). However, the two peoples
are historically unrelated and moved to their present sites from
opposite directions over 200 years ago. On reaching Kagoro, the
original migrants or Ankwei occupied a massif which later
provided excellent refuge from Muslim attacks. Farther north
the Kadara, pressed by Muslim from Zaria and from the Habe
vassal-state of Kajuru nearby, remained independent of Kajuru
but rendered tribute to Zaria, which raided when it was due.
In 1894-5 the Emir Yero attacked Ma'aveli, the leading settlement of Northern Kadara. The tribesmen dispersed in flight,
some to nearby Kadara communities, the majority to found new
villages at Kufana, Dan Bagudu, Kiamara, Dutsen Gaya, and
Rafin Kunu. In 1950, while internally autonomous, these new
settlements were all attached to Kufana, whose chief (*agwom*)
supervised their administration.

Thanks to their rocky refuge, the Ankwei maintained their
independence until the British came (Tremearne 1912). However, during the last century, Ankwei received refugees from

Katab, Kagoma, Kaninkwom, and nearby tribes of similar speech and culture, who fled from Fulani pressure. After an interval these immigrants were assimilated into Kagoro society as a moiety called Kpashan (Smith 1960: 139-40), subject to certain regulations. In return for land, they furnished token tributes of grain annually. They were excluded from active roles in the calendrical rites (ci) that sacralized land and people. They were forbidden to marry one another or to abduct the wives of Ankwei, being thus obliged to marry the latter's daughters. However, unless otherwise prevented by relations of kinship or community, Kpashan were free to abduct one another's wives, who were Ankwei by birth. Ankwei, the original occupants, continued to marry among themselves and to abduct one another's wives as before, while intermarrying with Kpashan. In their beleaguered state, both moieties participated equally in their common defence and in the tribal head-hunter's cult.

Kagoro and Kadara are hoe-farmers who supplement their staple grains with root crops. Possessing rudimentary technologies, both people lacked cattle, markets, and currency, and depended on hunting for meat. For defence, both tribes had nucleated settlements, thus demarcating communities sharply; and in 1950, the period to which these data refer, both retained this pattern. At that date Kufana and Fadan Kagoro, the communities I studied most fully, contained 1,800 and 2,000 persons respectively, Kagoro have since experienced notable changes, Kadara rather less so.

On pacification, the British placed Kagoro under a 'tribal chief' whom they supervised from Kafanchan, Jema'a. Not until 1930-3 did Ankwei ritual leaders protest against this secular administration; but by 1950 a *modus vivendi* obtained (Smith 1960). Christian missions, active at Kagoro since 1926, had by then converted about one-third of the adults and nearly one-half of the children; the old Ankwei ritual order was passing, and Kpashan were already the larger moiety. Among the Kadara, despite parallel mission efforts, Christian influence was negligible, and in 1950 traditional Kadara rites were unimpaired.

MARRIAGE REGULATIONS

Both Kagoro and Kadara have agnatic descent, prohibit marriage between agnates, proscribe cross-cousin marriage, esteem

153

polygyny, and prescribe virilocal residence. Both practise early betrothals for first marriage and observe similar modes of widow-inheritance. Lacking durable objects of value, bride-wealth in either tribe involved a long series of prescribed transfers. In Kagoro, standard payments of hoes and goats, known as *drangwan*, were required from men to ratify their paternal rights in each child at its weaning. Among Kadara, following infant betrothal, the groom's father and agnatic kinsmen perform farm service for the bride's kin at annually increasing rates. There also, husbands maintain their marriages and ratify paternity claims by set gifts to their affines. However, while Kagoro abhor premarital unchastity, Kadara welcome pregnant brides as demonstrably fertile. Both tribes observe similar institutions of secondary marriage (Smith 1953). All secondary marriages begin with wife-abduction. Normally the abductor has made the betrothal payments in advance to the woman's guardian (father, father's brother, or, rarely, mother's brother). In both tribes men are entitled to arrange successive marriages for their daughters or female wards without consulting the women's husbands, but without thereby terminating their marriages. Thus women can participate in several marriages simultaneously, though they may cohabit with only one spouse at any moment. In either tribe, only with her guardian's approval should a woman desert her current husband for some other. Then, to obviate paternity disputes, she should demonstrate non-pregnancy to some senior kinswoman at her next three menstrual periods. However, since the woman remains married to her former husband despite her removal, she is obliged to return to his lineage to undergo widow-inheritance on his death. Women could also rejoin their former husbands at any time without further payments, with or without the knowledge and formal consent of their current partner. On such occasions the woman reassumes all her wifely duties. Neither Kadara nor Kagoro recognize divorce or annulment; and in both societies widow-inheritance indicates the corporate character of marriages and lineage interests in them.

Secondary marriage is distinguished from primary marriage and widow-inheritance, and is regulated by identical rules in both tribes. Since these unions presuppose prior marriages, unwed girls cannot be taken as secondary wives. Secondary marriage is also forbidden between agnates anywhere, and within each local community. Thus wife-abduction is explicitly an inter-community as well as an inter-lineage affair. Men can neither marry the daughters of those whose wives they may abduct, nor inherit the widows of those whose daughters they may wed. Once abduction has occurred, antecedent relations of betrothal and intermarriage between the lineages concerned automatically change into collective relations of wife-abduction. Thus abductions are restricted to lineages that do not marry one another's daughters. Most betrothal-marriages are thus arranged within local communities; and most men live among their kin and affines, away from their rivals.

Among Kadara, real or potential affines address and describe one another reciprocally as *azaimi*. Men whose lineages practise mutual wife-abduction describe each other collectively and individually as *aformi*. *Azaimi* represents affinal alliance, *aformi* is the opposition of rival affines. *Azaimi*, *aformi*, and exogamy are symmetrical and mutually exclusive relations between corporate groups, each of which has its own unique distribution of these relations, widow-inheritance being normally restricted to the local exogamous lineage group. However, while *aformi* institutionalizes antagonism between particular lineages settled in different communities, *azaimi* entails insecurity for husbands within each community, since lineage norms authorize men to disrupt their daughters' unions. Lineages linked by *aformi* relations must have certain *azaimi* relations in common with particular descent groups; they compete as *aformi* for the daughters of their common *azaimi*.

The Kagoro equivalent of Kadara *azaimi* (affinity) is known as *niendi*; the Kagoro equivalent of *aformi* (affinal opposition) is known as *nendwang*. However, Kagoro exhibit two levels of exogamy. That which bans wife-abduction as well as intermarriage is called *bin* and characterizes agnatic kinship. Kpashan moiety exogamy differs from *bin* in allowing mutual wife-abduction between Kpashan of different communities. Like Kadara, Kagoro reserve widow-inheritance for local exogamous groups, and here also a single incident of wife-abduction immediately converts *niendi* relations into *nendwang* between the lineages concerned. Here also, men can only abduct women eligible to them as *niendi*. Thus in Kagoro, rival lineages compete

155

for their common affines. Under the moiety arrangements, some Ankwei are rivals, others are affines, and others are *bin*. With the sole exception mentioned below, all Ankwei and Kpashan are reciprocally *niendi*; and, beyond community boundaries, all Kpashan not linked by agnation are formally *nendwang* (rivals).

Secondary marriage presumes that agnatic groups reserve continuing rights over their kinswomen, and provisionally over the latter's issue. While these lineage reservations exclude annulment and divorce, they limit men's rights in their wives reciprocally. In either tribe relations of exogamy, marriage, and wife-abduction (*nendwang, aformi*) hold between corporate local descent groups as determinate collectivities.

LINEAGE ORGANIZATION

Among Kadara and Kagoro, lineage divisions are explicit and formalized. Special terms denote successive levels of patrilineal grouping. In Kagoro, *kwai*, and in Kadara, *ute*, refer equally to the dispersed patriclan and to its largest local divisions. Major segments within these largest localized lineages are described by Kagoro as *tusa* or *uli*, by Kadara as *anepa* or *erute*. These segments are further subdivided into minor segments called *ufam* at Kagoro and *aban* among the Kadara. Kadara *aban* are multi-family compounds containing households called *engau*, corresponding to the Kagoro *kyambwak*. Even these small units also contain named divisions. Such terminologies suggest such fixity in the identities and relations of these segments as to exclude their structural relativity. However, despite these parallels, the two lineage systems differ in certain ways.

While Kadara genealogies rarely extend two generations beyond the senior living males, among Kagoro even the Kpashan cite five or six deceased ancestors, and the Ankwei normally eight. This Kagoro stress on lineage genealogies contrasts sharply with Kadara indifference to them. The difference cannot be explained simply by Kadara dispersal from Ma'aveli, since at Kagoro immigrant Kpashan all assert elaborate genealogies. Evidently this divergence indicates that, while genealogy is critical to Kagoro conceptions of lineage, Kadara rely on other criteria.

In both tribes the mother's brother and his lineage are identified by a single term. The sister's son has a privileged relation with his mother's lineage and may settle permanently among them, or he may be claimed in infancy for non-payment of prestations required to ratify paternity rights. However, while Kagoro lineages are almost all eponymous, most Kadara lineages bear place-names or other descriptive terms such as Anigum or Anaregum, that is, the lineage of the *agwom* (chief). Further, Kadara compounds that house minor lineages generally bear the names of their current heads, not those of their founders.

Given their indifference to genealogy, Kadara make little use of lineage fictions. Kagoro, conceiving lineages in strictly genealogical terms, deny publicly that any agnatic group contains unrelated descent groups or segments attached by uterine ties. Despite the differential exogamy that generally distinguishes such assimilated segments, given their lineage axioms, Kagoro cannot avoid such public denials. Kadara encounter no such problems. Among them, lineages are validated by external identifications and by ritual connexions. An immigrant male, a sister's son, or wife's son born elsewhere, may be assimilated into a lineage by ritual and jural identification through continued co-residence. The lineal issue of such assimilated men maintain differential exogamy relations but, as Kadara exogamy excludes both marriage and wife-abduction, this restriction entails no positive deviation from the specific complex of affinal alliances and oppositions of the host lineage. Given their identical marriage regulations, these conditions affect lineage organization equally in both tribes.

In each tribe, irrespective of their genealogical or ritual status, autonomous patrilineal groups are distinguished by their individually specific combinations of positive relations of marriage and wife-abduction with one another. Though agnates neither intermarry nor abduct one another's wives, since each autonomous localized group maintains a distinctive set of relations of intermarriage and wife-abduction with specific lineages, it is distinguished by them as a discrete collectivity having common exclusive external and internal affairs.

LINEAGE STRUCTURE IN KAGORO

In Kagoro the marriage system has direct implications for lineage groupings, although these are formally defined by agnatic

157

genealogies that segment serially to segregate units of decreasing level and span. I shall illustrate the implications of these marriage rules for Kagoro lineages by six concrete cases.

Of the three original Ankwei clans, Mingio are probably the largest. All Mingio at Fadan Kagoro can trace common agnatic descent except the minor segment of Biniat, which descends from a Kumat man of that name and a woman of the Kabiom major segment of Mingio at Fada. Biniat are thus immediate 'sisters' sons' of Kabiom, and indirectly of other Fada Mingio. Being assimilated to Kabiom, Biniat observe all Mingio marriage regulations, including exogamy with Mingio living elsewhere. However, being of Kumat descent, Biniat also observe exogamy with the Kumat nearby. With this exception, Biniat practise the same affinal alliances and oppositions as other Mingio of Fada. Though no other Mingio at Fada observe exogamy with Kumat, Mingio assert publicly that Biniat are their agnates. Privately, the Mingio lineage head (*tienwhop*), who was also the community priest, explained the reasons for this anomaly and for these public statements.

The position of Kumat, another Ankwei clan, is also of interest. In 1929 Kumat formed a distinct patriclan, coordinate with their agnates, the Mungwop, also settled at Fada (Meek 1931, vol. II: 92). As agnates, Kumat and Mungwop observe common exogamy, though inheriting widows separately. In 1950 both Kumat and Mungwop asserted their unity, citing their common exogamy and descent. If publicly accepted, such reunion would reduce each unit to the status of a major segment and each of their major divisions to minor segments. However, Mungwop and Kumat maintain distinctive sets of marriage relations involving other descent groups. Kumat maintained affinity with the Ankwei lineages of Zafan and Ti at Kadarko, while practising wife-abduction with Kikwot there. Mungwop's relations with these Kadarko lineages were exactly the opposite. In consequence, despite their efforts to assert common identity within Fadan Kagoro, given their differential sets of inter-lineage relations, Kumat and Mungwop remained distinct clans to other lineages. These external differentiae also affected relations between Kumat and Mungwop. The two groups remained residentially separate, each with its own head. Each is a distinct unit of collective responsibility and holds exclusive corporate rights in its land, members, ritual, and widows. Thus whereas negative differences between Biniat and other Mingio did not obstruct their fusion, the positive differentiation of Kumat and Mungwop by their affinal alliances and oppositions blocks their asserted reunion.

In Kagoro, different levels of lineage grouping differ in their properties and structural significance As the largest localized agnatic group the *kwai* is identified by exogamy, by its uniform and unique set of affinal alliances and oppositions with other units, by residential concentrations, by its common head, eponymous ancestor, genealogy, and totems. At various seasons each *kwai* annually carries out collective action to harvest and thresh certain cereals. Each clan also maintains its shrines (*shwo*) for war and hunting rituals, including the purification of killers. Each has exclusive corporate rights in named hunting areas, and Ankwei clans have similar rights in ritual perform-ances of the calendrical cult. Further, each *kwai* initiates its boys separately in its own *obwai* cult, and has its own *obwai* shrine, priest, and ritual paraphernalia. To conclude each hunting season, each clan conducts its purification rites (*akanyam*) separately; and, formerly, in distress, each held its own *nainda* rites and ordeals to identify the sources of mystical misfortune (*nendyung*). The clan is also the widest unit of collective responsibility in kinship affairs and holds exclusive residual rights in the farm plots, house sites, and widows of its members, and in its daughters' offspring until filiation dues are paid. All lineage segments are bound by these conditions.

The major segments of a local lineage are segregated resi-dentially, genealogically, by distinct headships, and, symbolically, by shrines at which small game are shared. Men of the same major segment normally farm contiguous plots and should assist one another in disputes with members of coordinate segments. Each segment normally seeks to preserve its members' widows for internal inheritance, and each performs certain funeral rites for its members separately. However, though most localized lineages contain two major segments, many have three and some have four. A dichotomous organization of paired segments in balanced opposition is neither essential nor characteristic in this lineage structure. For serialized contrapositions to operate effec-tively, units should not be organized with such hierarchic rigour.

Each major segment contains two or more minor segments distinguished genealogically by their closer co-residence and by their first claims to the farms, compounds, house sites, widows, and personal possessions of their members. Members of minor segments share all newly made beer and meat of hunting with one another. Structurally, major and minor segments are distinguished by their positions *vis-à-vis* one another and their co-ordinates in the lineage hierarchy, despite similarities of functional capacity and organization. They differ in scale, complexity, and structural potential. By contrast, differences between autonomous local lineages and major segments are very marked. In declaring their unity, Mungwop and Kumat exhibit structural inconsistency since, although each should then revert from clan to segment status, thus redefining their constituent major segments as minor ones, each retains the structural status and properties characteristic of *kwai*. Such attempts by autonomous collectivities to change their status arouse wide public interest because of their implications for the structure of inter-lineage relations of marriage and wife-abduction, with which societal integration and boundaries are identified. They are accordingly obstructed wherever inconsistent with the necessary conditions of the social system. In effect, the relativity of structural units and relations is inconsistent with those differentiations on which the identities and articulation of these corporate lineages are based. Such differentiations obstruct those situational realignments of genealogically coordinate units that express their segmentary organization. Even though Kumat and Mungwop share public rituals at Fadan Kagoro, each unit retains its distinctive ritual role; their separateness is enhanced by their attempts at reunion.

Among the Kpashan of Kpak, the Nientswot, numbering 256 in 1950, and the Kabiyip, then 92 strong, observed common exogamy as agnates. Though both units shared purification rites and widow-inheritance, they were distinguished as patriclans by all others, following a single divergence in their external relations. Kabiyip intermarried with the anomalous Sukurak of Kukum, with whom Nientswot practised abduction. Marriage relations maintained by these Sukurak, a Kpashan clan, probably antedate the present moiety regulations.

At Kpak also, Micen numbering 222 souls were agnates of

Kanwai, the smallest Kagoro *kwai*, which contained 9 persons in 1950. Though Kanwai and Micen conducted all their clan activities together, like other Kagoro, they recognized their separateness, which followed on a single difference in marriage relations. Formerly a minor branch of Micen, Kanwai abducted a wife from the Kpaguwak of Kukum, an Ankwei group, thus breaching the historic ban on inter-moiety wife-abductions and initiating a struggle that publicized the event. When Micen dissociated itself from Kanwei's action, the latter was publicly distinguished as a separate unit of collective responsibility in inter-lineage relations, and so became a *kwai*.

At Fadan Kagoro the Kalahu, a Kpashan clan which holds the tribal chiefship, consists of three genealogically unrelated and ritually distinct major segments, Kamang, Bafwei, and Tukum, that inherit their widows separately. Originating among the Kutrok of Kpak, Bafwei and Kutrok maintain exogamy and joint rights of widow-inheritance, though I know of no such cases. However, as Kpashan within the same community, Bafwei, Tukum, and Kamang can neither intermarry nor abduct one another's wives. Further, neither Tukum nor Kamang, among whom the Bafwei settled on moving from Kpak to Fada, had abducted any wives from the Kutrok of Kpak. Given their residential contiguity, the three lineages were therefore assimilated into a single clan, Kalahu, by other lineage groups with whom they shared common marriage relations. This assimilation developed despite differences of descent among the units concerned. Tukum and Kamang have thus adopted Bafwei exogamy with Kutrok, to share uniform marriage relations.

These cases show that *uniformities* of marriage relations identify groups Kagoro regard as clans, while *differences* of marriage relations distinguish such units, irrespective of genealogical linkages, numbers, and levels of internal segmentation. Since marriage alternatives are mutually exclusive, symmetrical, and bind autonomous lineages, all are directly concerned with the boundaries and identities of each, to maintain the system of collective relations on which the societal order rests. In consequence, Kagoro lineages are defined by these external differentiae; they cannot alter their public status, alignments, or identities independently, as segmentary principles require. The structural relativity of lineage units is overridden by the system

161

of differential marriage relations that determines their identities; and perhaps this is why their internal organization presents an ideal hierarchy.

The Mingio at Kpak illustrate the force of these extrinsic conditions. These Mingio, locally known as Ankpen, observe exogamy with Mingio elsewhere. In 1950, during the tribal census of lineage groups, segments, relations, and personnel on which this summary is based, Ankpen asserted their division into two independent groups, the Kusak of 89 souls and the Kasa'a of 90. While together they still constituted an exogamous unit, each group conducted its own rites of purification, initiation, and expiation separately and had a separate shrine for hunting and war. Each had its own head and inherited its widows exclusively. No lineages at Kpak challenged the claim of Kusak and Kasa'a to rank as separate clans, since this entailed no change in the community system of marriage relations. However, these claims to separate independent status were unanimously rejected by the tribal assembly, precisely because Kusak and Kasa'a observed identical relations of affinity and wife-abduction with all other clans throughout Kagoro. For this reason, Mingio and other lineages outside Kpak categorically identified the two units as coordinate major segments within the Ankpen. In short, lineages can neither alter their public status merely by processes of internal segmentation, nor can they avoid such differentiation, once they are distinguished by external relations of abduction and marriage. Marriage regulations differentiate or identify lineages as collective units, irrespective of their numbers, genealogical character, and internal alignments. Such differentiations are of direct significance to all other *kwai* engaged in this marriage system; in consequence, all lineages are concerned with one another's boundaries, identities, and external relations. Though these lineages are ideally based on agnatic descent and co-residence, Kagoro mis-state and misunderstand their nature in stressing their genealogical basis to the exclusion of marriage.

At Kagoro, community obligations override lineage and moiety loyalties, wherever both are engaged. All Kagoro communities are multilineal and most contain Kpashan and Ankwei in approximately equal numbers. For defence against foreign foes such as Kaje, Ganawuri, or Fulani, and for rituals in such emergencies as famine or epidemic, the small tribal territory was divided into three unequal areas called *bin*, each under the ritual jurisdiction of its senior Ankwei priest, the *tiebin* (pl. *niebin*). In the sporadic struggles over alleged theft or wife-abduction, each community fought as a unit once its war-horn was blown, until the community priests (*nienci*, sing. *tienci*) intervened to halt the fray. Such fighting recurrently demarcated community boundaries and reinforced their several solidarities. In these encounters, members of opposite moiety avoided one another, and agnates on opposing sides directed their blows elsewhere. Thus in the disputes generated by wife-abduction, clans and moieties were neither isolated nor contraposed. Moreover, within each community, disputes only engaged the agnates of their principals up to the relevant level of lineage grouping. As elsewhere, conventions regulated the weapons appropriate for disputes of differing social range; these and other rules were jointly enforced by the village priest and local lineage heads with fines and other punishments. Thus in the political and legal spheres, lineage autonomies and oppositions alike were restricted by conditions of community structure. Affinally opposed lineages had thus no chance to feud in isolation or with their affinal and agnatic associates; communities furnished the principal units of social solidarity and contraposition. Inter-lineage strife was immediately converted into inter-community fights until stopped by the village priests. The political preconditions of segmentary lineage alignments were excluded by the overriding obligations of communal unity, these communities being the largest local groups within which abductions were proscribed.

KADARA LINEAGE ORGANIZATION

Kadara share the marital arrangements found in Kagoro, and their lineages are similarly affected. In either society some agnatic groups are widely dispersed, and all localized descent groups are internally segmented. In addition, Kadara lineages have to meet important ritual requirements. Though they lack the moiety divisions and two modes of exogamy found in Kagoro, Kadara communities divide into two halves known as *abanizum*, one of which contains the lineage of the village priest, the other that of the chief. Though such groupings are only

163

effective in certain ritual and age-set activities, they express Kadara distinctions between ritual and secular action and leadership. These *abanizum* have no exogamous or moiety connotations.

Unlike the Kagoro *ci*, Kadara ritual centres on ancestors, two of whom are recalled annually in each community, one by each division, for the final funeral rites held between *eguro* in February-March and *otron* in August. Normally, in each village one recalled ancestor is female (*akra*), the other male (*atururu*). Known as *ahwasasen*, these returned ancestors are elaborately masked representations whose secret nature is stringently taboo to women, strangers, and the uninitiated. In the daily dances held at this season, each leads those sections of the community age-sets (*ufro*) that belong to its division.

Every eighth year Kadara initiate a new age-set (*awolegum*, *ufro*), segregating the novices for eight to ten weeks in nearby bush under the local lineage (*ute*) that has ritual jurisdiction over forest and waste. All males should undergo initiation before puberty. For defence, large-scale hunts, road clearance, and wall-building, Kadara relied on their age-sets, the senior directing the junior. In Kajuru District, Kadara communities were also grouped in two divisions that pursued their annual ritual cycles and initiated their age-sets in fixed orders. None the less the local communities, in which bloodshed and secondary marriage were both prohibited, formed the widest effective units of their social system. Each community initiated its age-sets separately; and, although equivalent, sets from different communities seem never to have combined. Thus, despite their weak village chiefships, Kadara were even more fragmented than Kagoro, whose three senior Ankwei priests (*niebin*) sometimes acted together in tribal emergencies, such as smallpox or famine.

In Kadara communities, patrilineages are grouped in ritual associations known as *ategburu* which also serve as village wards. The lineage composition of these ritual groups at Kufana in 1950 is given opposite, each being named after its ritual leaders.

At Kufana the ritual groups headed by Anigum and Anegepon form one community division, while those headed by Anigile, Anaberetan, and Anekyum form the other. The village chief is from Anigum, the village priest from Anigile. In 1950 the 17 Kufana patrilineages averaged 54 males each; the five ritual

ATEGBURU	PATRILINEAGES	COMPOUNDS	HOUSEHOLDS
Anigum	Anigum	5	12
	Anaboahwhah	6	25
	Anafishie	3	15
	Anekekow	1	3
(total)	4	15	55
Anegepon	Anegepon	3	10
	Anakyum	1	3
	Anukwasali	3	8
	Anadai	2	4
(total)	4	9	25
Anigile	Anigile	4	11
	Anumabe	3	16
	Adaru	2	7
	Anoahwhanum	3	7
	Anugima	?	?
(total)	5	12 +	41 +
Anaberetan	Anaberetan	2	13
	Anehurola	3	14
(total)	2	5	27
Anekyum	Anekyum	1	3
	Anilup	3	15
(total)	2	4	18
TOTAL	17	45 +	166 +

groups 183; on average each compound contained about 3.5 households. Given Kadara indifference to genealogy, the compound represents the normal limits of demonstrable agnatic kinship.

Ategburu are agnatically heterogeneous associations of locally contiguous lineages for ritual and social purposes. As primary subdivisions within the community, they provide its administrative wards, each component lineage having its own sub-warden. In community age-sets, boys are organized in separate sections, first by ritual groups and then by lineage.

Though Kadara often describe these ritual groups as clans, the two types of group differ profoundly. Of the five Kufana ritual groups listed above, only that led by Anaberatan was exclusively agnatic. In the Anigum group, Anekekow are unrelated to all others; so are Anoahwhanum and Anugima in that led by Anigile. In the Anegepon group only Anakyum and Anegepon are kin, Anadai and Anukwasali being unrelated. Anekyum and Anilup are also not kin. Anafishie and Anaboahwhah are junior collaterals of Anigum, which leads their group. In relation to Anigile, so are Adaru and Anumabe. Anakyum is likewise a junior collateral of Anegepon. Thus *ategburu* may include unrelated lineages or others linked as senior and junior collaterals, yet all have equivalent status as coordinate units. Occasionally segments of a single patrilineage are attached to different ritual groups. Thus in Kufana one compound of Anoahwhanum participates in the Anegepon group, the remainder in that led by Anigile.

Marriage prohibitions attach to agnatic kinship, not to membership in ritual groups. For most purposes Anaberetan and Anehurola form a distinct ritual group, while joining the Anigile group for others. Anaberetan and Anehurola are linked to Anigile, Adaru, and Anumabe as agnatic collaterals. In this case, segmentation closely approaches fission. Anaberetan and Anehurola, while observing common exogamy, intermarry with all the Anigile group despite agnatic ties. Anoahwhanum and Anugima, being unrelated to Anigile, Adaru, Anumabe, Anaberetan, or to one another, intermarry as freely within their ritual groups as beyond them. Likewise, Anekekow intermarry with the exogamous agnatic group of Anigum, Anaboahwhah, and Anafishie. Anekyum and Anilup also intermarry. Within the *ategburu* led by Anegepon, Anadai and Anukwasali could marry one another or Anakyum and Anegepon, an exogamous agnatic pair. Segments of Anoahwhanum attached to the groups led by Anigile and Anegepon maintain mutual exogamy, as also do certain agnatic groups that claim common maternal origin. Thus despite Kadara attempts to identify them, their ritual and descent groups differ profoundly.

Each autonomous agnatic group maintains exogamy, exclusive widow-inheritance, and a unique combination of affinal alliances and oppositions with similar units. Collateral lineages such as Anafishie, Anaboahwhah, and Anigum, although observing common exogamy, are distinguished by their differential sets of affinal alliances and oppositions. Within each ritual group, lineages preserve their separate identities and interests. Each lineage is a distinct unit for certain ancestral rites, residence, widow-inheritance, headship, and distribution of the 'meat of hunting'. While maintaining agnatic links or ritual alliances, these lineages are clearly segregated as coordinate units. However, despite differentiation in ancestral worship, other ritual considerations prescribe their collaboration.

Though the ritual leaders in each group enjoy precedence, the associated lineages are all substantively equal. Such equivalence is unaffected by differences in their numbers or genealogical relation. Anekekow and Anakyum remain distinct, though each occupies only one compound. Given their distinct descent and marriage relations, even these small groups represent separate units of collective responsibility, formally identical with those that lead the ritual groups to which they belong. Moreover, although, at Kufana, Anekyum lead the ritual group in which Anilup are the majority, at Dan Bagudu where these two lineages are also linked, their relations are reversed. There, although a minority, Anilup lead the group in which Anekyum predominate numerically. In all cases, the ritually senior lineage of an *ategburu* is that which possesses the essential means for recalling ancestral and age-set spirits for certain calendrical public rites. Thus, besides their differentiation through marriage relations, Kadara lineages are simultaneously differentiated by their varying ritual endowments and aligned by their particular ritual needs. The affiliations of Anekekow, Anadai, Anoahwhanum, Anugima, Anilup, and Anukwasali in ritual groups at Kufana all reflect these ritual imperatives. To conduct recurrent rites they regard as indispensable, lineages that lack the necessary ritual instruments must associate in exclusive continuing relations with those that have them.

Normally, this ritual association presumes contiguous residence of the linked units. In such conditions, lineages distinguished by their specific marriage relations, their internal autonomy and ancestral spirits, preserve ritual ties with senior collaterals who retain the ritual heirlooms of their clan. Thus despite intermarriage, Anaberetan retain their ritual links with

167

Anigile. Ritual links accordingly restrict lineage segmentation and regulate alignments by enjoining stable associations for critical recurrent rites. Moreover, as the major community units, these ritual groups furnish the essential framework for the communal initiations and age-set organization, for hunting, defence, and village administration. Only those lineages such as Anoahwhanum, which lack both the necessary ritual objects and agnatic ties to others that have them, are free to subdivide and realign among differing ritual groups in response to purely internal pressures. Even then, Anoahwhanum remain a single entity in inter-lineage marriage relations, though they no longer unite for internal affairs. In effect, lineage location, segmentation, and ritual affiliations are subject to two sets of structural differentiae: those ritual conditions that govern community organization, and those marriage alternatives that simultaneously segregate and align communities and agnatic units.

Within a ritual group, each lineage has its own ritual and secular leaders. The latter is normally an active man of middle age, chosen by the lineage head and elders. The lineage head (*anekute* or *anekwun*) is normally its oldest living male. His activities and authority are ritual and advisory, while his junior colleague, the secular head, acts as the group's executive, directing its age-set and administrative affairs. This division between ritual and secular leadership of lineages parallels that between the village chief and priest, around which the two community divisions are grouped. Within the ritual groups, ritual and secular leadership rests formally with that lineage which holds the essential instruments of collective ritual; but, in either sphere, the group's affairs are administered through councils of lineage representatives. Thus lineage autonomy is restricted by ritual ties to such spheres as marriage relations, widow-inheritance, reallocations of lineage land and house sites, burials, and internal age-set or administrative arrangements. Each descent group conducts separate ancestral and hunting rites, undertakes such periodic tasks as farm clearing or cultivation, and builds its compounds alone. Since lineage compounds are usually adjacent, intra-lineage disputes are routinely settled by the senior men. Disputes between members of differing lineages within the same ritual group are conducted through their representatives in the unit's secular or ritual councils. Thus lineage disputes within ritual groups tend to mobilize neutral members who normally impose an acceptable compromise. Similarly, disputes between lineages attached to different ritual groups stimulate their neutral members to seek some acceptable solution, since, given their mixed composition, diverse functions, and equivalent positions in the age-organization and village administration, ritual groups cannot unite in mutual opposition. In serious disputes between ritual groups, the Anigile village priest might intervene with the support of neutral groups and the village chief. In intra-community disputes, metal weapons were forbidden, but I learnt of few such fights, and no ensuing deaths, perhaps because the ritual groups and age-organization enabled men of senior generation to enforce traditional norms on their juniors by appropriate ritual and secular means. The age-organization further limited occasions for intra-village dispute by prescribing fraternity among age-mates and deference to seniors, irrespective of lineage membership. The community organization also subordinated lineage loyalties and autonomies to the needs of ritual groups, which furnished the framework for age-sets and provided the essential intermediate organization between lineage and community.

Between communities, hostilities were canalized in interlineage relations of wife-abduction with their contingent paternity disputes. Here, as at Kagoro, lineages engaged in mutual wife-abduction were prevented from feuding in isolation or with lineage allies; once violence occurred, retaliation was obligatory for the local lineage and for the age-set of the injured party, while all other lineages in his ritual group remained neutral, as required by their individually specific relations of exogamy, marriage, and abduction. In asserting collective responsibilities for their members on such occasions, age-sets tended to equalize the relative strengths of the contraposed lineages and to extend their dispute to community levels without, however, engaging the communities concerned as total units. Thus lineages were neither isolated nor united by opposition within or beyond community limits. Other corporate groupings interposed to forestall this, thereby restricting lineage autonomies and excluding segmentary alignments.

Kadara rituals integrate ancestral worship with communal rites that sacralize and initiate age-sets. The ancestor cult presupposes certain sacred objects for its calendrical rites, when many people should participate to ensure their success. Since essential features of this cult are hidden from the uninitiated, Kadara lineages depend on one another to preserve the mysteries essential for their common welfare. These ritual secrets centre on spirit representations (*ohuma*) and on certain instruments inherited from ancestors and ultimately attributed to God (*Onum*, the sun). While junior lineage segments may never have possessed these instruments, other lineages probably lost their direct possession during the flight from Ma'aveli. For example, those Anilup who fled to Dan Bagudu took the Anilup ritual objects with them, and other Anilup who came to Kufana consequently lack them. Such impoverished units cannot make good their ritual deficiencies by manufacture or purchase: Kadara say that newly-made substitutes can have no ritual validity, since they lack sacralizing ancestral use and divine origin. This belief effectively discourages the ritual segregation of lineages which could threaten or destroy the ritual units on which these communities and their age-organization depend for cohesion. If Kadara lineages were all ritually independent, the community age-organization, which presupposes their stable groupings for ritual action, could scarcely obtain in its current form. It is more likely that in such conditions Kadara lineages would initiate their youth separately, as Kagoro do in their *obwai* cults, thereby frustrating the preconditions of this communal age-organization.

Of these ritual necessities the bullroarers, trumpets, *iholi* flutes, *ahupe* pods employed in mortuary rites, and the *ibini* drums of clanship are apparently crucial. Without them, neither the age-set nor the ancestral spirits can be recalled, since the bullroarers, *iholi* flutes, and *ahupe* pods represent their voices and movements, while *ibini* and the trumpets are required to summon them. Thus, without these five musical instruments, neither the final funeral rites nor the annual visits of age-set spirits (*ibeigbum*) in September–October can occur.

While each distinct lineage has its own ancestral shrine (*esan*), *kutu* drum, tomb, and burial-flutes (*ahusha*), and all but two have ritual huts, in Kufana only those that led the five ritual groups had their own bullroarers, trumpets, and *ahupe* pods; and of these leading lineages, only four held ancestral drums of clanship, Anaberetan borrowing the Anigile drum as necessary. Further, only Anigile and Anaberetan at Kufana possessed *iholi* flutes, and only four local lineages could recall the age-set spirits. Of fifteen ritual instruments, two lineages that led ritual groups held thirteen each, two fourteen, and only the Anigile retained all. By contrast, of ritually dependent lineages, five each had only four objects, two possessed five, and two had six. Given Kadara ritual and belief, such parallel distributions of essential instruments and ritual capacities simultaneously differentiate lineages and enjoin their continuing cooperation in ritual groups for cult and age-set activities. Thus the conditions that differentiate lineages in ritual capacity restrict their autonomies and prescribe their association to meet common needs; and, although these ritual differentiations and combinations proceed independently of secular differentiations in the marriage system, both sets of conditions identify lineages by exclusive and specific external relations that deny the structural relativity prerequisite for their situationally variable segmentary alignments.

CONCLUSION

These synopses show that in Kagoro and Kadara societies the segmentary capacities of localized patrilineal groupings were deflected and suppressed by other principles of structural differentiation. Despite the differences between Kagoro and Kadara conceptions of lineage, in both societies identical structural conditions exercised identical effects on these two lineage systems. Both societies practised identical patterns of marriage; in both, lineages engaged as collective units in identical sets of mutually exclusive marriage relations – exogamy, affinity, and wife-abduction. In each society, local patrilineages are accordingly distinguished by their unique sets of marriage relations, irrespective of strictly genealogical criteria; and, in either case, these external differentiae preclude the situational realignments of descent groups in segmentary contrapositions by individuating their collective identities, boundaries, and relationships. In both societies, lineage oppositions within communities were restrained and overruled by communal norms; in both, violence and wife-abduction were prohibited within communities. Moreover, lineages settled in different communities could not pursue hos-

171

tilities in isolation or in segmentary alliances. At Kagoro such inter-lineage violence opposed communities as units; among Kadara, such disputes mobilized the age-sets as well as the lineages of their principals, thus generalizing the conflict to other groups interested in its resolution, without disturbing the intricate network of inter-lineage marriage alignments.

Despite their similar multilineal community bases, both societies also exhibited significant structural differences. Lacking age-organization, Kagoro rely for tribal cohesion on their moiety and territorial divisions (*bin*), calendrical rites (*ci*), dispersed patrilineages, and alternative marriage relations, and identify lineages by genealogy and residence. Among Kadara, as Anoahwhanum illustrate, lineages retain external unity despite divided residence, ancestral worship, and genealogy, so long as their members observe uniform marriage relations. Lacking tribal unity, Kadara rely for community cohesion on their ritual groups and age-set system. In both tribes, wife-abduction and violence characterize inter-community relations; within Kadara villages, lineage autonomies and alignments were governed by necessities of ritual and age-organization on which communal boundaries and integration depended. Segmentary relations between lineages were accordingly inhibited. In Kagoro, moiety regulations excluded wife-abduction and contraposition between Ankwei and Kpashan lineages, while communal norms subordinated lineage autonomies and regulated their alignments. It seems, then, that similar conditions of structural differentiation exercise similar restraints on the segmentary'capacities of patrilineal groupings in these two acephalous societies, while differing conditions of structural differentiation have differing effects. In either case, non-genealogical principles of structural differentiation effectively obstruct segmentary processes of alignment among the lineages on which these societies are based.

NOTE

1. I first visited Kadara and Kagoro in 1950 on a studentship from the Colonial Social Science Research Council, and again in 1959 while attached to the Nigerian Institute of Social and Economic Research. My thanks are due to both these bodies.

Differentiation and the Segmentary Principle

In 1950 Kagoro was administered as an independent District of Zaria Province. In 1954 the District was transferred to Plateau Province, and since then, with Jema'a, Jaba, and Moroa, has formed the Jema'a Federation of Native Administrations. By comparison, Kadara administration developed little between 1950 and my third visit in 1964. The present account refers to the situations observed in 1950, when some changes had already occurred under the British administration. Hence, in this paper, 1950 is the ethnographic present.

For summary ethnographies of these tribes, see Gunn 1956: 88-103 (Kagoro) and 122-37 (Kadara).

© M. G. Smith, 1969.

REFERENCES

FORDE, C. D. 1938. Fission and Accretion in the Patrilineal Clans of a Semi-Bantu Community in Southern Nigeria. *Journal of the Royal Anthropological Institute*, **68**: 311-88.

— 1939. Government in Umor. *Africa*, **12** (2): 126-62.

— 1947. The Anthropological Approach in Social Science. *The Advancement of Science*, **4** (15): 213-24.

— 1961. The Governmental Roles of Associations among the Yakö (Munro Lecture). *Africa*, **31** (4): 309-23.

— 1962. Death and Succession: An Analysis of Yakö Mortuary Ritual. In Max Gluckman (ed.), *Essays on the Ritual of Social Relations*. Manchester: The University Press, pp. 89-123.

GUNN, H. D. 1956. *Pagan Peoples of the Central Area of Northern Nigeria*: Ethnographic Survey of Africa, Western Africa, Part XII. London: International African Institute.

MEEK, C. K. 1931. *Tribal Studies in Northern Nigeria*, Vol. 2. London: Routledge & Kegan Paul.

SMITH, M. G. 1951a. Social Structure of the Northern Kadara. Unpublished MS.

— 1951b. The Social Organization and Economy of Kagoro. Unpublished MS.

— 1953. Secondary Marriage in Northern Nigeria. *Africa*, **23** (4): 298-323.

— 1960. Kagoro Political Development. *Human Organization*, **19** (3): 137-49.

THOMAS, N. W. 1925. The Languages. In C. K. Meek, *The Northern Tribes of Nigeria: An Ethnographical Account of the Northern Provinces of Nigeria together with a report on the 1921 Decennial Census*. London: Oxford University Press, Vol. II, pp. 132-47.

TREMEARNE, A. J. N. 1912. Notes on Some Nigerian Headhunters. *Journal of the Royal Anthropological Institute*, **42**: 136-200.

Phyllis M. Kaberry

Witchcraft of the Sun

Incest in Nso

I

The Kingdom of Nso in what is now West Cameroon is an interesting example of a society in which, although traditionally there was a complex superstructure of government with considerable authority vested in the hands of the *Fon* (king), localized patrilineages were the smallest political units. They varied in size from twenty to seventy members, and most of the male and unmarried female members of a lineage resided in a compound under the authority of a senior lineage head, who had the title of *fai* (lord), or of a junior lineage head, *shey* (lordling). A number of such compounds, representing lineages of different patriclans, constituted a village. Lineages functioned, and still do in many cases, as economic, judicial, and religious corporations. Nevertheless there was a marked emphasis on affinal and uterine ties.[1]

The patrilineage was exogamous, and sexual intercourse between members was regarded as incest, *virim ve shuivi* (literally, witchcraft of the sun), and was subject to mystical sanctions. Moreover an individual could not marry into the patrilineages of the mother, mother's mother, and mother's mother's mother. These lineages were also called 'houses of sacrifice', because an individual was believed to come under the influence of the ancestors connected with them and might, on occasion, have to have a sacrifice performed on his or her behalf by the lineage head concerned. Members of these lineages were regarded as kin, as being 'one blood'. Some Nso said that sexual intercourse with any of the members of these three lineages was incestuous, though the degree of heinousness of the offence depended on closeness of relationship; other informants classified intercourse with the mother, mother's mother, and mother's mother's mother and their respective close kin as incestuous, and regarded intercourse with other members of the lineages concerned as a very reprehensible form of fornication or adultery. Sexual relations with the full sister or half-sister of a wife were also incestuous, and hence sororal polygyny was ruled out. Lastly, intercourse with a person who had married into a person's own lineage, or with women who had married into the lineage of the mother or that of the wife, was considered incestuous. The seriousness of the offence and the horror with which it was viewed varied with the status of those involved – rank, age, generation, closeness of relationship, and whether a woman was single or married.

Literate Christians were in complete agreement that the Nso term for incest (as for example, sexual relations between brother and sister) was *virim ve shuivi* (witchcraft of the sun). In contrast to those heterosexual offences which were classed as 'witchcraft of the sun', fornication and adultery between individuals who did not fall within the prohibited categories were termed *kinjang* (literally, 'the calling' of a woman). *Kinjang* was not associated with mystical sanctions, and the degree of condemnation depended on whether it was fornication or adultery. Young girls before marriage frequently had love affairs, and providing discretion was observed and pregnancy did not result the practice was condoned.[2] Indeed, just prior to her marriage, a girl would be secretly counselled by her mother to pay a final visit to the lover so that he would not bear any resentment towards her. This custom of a last meeting with lover or lovers was called 'warming the village'. Once, however, a girl was married all such affairs had to come to an end. Adultery led to a quarrel and estrangement between the guilty man and the husband, who would also be within his rights in giving his wife a beating. But sooner or later interested parties would seek to reconcile the two men and they would drink wine together and share a kola nut. It should be noted, however, that adultery with the wife of the *Fon* was both an act of sacrilege and a crime, and in the past both culprits were put to death.

The application of the term 'witchcraft of the sun' to a wide

176

range of heterosexual offences did not spring from any prurience about sex as such, and an understanding of this phenomenon must be sought in terms of social structure and cosmological beliefs. Long ago, Firth, in discussing incest and other sexual offences in Tikopia, suggested that 'the incest situation varies according to the social structure of each community, that it has little to do with the prevention of sexual relations as such, but that its real correlation is to be found in the maintenance of institutional forms in the society as a whole, and of the specific interest of groups in particular' (1936: 340). Much more recently, Goody has re-examined theories about incest prohibitions and other sexual offences, and has demonstrated that anthropologists have often in the past carried over into the analysis of sexual offences the concept of incest, as viewed in our own society. He considered (1956: 293-4) that, in most societies with unilineal descent, prohibitions on sexual intercourse are grouped together, depending upon whether they are:

(i) with a member of the same descent group (intra-group sexual prohibition),

(ii) with the wife of a member of the descent group (group-wife prohibition),

(iii) with another married woman (extra-group prohibition).

The last he categorizes as common adultery, that is non-group adultery. The first is incest, but the second he categorizes as group-spouse adultery even when, as among the Tallensi, 'sexual relations with a sister or daughter are so much less reprehensible than incest with a wife of the lineage' (see Fortes 1949: 114). Goody himself suggests that 'the word incest be retained for the category of offences inside the group. . . . The group-spouse category should be associated with adultery rather than incest, for at the core of the prohibition lies the fact that the woman is *married* into the group; the taboo depends on her married status' (Goody 1956: 294).

However, in attempting to explain the heinousness of group-wife adultery in societies with patrilineal descent, Goody again draws on the exposition given by Fortes. Among the Tallensi, sexual intercourse between a man and the wife of his father, brother, or son is severely reprobated, and, unless confession and ritual reconciliation take place, the offender will be struck down by the ancestors (Fortes 1949: 113). The reprobation, according to Fortes, is due to the fact that such offences 'cause deep and irreconcilable "enmity" (*diung*) between father and son, brother and brother, and this is a mortal blow to the solidarity of the family and the lineage' (ibid.: 113). Goody generalizes this statement and says where there is strong condemnation of group-wife adultery in societies with patrilineal descent, this is because 'the category of "wives" is of fundamental importance to the descent group because it is through them that the continuity of the clan is obtained. Hence illegal intercourse with the wife or another member of the group is treated most severely' (1956: 296).[3]

Goody's category of offences with the group-spouse is an important one, and my own essay owes much to his stimulating analysis of the problem. But, in classifying offences an incest or adultery and fornication, I would place even more emphasis than he does on the concepts of the society concerned. In some societies incest may be only an intra-group offence; in others it may be an offence not only within the descent group, but in other groups as well with whom a man has some relationship; in others again, it may involve non-group relations. As far as the Tallensi are concerned, Fortes has described sexual intercourse between a man and certain women who fall into the group-wife category as incest, and his evidence is such that he should, in my opinion, have the last word! It should be noted, however, that there is no Tallensi term for incest as distinct from other heterosexual offences, though there are profound differences in attitude towards certain types of sexual offence. In Nso, on the other hand, intercourse between siblings is 'witchcraft of the sun'; and, as I have indicated, this term is applied to other heterosexual offénces not only within a person's patrilineage but also in other lineages with whom he has uterine or affinal connections. What is needed is a broader definition of incest than that put forward by Goody, and I would prefer that the one given in *Notes and Queries on Anthropology* be expanded to include some relations of affinity since it is pointed out there that 'in some societies unions with certain persons related by affinity are also considered incestuous' (1951: 113). The definition would then run: Incest is sexual intercourse between individuals related in certain prohibited degrees of kinship and/or affinity. In making an analysis of Nso concepts of incest, it must be stressed that their kinship and political system is complex and that here I can do no more than indicate some of the variables which must be taken into account. However, before doing this, it remains to clarify what is entailed in the concept of *virim ve shuivi*.

Virim ve shuivi is a term which is applied only to incestuous relationships; it means literally 'witchcraft of the sun or day' in contradistinction to 'witchcraft of the night' (*virim ve vitsë'ë*). 'Witches of the night' are evil persons who bring misfortune, sickness, and death, more especially to agnates of whom they are envious or to individuals whose office and power they covet. Witchcraft is said to reside in the belly and may come forth at night in the guise of a nightjar. Witches are said 'to eat people' (*kfër wir*) so that the bodies of such people eventually weaken and they die. When informants were asked to explain why incest is called 'witchcraft of the sun' they offered a number of reasons: unlike 'witchcraft of the night', witchcraft of the sun can be seen; if a brother and sister have intercourse they do wrong deliberately, knowing that it is a sin which not only brings trouble on themselves but imperils the safety of their kin. It is like 'witchcraft of the night' because it is as though the culprits were eating one another and they would, unless action were taken, not only die or go mad but in some cases bring death to their children and other members of the compound or compounds involved. It is described not merely as bad (*bi*) or dreadful (*be'emi*), but as revolting or disgusting (*ko'oi*, a term also applied to a corpse found in decayed state, to excrement, suicide, and leprosy). Some said it is an offence against the Earth (*njo nsaiy*), but all agreed that it was an offence against the ancestors and would be punished by those of the lineages involved. If children are born of an act of incest between kin they will die because their parents are of 'one blood'. My attempts to get further elucidation of what is involved in some of these statements were not successful, but there was agreement that certain types of incest are far more heinous than others; and that, if illness and death are not to be visited upon other members of the compound, the culprits or sometimes one of them must be driven away. In other types, such as that between agnates of the same generation or that between a lineage head and a female of his lineage, a rite called *nsëlaa* (literally, stinging of the compound) could be performed, the wrong expiated, and the Earth and the ancestors appeased. The term *nsë* means to sting and is used for the stinging by a bee. I was unable to get any adequate explanation as to why this rite of expiation was called the stinging of the compound, except that its performance safeguarded all members.

II

Nso is the largest of the chiefdoms in West Cameroon. It lies at the eastern end of a high plateau known locally as the Bamenda Grassfields; and, at the time of the last census in 1953, had a population of *c.* 50,000 (exclusive of the associated brother-chiefdom of Oku). Its present population is estimated to be in the region of 105,000. At the heart of the kingdom is the capital, Kumbo, where there are the palace, the headquarters of some of the more important associations, a market, and a large resident population. Beyond the capital are a number of villages of which eight are sub-chiefdoms conquered during the nineteenth century. The latter have their own language and differ in custom, particularly in regard to marriage. Here I am concerned only with the Nso people proper.

The Nso people are divided into four ranked status categories (formerly five when there were slaves): close kin of the Fon (*wonto*, literally, children of the palace); cadet royals (*duiy*); free commoners (*mtar*); and retainer commoners (*nshilafsi*), who are liable to a period of service in the palace if males, or to be taken as wives if females (Kaberry 1952: 288-9). The royal category of *wonto* includes descendants of any ruler down to the fourth generation through males, and to the third through females. At the fifth generation in the male line, progeny rank as cadet royals, *duiy*. The category of *mtar*, in popular estimation, includes the descendants of those who freely offered their allegiance to earlier kings in return for symbolic privileges – the retention of the leopard pelts after their presentation to the Fon, and freedom from recruitment to retainer duties at the palace. Moreover, *mtar* lords alone have the right to marry princesses; they freely give women to the Fon as wives, and it is from among the children of such women that a Fon is chosen. The rank of a lineage, as opposed to other lineages, is determined by the status of its lineage head, but within a lineage a few of the members may be of different status. Thus in a *mtar* lineage, if one of the wives of the lineage head is a princess her children would rank as royals, though in many other respects they are members of the lineage; similarly, the children of a wife of retainer status would rank as retainers. In this essay it is not possible to discuss in further detail the way in which status categories affect the control exercised by lineage heads over their dependants, and for simplicity of exposition I shall be concerned here only with lineage heads and their dependants who are of full *mtar* status.[4]

The Nso patriclan is not an exogamous unit, and its members are dispersed throughout a number of villages. In each clan there is one lineage head who ranks as ritual and ceremonial *primus*. Some of the larger clans are divided into two or more sub-clans; in each sub-clan one lineage head is regarded as senior in rank. The latter would be consulted about succession to vacant lineage headships and he has a role in the installation ceremonies; he may also be called on to arbitrate and make peace when trouble occurs between dependent members of a lineage and their lineage head. But he is in no sense a political overlord. Lineage heads may have a direct and not mediated relation with the Fon in matters which concern themselves and/ or their dependants. The importance of lineage heads in the political structure affects the status of a village head. Unless the village head is also a state councillor, he ranks merely as *primus inter pares* among the lineage heads resident in his village. With their help he arbitrates in civil disputes, reports the presence of foreigners to the Fon, and transmits the Fon's orders given out on market day and at meetings of the palace drinking club (see Chilver and Kaberry 1966: 118-19).

A lineage head is also *talaa*, father of the compound, and receives the respect and obedience due to a father. Irrespective of place of residence and age, all members of the lineage are either his 'sons' or 'daughters'. The children and grandchildren of female members of the lineage are also subject to the influence of his deceased predecessors and, on occasion, he may be called on to make sacrifices on their behalf. In addition to his priestly duties, he settles disputes, administers tracts of land vested in his lineage, requisitions labour for path-clearing, bridge-building, the cutting of thatch for his houses, and the cultivation of his mensal farm. He inherits most of the wealth (kola trees, raffia bush, livestock, guns, money, etc.) of his male dependants of *mtar* status, irrespective of their place of residence, and he arranges who in the lineage is to inherit their widows. (His own widows are inherited by his successor.) When the descendants of a man, who for various reasons has established a compound of his own either in the same village or elsewhere in Nso, request that they have their own lineage head, his approval is normally required before the Fon selects and confers the title of *shey* (lordling) on a man of the compound concerned. In theory, two or more generations should elapse before the title of *shey* is elevated to that of *fai* (lord) (Kaberry 1952: 30 ff.).

Lastly, and most importantly, a *mtar* lineage head has a decisive voice in arranging, with one exception, the marriage of females of *mtar* status in the lineage. The exception is the marriage of the first-born daughter of any union in the lineage; this is arranged by the head of the girl's mother's lineage, though in other respects the girl ranks as a member of her father's lineage. The lineage head who controls the marriage also has first claim on the services and gifts which the groom has to make to affines both before and during the course of his marriage, though the girl's mother will receive assistance as required. In Nso proper, there is no payment of bridewealth in the traditional form of marriage: a man as suitor and later as a husband is bound to make gifts of, for example, livestock, wine, and food, and to render help in such matters as housebuilding and harvest (Kaberry 1952: 114-15). The absence of payment of bridewealth may well be one of the factors bound up with the rights exercised by a lineage head over the first-born daughter of any woman of his lineage, and with the closeness of ties with the descendants of women of the lineage who are referred to as 'sisters' sons' (*wonjemer*).[5]

From this account it can be seen that the patrilineage in Nso is a strongly corporate unit under a head who, if he is accountable to living members and to his ancestors, is also directly responsible to the Fon. To the best of my knowledge, nowhere else in the Bamenda Grassfields do lineage heads exercise such extensive authority; but nowhere else does a ruler exercise such influence on their appointment. The Fon not only controls the formation of new lineage corporations under titled heads but also the selection of such title-holders. He delegates to men (usually one or two palace stewards) the task of making inquiries among members of the lineage concerned, and also among notables of the sub-clan, clan, and neighbourhood, about the qualifications of eligible candidates. The Fon's delegates report back to the Fon, who then makes a choice and orders them to seize the man and place him on a stool in the presence of members of the compound. Once installed, the lineage head's personal name cannot be called by anyone except the Fon. His authority derives from his roles as 'father' of the lineage, as a priest in the ancestor cult, and as the Fon's delegate. But he is expected to exercise the responsibility and care of a father; if he flagrantly disregards his duties and wastes the assets of his lineage, his people, when all other measures have failed (including consultation with titled 'sisters' sons' of the lineage), may request the Fon to destool him. If the Fon is satisfied that their case is a just one, he sends his stewards or members of the regulatory society (*ngwerong*) to remove lineage head's cap and to call his personal name, thus reducing him to the status of an ordinary man (Kaberry 1959: 379-80).

For an individual, his membership of his patrilineage is of great importance: through it he derives rights to arable and residential land, to assistance in economic, judicial, ceremonial, and ritual matters. Unless he has quarrelled and moved away, or has insufficient land for a growing family, he lives in close association with his agnates and is subject to the power of his agnatic ancestors. Intercourse with a female agnate is regarded as incestuous. If two unmarried siblings (full or classificatory) commit incest, the rite of *nsëlaa* must be performed or death will come to the culprits and members of the compound. I myself did not witness the rite, and the versions given me by a number of informants differed in minor details, such as the actual words spoken by the culprits and the ritual officiant. However, all accounts involved a confession of wrongdoing by the culprits. Only one person said that the culprits would not be struck on the back with the scapegoat, but he too stressed that the culprits would strike the goat, thereby transferring the evil that had been done to the goat. Another man said that all present in the compound would hold the rope attached to the goat, otherwise the guilty would fear to confess their wrongdoing.

Usually a 'sister's son' (at two or more generations' remove) is called upon to do the rite; failing him, a stranger who has the knowledge. Members of the compound assemble in the evening in the main courtyard and the lineage head provides a goat to which is attached a rope. The ritual officiant gives an infusion of medicinal herbs to the culprits and to all those who have been associated with them to cleanse them of impurity. Then the guilty pair hold the rope attached to the goat and strike the goat, saying: 'The wrong which has been done, let it be removed today.' The officiant picks up the goat, strikes the culprits on the back with it and says: 'The wrong which was committed, I have removed today.' Then he takes away the scapegoat (*bvëïy ye dzëvin*, literally, the goat that is beaten). Informants said the goat was beaten 'so that the bad thing should go forth from the compound'; the goat could not remain in the compound or be eaten by its members because in that case the evil of the offence would remain in the compound. Lastly, the officiant had either to be an unrelated medicine man or a distant 'sister's son'; it could not be the son of a woman of the lineage since he is 'a son of the compound' (*wan o laa*).

Incest committed by persons of different generations is far more serious in that, with one possible exception, expiation is impossible. In the case of sexual intercourse between a man and his father's sister, the man is driven away from the compound, and both he and the woman would be likely to become mad. If a man, even if he is lineage head, commits incest with his daughter, his marriage with the girl's mother is abrogated, and the latter will take her daughter and other children away permanently to her natal compound. To remain in the husband's compound would bring misfortune to all, particularly to the woman and her children. The marriage is also dissolved if the woman's husband's brother has intercourse with her daughter. As to what would happen if a lineage head had sexual relations with an unmarried woman (other than his own daughter) of his lineage, opinion was divided. Some said that the rite of *nsëlaa* could be performed (some account being taken of his rank); others declared that no expiation was possible. The marriage between the girl's mother and her father would be dissolved; and, as in the case of incest between father and daughter, the girl and her mother would leave the compound for good. All were agreed that it was a most heinous offence because, in committing it, the lineage head had failed to fulfil his highly responsible role of 'father of the compound' (*talaa*).

As far as prohibitions on sexual intercourse with women in the category of group-wife are concerned (and I exclude from this category a man's own mother), there was general agreement that a breach of these is witchcraft of the sun, but here again the severity of both mystical and secular sanctions is related to generation, closeness of relationship, and rank. In increasing order of heinousness the offences are as follows: (*a*) intercourse with the wife of a brother; (*b*) intercourse with the wife of a father (who is not himself a lineage head); (*c*) intercourse with son's wife; and (*d*), most serious of all, intercourse with the wife of a man's own lineage head. In the cases of (*a*), (*b*), and (*d*), the male culprit is driven away from the compound and no expiation is possible. (One very knowledgeable informant said that in the case of (*d*) the guilty *fai's* wife would also be driven away). As far as (*c*) is concerned, *nsëlaa* would be performed if a *fai* had intercourse with his own or a classificatory son's wife; if this was not done, the *fai* and the people of the compound would sicken and die. Unfortunately, I neglected to ask what would happen if the culprit is not a lineage head, but it is almost certain that he would be driven from the compound.

When Nso were discussing the seriousness of heterosexual offences between members of a lineage and between a man and a group-wife, they emphasized not merely the factors already noted (closeness of relationship, generation, and the obedience due to a person of rank), but also the mistrust and dissension that these offences created within the compound. As we shall see later, great stress is laid on good relations with matrilateral kin, but before describing these it should be noted that there are two other types of incest which are connected with affinal ties and which lead to a dissolution of a marriage. If a man has sexual intercourse with his wife's full sister or half-sister, or with a woman married into the wife's patrilineage (i.e., in Goody's terminology, a 'group-wife' of a man's wife's patrilineage), the marriage between the man and his own wife is abrogated. Here again, the wife's ancestors would bring suffering and death to the wife and her children if they remained in the man's compound.[6] Lastly, as pointed out earlier, if a couple have married and it is subsequently discovered that they are in fact kin, however distant, the marriage is dissolved. The offence is not called incest since it has been committed unwittingly; but if the marriage continues it becomes incestuous and both the woman and her children are no longer under the protection of her ancestors and are likely to die.[7] She cannot, however, marry again, though it would be possible for her to take a lover; any children born of such a union would belong to her own patrilineage.

With the exceptions noted above, the traditional form of marriage is indissoluble. If a woman leaves her husband and continually refuses to remain with him, then any children she may bear subsequently belong to her husband's lineage.[8] Although widow-inheritance is practised, as we have noted above, it is incestuous for a man to have intercourse with the wife of an agnate while the latter is alive. Yet it would be wrong to think of the woman as being incorporated into her husband's lineage. She maintains ties with her own lineage, receives assistance, has rights of usufruct to lineage land, and remains under the care of her ancestors. Through the system of marriage prestations and services, there is frequent association between her husband, herself and her children, and her own kin. Her children are in some respects and in some contexts regarded as members of her lineage, as 'children of her compound'. It is significant that, in the Nso beliefs about conception, the man and woman are thought to play an equal role in the making of the embryo: children derive flesh and blood from both parents. Children come under the influence of the ancestors of the mother's lineage and of the lineages of her mother and her mother's mother. Any quarrel between a person and the mother's kin or between a person's father and her kin creates a situation in which, when a sacrifice is required to her ancestors for her children, it will be ineffective unless reparation is made. Indeed, without reparation, the sacrifice would not, said most informants, be performed at all.

Intercourse between a man and his mother's brother's daughter or his mother's sister's daughter is equated with intercourse between siblings, and most informants said that the rite of *nsëlaa* would have to be performed. If a child is born of such a union it would in any case die. Intercourse with a group-spouse of the mother's lineage is also an act of incest, and the mother's lineage head would henceforth refuse to perform any sacrifices for the 'sister's son'. The most reprehensible form of incest is intercourse between mother and son; indeed, some informants found it difficult to believe that it ever happened at all, and were profoundly shocked when others present said that they had heard of cases in the past. This is regarded as so terrible that it could only occur if a 'witch of the night' transformed the appearance of a woman's son so that he looked to her like her own husband, and she therefore accepted her son as her husband. Both she and her son would be expelled from the compound: the son would become mad and the woman would die. The same also occurs if a man has intercourse with his mother's own sister.

As noted earlier, Goody, in his discussion of incest and adultery, would place a man's own mother in the group-wife category, and account for the heinousness of the offence because in a patrilineal system 'the mother is the closest *wife* of a clansman of *senior* generation' (1956: 296). But at least in the case of Nso (and I would suggest in most societies with patrilineal descent), the mother cannot be regarded as a group-wife. The relation between a man and his mother is not merely the closest which he has with any woman married into his patrilineage, it also differs in *kind* from his relationship with women married to other agnates. There is the tie of blood which, as I have said, is stressed by all informants. Through his mother he becomes a kinsman to her kin and subject to the power of her ancestors. In other words, through his own mother he has ties of complementary filiation with her kin and occupies a special status in her lineage. He has no such comparable relations where other women married to his agnates are concerned. Some mention has already been made about the importance of uterine ties; here I set them forth in more detail.

In Nso there is no privileged aggression between a man and his mother's agnates; indeed, he must respect those of her generation and that of her father. But a person receives assistance, gifts, and hospitality from his mother's agnates, though he has no right to take property without permission. In other respects, however, it is not so much a person having a shadowy claim, because if his mother had been a man he could have exercised rights in her descent group fully. It is because of *her* sex that he stands in a special relationship to her agnates. He is

187

her child, he is 'one blood' (as the Nso say), and therefore in some respects a member of her lineage.[9] Moreover success in hunting, a typically male pursuit, is transmitted through females and is affected by the maternal ancestors. Thus, on the death of a woman, her husband and/or her brother pray at her burial that she goes in peace and does not bring misfortune to her sons when they go hunting. When a youth catches his first game, he presents it to his own mother's father or mother's brother, or failing them the head of her lineage, and receives a spear in return. Neglect to present the game would imperil his chances of future success in hunting. In certain hunting lodges, part of the ceremonial at a meeting involves the participants calling out the name of the lineage of their mother's father.

As already described, a first-born daughter of a woman is given away in marriage by her mother's lineage head. So close is the tie between a man and his mother's lineage that he may be selected as head of her lineage in the absence of a suitable candidate. Here again, the explanation given is that he is 'a child of the compound' (*wan o laa*), though permission would also have to be obtained from the head of the man's own patri-lineage. Again, when a man is installed as head of his own father's patrilineage, he has to go with members of his lineage to the compound of the head of his mother's lineage who, in this context, is called *taryi* (father of the mother). He takes as gifts a female goat, a cock, a hen, wine, and firewood; and the mother's lineage head then sacrifices the fowls and part of the wine to request the blessings of the maternal ancestors on the 'sister's son', who has become a lineage head. He also removes the sister's son's cap and gives him a new one, as well as pre-senting him with a stick of ebony for the performance of sacri-fices. Without this sacrifice being performed by the mother's lineage head, the new office-holder can neither successfully carry out sacrifices to his own agnatic predecessors nor sacrifice to them on behalf of sisters' sons of his lineage. If he did so he would sicken and die. My informants were quite specific that the power to sacrifice to ancestors derives in part from the mother's line. Even the Fon of Nso when he succeeds to the kingship must send the gifts for sacrifice to his *taryi*, that is, to the head of his mother's lineage. He does not go himself but entrusts the sacrificial offerings to one or two minor priests who belong to cadet royal lineages. If this is not done, the Fon cannot carry out sacrifices to the royal dead.

Lastly, while full sisters' sons are regarded in some respects as children of the compound, more distant sisters' sons, who are at some two or more generations' remove and are themselves lineage heads, are believed to have the power (*sëm*) to detect 'witchcraft of the night' practised against a lineage head by his own envious agnates. They tie the suspected witch and, if convinced after inquiry that he is guilty, drive him from the compound. If the lineage head then dies, the witch would be handed over to the four 'sisters' sons' of the Fon (*wonjemer ve fon*) for further inquisition. If found guilty, he would formerly have been put to death by the regulatory society (*ngwerong*). These four titled men are drawn from four *mtar* lineages and are said to be descended from the sister's sons of earlier rulers. They have the duty of protecting the Fon against witchcraft, are present at sacrifices of expiation at the palace, keep the royal grave-huts in repair, pave the graves of the seven state councillors who belong to royal cadet lineages, and also those of the seven minor priests who are drawn from royal cadet lineages.[10]

It is not possible in this essay to give other examples of the close relations with uterine kin. What should be clear is that marriage, with the exceptions I have mentioned, is indissoluble and establishes enduring ties between a woman's children and her own body of kin. The patrilineage is a strongly corporate unit (whether or not one adopts the definition of corporateness put forward by Maine, Weber, or Radcliffe-Brown), but through marriage the lineages of the two spouses play as it were complementary roles in the welfare of the offspring of the union. In the light of this, it is not surprising that sexual relations with members of the mother's lineage are regarded as incestuous, and that a man through sexual misdemeanour with close female kin of his wife or with group-wives of her lineage may imperil not only his own children but the marriage itself.

III

In conclusion, then, one may say of Nso that the categorization of a wide range of heterosexual offences as incest can be understood in terms of their cosmological beliefs, the nature of the patrilineage, marriage, and ties of complementary filiation. These offences are sharply distinguished by the Nso themselves from fornication or adultery with women who do not fall within the forbidden categories.

Unfortunately, limitations of space preclude a discussion of all the implications of the material presented, and I can touch on some of them only briefly.

Firstly, Nso presents a somewhat anomalous case in view of the controversy among anthropologists about factors affecting the stability of marriage. Among those which have been stressed in accounting for a low divorce rate are 'strong' patriliny, high bridewealth, and close association (if not almost incorporation) of women with the groups into which they have married.[11] In Nso, traditional marriage, apart from very few exceptions where its continuance would constitute incest, is indissoluble; women are closely associated with the lineages into which they have married and there is widow-inheritance, but their children have important ties of complementary filiation with maternal kin; patrilineages are strongly corporate groups; there is no bridewealth proper, but traditionally only a series of prestations and services from men to the lineage heads of their wives and, to a less extent, to other affines such as mothers-in-law.

Secondly, Goody has made an important contribution to social anthropology not only in his analysis of concepts of incest in certain societies with patrilineal or matrilineal descent, but in insisting that incest should be considered in relation to other heterosexual offences and that these should be viewed against the structure of the society (1956: 304). I would, however, suggest that in classifying certain offences as incestuous the anthropologist must firmly take into account the concepts of the people concerned, their attitudes, and the nature of the sanctions involved. We should not therefore limit the concept of incest to intra-group offences as Goody and some others have done, but broaden our definition: incest is sexual intercourse between individuals related in prohibited degrees of kinship and/or affinity.

The need to adopt a wider definition of incest does not spring from a consideration of Nso material alone. As already noted, Fortes uses the term incest for sexual relations between a man and his father's or his brother's or son's wife among the Tallensi. Unless confession and ritual reconciliation take place the culprit will be struck down by the ancestors; even so, if the culprit is a son he will never be able to offer a sacrifice to his father with a clear conscience; if he is a brother he will not be able to sacrifice together with his brother or inherit his wife (Fortes 1949: 113). Among some of the Ibo, 'adultery' within the kin group was an abomination, an outrage on *Ala* (the Earth) and therefore a matter affecting the public. At Ngoidi, when a man committed 'adultery' with the wife of a member of his patrilineage, the offence was reported to the priest of *Ala*, who then called the town elders to a meeting. The culprits had to confess, and a sacrifice was made both to *Ala* and the ancestors, who were told: 'We will rid the land of the presence of these two who committed an abomination.' The male culprit was sold as a slave to Arochuku, and the woman was returned to her people. In the Mmaka section of the Ibo, gifts were offered to *Ala* and a sacrifice performed to remove pollution from the land; the culprits were exiled from the community (Meek 1937: 218-19). Ardener, in discussing sexual offences among another group of Ibo, the Mba-Ise of Owerri Division, refers to 'degrees of incest'. Major segments of the maximal lineage are exogamous. 'In the smallest lineage segments intercourse with the wives of other male lineage-members is controlled almost as stringently as intercourse with lineage-sisters' (1959: 128).[12]

Among the Nuer, it appears that for a man to have sexual relations with the wife of a 'bull' is at most an incestuous peccadillo (Evans-Pritchard 1951: 45). 'Bulls' are *paternal* half-brothers, *paternal* cousins, and *paternal* half-brothers of the father (my italics). But the Nuer consider that, apart from the wives of these paternal kinsmen, it is incest (*rual*) to have intercourse with the wives of any close living kinsman. The worst incest is with wives of the father (even if he is a ghost-father), the father's *uterine* brothers, *uterine* brothers, sons and *maternal* uncles (my italics) (1949: 91-2).

As stated earlier, in Nso, a man's mother cannot be placed in the group-wife category, the relationship being different *in kind* from those with the wives of agnates. The same would apply to many other communities with patrilineal descent; moreover, in some of these, sexual relations with the members of the mother's patrilineage are regarded as incestuous. Among the Tallensi, Fortes says that incest with own mother is regarded as such a

191

monstrous iniquity that only the mentally deranged could commit it. In the case of incest with full (*soog*) sister there is a feeling of horror. Moreover, she 'perpetuates their mother's uterine line and therefore stands for the indestructibility of the unique bond between mother and child. Sexual intercourse with her would be almost like incest with one's own mother; and this feeling is extended to distant female uterine kin (*saaret*) as well' (1949: 112). Lastly, a man cannot marry his true mother's brother's widow, for this would be incest (ibid.: 277).

Goody discusses some of the material on the Nuer published by Evans-Pritchard and Howell, but he concentrates mainly on offences within the patrilineage and with group-wives of the patrilineage and does not deal adequately with offences affecting matrilateral kin. As among the Tallensi and the Nso, incest with own mother is regarded as the worst offence, and informants said that if it occurred death would follow. Incest with paternal half-sister is bad, but with uterine sister it is terrible. Incest with mother's brother's daughter or mother's sister's daughter is worse than that with father's brother's daughter or father's sister's daughter (Evans-Pritchard 1949: 94-5). One of the worst forms of incest is with the mother's brother's wife: Evans-Pritchard recorded two cases and in one the offender died of *rual* (ibid.: 91, 95). The Nuer make sacrifices to avoid the consequences of incest; the heinousness of the offence is related to the thing sacrificed. For less serious breaches of the rule, a yellow fruit may be cut in half; but for really bad incest (*wal ruali*) a goat, sheep, or sometimes even an ox is cut in two. The culprits must drink incest medicines infused in the gall of the sacrificed animal or retribution follows swiftly (ibid.: 96).

What emerges from the Nso material and from the brief references to some other societies with patrilineal descent is that, while a range of offences may be classified as incestuous by the people concerned, there are nevertheless marked differences in the degree of heinousness of some sexual offences as compared with others. Finally, in making an analysis of heterosexual offences and of incest in particular, it is not sufficient in Nso to stress the corporateness of patrilineal descent groups and the need to preserve their unity, and I would suggest that in many cases this also applies to other systems with a similar kinship structure. The Nso do not live by patrilineages alone. Marriage, the elementary family, ties of complementary filiation with maternal kin, and cosmological beliefs also have a bearing on the concepts of sexual offences, and a full understanding can be reached only by taking these into account.

NOTES

1. My most intensive research in Nso was carried out in 1958, with much briefer periods in 1960 and 1963. For financial assistance I am indebted to The Trustees of the Leverhulme Research Awards (1958), to the Wenner-Gren Foundation for Anthropological Research (1960), and to a Hayter Travel Grant (1963). This research would not have been possible had not Professor Forde granted me leave of absence from the Department for the purpose. I am deeply grateful to him for the assistance, encouragement, and interest which he has always shown in my research during our many years of friendship.

2. No stigma attached to the child of an unmarried girl, but it belonged to the lineage of its mother. A woman who left her husband and resisted all attempts to make her return might become a prostitute (*wiiy saki*). Such conduct was regarded as immoral; but, in daily contacts with individuals, reactions depended, as might have been expected, on the personalities of those concerned.

3. In this essay I am concerned with a society with patrilineal descent. However, Goody in his article suggests that in a society with matrilineal descent, such as the Ashanti, 'Social reproduction . . . is obtained not through wives but through "sisters", the female members of the clan. Hence it is interference with *their* sexuality that constitutes the most heinous heterosexual offence' (1956: 296).

4. The daughters and grand-daughters of a princess are given away in marriage by the Fon.

5. In most of the sub-chiefdoms of Nso, bridewealth is paid and a lineage head has no rights over the first-born daughters of females of his lineage. The Nso proper regard this payment as a form of 'purchasing' a woman and are contemptuous about the practice. They stress that their own system involves the maintenance of close relations with the wife's kin. However, when divorce became possible under British administration and also subsequently, most men began to keep a record of all gifts and services rendered to affines during the course of the marriage so that they could reclaim their value in the event of divorce.

6. Intercourse between a man and an unmarried girl of his sister's husband's lineage is regarded as a serious form of fornication, but not incest.

7. This attitude to the offence, which in the first place had been committed unwittingly, suggests some similarity with Nuer attitudes. Among the

193

Nuer 'it is felt that no ill effects will follow an infraction if the incestuous pair were unaware that they were breaking it' (Evans-Pritchard 1949: 97). There are other similarities too. Among the Nuer 'if ignorance is regarded as an extenuating circumstance, the presence of children increases the danger . . . *Rual* will kill the children' (ibid.).

8. If a woman before a legitimate marriage contracts a union with a man against the wishes of her lineage head, she is regarded as a concubine (*wiiy o cemin*), as distinct from a woman given in legal marriage (*wiiy o foone*). Any children she bears belong to her own lineage head.

9. Goody's concept of the 'residual sibling' is a useful one but does not altogether apply in the case of Nso. He claims that in patrilineal systems a woman is a residual sibling who 'has as it were a submerged claim to the property of the patrilineal group and thus her son, while having no full claim to property and office, has a shadowy claim and this may be expressed in a standardized form of aggressive behaviour or privileged aggression' (1959: 80-82). Unfortunately, there is no space to discuss his concept further here.

10. In the case of lineage lords in Nso, their own respective 'sisters' sons', who are themselves lineage heads, will pave the graves.

11. For a recent discussion of the various factors affecting the stability of marriage, see Lewis (1962: especially ch. 8).

12. I am indebted to Edwin Ardener for drawing my attention to the Ibo data.

REFERENCES

ARDENER, E. 1959. Lineage and Locality among the Mba-Ise Ibo. *Africa,* **29** (2).

CHILVER, E. M. & KABERRY, P. M. 1966. *Notes on the Precolonial History and Ethnography of the Bamenda Grassfields.* Mimeographed for private circulation. Now published (1968) in a revised form and with a new title – *Traditional Bamenda.* Buea: Government Printing Press.

EVANS-PRITCHARD, E. 1949. Nuer Rules of Exogamy and Incest. In M. Fortes (ed.), *Social Structure: Studies Presented to A. R. Radcliffe-Brown.* Oxford: Clarendon Press.

— 1951. *Kinship and Marriage among the Nuer.* London: Oxford University Press.

FIRTH, R. 1936. *We, The Tikopia.* London: Allen & Unwin.

FORTES, M. 1949. *The Web of Kinship among the Tallensi.* London: Oxford University Press for the International African Institute.

GOODY, J. 1956. A Comparative Approach to Incest and Adultery. *British Journal of Sociology,* **7** (4).

GOODY, J. 1959. The Mother's Brother and Sister's Son in West Africa. *Journal of the Royal Anthropological Institute,* **98**.

KABERRY, P. 1952. *Women of the Grassfields: A Study of the Economic Position of Women in Bamenda, British Cameroons.* Colonial Research Publication No. 14. London: H.M.S.O.

— 1959. Traditional Politics in Nsaw (Nso). *Africa,* **29** (4).

LEWIS, I. M. 1962. *Marriage and the Family in Northern Somaliland.* East African Studies No. 15. Uganda: East African Institute of Social Research.

MEEK, C. K. 1937. *Law and Authority in a Nigerian Tribe.* London: Oxford University Press.

PART IV

Expression of Values

Clara Odugbesan

Femininity in Yoruba Religious Art

People who are familiar with Nigerian traditional art may have been struck by the femininity of some Yoruba ritual staffs: *Shango* staffs, *Ifa* staffs, and *Eshu* staffs (*Plates A, B, C*).

Much has been written about the Yoruba – one of the major tribal groups (or nation within nation) in Nigeria.[1] They inhabit the western portion of the forest belt which stretches across the whole of southern Nigeria. The humid tropical environment has allowed them to be cultivators to the exclusion of the nomadism of the savanna belt to their north. The cultural unity of the Yoruba has been attributed to their long-established and single origin, some writers even attempting to trace their origins to ancient Egypt. This unity is reflected in religious beliefs that still remain a focus for Yoruba as far afield as Dahomey, Cuba, and Brazil.

Yoruba religion is made up of a corpus of complex ideas about the universe and its historical origin. The latter is expressed in the form of myths about Oduduwa. One version styles Oduduwa as a mother-goddess, 'the progenitor of the Yoruba race', whose husband is Obatala, the god of creation. More popular myths regard Oduduwa as being male, with a wife Olokun, the goddess of the sea. In both versions a dualism is expressed, between earth and sky or between land and sea. In the former, the union is usually symbolized by two white calabashes closely fitted together one on top of the other.

The complex relationship between history, religion, and cosmology can be seen with reference to Shango, the legendary third king of Oyo. During his rule Shango attempted to rid himself of potential rivals by setting his lieutenant chiefs against each other. Two of the more powerful chiefs, however, maintained their influence, and Shango finally, in a state of dejection, hanged himself. It could not be admitted that a king of Oyo had behaved in this disgraceful way, and his subjects announced, therefore, that Shango still lived and was responsible for thunder and lightning.

While on earth Shango had several wives, the most faithful being Oya, who stood by Shango during all his misfortune. After the tragic death of her husband, she returned to her former home (Nupe country) where she transformed herself into the present river Niger, which is still worshipped. Thus Oya rose to the rank of goddess of the river Niger, to which the Yoruba have given her name.

But it is thunder and stormy wind, not thunder and river, which occur together in the universe. Thus an informant told me that Oya manifests herself in the form of strong seasonal winds that precede the thundery rainy season. Oya, as the wife of Shango, comes as wind to sweep the path along which Shango will tread when he arrives in the form of thunder and lightning marking the beginning of the monsoon rains in the tropical forest. The human Oya, as wife, was supposed to have kept her courtyard spotlessly clean whenever Shango approached the doorsteps, for Shango never moved in dirt. Idowu (1962: 91) also quotes Oya's praise names, which suggest a similar idea about the ethereal attribute of Oya: 'The rushing wind that tears down trees from the top'; 'One who causes a heavy dark cloud but brings no rain.'

Not only Shango and Oya feature prominently in Yoruba cosmology. Concepts behind the worship of Eshu and Ifa divination are also fundamental to the Yoruba view of the world. One of the Ifa utensils – the tray or board, which is usually square or round – is supposed to represent the world as the Yoruba conceive it. The Yoruba, like people of ancient times in other parts of the world, believe that their little environs constitute the world. Thus the world which the face of the Ifa tray represented was the town of Ife, and this 'square' world widened gradually and still continues to widen into the bigger world we know today. It is perhaps not a coincidence that the proper noun 'Ife' is a compound of the verb *fe*, to expand, to extend, to widen.

This square world is controlled by four supernatural forces, each presiding over areas equivalent to the four cardinal points (Frobenius 1913, vol. 1: 264): Shango, to whom we have already referred, has his domain in the west; Eshu, to be dealt with below, operates in the east. To the south is Obatala (the god of creation already mentioned); and the god of war, Ogun, rules over the north. These four sections of the 'world' are linked up in the chief verses of *odu* recited during the Ifa divination. One legend says these verses came out of the mouth of Orunmila (see also Clarke 1939: 235) whose face, with what has been described as the 'all-seeing eyes', is said by some diviners to be that depicted at one, two, or four points on the edge of Ifa trays. Yoruba legends depict great rivalry between Eshu and Orunmila, Eshu claiming the right to hide people in misfortune, while Orunmila offers them certainty through divination and sacrifice (Frobenius 1913, vol. 1: 232). What appears a more logical conclusion is that the world comprehended and revealed by Orunmila has uncertainties ascribed to intervention by Eshu, who has to be reckoned with. Hence Ifa, the cult of Orunmila, is operated hand in hand with ritual observances for Eshu (cf. Idowu 1962: 80). This complementary role played by Eshu in Ifa divination can be illustrated by the fact that when the diviner casts the sixteen palm-nut kernels for his oracle, he keeps a seventeenth object – a little ivory head (*olori Ifa* – the chief of Ifa: Fagg 1963, plate 96) which depicts Eshu – on the edge of the tray. Secondly, portions of sacrifices brought by clients are donated to Eshu for himself, or for him to 'carry' to the appropriate god, Eshu being the intermediary between the gods and men.

The roles of Eshu and Ifa within the cosmological system of ideas are diametrically opposed to one another. Ifa is a system whose function is to promote orderliness in the world, one that corrects all wrongs by mediating between men and gods for good, and produces certainty where there is uncertainty. Eshu, on the other hand, is associated with disorderliness and confusion; 'he is the externalization of the difficulties of conforming' (Wescott 1962: 353). He is the equivalent of the 'tempter' rather than the 'devil' in Christian ideas; hence he has been best referred to as the 'trickster'. Both Eshu and Ifa mediate between men and their gods; but while one (Eshu) disrupts relationship between them, the other consolidates it.

Having discussed the ideas surrounding Ifa, Eshu, and Shango, we can now describe the respective cults with special reference to their social functions, and the possible interpretations of the cult objects which are the immediate concern of this essay.

IFA

Ifa is regarded not as a deity to be worshipped, but as an oracle from which people try to obtain certainty from uncertainty in any human problem ranging from the choice of a chief or a king from among prospective candidates, to the choice of a husband or wife or a site for a building, or to the request for the gift of a child. In most religions we find that attempts are made to represent the god being worshipped by concrete idols. For example, the Children of Israel preferred a visible god and so were tempted to and did make a metal image in place of their God (Deuteronomy 9); the Buddha is represented; Diana and Venus, Christian saints, etc., are represented. No image is worshipped in Ifa, however, although the cult objects carry images of Eshu and of Orunmila's face, both of whom are conceived as being of the male sex. There is another important Ifa cult object – the Ifa rattles or bells, which form a class of distinguished works of art among the Yoruba. These staffs or bells (e.g. in Plate A1) are usually made of carved ivory, but recently they have been made of wood, either left plain in the middle with incised symbolic patterns at the extremities, or depicting a kneeling figure, which may be male or female.

The kneeling position is a sign of worship in most religions, or of salutation in a social context; and, in view of the fact that the *Babalawo* – the Ifa divining priest – uses the pointed tip of the staff, to tap the edge of the tray every morning to attract the attention of the deity controlling Ifa (i.e. Orunmila), the kneeling posture on the Ifa staff may well represent an act of worship by both male and female. (Worship, of course, also involves respect, and the curtsey is usual among Yoruba women as a way of showing respect to their elders). The process of Ifa divination not only consists of consultation and sacrifice, but also involves prayer; and for these three acts the client, whether male or female, must assume the kneeling position, although the Ifa priest himself remains seated. This fact probably accounts in part for the kneeling posture of the figures sculpted on the ivory staffs.

We must now seek an explanation for the large number of

female rather than male representations on the Ifa staffs, particularly as Ifa is a cult controlled by men. This involves examining the different contexts in which women play active roles in the cult. Women of the household of the Ifa priest attend a kind of 'family prayers' every morning, whereas other followers of Ifa assemble as part of the congregation every five days for the special prayer. During prayers, women and children hold each of the rattles placed at the Ifa shrine, and at the end of each petition they shake them (like the ringing of a bell) as a symbol of sanction – 'so be it' or 'amen'. Another occasion when women use the staff is during the Ifa festival, when men beat the gongs and women shake the rattle at rhythmical intervals. Thus the Ifa rattles function as female musical instruments.

Women also feature as suppliants in the Ifa cult in another context. It has been observed that quite a number of clients of Ifa priests are women who desire to bear children. The Yoruba have no single fertility cult, but they can request children from any of their gods. Often the Ifa oracle reveals which of the gods is to be worshipped and by whom the suppliant will be blessed with a child. Ifa itself, however, provides children, as is evident from various Yoruba names prefixed by *Fa*, which is an abbreviation of *Ifa*. Such names are Fabunmi (Ifa gave me), Fashanu (Ifa had mercy), Falope (to Ifa belong thanks), Fakorede (Ifa brings good). The questions then are whether the kneeling female figures on Ifa staffs bear witness to the important fact that women constitute the majority of clients of Ifa priests, and whether fertility is one of the major problems for which they consult Ifa.

There is another aspect to the kneeling female figure (*Plate A*1): she is holding a sacrificial chicken in her right hand – a very realistic representation. Sacrifice is probably the most significant aspect of Ifa divination, for one's request is not granted without some kind of offering (Bascom 1941: 45). The idea of sacrifice is common to all Yoruba cults, although it is not often so explicit on other carved cult objects. It should be noted that newly carved Ifa staffs do not give a full representation of the actual event. The sacrificial role of women is further exemplified in an uncommon wooden carving, which has been used for the worship of Erinle, god of the forest. Thus *Plate A*2 depicts a pregnant woman (pair to a male figure) holding a sacrificial chicken. The second figure (*Plate A3*) represents the husband, holding in his left hand a kola nut, which he would split and toss before the god of the forest to express his request (probably for safe delivery of his wife) or his gratitude, before sacrificing the chicken. This couple may have started by consulting the Ifa oracle, which would have revealed to them that it was necessary for them to worship and sacrifice to the god of the forest before the safe delivery of a child could be assured. Could these two carvings have been a record of actual events, representing the people involved?

In the case of Ifa divination, where no goddess or priestess is involved, the representations on the staffs appear to be a record of beneficiaries of Ifa – particularly if the objects were carved by clients as gifts to the priest in appreciation of the successful consultation. The figures would still be depicting clients if they were commissioned by the diviner himself to advertise his specialization in fertility consultations. There has also been a suggestion that those female figures carved with a special 'royal' necklace, called *ide*, represent *Odu*, that is to say, oracular utterances personified as wives of Ifa; but other evidence shows that the *Odu* are to be regarded as kings, and not as goddesses (McClelland 1966: 425). If he has various representations on his staffs, the Ifa priest perhaps uses the one appropriate to the sex of his client. The subject-matter of consultation varies so widely that he could not possibly carve a staff for each topic. He uses instead small identifying tokens placed at the edge of the divination board.

ESHU

Eshu is, as a deity, more of a personage than Ifa, and so every attempt is made to locate him in a particular object. Hence the trickster is represented as a male figure, with or without beard, smoking a pipe or blowing a whistle. He usually has long phallic hairdressing. The figure sometimes rides a horse, since he is a 'messenger' of the other gods. The strings of cowrie shells which hang down some Eshu figures have also been regarded as bearing reference to his role as messenger, being his 'errand fee' – *owo iranse* (see also Wescott 1962: 346), for a slightly different interpretation). Representations of Eshu may be in a kneeling position or they may consist only of a bust.

A1 Ifa staff: a rattle, depicting kneeling figure with chicken in right hand. Ivory. Height $13\frac{1}{2}$ in.; diameter at base $1\frac{1}{2}$ in. Nigerian Museum

A2 Expectant mother going to sacrifice to Erinle, a forest god. Wood. Height $28\frac{1}{4}$ in.; Front to back $5\frac{3}{4}$ in. Nigerian Museum

A3 Pair to A2. Wood. Height $27\frac{1}{2}$ in.; front to back $4\frac{3}{4}$ in. Nigerian Museum

B Eshu staff. Wood. Height 13½ in.; width at back across shoulder 3 in.
Nigerian Museum

c1 Shango staff, depicting the double axe and a kneeling woman with child on back. Wood. Height 17 in.; front to back 3 in., width of axe at top 5½ in. Nigerian Museum

c2 Shango staff, depicting kneeling woman with hands clasping breasts. Wood. Height 12 in.; width at shoulder 2½ in. Nigerian Museum

Eshu is supposed to be very short in stature, and the Yoruba are often sarcastic in his praise-names. This sarcasm is what Wescott regards as 'conflicting pictures of Eshu' (1962: 341). 'Knowing' very well that Eshu is a dwarf, the Yoruba ironically describe him as a tall person whose head shoots above the level of the groundnut plant: groundnut is, of course, a creeping plant which rises only a few inches above the ground.

Devotees of Eshu may be associated with various types of representation. One is a shrine – in the form of a mound or stone (usually in a market-place) – on which libations of oil are poured. A second representation is the carved image of Eshu as a complete male figure ornamented with cowrie shells and placed at the entrance of the shrine of other gods. A third category is the mobile Eshu hung round the neck by leather thong or hooked over the shoulder by its curved hairdressing; and there is the little head and limbless torso dangling from the wrist of devotees. The other two groups of mobile Eshu may be representations of either sex, and they may be carried in pairs of both sexes; some of those hung round the neck are quadruples of Eshu. Some of the mobile cult objects carried by Eshu devotees are in the form of rattles that could be held in the hand (*Plate B*) by dancers (cf. Shango staffs below). Quite a number of these staffs bear a kneeling female figure.

What interpretation can we give to the kneeling female figures on Eshu staffs? There is no doubt that, as in the case of Ifa staffs, they do not represent a goddess. Unlike Ifa, however, there are possibilities that these figures may represent priestesses or devotees of Eshu, whereas in Ifa they more probably represent clients of the Ifa priests, who are not necessarily devotees and who make only occasional visits to the Ifa priests at moments of anxiety and uncertainty in their lives. It should be emphasized at this point that whereas Ifa is a divination *skill* acquired only by those *few* who learn the art, Eshu is a household god for whom *any* member of the community could erect a shrine. Therefore the Ifa remain in the custody of a few priests; whereas anyone who professes to be a devotee of Eshu may carry an Eshu staff in the same way that a priest may carry an Ifa rattle, i.e. to announce his approach, and also as a symbol of his calling.

It has been noted that divination is a male occupation. Although females have been said to engage in it, their process of divination is different. They use cowrie shells instead of palm kernel nuts and the Ifa chain (*opele*).

The devotees of Eshu, male and female, play similar roles in the cult to those played by Ifa priests in the Ifa cult. For example, they are the recipients of sacrificial offerings. Devotees of both sexes carry Eshu figures round the neck for alms, but their roles are separated, men performing the vigorous dances at an Eshu festival and women singing the praise-songs. The propitiation of the god by sacrifices, however, may be the duty of a priestess such as the *eni oja* – woman in charge of the market – in Oyo (Johnson 1921: 66; Morton-Williams 1964: 258). Her function was to pacify Eshu so that he would not stir up trouble in the market-place. Thus the female figures on Eshu staves could be regarded as representing one side of the dualistic element in the cult – the priestess. However, there is every likelihood that they also represent the female worshippers themselves, for whom the staff acts as a symbol of identification in public.

SHANGO

Shango, like Ifa, is more institutionalized than the Eshu cult, in the sense that it requires more skill and devotion, and that members of the cult are a chosen few. The Shango festival is an annual communal celebration, although Shango priests operate all the year round, in groups, for specific social functions such as completing the death (by hitting with a club) of anyone struck half-dead by lightning. They perform rituals at the site of death and collect the victim's property in the name of Shango.

Shango has priests and priestesses. But, whereas men when they are 'possessed' by the god at festivals dance most vigorously, most of the women votaries dance gently and sing praise-songs. Women do not perform what appear to be dangerous magical feats such as thrusting iron rods through the tongue or under the eyeball, as described by Ulli Beier (1959: plates 57 and 58).

The Shango staffs to be interpreted are shown in *Plate C.* It should be emphasized that these staffs with female representations are used for the worship of a god, and not of a goddess, so again we are faced with the problem of whom the figure represents. Returning to the dual role of Shango and his wife, would it be acceptable to regard Oya as the woman depicted on Shango staffs, as in fact a number of informants have stated? Oya could be represented on a Shango staff because she is the faithful deified wife of Shango, and because, as water, she is a symbol of fertility.

A second interpretation of the images on the staff is that they probably represent priestess or female devotees who had consulted Shango for fertility purposes, or had been blessed by Shango. Evidence of such blessing is the personal names which are prefixed by 'Shango' as in the case of Ifa and Eshu. Examples are: Shangotayo, (it is worth rejoicing about Shango), Shangoyele (Shango befits the house), Shangowanwa (Shango has come to me), Shangoloni (Shango owns him or her).

*Plates C*1 *and C*2 could be given either interpretation: i.e. *Plate C*1 with a child denotes that Oya is the giver of children or the figure may represent a devotee who had been blessed with a child. *Plate C*2 may also represent Oya offering herself as mother of all, in the way that old Yoruba women express affectionate delight at the sight of a person they love by raising both breasts, as shown in *Plate C*2. Therefore it could be an act of self-offering on the part of Oya to all, as mentioned above, or on the part of a devotee offering herself to Shango. The writer once received a warm welcome from an old grandmother by her act of raising both breasts and offering them to the guest, not to feed, but to express absolute affection.

It is not unexpected that a theme recurring in three different contexts should have a similar interpretation, particularly since it is the work of art of a single group of people – the Yoruba. The Ifa staff depicts the female client with her sacrifice; the Eshu staff bears the image of the devotees and perhaps of priestesses; while the Shango staff represents either the goddess Oya or the female devotee. We can now raise a few questions.

Do the Yoruba believe that greater attention should be given to carving female devotees rather than the god himself, or the goddess herself? Perhaps this is so; for there are other examples of cult objects which are reproductions of devotees rather than of a god or goddess. For example, *edan Ogboni*, anthropomorphic cast-metal staffs, are representative of the owner-members of the Ogboni secret society, who carry the *edan* during a cult or on special occasions: e.g. *edan onirungbon* represents a member with beard; female *edan* represents a woman member. Another example is the set of *igbin* drums depicting either male or female figures that may be devotees who dance at festivals. (Originally the set of drums was named after the four wives of Obatala: Beier 1963: 58; and there is some likelihood that they are the female figures represented on many of the drums). In a similar manner we may regard 'every little naked Mesopotamian terracotta' of which Seltman wrote that it 'does not necessarily represent Ishtar, but is rather a permanent substitute for the female votary who, having worshipped the goddess, leaves the terracotta behind in the shrine' (Seltman 1956: 30).

A further argument in favour of the view that these figures represent devotees rather than goddesses is as follows: the pertinent question has been raised whether the Yoruba ever intended any carving to represent any of their gods, leaving aside the consideration that if a couple of gods were depicted the other four hundred might be jealous. European missionaries who came to West Africa probably ascribed the idea that they represented gods to the carvings which the Yoruba placed in their shrines as decoration, rather as statues of saints are placed in some churches. Perhaps there are three exceptions that are likely to be representations of gods: these are the face of Orunmila on Ifa trays (Frobenius 1913: 249), the Abraxas-like figure with mudfish legs (Fagg 1963: plate 98; Frobenius op. cit.: 207, fig. 6); and perhaps the figure of Eshu (Fagg op. cit.: plate 97).

The significance of the kneeling posture in sculpture was discussed earlier. The love for this posture, and the ease with which it is carved, seems distinctive of traditional Yoruba art, for similar examples in Nigerian or other art are very rare. It is not, however, unique to them in African sculpture. The Baluba of the south-eastern Congo have produced examples by way of a chief's stool with kneeling female figure (cf. Leuzinger 1960, plate 60: 202), and a kneeling female figure with bowl (Wingert 1962, fig. 37: 168). As well as the kneeling posture, we may briefly examine other characteristics of the carvings to see whether they are meaningful, or whether they are simply decorative.

One obvious feature is the position of the hands. It is difficult not to read meaning into the position of the hands in terms of overt expression not only of a female physical attribute but also of innate fertility, or in terms of self-offering, as described on page 207 above. Another interpretation of the hands on breasts is that the devotee represented is a nursing mother. Hands on the solar plexus may signify an expectant mother. Some hands are engaged in activities, which need no explanation, such as holding a bowl of offerings or holding objects symbolic to the cult.

One other important feature of the female figures is their nudity. It has been observed that they are carved nude. The female devotees in actuality always wear a skirt, even if their tops are bare. The Yoruba, therefore, do not seem to practise cult-nakedness in the manner described by Seltman with reference to some prehistoric figurines (Seltman op. cit.: 30 ff.), and the problem must be left unsolved.

On the whole, the cult objects described in this paper give the impression that the Yoruba realize the need for their religion to maintain and express in the imagery of male and female the dualistic element of the natural or cosmological order. When asked why female figures are depicted on carvings, the Yoruba themselves offer explanations that sound rather psychological, as the following: *Owo ero lowo obinrin*, meaning that the presence of a female or a female cult object facilitates success, has a 'cooling' effect. Thus, in the case of Ifa, the female figure facilitates favourable results during consultation. The writer was in fact informed that one particular *Odu Ifa – ose tura* – warned Ifa priests that women should not be kept outside the cult if they were to be assured of its smooth running. In the case of Eshu, the feminine influence helps to pacify the deity; and, in the case of Shango, the sight of females eases a tense atmosphere. Further, the representation on Ifa staffs may perhaps be viewed as a means of solving the conflict in men's mind between their reluctance to accept females as Ifa priests, and the realization that the success of the cult needs the females' blessing!

NOTE

1. Quite a large body of material is in the form of articles, apart from some main reference books such as Forde (1951), Frobenius (1913), Johnson (1921), and Lloyd (1962).

ACKNOWLEDGEMENT

The writer is grateful to the Nigerian Department of Antiquities for providing facilities.
The plates are reproduced by courtesy of the Nigerian Department of Antiquities, Lagos.

REFERENCES

BASCOM, W. R. 1941. The Sanctions of Ifa Divination. *Journal of the Royal Anthropological Institute*, 71.
— 1942. Ifa Divination. *Man*, 62.

BEIER, H. U. 1959. *A Year of Sacred Festivals in one Yoruba Town.* Lagos: *Nigeria Magazine.*

CLARKE, J. D. 1939. Ifa Divination. *Journal of the Royal Anthropological Institute*, 69 (2).

FAGG, W. 1963. *Nigerian Images.* London: Lund Humphries. New York: Praeger.

FARROW, S. S. 1926. *Faith, Fancies and Fetich, or Yoruba Paganism.* London: S.P.C.K.

FORDE, C. D. 1951. *The Yoruba-Speaking Peoples of South-western Nigeria.* Ethnographic Survey of African, Western Africa, Part IV; London: International African Institute.

FROBENIUS, L. 1913. *The Voice of Africa*, 2 Vols. London: Hutchinson.

HERSKOVITS, M. J. 1938. *Dahomey, An Ancient West African Kingdom.* 2 vols. New York: J. J. Augustin.

IDOWU, E. B. 1962. *Olódùmarè, God in Yoruba Belief.* London: Longmans.

JOHNSON, S. 1921. *The History of the Yorubas.* Lagos: C. M. S. Bookshop.

LEUZINGER, E. 1960. *Africa.* Art of the World Series. London: Methuen.

LLOYD, P. 1962. *Yoruba Land Law.* London: Oxford University Press.

LUCAS, J. O. 1948. *The Religion of the Yoruba.* Lagos: C.M.S. Bookshop.

MCCLELLAND, E. M. 1966. The Significance of Number in the Odu of Ifa. *Africa*, 36.

MORTON-WILLIAMS, P. 1964. An Outline of the Cosmology and Cult Organization of the Oyo Yoruba. *Africa*, 34 (3).

Femininity in Yoruba Religious Art

SELTMAN, C. 1956. *Women in Antiquity*, London: Thames & Hudson.
VERGER, P. 1956. *Dieux d'Afrique*. Paris: P. Hartman.
— 1957. Notes sur les cultes des *Orisa* et *vodum*. Dakar, *Mem.* IFAN, 51.
— 1960. Nigeria, Brazil and Buba. Lagos: *Nigeria Magazine*.
WESTCOTT, J. 1962. The Sculpture and Myths of Eshu-Elegba, the Yoruba Trickster: Definition and Interpretation in Yoruba Iconography. *Africa*, 32 (4).
— & MORTON-WILLIAMS, P. 1962. The Symbolism and Ritual Context of the Yoruba 'Laba Shango'. *Journal of the Royal Anthropological Institute*, 92 (1).
WINGERT, P. S. 1962. *Primitive Art*. New York: Oxford University Press.

Robert Brain

Friends and Twins in Bangwa

I

The Bangwa are a group of Bamileke chiefdoms in the eastern highlands of Mamfe Division in West Cameroon.[1] During my stay there, one of the terms I had initial difficulty with was *eshua*. The Bangwa who spoke English translated it as 'friend'. Yet, as I began to acquire my own 'friends', I realized that the relationship involved more than one of mere mutual intimacy.

Most Bangwa, who asked me if I was their friend, wanted to know if I was born at roughly the same time as themselves; if this were so, a man (or a woman) automatically became my friend and we used the reciprocal term, *eshua ga* (my friend). We also assumed a hail-fellow-well-met relationship and I adopted a more intimate attitude with his wife (whom I called 'wife of my friend') and his children. I began to assume that the primary referent for the word *eshua* was age-mate and that there existed a form of institutionalized friendship between those persons born at the same time. Yet, in Bangwa, there are no age-grades like the *manjong* warrior associations of the Bamileke and Bamenda peoples. The relationship between age-mates who are 'friends' involves mutual rights and duties but no allegiance to any form of grouping.[2] It is a voluntary relationship: over the years a man chooses, from among his age-mates, one or two close friends who become his close allies in social, political, and economic ventures.

Nevertheless, many of my self-declared friends in Bangwa were not of my age-group; many were much older. Most of them, when calling me *eshua ga* (my friend), implied that we stood, in some way, on a footing of equality. When I received a title in the complicated system of Bangwa title-holding, people who held the same title and had the right to attend the same societies began to call me *eshua*. Chiefs and sub-chiefs of the same rank but from widely separated areas called each other *eshua*; on the dancing field such men expressed their relationship by clashing cutlasses above their heads. Women who are also of the same rank, such as a chief's first wife and a titled royal daughter, embrace in a formal expression of their 'friendship'. Men who do the same work and have the same amount of wealth may also be friends in this sense.

Again, I had friends who were in no sense my equals. These were more sentimental attachments than relations ascribed through birth or position. Thus one sub-chief, who took a great interest in my activities and personal life, became known as my good friend (*mbong eshua*). Small children I became attached to and who haunted my house were termed the white man's friends. Among the Bangwa themselves there is evidence of many friendships, based on affection or common interests.

Blood-brotherhood is not to be confused with the Bangwa notion of friendship. Blood pacts were made in the past and are occasionally made in a slightly different form today – usually between two men for a specific and temporary purpose, such as a warlike mission or a commercial venture. Cuts are made in the forearms of the partners and the blood mixed and eaten with a segment of kola nut or a glass of wine. True friends would not need to undergo this kind of ritual and a man would be offended if his friend asked him to do so. Today such pacts may be made by two persons if one wishes to swear another to secrecy over a certain matter. In the past, chiefs made temporary political alliances in this way. In the 1890s Conrau, the first representative of the German colonial power to visit Bangwa in search of trade articles and plantation labour, made a pact with the chief of Fontem, the two drinking from a bottle of gin mixed with their blood. Conrau left Bangwa with labourers for the southern plantations. When he returned a year later, without the men, he was deemed to have broken his side of the bargain; in the quarrel that ensued he lost his life.

Friendship, therefore, in Bangwa, although institutionalized, has many aspects. It may be ascribed through birth; the term *eshua* is then qualified and becomes *eshua nzo*, friend by birth. Both sexes have ascribed friends; and men may have friendships with women based on the fact that they were born near the same time. Friendship may be acquired later on in life through achieving equality of status with another man or woman. This type of friend is called *eshua manze*. A third type of friend, called *eshua nti* or *mbong eshua* (friend of the heart or good friend), is a friend acquired through mutual liking. I have used the word 'friend' throughout this essay since the Bangwa do not frequently distinguish these three types and because it is a more comprehensive term than age-mate or equal. Moreover if the relationship flourishes, however it began, it becomes primarily one of friendship.

Equality, in some sense, is the main ingredient of the Bangwa notion of friendship. It cuts across the basic inequalities between the sexes and different age and status groups. In relations between friends who are age-mates the usual inhibitions between the sexes or between an aristocrat and a commoner are relaxed. In relations between two men of equal status, the respect ordinarily due to the older man is relaxed. And in relations based on mutual affection, differences of both age and rank are forgotten. Friendship allows increased social and economic opportunity outside the fields of kinship, without degrading individuals in patron-client type relations. Friendship also provides valuable emotional outlets that are not usually found in the world of kinship.

II

In Bangwa the only true equals, and therefore the best friends, are twins, born of one womb, at one time, and sharing the same rank. They are the only persons in a kin group, even a nuclear family, who are allowed to use each other's personal name in conversation. All other siblings use the terms 'elder sibling' (*ndega*) or 'our child' (*mwogwüh*), and age differentiation is given expression in formal etiquette even between full siblings. The reciprocal term for twins is 'my friend' (*eshua ga*). Twins are friends and equals, having shared their mother's womb for nine months, or often, according to the Bangwa, much longer. Before birth they roam the world of spirit children for indefinite periods before conception.

Twins are called 'friends' as equals; but as peculiar beings

215

they are known as *befak* (sing. *lefak*). Duality is implied in neither word. *Lefak* is used for a child delivered by breech birth, with a caul round its neck, with six fingers – any child in fact who exhibits physical or, later, psychological abnormalities. Twins are wonderful children, likened to 'spirit beings' and called 'children of the gods'[3]. They are thought to be endowed with the gift of seeing their way back to the world of unborn children (*efeng*). Children are sometimes converted into the twin (*lefak*) category after long bouts of illness. Once their propensity for dying has been removed ritually, they remain twins. Twins, of all sorts, have special gifts and are considered very highly. Chiefs choose 'twins' to succeed them. The parents of twins assume special titles (*anyi* for the mother, *tanyi* for the father) which give them the right to take up ritual office or practise as diviners.

Efeng, the world of unborn children, was described to me as a vast black cave, peopled by the spirits of children who wander around in pairs or groups looking for suitable parents. The Bangwa believe that the supply of children's spirits is constant, being replenished constantly by the spirits of dead Bangwa who are reincarnated in their descendants. Ideas about *efeng* and reincarnation are vague and very variable. Children have to be seduced from *efeng* into their mother's womb. In some cases they go in pairs and are born (in the ideal case) as twins. If this happens and no special ritual is performed, one of the twins' parents or their grandparents must immediately die to correct the imbalance in *efeng*. It is, however, rare for the spirit pair to agree to enter a single womb. Tastes differ and twins often separate at the last minute. Some enter a womb and remain there for some time before one decides to return to *efeng*. A child who has been convinced by his parents that life with them will be the best thing for him may be tormented by his twin, who lurks in the shadows or the fire burning in the hut of the pregnant woman, trying to seduce him back to *efeng*.

One man, telling me the story of his childhood, began it in the antenatal world of *efeng*, where he was travelling with his friend and twin. Looking around for a comfortable home and agreeable parents, he decided to enter the 'belly' of his father before transferring in the latter's semen to the womb of his mother. His friend refused to accompany him, but, furious at having been left, tormented the child in the womb, bringing considerable pain to the mother who suffered a long and painful pregnancy 'which lasted for two years'. Towards the end of the pregnancy the unconceived twin hid in the woman's eye, forming an ugly sty. Finally this twin left the woman's eye, entering the womb of a woman of the village who gave birth to a bouncing girl a few months later. On the advice of the diviner, who recounted this story of the twins' separate births when one of them became ill, the two children were formally declared twins (*befak*), became friends (*beshua*) – a relationship which has lasted until sixty years later.

The point of this story is to indicate how concepts of twinship are linked with those of friendship. This man was explaining 'friendship' to me. Children who are born without a twin are considered to be in a dangerous state; pairing them with a friend removes the danger that they will be seduced back to *efeng*. Another friend of mine, constantly ill as a child, was taken to the diviner who declared that the child was suffering because his friend (*eshua gi*) had been conceived in the womb of another woman and, owing to a quarrel between the spirit children, the pair had not been united. Nor had their full status as twins been recognized. The two children were declared twins, the usual rites were carried out, and their mothers assumed the status of *anyi*; the two men have been 'friends' since that time. Other children, who exhibit signs of chronic illness, are said to suffer from the tormentings of their 'friends' in *efeng* who have not agreed to be born and who continue to seduce their friends along the road to *efeng* and the carefree life of the unborn children. The parents of such a child call in a ritual expert (*tanyi*, 'father of twins' himself) to perform a ceremony to cut him off from his friend. An effigy is made of the child from a plantain stem; a deep pit is dug; the child is placed inside as if at a burial, but at the last minute before the pit is filled in the child is whisked out and replaced by the effigy. In this way the unborn twin is fooled and will cease preying on his 'friend'.

The closest of friends are therefore twins, or children who travelled together as twins in *efeng*. On the whole, children are linked by their parents with other children born at roughly the same time. The same day is preferred, but friendships are encouraged between children born during the same season or even year. My interpreter told me that his father considered his friends too few when he reached the age of five or six. One day when they were walking together in a neighbouring village they met a small child of his age, whom his father swore resembled his own son in every aspect. They must have been twins in *efeng* he declared; the two children were formally declared twins. Their hair was allowed to grow long and was dressed in two peaks like twins; and they made a formal parade through the market, well-oiled and dressed in identical fine cloths, like twins' 'coming-out' after a 'fattening' rite and ceremony. Forty years later the two men had remained firm 'best friends'.

III

During childhood and adolescence friends associate in an informal way. For most people, unlike my interpreter, friendship is entered into without any kind of ceremonial. The importance of the relationship, however, is impressed on them by precept, proverb, and story. It is a relationship which is always extolled, friends being told how they should support each other at all times, and exchange small gifts. Parents encourage their children to develop relations with age-mates and friends. Gradually a young boy or girl begins to select from among several age-mates a friend of the same sex whom he can trust absolutely. Confidences are exchanged, secret ambitions discussed. Young boys go hunting together, girls discuss their future husbands. Lads plan amorous adventures, depending implicitly on the connivance of their friends in troubles they may have within the village or compound.

Sexual education is acquired casually. There are no formal puberty rites for groups of boys or girls. Girls are married shortly after puberty or as their breasts 'begin to drop'. Once a girl, in a group of age-mates, is considered ready for marriage the parents of her age-mates prepare to arrange for the weddings of all their daughters, whatever their physical maturity, although a very immature girl may be 'fattened' for seven or nine weeks, on the advice of a diviner. A girl is accompanied at her wedding by two age-mates or friends who attend her through the lengthy ceremonial, bathing with her and anointing her with camwood and oil before she is taken to her husband's sleeping-hut for the first time.

Men marry much later than women. Throughout the long process of betrothal and marriage a man is supported by his friend, who acts as go-between in relations between him and his affines. Bridewealth arrangements are discussed by the go-between with the bride's matrikin and four patrigroups, her own and three other matrilaterally related patrigroups who have bridewealth rights in his fiancée.[4] Nowadays young men who work in the southern towns or plantations send their friends back to Bangwa to arrange their marriages. Almost inevitably this involves the tricky business of arranging the divorce of the young woman from a husband who had been betrothed to her at her birth, and repaying to him all the bridewealth he has given to her kin and marriage guardians since that time.

Bangwa men have fleeting sexual relations with girls, but never confuse a love affair with a relationship of friendship with a woman, formed in early childhood. Men and women of the same age are not necessarily of the same social age; this in itself precludes the notion of sex. Youths, on the whole, are not considered sexually or socially mature until many years after their girl 'friends' have married and had children. The difference in poise and physique between a youth of twenty and a matron of the same age is often remarkable. A young man usually becomes betrothed to his first fiancée in his early twenties, while she is still a child; when he first marries, his female friend may be a grandmother. Sometimes a woman will give one of her own daughters the name of her own friend (boy's and girl's names are interchangeable), and this gives the friend the right to first refusal of the baby's hand in marriage. Thus a friendship between persons of both sexes is always of the *eshua nzo* (friends by birth) variety and precludes sexual relations. This friendship does not differ much from the informal relationship of companionship between men. When a man is with his woman friend the relationship between them is immediately apparent, since the woman relaxes her usual attitude of deference which she assumes in the presence of men of any age or rank. They are permitted to joke, eat together (usually tabooed between men and women), and talk frankly. In the market they exchange kola nuts and gifts freely.

Friendship between two women is not institutionalized to the extent it is between men, although women know their age-mates and have special friends among them. Perhaps a woman's closest friend or friends are those who were married at the same time to the same husband. As co-wives of an important polygynist they would have shared the same seclusion, but after their wedding; they share farming chores, care for each other's children, mourn their death, gossip, and share small domestic tasks in the compound. After their sons and daughters have grown up and left the compound, they grow old together; the death of one is a bitter blow. Other women friends, separated by marriage, visit each other at important *rites de passage*, bringing members of their local women's society gifts of food, firewood, etc. Some women friends farm together, often travelling long distances to work a groundnut or cocoyam plot in the friend's village.

Friendship does not falter; its rights and obligations do not concern matters that lead to enmity. They are not involved in affairs of property. Friends who are non-kinsmen are not accused of bewitching each other (although to the best of my knowledge a person is not accused of bewitching his twin). The relationship is seen as one of reciprocal advantage: there is nothing to be gained by betraying a friend. A man has complete freedom of his friend's compound and receives lavish hospitality when he visits. Friends tell each other details of personal and family affairs which they would keep from a brother or other kinsman. A friend is the person who is absolutely trusted. Old Bangwa men wax long on the virtues of friendship. 'My friend can lie in my wife's bed,' said one old man, implying that a friend could never betray another by seducing his wife. It can be said of few other men. At dances men are permitted to dance with their friend's wives, a rare privilege. To sleep with a friend's wife is considered the most heinous of sins; it brings mystical danger automatically on to the head of the wronged husband.

Friends attend any family discussions or disputes and give the benefit of their impartial advice. They attend *rites de passage* as a matter of course. A man's sons will call his friend as soon as he is critically ill. A friend is considered to be the best person to calm an old man's rage. Friends can be relied on to support a man in trouble even when kinsfolk and neighbours have withdrawn: this is noticeably so in cases of accusation of intragroup witchcraft or adultery. They also execute less pleasant tasks, such as recovering debts, or demanding the repayment of bride-wealth when a wife divorces. A man may well be asked to perform the autopsy for witchcraft on his friend's dead children. When a man loses a close relative he is attended by his age-mates and friends at the mortuary rite; they perform the masquerade he arranges in honour of his dead kinsman. If any-one quarrels with a person, his friends are automatically in-volved. One chief, whose young wife was stolen from his com-pound, banned the seducer and his friends from the village; he naturally assumed that a man and his friends perpetrated such an action in concert.

A man's friend is sometimes made, formally, the surrogate father of one of his children. A boy or a girl is presented to one of the parents' friends as his or her 'child'. The surrogate parent looks after the child's interests, particularly during adolescence and young manhood. A godfather may be asked to act as a go-between in the betrothal arrangements of his 'child' and the latter's prospective affines. The Bangwa explain this institution, which is by no means universal, as a means whereby harassed fathers (in polygynous compounds) share paternal duties with a friend whose responsibilities are fewer. It is also a device whereby a young man can partake of another's knowledge or other advantages without his being a kinsman: for example, if his father's friend is a blacksmith, the child may learn his craft. Since fathers are authoritarian and somewhat distant figures, his friend may act as a confidant and adviser to his children.

Friendship is given physical expression. Youths who are friends hold hands when walking the village paths. Old men embrace their friends when they meet in the market. To the old, friendships are specially valued; the older they grow the more hours they while away, visiting their friends, chatting over legal cases, marriage disputes, politics, etc. The most bitter complaint of an ageing man is that he has grown so old he no longer has any friends to talk to.

IV

I shall consider in more detail the role of friends during a man's last years, the making of his will, his death, and the succession and inheritance of his status by his heirs. In illness a man turns to his friends for help. An old man is in constant fear of witchcraft attacks, sorcery, and other mystical dangers from kinsfolk and neighbours. When critically ill, these fears require him to be put away privily, where he will be attended by a servant, a favourite daughter, and one or two of his closest friends. The symbol of injunction of the secret society, *tro*, is placed outside the house to warn off intruders. The advice of doctors and diviners is sought secretly by his friends, and all hint of the serious nature of the illness is kept from his family, particularly his sons.

A man's will is made, either orally or in writing, during his last illness. His wishes are confided to a small group of trusted friends and other witnesses. Besides friends, a man's will may be heard by a favourite daughter, a sister's son, a retainer, and perhaps a trusted son-in-law. Bequests may be very complicated: his widows, marriage wards, palm groves, livestock and cash are divided among his sons and close matrikin. Miscellaneous properties are bequeathed to distant kin. The bulk of the property, including patrigroup paraphernalia, is inherited by the man's primary heir. Patrigroup members are banned from hearing the will and a man's sons will, on no account, be informed of its contents. A man fears the rapacity of his brothers and disappointed sons. For this reason his friend, the executor of his will, keeps all details of the will secret until arrangements have been made for the disposal of his property, the payment of debts and death dues to the dead man's chief and his marriage guardian. If the preparations are not ready, the man's death is kept secret for a time to prevent the inevitable commotion that occurs after a wealthy man's death – widows fighting for their sons' interests, patrikin snatching property, sons attempting to seduce their father's widows.

A man depends on his friend, as executor of his will, to see that his dying wishes are carried out. Bequests are distributed, often in face of the hostility of disappointed kin, grasping chiefs, and influential patrikin, all of whom try to further their own interests at the expense of the successor. A friend is not a beneficiary so his own interests are not concerned. A dying man, whatever his status, is primarily intent on perpetuating his name after death. Succession is from father to son, and a man's status as an ancestor and founder of a patriline is guaranteed only if he is succeeded by a son. If a collateral succeeds, the dead man's property is merged with that of the successor and his status as founder of a skull cult lost for ever. Because of the strict father-son succession rule many men die while their heirs are still young. Before his death this child will be placed in the care of one of his friends. This man, the heir's guardian, manages the estate, provides a sexual partner for the widows who remain in the compound, and watches over the education of the child until he reaches maturity. Both the estate and the heir are considered to be in a dangerous position during these years, since kinsfolk will attempt to claim widows and properties. The heir lives with his guardian; the jealousy of his mother's co-wives would be considered too bitter for his safety. When the youth formally succeeds to his father's status a wrangle frequently occurs, since the temporary compound head has become firmly ensconced in his role. Physical force may have to be brought to bear to dislodge him.

Some men die with no male heirs. In this case the position is even more tricky. His friend may arrange for the man's widow or widows to remain in the compound, take a lover, and bear children for the dead man, one of whom will succeed. In other cases, in order to continue a dead man's name, a slave is named successor or even a daughter's son. These situations are not uncommon; patrilineal collaterals of the dead man will struggle even harder to merge the late man's property with their own, and the role of loyal friend in supporting the man's successor is of great significance.

The heir's guardian's last public act, in conjunction with the successor and the man's kin, is to arrange for the mortuary rites of his late friend. These rites jurally establish the position of the heir as head of his patrigroup and custodian of patriline skulls. The dead man's skull is exhumed, medicated, and placed in the sleeping-house of the compound head. A sacrifice is made, attended by all patrigroup members, who declare their allegiance to their new head. In the compound courtyard a spectacle is arranged. The societies to which the dead man belonged bring their music, dances, and masquerades. The heir entertains them and he is formally initiated into his father's role in the society. His guardian, his father's friend, brings his own group, mem-

bers of which are also entertained by the heir. Even after the
final mortuary rites the relationship between the guardian and
the young man may continue. Alliances between patrigroups,
cemented by marriage exchanges over many generations, have
originated in this way.

A man's successor does not enter into the fulness of his powers
until the supernatural talents of his late father have been added
to more mundane ones associated with running a compound and
estate. A man's witchcraft potential is inherited by his successor
along with patrigroup property. This power is taught to a man's
heir in many devious ways while the child is growing up. 'It is
our education,' said one man. The talent he learns is involved
with witchcraft and shape-changing, at which the Bangwa are
great adepts. If a man dies before his heir is old enough to have
learnt the tricks of this trade, he asks a retainer (in the case of a
chief) or his best friend (in the case of a commoner) to hold
these powers in trust for the young man. They are spoken of as
being kept in a 'bag of the country' or in the physical manifesta-
tion of a twisted root. Friends cannot bewitch each other. But
they are expected, from the very nature of their relationship, to
indulge in witchcraft and shape-changing activities together.
Friends join the same covens and incur flesh-debts on each
other's behalf. Men are sometimes accused of killing their
children through witchcraft, not to satisfy their own lust for
flesh but to please their friends. A man's friend is thus a good
person to guard his witchcraft potential and hand it to his heir
when he is old enough to use it wisely.

V

Friendship in Bangwa provides many economic and social
opportunities that are not available within kin groups. In any
case, the important segments of Bangwa society for dealing with
economic and political processes are not groups of kin but territorial groups under chiefs, sub-chiefs, and village heads, abetted
by innumerable associations. Kin groups are not localized; the
Bangwa do not live in extended families. There is no corporate
lineage organization and the idiom of kinship does not underlie
the political and economic framework of society. Economic

factors play a large part in the emphasis placed on extra-kin relationships. The Bangwa economy is far from being the purely subsistence one often associated with simple societies, where farming is a cooperative venture and sharing forms the basis of exchange. The Bangwa operate, and operated in pre-colonial days, a market economy; they are highly acquisitive and property-conscious. Their role in the past as important middle men in a profitable trade in slaves, guns, salt, and European goods between the forest lands and the savanna gave individuals many chances of acquiring wealth quickly. Opportunities for gain existed outside corporate kin groups and even local communities. Trading brought them into contact with different people and ideas. A higher value was placed on the acquisition of goods and status than on the maintenance of good relations between kin.

Friendship relationships (like *compadre* relationships) have considerable advantages in a situation of this kind. They allow increased social and economic opportunities and provide an outlet against close, restricting obligations imposed by kinship. Bangwa gain few material advantages through membership of a patrigroup or matrigroup. After the death of his father, a man if he is not the successor must make his own fortune, pay bridewealth for his own wives, and attempt to found his own patrigroup and patriline. In the past, men made quick fortunes trading slaves in exchange for European goods. Individuals formed trading friendships both within Bangwa and in the Bamileke Grasslands, where the slaves originated, and in the forest markets which had access to European goods. Young men pooled capital and joined with friends to organize long-distance trading expeditions. Chiefs traded as well, through retainers. They established friendships and alliances with neighbouring chiefs to further trading opportunities. Chiefs who were born at the same time could become personal friends (*beshua nzo*) as commoners did. Chiefs who formed such friendships had privileges in each other's markets; they also exchanged daughters or wards as wives. One of the most important obligations of a chief's friend was to supervise the installation of his successor after his death. In Bangwa such a man arrived at the palace immediately he heard of the death, took charge of the compound, arranged the mortuary rites, and saw to the crowning of the heir. To prevent spoliation of his friend's property he would place a strong man in charge of the compound during the months the new chief spent in seclusion.

In the early years of British Trusteeship, when the trade in slaves had been successfully abolished, the Bangwa continued to trade European goods, bought in south-east Nigeria, in the innumerable Bangwa and Bamileke markets in exchange for colonial currency. Friends tell how they formed partnerships, trekking down the mountain slopes and through the empty forests for weeks at a time to bring the valued goods from the coast to the interior. Alliances were formed between friends rather than kin, since the latter tended to quarrel. Many friendships which flourished in the sixties were the fruit of these early partnerships. Since 1962 when West Cameroon, formerly the Southern Cameroons under British Trusteeship, elected to be 'reunified' with East Cameroon, the source of these trade articles has dried up. Trade is now mostly local, in palm-oil, surplus crops, wine, and livestock. Young men have fewer opportunities for making spectacular profits with the curtailment of long-distance trading. Yet small stores have recently been opened in the market squares, frequently owned jointly by friends, who acquire together exclusive agencies from large Indian and Lebanese stores in the southern towns.

Friendship, an old institution in Bangwa, has enabled young men to cooperate easily and adapt to modern market competition. The few young men who are not traders, and have resisted the compelling urge to leave their mountain homes for the El Dorado of the southern plantations and towns, have recently begun to plant coffee and cocoa farms or continued to work oil palm. In all these occupations young men cooperate on the basis of friendship. Profits are frequently pooled and savings clubs joined. These young men help each other to build their European-style houses, plant their plantain groves. They form dance groups and meet regularly for political discussions. In all these groups, special friendships between a man and his friend by birth (*eshuo nzo*) still exist.

NOTES

1. My first field trip to Bangwa (1964-65) was made possible by a field research assistantship from University College London and grants from the Wenner-Gren Foundation for Anthropological Research and the Trustees of the Horniman Fund. In 1967 I had a Hayter Travel Grant. During both periods I was granted leave of absence from University College by Professor Forde, who gave me throughout practical assistance and much-needed advice.

2. Dr Kaberry informs me that great value is attached to personal friendships throughout the Bamenda Grassfields. In African ethnography very little has been published on friendship, as distinct from bond friendship and blood-brotherhood. There is, however, some material in Driberg (1935), Goody (1962), Herskovits (1938), and Wilson (1951).

3. Twins in many parts of the Bamenda Grassfields to the north of Bangwa are referred to as 'children of God' and undergo rituals after birth. In Nso a child born with a caul around its neck is also regarded as a twin (personal communication from Dr Kaberry).

4. Marriage payments and their relation to the complex descent system are discussed in the writer's article, 'Bangwa Marriage Wards', *Africa*, 1969 (in press).

REFERENCES

CHILVER, E. M. & KABERRY, P. M. 1966. *Notes on the Precolonial History and Ethnography of the Bamenda Grassfields* (mimeographed). Reissued 1968 in a revised form under the title *Traditional Bamenda*. Buea: Government Printing Press.

DRIBERG, J. H. 1935. The 'Best Friend' among the Didinga. *Man*, 35, art. 110.

GOODY, JACK 1962. *Death, Property, and the Ancestors*. Stanford: Stanford University Press; London: Tavistock.

HERSKOVITS, M. J. 1938. *Dahomey*, 2 vols. New York: Augustin.

WILSON, MONICA 1951. *Good Company*. London: Oxford University Press.

Victor W. Turner

Symbolization and Patterning in the Circumcision Rites of two Bantu-speaking Societies

INTRODUCTION

In this paper I wish briefly to compare certain key symbolic features of the rites immediately preceding or succeeding male circumcision in two widely separated Bantu-speaking societies, the Gisu of south-east Uganda and the Ndembu of north-west Zambia. I spent nearly two and a half *years* in the field among the Ndembu and only two and a half *months* among the Gisu, but I have been fortunate enough to have been permitted by Dr Jean La Fontaine of London University to have access to her un-published data on the Gisu. Together with her published accounts, these data constitute a comprehensive account of Gisu social organization. With this excellent background, I was able in the field to focus maximum attention on the symbolic structure and semantics of the circumcision rites themselves. I observed about a dozen circumcision rites in central and southern Bugisu from July to September, 1966. In writing this paper I have benefited greatly from the comments and criticism of my col-league and clansman, Dr Terence Turner, of Chicago University.

Brevity makes for oversimplification but, since this is in-escapable here, let me say now that I wish to compare in each society an array of three symbols that have importance just before or immediately after the time of the circumcision opera-tion. Among the Gisu the three symbols used before circum-cision consist of finger millet yeast, chyme from the stomach and intestines of a slaughtered goat, and mud; animal, vegetable, and mineral, so to speak. The Ndembu symbolic triad, promi-

R   229

nent at and just after the operation, consists of a tree that exudes a milky white latex, a tree that secretes a colourless gum, and a tree that secretes a dusky red gum. Both these symbolic triads are rich with reference, explicit and implicit, avowed and unavowed, to many features of the social structure, culture, and ecological setting, and to human and animal biological processes. Moreover, each symbol in each triad provides the focus for a cluster of ritualized activities that marks a distinct stage in a novice's transition from culturally defined immaturity to the beginnings of maturity. At one level of reference, each symbol relates to important modifications in social relationships. By and through them social ties are being formally broken, created, or changed. Additionally, master values and principles of society are being reaffirmed – sometimes in situations where they appear to be threatened – or brought into new relationships with one another. But to throw into high relief the character of each triad, I propose first to describe a number of features of their respective containing cultures.

Although Ndembu and Gisu belong to a single major linguistic group and although both cultures have circumcision rites and reveal a common flair for the exegesis of symbols, it would perhaps be hard to find two sub-Saharan African peoples more different, even antithetical, in many cultural domains. Let me list some of these differences. The Ndembu are few in number (*c.* 18,000) with a low population density (4-6 per square mile); the Gisu must now number over one-third of a million in Bugisu District alone – they are penetrating other districts in considerable numbers – with an average density of at least 250 per square mile of cultivable land, rising in parts of the Manafwa valley to more than 700 per square mile. With these differences go differences in degree of pressure on resources: in Bugisu there is now almost no uncultivated land, whereas Ndembu territory is mainly uncultivated bush with scattered pockets of cultivated land.

These demographic factors affect both the siting and the symbolism of the circumcision rites, for the Ndembu seclude their novices in lodges far from the inhabited territory, and make an important ritual distinction between the domestic and wild domains, while the Gisu, with hardly any bush to speak of, seclude their novices within the lineage dwelling-areas and do not make a symbolic distinction between bush and residential area. The Gisu, whose land is blessed with rich volcanic soil and two rainy seasons, are relatively prosperous agriculturalists who produce in addition to such long-established crops as millet, corn, and bananas, lucrative modern cash crops, such as coffee, cotton, and tea. Their homesteads are widely and fairly uniformly dispersed over the whole territory which mainly consists of the western slopes of Mount Elgon and its foothills – though many now inhabit the lower, dryer, and comparatively less fertile plains at the foot of the mountain. The Ndembu, by contrast, live in small, circular nucleated villages, containing on average some thirty people, which are grouped into clusters or vicinages of some six to fifteen villages. Gisu huts, but not Ndembu ones, are dispersed among their cultivations. Between Ndembu vicinages are tracts of wild, uninhabited bush suitable for hunting and gathering. The Ndembu who are plateau-dwellers, have few cash crops, and subsist mainly on manioc, finger millet, and corn. The Gisu practise *sedentary*, the Ndembu *shifting*, cultivation. Gisu homesteads tend to be fixed and immobile, Ndembu villages unstable and mobile. Gisu keep some cattle and a fair number of goats and sheep. Ndembu have no cattle and but few of the smaller livestock.

With such divergent demographic and ecological backgrounds, it is hardly surprising to learn that Gisu and Ndembu social systems also differ significantly. Gisu are *patrilineal* and virilocal, Ndembu *matrilineal* and virilocal. In other words, with regard to the relationship between descent and post-marital residence rules the Ndembu, in Lévi-Strauss's terminology, have disharmonic, and the Gisu harmonic, systems. The Ndembu village is in constant tension between matriliny and virilocality, for men strive to keep their sisters and sisters' children with them to maintain village continuity and, at the same time, to keep their wives and their own children with them to increase their personal support within the village. But virilocal marriage pulls sisters out of villages, while matrilineal descent brings them back to their kin at the cost of broken marriages – as is attested by an exceptionally high divorce rate, even for Central African matrilineal societies. Matriliny is, therefore, opposed to patrilaterality in this competition for village personnel. In the 'harmonic' Gisu system this particular type of strain does not exist. Here the emphasis is shifted to a tension between local particularism, most signally represented by membership in the small, but structurally cohesive, minimal patrilineage, the *sikuka*, which is a land-holding unit, and loyalties to wider territorial groupings.

Again, among the matrilineal Ndembu, women, so important in descent, appear as the ritual equals of men. Among the patrilineal Gisu, women never attain to more than a junior status in the jural and ritual systems, though their personal influence is, of course, formidable. But this jural inferiority is counterbalanced to some extent by the fact that it is precisely through women that the self-sufficiency of the local patrilineage is broken down and the wider society, as it were, invades the particularistic segment. Thus links, structurally inferior to those of patriliny, created by the marriages of women and continued subsequently through matrilateral kinship, contrast with the hard jural rights vested by localized patriliny. This 'hardness' reaches its maximum in highly tense relations between father and son. Dr La Fontaine has constantly stressed the aggressive character of this relationship, as seen, for example in her recent article in *Man* (1967), in the high incidence of parricide in Bugisu. Much of this tension is due to the rule that a man must give his son a piece of land after the latter's circumcision; and, as we have seen, pressure on land is intense. On the other hand, a wealthy mother's brother, in need of local political support, may not infrequently allocate land to his nephew; thus, in the relationship between brothers-in-law we see reflected the tension already noted between patrilineal segment and society at large.

A major source of local lineage segmentation among the Gisu is polygyny. The weakest link in the lineage structure is between seminal brothers. Segmentation between the sons of one father by different mothers takes place approximately every third generation. Since mutual accusations of witchcraft between halfbrothers precede and accompany segmentation, it is clear that this process constitutes a moral and ideological as well as a practical problem for Gisu society. The major requirements for founding a new localized patrilineage are, first, a plot of land separate from that controlled by the original lineage head, usually the father or older brother, and, secondly, a family preferably polygynous. If a man can obtain land from his maternal uncle or additional supporters from his nephews, the link between mother's brother and sister's son as well as the father-son relationship can clearly be exploited to the man's secessionist advantage. I mention these considerations to stress the strong ambivalence of the father-son tie, especially as it affects circumcision. For, on the one hand, patrilineal values are reinforced through the affirmation of the son's adult male status in the symbolic environment of his patrilineal homestead, values which signally include the authority of father over son; while, on the other hand, that very son is endowed with higher jural-economic status, obtains extended rights over land, and a sounder economic base for his marriages. Thus, as La Fontaine again has argued (1967), he is now potentially his father's equal and threatens his father as the potential founder of a new local segment.

It should be pointed out that Gisu society is 'achievement-oriented' for males who have undergone circumcision. La Fontaine has demonstrated how both wealth and political position depend principally upon a man's own efforts – the Gisu *mukasa* is in certain respects closer in concept to the New Guinea 'Big-Man' than to the classical African chief or village headman. Lastly, the political system of the Ndembu is a hierarchical, though largely expressive-symbolic, structure of ascribed political positions consisting of a senior chieftainship, four sub-chieftainships, and a number of historically important village headmanships. Rights to succeed to each of these offices are bestowed by matrilineal descent. The major chieftainships obtain their title from the source of all Lunda political authority and high office, the *Mwantiamvwa*, who reigns in the Congo. In practice, most villages enjoyed in the past considerable political autonomy, but the symbolic hierarchy periodically became visible at the funerary and installation ceremonies of senior chiefs, in which each sub-chief played a specific ritual role. Thus, among the mobile and scattered Ndembu, there was a fixed ritualized hierarchy of political rule, while, among the stable sedentary Gisu, political power depended upon achievement, charisma, and the acquisition of economic resources and followers.

CIRCUMCISION RITES

Differences in the circumcision rites may be correlated with structural differences. The Gisu rites are performed every other

233

year and spread over the whole year. They are performed at different times in different maximal lineages, which have their traditional order of performance, each following on after the end of the rites in the preceding lineage. The actual operation takes place after the main harvest, which lasts from June till September. The rites do not group boys into any formalized system of age-sets on which a military or political organization is based, though each year is known by a topical name, and long sequences of such names can be remembered by elderly men. In each circumcision period the rites embrace the whole of Gisu and especially since independence they have acquired a militantly nationalistic character, serving as a marker of Gisu identity. The Ndembu, on the other hand, whose tribal unity is especially symbolized in its system of traditional chieftainships, perform their circumcision rites on a localized basis. Here the appropriate social field is the vicinage. Moreover, the rites are not performed at regular intervals, but only when a sufficient number of boys of appropriate age have accumulated in the localized village cluster. Most Gisu boys are circumcised after puberty, though the actual age varies in different areas. In the hills to the north, where significantly pressure on resources is greatest, the age was formerly between eighteen and thirty-five; in the southern plains the age was appreciably lower. La Fontaine attributes both the higher age and also the greater severity of the operation in the north to the greater tension between father and son there, due to pressure on the land and its more intensive utilization for the growing of cash crops. However this may be, the age of circumcision among the Ndembu is much lower than in Bugisu. The novices of today are commonly about 8-10 years old and rarely over 14-15. My information indicates that even in the pre-European past the average age of circumcision was consistently pre-pubertal. Ndembu often circumcise brothers together, and an older brother may act as their guardian during seclusion. Gisu brothers are never circumcised in the same year, and indeed may not be initiated in successive circumcision periods.

Consonant with the post-pubertal age of Gisu circumcision is the view that the operation is in an important respect an ordeal, a trial of courage and manliness – a view that Gisu share with many East African Nilo-Hamitic pastoralists such as the Sebei and Nandi. It is the moral test of a manhood already physically achieved, as well as the entrée into political and economic arenas of achievement. *Per contra*, the Ndembu novices are expected to cry out in pain, although the braver of them may receive a ritual title during the rites of reaggregation. Since many of them are less than ten years old, it is not expected that they should display fortitude.

Gisu novices are circumcised in an open-ended shelter, erected for the occasion, at the homestead of each novice's senior male relative in the patriline. Most Gisu boys are circumcised individually or in pairs. Women may attend the operation, usually on the fringe of the critical throng who come to assess the novice's degree of bravery. Ndembu, on the other hand, are circumcised in the deep bush. All the eligible boys in a vicinage are circumcised on the same occasion by a team of circumcisers working side by side. Women are strictly prohibited – on pain of death – from attending.

We might now ask why it is that the Gisu rites are performed mainly for individuals in the particular context of the local patrilineage, with women present, while the Ndembu rites are collective affairs, performed in the wild, with women excluded. In the Gisu case, there seems to be at this critical point in the total circumcision ceremony an attempt to adapt the rites to effecting the passage from social immaturity to maturity within the specific context of the minimal patrilineage. Yet, as we have seen, the rites are also tied in with a cyclical pattern of successive performances which emphasize tribe-wide values, including those set on virility and patriliny. It would seem that the cyclical pattern of rites operates as a symbolic bridge between the specificity of the individual performances, rooted as they are in localized minimal lineages, and the values crucial for Gisu society as a totality. On the other hand, the Ndembu rites seem to operate in the direction of limiting the narrowness and exclusiveness of attachment to matrilineal villages by uniting in a single male moral community of suffering all the pre-pubertal boys of a given vicinage. The rites are here not so much a bridge between the part and the whole as an indicator of a social level (the vicinage) intervening between the part (i.e. the village) and the whole (the Ndembu people).

As regards the inclusion of women in the Gisu rites and their exclusion from the Ndembu rites, the following structural considerations may be relevant. In matrilineal societies jural and political authority is commonly transmitted from man to man, even although group placement is through women. Furthermore, among the virilocal Ndembu, *local* communities tend to be articulated by relationships between *males* – brother to brother, male matrilateral ortho-cousin to ortho-cousin, father to son. Here male authority combines with virilocality to exhibit masculine solidarity as culturally autonomous and antithetical to all relationships primarily based on matriliny. Matrilineal ties, seen from the perspective of what may be called the virilocal community, perpetually threaten to dismember that community. Again since succession to office is matrilineal, close male matrilineal kin are thrust into contention for office by the very principle that places them socially in lineages and villages.

Thus the Ndembu rites abstract male communality from the total social system, divesting it as far as may be of matrilineal and even feminine attachments and attributes, and create an idyllic sylvan unisexual community – whose only reality is a transient ritual one, though something of its character continues to invest secular village structure. In this domain, as we have seen, virilocal marriage consistently exports female matrikin from each village and retains male matrikin, while a significant percentage of sons reside as adults with their fathers.

In the Ndembu bush camp, therefore, the roles most importantly ritualized are precisely those which form the vertebrae of the virilocal community, i.e. brother, father, and son.

The Gisu circumcision rites, on the other hand, do not so blatantly segregate masculinity from femininity, or patrifiliation from matrifiliation. Rather, they assert the paramountcy of patriliny in the very heart of the inhabited, structured domain. Moreover, they also assert the supplementary, buttressing character of other principles of affiliation, such as affinity and cognation. Ndembu, through circumcision, spatially segregate boys from the women's sphere, the kitchen, to make them over to the men's sphere, the central village shelter where legal cases and administrative matters are discussed. Indeed the foreskin is explicitly likened by Ndembu to the *labia majora* – it is regarded as the feminine portion of a male child, to be removed from him pre-pubertally, so that he may be absorbed, as speedily as may be, in the male system of authority and into the masculine moral community. Previously he had been polluting to the ritual personae of circumcised men – now he has been moved from impurity and danger to purity and male sacredness. *Pari passu*, Ndembu segregate male authority from matrilineal descent, and polarize virility against femininity.

Gisu circumcision, unlike that of the Ndembu, where it is only one of many kinds of rites, is the 'high spot' of their entire ritual system. Ndembu circumcision is competitive with many other kinds of rituals – including the girls' puberty ceremony, which significantly is performed *in* the village milieu, just as Gisu *boys'* initiation is. But Gisu circumcision has two major aspects: it is an index of pan-tribal solidarity and in this respect the phase leading up to the operation has something of the character of a harvest festival; but it is also a life-crisis ritual indicating the status elevation of a male individual both within the wider setting and also – and crucially – within the patrilineage. These aspects will emerge in finer detail when we consider the symbolic triad I mentioned at the outset. But first it is necessary to say something about the main events preceding the day of circumcision. There are four major phases of the rites:[1]

1. The first, from January to June, is 'occupied entirely by dancing' on what La Fontaine calls the 'village greens' of each maximal lineage's territory. The novices are instructed in singing and dancing by expert 'song-leaders'. They are dressed in a complex traditional costume, each item of which has symbolic value, but the ensemble mainly stresses matrilateral structural connexions.

2. The second phase 'begins soon after the main agricultural work of sowing and weeding the crops is over' – the novices go round the country in troupes, accompanied by their sisters and other kin and neighbours, dancing and singing, led now by one of themselves who sings the solo lines while the others sing the chorus. This is the time when they visit all their relatives, both patrilineal and matrilateral, near and distant, spatially and consanguineally, culminating in visits to their senior fathers' sisters. During this period the roads and byways of Bugisu are filled with turbulent chanting troupes of *basinde* (novices) and their kin, colourfully dressed and caparisoned, who sometimes travel many miles in this otherwise highly localized social system to visit remotely dwelling kin. The whole country is temporarily woven together by the busy shuttle of the rites – normally Gisu call fellow-tribesmen from another part of the same hill by the term for 'stranger'.

3. The third phase starts a few days before the operation takes place. Dancing is intensified and sometimes continues all night, and the whole community, including elders, now participates. The novices hardly sleep at all but dance and sing continually and are plied with beer – they are held at this time not to be responsible for their actions, which are wayward and wild.

4. The fourth phase consists of final preparations for the rites, during which the maximal lineage elders clean out the sacred groves of patrilineal ancestors, rebuild shrines in them, and sacrifice a chicken and beer. The grandfathers of the novices, or the persons under whose ritual jurisdiction the novices come, make similar sacrifices to the ancestors in their own – usually minimal lineage – compounds. Each novice then goes to his mother's brother (the one linked to his mother through bridewealth – the bridewealth received for the mother was paid by that uncle for his bride) to ask formal permission to be circumcised and to receive the blessing of the maternal ancestors. The mother's brother usually gives the novice a present of a cow, which is killed to feed him during his early seclusion after circumcision. Sometimes a skin cape from this beast is worn during circumcision by the lad, who is said to be held up by it if he shows signs of weakness or trembling – here again the supportive and buttressing role of matrilateral ties seems to be symbolized.

The profile of the rites has approximately the shape of a Gaussian curve; they begin in the localized minimal lineage, ascend, first to the maximal lineage territory, then to the Gisu nation, descend once more to the maximal lineage territory, and culminate as they began in the localized patrilineage. Throughout, patriliny is stressed, but the efficacy of this principle is attenuated during the ritualized wandering over the land to rise again to dominance at the site of the operation. Patriliny, however, is not a uniform concept; it includes a variety of relationships and attributes. The often fictitious patriliny that provides the widest frame of territorial organization must be distinguished from the traceable patriliny of the minimal lineage, while the father-son bond differs from both. These facets of patriliny receive expression in the symbolic triad I mentioned at the beginning of my essay.

The Gisu rites involve the successive smearing of the limbs and trunks of the novices with glutinous, adhesive substances that harden as they dry – millet yeast, chyme, and mud – in con-

238

trast to the Ndembu removal of novices from one symbol after another. Detachment of Ndembu boys from childish dependence on the mother is represented by each boy's circumcision under the milky latex-secreting *mudyi* tree. Passing them over the *muyombu* tree – standing for the ancestors – represents ritual death from the past. But placing the boys on the red-sap exuding *mukula* tree does symbolize incorporation into the wider male moral community. I have discussed the symbolism of these rites in some detail in *Essays on the Ritual of Social Relations* (see Gluckman 1962) and in *The Forest of Symbols* (1967). Here it is sufficient to say that the Ndembu rites are separative – they signify the detachment of ties between males from predominantly matrilineal links – especially those between males and females. The opposite is true of the Gisu – their rites involve the association of matrilateral and cognatic links with those based on patrilineal descent, including cognatic links between males and females.

This association of bonds is concretely represented in Gisu rites on the morning of the day of the operation. First, the boy's father slaughters a goat in the compound of the organizer – usually a senior agnate of the novice. The goat is skinned by another male member of the local minimal partilineage who had been brave at his initiation. The goat's internal organs are inspected by a knowledgeable elder who divines from their form, texture, and position and from the presence or absence of alien substances whether the operation will be successful or not. The novice's head is shaved by his father's sister, whose own head has been shaved by her brother's daughter. Then the novice's paternal grandfather takes chyme from the goat's slit stomach and smears it on the lad's chest, back, and legs, admonishing him to stand firm during the operation. Then he takes finger millet yeast (*kamamela*) and smears it over the chyme. He also smears a full or classificatory sister of the novice with yeast – but *not* with chyme – saying 'This makes you the wife of X (the novice)'. La Fontaine mentions that the father's sister is also smeared with yeast, but I did not observe this in southern Bugisu, where the yeast was applied before the chyme. The father's sister receives a large piece of the sacrificed animal, the sister or sisters, smaller pieces, but most of the meat is reserved for the novice to eat during seclusion in the first days of his convalescence. The novice, accompanied by his older agnates, sisters, and small children, then dances round the neighbourhood following an irreversible path – to indicate his irreversible intention to be circumcised – and in the course of which he descends to a valley or plain where, with all other novices of the maximal lineage territory, he is smeared with mud moistened by water that has welled up from under the ground – representing both the cooling power and fertility of the earth itself.

These three smearings stand for different types of social relationships – though they stand for other things as well. The chyme, taken from a goat given and sacrificed by the novice's father (who is, it must be remembered, 'sacrificing' his full authority over his son, and, maybe, a piece of land besides) and skinned by an agnate, is applied by a paternal grandfather or other senior local lineage kinsman. It is everywhere operationally associated with patriliny and fatherhood. It is said to 'harden the boy's skin' so that he will not tremble in his limbs when being cut. Chyme has other links with virility and a virile member as well, which I have no time to discuss. I might add, however, that, among the Gisu, goat's chyme is regularly used to augment auspiciousness, sheep's chyme to avert or dispel inauspiciousness.

Finger millet yeast, on the other hand, has many connexions with motherhood, wifehood, and femininity. It is said to have come with the ancestor of the Gisu, Masaba, from the east to the Mount Elgon region. Finger millet is associated with the centre-pole (*inzeko*) of a hut. The millet spirit, Murabula, is thought to dwell in it. When women plant the millet crop they take the first grain from a basket, known as *ikhorera*, which is kept near the centre-pole, as are the hoes with which the crop is planted. Whenever finger millet beer is brewed it is brewed just beside the centre-pole. After the harvest the first fruits of finger millet are tied to the centre-pole, while beer made from it is placed in a small pot for the Murabula spirit. When a woman is in labour it is thought that she will have a better delivery if she grasps the centre-pole in both hands. Likewise, while her son is being circumcised a mother must, in a sort of counter-couvade, grasp the same pole as he is being born into manhood 'through the knife' and its pangs. Interestingly, beer is brewed beside the centre-pole from the same lot of yeast that has been smeared on the boy to strengthen him for his ordeal. This will be shared by his paternal and maternal kin – first of whom being the mother's brother – three days after the operation when the boy is allowed to leave the seclusion hut prepared for him in the compound. Clearly, then, maternity, femininity, wifehood (for the wife is the centre of each dwelling), and matrilaterality are connected with the yeast symbolism as well as fertility. In the latter connexion, informants told me that the novice is smeared with yeast because it starts the fermentation of beer and thus will make the boy's heart also ferment or 'bubble up (*khututuba*) with courage for circumcision'.

To cut a long story short, the successive and mingled smearings seem to represent the ritual identification of several broad principles of social organization; patriliny, matrilaterality, affinity, and territory. The sister is identified with the wife, Gisu say, because she brings in the cattle with which the novice marries his own wife. Gisu also explain in this way the fact that they call sister's child 'child', and do not have cross-cousin marriage – though they know that other Ugandan peoples do. The father's sister is important in a similar way, for it was due, they say, to the cattle she brought into the minimal lineage that the novice's father was able to marry his wife, the novice's mother – now suffering symbolic pangs at the very heart of the finger millet symbolic complex. The mother's brother represents the other side of this equation, for it was with the cattle brought in by the novice's mother – coming from the novice's minimal patrilineage, in fact – that he was able to marry and raise children for *his* lineage. Gisu have told me that it is in gratitude for these marriage cattle that he kills a cow for his sister's son, and in some areas gives him a cloak from its skin and a rib cage to keep him steady during the painful operation.

I have no time to spell out in detail the complex and subtle interrelations between different aspects of matrilaterality, affinity, and other extra-patrilineal modes of interlinkage represented by the symbolism of smearing and the statuses of the smearers and the smeared. But it does appear as though virtually the entire range of a novice's relatives take part and that a symbolic field is generated in which values, loyalties, and relationships wider than the localized patrilineage form interdependent

241

parts. Yet the main axis is still the principle of patriliny – for a rite which in its cycle moves around almost all Bugisu culminates in the lineage compound.

I mentioned the ambivalence and indeed open aggressiveness in some situations in the father-son relationship. La Fontaine has argued from her numerical data that a greater severity of the operation in north Bugisu correlates with the greater pressure on the land there than in the south. She interprets this as due to greater reluctance on the father's part to part with a piece of land to his son, as he must do when the lad has been circumcised. She has also found that the average age of circumcision is higher in the north and explains this fact in the same way. My own observations show that fathers play an inconspicuous role while the operation is actually being performed, and may even disappear from view. This is in marked contrast to the Ndembu situation where fathers stand guard over their children while the circumciser performs what is a much less painful operation than in Bugisu – where not only is the foreskin severed but the inner lining of the prepuce is slit in a second part of the operation (in the north sometimes two hours after the foreskin has been removed) and all subcutaneous tissue covering and surrounding the gland is removed. Ndembu fathers also feed their sons as though they were infants while they sit bleeding on the red *mukula* log of achieved male maturity. On the other hand, the jurally important male senior, the mother's brother, plays an inconspicuous role among the matrilineal Ndembu at the time of the operation.

Thus, to summarize: among the patrilineal Gisu, the central principle of the localized minimal patrilineage assimilates to itself, in appropriate symbol and mime, all other Gisu principles of consanguinity, affinity, and territoriality, yet liberates the novice from strict and specific paternal authority; while among the matrilineal but virilocal Ndembu, a sharp symbolic separation is made between relations among men and ties of men to women – with an emphasis on paternity as the mediating link between particularistic, local ties of family and matrilineage and the broader comities of vicinage and tribe. The two symbol triads I have discussed are complex semantic systems that would take a book fully to explicate, but I would argue that an important key to the central meaning of both is to be found by considering them in their operational social settings and in their processual character as both indices and agencies of change in the structure of social relations.

La Fontaine has suggested in her unpublished Ph.D. thesis (deposited at Cambridge University) that the Gisu fall midway between societies in which the segmentary lineage system has politically integrative importance and societies in which age-set organization – often accompanied by circumcision – is politically paramount. In the first case the localized patrilineage has great importance, in the second its importance is reduced – sometimes even to the point of ineffectiveness – by the horizontal tie of age-set affiliation. I would like to suggest that such features of Gisu circumcision as its powerful affectual accompaniments and tribally focal character are more than reflections merely of a tense father-son relationship, but rather represent an irresoluble conflict between disparate *world-views*. On the one hand, the universalistic and egalitarian ethos of an age-set system; and, on the other, the localized particularism and gerontocratic authoritarianism of a narrowly patrilineal system. In brief, the conflict is not between kinship positions in a single type of system but between a 'vertical' and a 'horizontal' type of system, where the pivotal relationship under inter-systemic stress coincides with the father-son relationship. In this kind of social field, matrilaterality may well be 'overdetermined', or may 'compensate', in its horizontal bonding function, for the absence of the age-set organization that accompanies circumcision and other kinds of initiation in many societies not so far from Bugisu, such as the Sebei, Nandi, and Karimojong.

NOTE

1. This account is based on J. S. La Fontaine's description in *The Gisu of Uganda* (1959: 41-6).

REFERENCES

GLUCKMAN, M. (ed.) 1962. *Essays on the Ritual of Social Relations*. Manchester: Manchester University Press.

LA FONTAINE, J. S. 1959. *The Gisu of Uganda*. Ethnographic Survey of Africa: East Central Africa, Part X. London: International African Institute.

— 1967. Parricide in Bugisu: a study in intergenerational conflict. *Man*, n.s. 2, no. 2.

SCHNEIDER, D. M. & GOUGH, K. (eds.) 1961. *Matrilineal Kinship*. London: Cambridge University Press; Berkeley and Los Angeles: University of California Press.

TURNER, VICTOR 1967. *The Forest of Symbols: Aspects of Ndembu Ritual*. Ithaca: Cornell University Press.

Jan Vansina

The Bushong Poison Ordeal

'After two hours' marching and our hearts so glad with the prospect of getting safely into the first Bakuba town, we suddenly ran upon an excited crowd of people, most of them armed with spears, bows and arrows. I called an immediate halt to my caravan. The armed force showed no signs of fight but rather to run away. Bope, my Bakuba friend, explained that they were giving a witch poison, and they never administered the deadly drug inside their towns, but far out on the plain. On this information I started for the crowd, saluted them in their tongue and to my horror as I drew near they were slowly driving a woman to whom they had given the poison. She ran about fifty yards, staggered, reeled and fell with a thud. A shout went up from them all, "Naki! "Naki!" (Witch! Witch!). At once the witch doctor, a great, strong man, with eagle feathers in his hair, a leopard skin around his loins, leaped upon the woman's neck and crushed out the remaining life. Like a shot the men were off, and returned with loads of dry wood, placed the woman's body on the pile, poured on palm oil and stuck a torch to the heap. . . . My friend Bope explained that someone had died in a nearby village and they believed that the woman was the guilty party who had bewitched her. For if she had not been guilty, he said, the victim would have vomited the poison' (Sheppard 1892: 92-3).

This is an early description of the poison ordeal of the Bushong, the dominant tribe of the Bakuba group in the Congo. Common throughout Central Africa at the time when Europeans appeared on the scene, inevitably the poison ordeal was frowned upon from the beginning. Its most obvious function, as a judicial procedure for the conviction of witches and sorcerers, has been well understood. But for the Bushong, the poison ordeal is the most powerful rite they know. It has as its ambitious aim to eliminate evil and death. Much more than a judicial procedure, it is also a meeting of the supernatural with the human. In some

s

respects it even shows some parallels with human sacrifice, the witch being seen as victim. In its form it is a dramatic *rite de passage*. Its elaborate ritual character has hitherto remained unsuspected, mainly because public resort to the ordeal was suppressed from the beginning. Sheppard, the very first visitor to enter Bushong territory, remarks:

'I kept a close watch on the witch doctors, but I presume because I had preached so much against the wicked custom, they did not have a public test. I fear though that they went off secretly into the bushes or high grass and carried out their custom' (1892: 130).

In 1908 Commandants Decock and Gustin had already reported that poison ordeals were being suppressed. In fact, they survived to around 1931 and were then replaced by others. But, on the eve of independence in October 1959, 58 Bushong villages out of a total of about 120 suddenly held public poison ordeals. It was reported that about 500 persons had been involved, most of them women, and that 255 escaped and 250 were killed. This indicates that the chances of dying and of escaping were about the same, a question which has given rise to some controversy in the past (*Courrier d'Afrique*, 1960). Since I had worked in the area, one of my former aides was able to send me information, on which the present paper is based.[1]

The Bushong believe in both witchcraft and sorcery, but the ordeal deals only with suspected witches. Sorcery which involves the use of medicines and fetishes to kill enemies, is said to be used mainly by men in positions of wealth or authority to further their ambitions. Witchcraft, which is usually thought to be innate, is also believed to be acquired – but it is not known how. It is supposed to be used mainly by women, without power or authority, out of sheer jealousy or to satisfy grudges, the latter being clearly the outstanding motive. It is typically the aggression pattern of the weak and defenceless.

A witch always tries out her powers first on chickens or dogs before she begins to kill humans. She also has a life-container or *ndyeemy*. This can be any object to which the witch has given her life-power so that she will escape death, even when given poison, since every witch fully expects to be discovered one day. The life-container can be a simple object like a pot, a box, a stick in the wall, but it can also be a more elusive item: the water in a pot, an insignificant pond in the woods. Sometimes the life-container is swallowed, and then only a diviner can remove it. Indeed, in 1953 I saw an apparently dead woman vomit a string of beads, said to be her life-container.

Beliefs in witchcraft and sorcery are constantly fed by gossip concerning the weird antisocial ways of witches, speculation as to the cause of a person's death, and by frequent dreams about witches. Even in 1953-6, the wide currency of such talk indicated the strength of the beliefs involved. They also led directly to the outbreak of ordeals in 1959 when the untested informal gossip became transformed into formal accusations.

Accusations fall into two categories according to whether the clan or the village is involved. The head of a matriclan can agree to an ordeal for one of his members. Either he himself or another older member accuses a junior in the clan, or an outsider asks formally for a particular individual to submit to the ordeal. No clan section dares to refuse such a request for fear of being known as 'killers of men and protectors of criminals', and ultimately of being chased out of the village, as has sometimes happened according to clan histories. However, should the person survive then the accuser must pay blood-money or have one of his own group submit to the ordeal. In either case, the ordeal cannot be said to have resolved the tensions between accusers and accused. These do not vanish, whatever the outcome of the ordeal. As my informant writes, 'You see very well that hatred and grudges will settle permanently between them.'

The other type of accusation is brought by the head of a village, after failure in hunting or fishing, and especially after repeated deaths. The village council meets and agrees that the cause must be sought. Each clan section that is represented on the council then nominates one of their number to be submitted to the ordeal. Spouses of clan members whose own lineages do not reside in the village cannot be subjected to the test. Neither can slaves or women given as pawns (*ngady akan*), unless their master agrees.

It is readily apparent that witchcraft accusations are made only by persons, functioning below the political level of chiefdom, that is, within the village and the clan. Conversely, sorcery accusations are made and acted upon at the chiefdom level or higher; the village court can also handle sorcery cases, but seems to do so very rarely. Accusations are never made on the spur of the moment, even for the first type. The correct procedure is to wait and to accuse only after death or similar disaster has struck, recalling then all the disputes in which the accused has been involved and all the gossip about him or her.

The poison ordeal is a social drama for the community but it is not a spontaneous drama. In its timing, as in its development, it follows standardized rules. It may be that in pre-colonial times there was a small ritual marking the accusation. Sheppard (1892: 121-2) describes how 'witchdoctors' with painted bodies, feathers in their hair, leopard-skins on their bodies, brandishing knives and ringing bells, would run up and down a street in the capital, stopping and hooting at every door, until by some imaginary force they were stopped at someone's door, and thus 'discovered' and accused the witch. The suspect was then taken to the witches' house, a special shed in almost every village, and would remain there to be visited by friends and relatives until the day for the ordeal drew near. This was set for a day when 'the marketers would come in from the country'. In 1959, the delay between accusation and trial by ordeal was from two days to a week, and the accused was no longer secluded in a special shed.

During the delay, the accusers go to the diviners, a minimum of three divinations being regarded as satisfactory to find out where the prospective witch is hiding her life-container. They also call on the poison-officiant (*nsheky*). A supervisor of poison for the country, the *nyim ansheky*, resides at the capital. If there is a resident poison-officiant in the village, he will administer the poison; otherwise an outsider is called in. To be a poison-officiant is a delicate matter, for an accused witch is expected to try to kill him before her own trial if she knows his identity. On the other hand, if the poison-officiant is too friendly with the accused, he may be suspected of attempting fraudulently to manipulate the ordeal in her favour. In a trial held in 1959 none of the six women accused died, but the officiant fell ill. Foul play was alleged for, although the women escaped, they did not vomit any bile, a sign that they were not really innocent. Therefore the officiants generally avoid the accused during this period. As for the accused themselves, the Bushong point out that they generally know in advance if they will survive or die, and prepare accordingly. In 1960 there was a case in which two witches had carefully and spitefully torn up every note of money they had hoarded.

The evening before the ordeal the friends of the accused shave her body completely and bring her the ceremonial funerary gifts. (This parallels exactly the procedure when a natural death has taken place.) The person is now separated from the living. This shaving of the head was reported in 1899 (Wharton 1962: 48-9). Meanwhile the accuser goes to the poison-officiant to pay him for the ritual just as one would pay any other specialist. The fee is 100 cowries and 20 more for 'the search in the grass', an allusion to the last act of the officiant in the ritual. The officiant is also told by the accusers where they think the life-container is hidden. Later in the evening the accused brings a calabash of palmwine to the officiant, an act formally analagous to the giving of wine to visiting chiefs. By this gesture the accused accepts the authority of the officiant.

The following morning the officiant goes to the poison-bearing tree (*bupweemy*) in the forest and addresses it as follows:

'You, Tembong of the clan Latum, the place where God was born. When he returned to the village, he carried lumps of kaolin. If truly the suspect is a witch, kill her! If she is innocent, save her!'

Then he cuts a rectangle of bark fairly high up the trunk and lets it float down on the air. Which way it falls indicates guilt or innocence. He does this twice over. But even if the bark shows innocence, the poison still has to be administered, for the public ritual is as much a vindication as it is a trial. This particular oracle of the falling bark was still carried out around 1940.

The officiant then gathers enough bark for his purpose, returns to the village, and seats himself at the back of the village. The spatial aspects of the ritual are that the inside of a village represents the orderly community, the bush is nature, and the side or back of the village is the marginal area, perfectly suited for this sort of *rite de passage*. Then, surrounded by the villagers, he pounds the stuff in a small mortar, stopping from time to time during the pounding to show graphically how the witch will totter and stumble and how she will die. This is done so that the poison may learn how to kill. Meanwhile the onlookers sing nine songs. Never more than nine are sung, for nine is the correct ritual number. The songs must relate to the nature spirits and the Creator. The actual choice of songs is left to the participants. Typical first lines of songs sung in 1959 were:

'The older person is the Creator' (he finds out)
'Here they are, those who totter' (the witches)
'Why don't you do away with the witch who stands in the middle of the villages?'
'Glory to the Creator'.

These are probably the complete texts of songs, apart from 'Ye, ye, ye' or 'O, O, O' at the end. The songs are supposed to tell how a witch plies her craft, thinking she will remain undetected. Finally, when the bark has become a fine powder, the bystanders may taste some of it with a little water. This satisfies their curiosity and shows them by its taste that there is indeed poison in the brew.

The next stage opens when the officiant takes two knives and calls out loud three times for the accused: 'Witch.' His posture expresses symbolically danger and death, and is very similar to that of the person who leads young male initiates into the tunnel which will kill them as *nnup*, 'children', and transforms them into adults (Vansina 1956: 141). By this time the suspect has donned her funerary clothing in her house, and is waiting behind the building. She now goes towards the officiant and answers at the third-call: 'Yes'. The officiant calls: 'Come quickly, like your brother the fieldmouse.' He then seats himself on a mat near his mortar while the suspect kneels in front of him, a scene recalling the attitude of a subject in front of his chief and his court.

Then the accused takes an oath swearing, for example: 'Since my mother delivered me, since my father educated me, if ever I bewitched a chicken or a dog and then a man, who has a right to live, or if I was jealous about wealth, let the poison cut my heart, untie my liver, strike my forehead to the ground.' In 1892 Sheppard's interpreter translated the oath simply as follows: 'If you are guilty, you'll die; if not, you'll be saved.' And, by 1953, the oath was replaced by a formula intoned by the officiant of a new cult, called *Miko mi Yool* (see below), before he put his powder (possibly still the bark of the tree) (*ipweemy*) in the food or drink of the victim: '*Pok Ibaan* (diviner of the king), *Miko mi Yool*! If it is a witch, if it is a criminal, cut her heart, slice her lungs, *pr, pr, pr, bu* (the last syllable means: she has lost her case) *shwee(ter)* (for good); kill, *yo, yo, yo* (for ever).'

This is the formula which will make the poison effective, for, like any other magic, *ipweemy* cannot work 'if it is not spoken to': it has already learned to kill from the miming of the officiant; it now learns the rules of the ordeal. The substitution of this formula for the oath of the accused suggests that the latter also had a role in activating the poison.

After this, the officiant reads a motto, the ceremonial words of the ordeal, which is like a praise-song, as one of my informants put it. It consists of three stanzas, linked by a refrain, and probably shouted by all: '*Kashakaama, Kieenc a!*' (attention, the Law, ah!), a cry also used to punctuate formal speeches by the king (see Jacobs & Vansina 1956). And since, according to Sheppard (1892: 92 and 121), the officiant wore eagle feathers, a leopard-skin, and an iron bell, all chiefly regalia, this expresses further the regal and judicial aspects of the ordeal.[2] Broadly interpreted, the first stanza describes the illness brought by the witch and warns that the truth will be revealed. The second summons the sun, whose nine spirits are said to have made the ordeal, and tells the accused that she cannot escape and cannot refuse the ordeal. The third appeals to the *ipweemy* poison to gather its strength, states that the cause of calamities will be discovered, and warns the accused again that there is no escape.

During the recitation of the motto, the accused drinks three small saucers of poison, followed by one of plain water, called 'the cup of *Ngaan*' after a former god of the water in which the Bushong no longer believe.

Immediately afterwards the following dialogue occurs:

Q. (Officiant) 'Did you have any pains before taking the poison?'
A. (Accused) 'No.'
Q. 'Did you have trouble with your eyes?'
A. 'No.'
Q. 'And if it should happen that you tell us that your view is blurred, what should we think?'
A. 'Then judge me a witch, who will die.'
Q. 'Did your legs hurt?'
A. 'No.'

Q. 'So, if you start to totter?'
A. 'It will be the sign of my leaving the world.'

The questions ascertain that there will be no misunderstanding about the interpretation of the symptoms of poisoning. They test the resolve and the cooperation of the suspect.

In the next episode the accused is asked to assume a ritual name, and it is believed that this name will be a forecast of things to come. The same is done in rituals of enthronement for kings or high dignitaries. It is curious that the accused often seem to take ritual names implying their own guilt, and do not always seek to vindicate themselves at this stage. The same problem is raised in the history of European witchcraft. Why did some of them confess without any pressure? It seems that among the Bushong some people believe in their own witchcraft. Examples of ritual names actually adopted in the 1959 ordeals are the following:

'Thief of cassava leaves, never missed a chance' –
admission of guilt;
this accused died in the ordeal.

'Be friendly with the forest and receive a gift' –
denial of guilt;
this accused survived the ordeal.

'Boundaries of the village, you won't escape' –
admission of guilt;
the accused died.

'The bird with fine plumage rests away from the road' –
ambiguous, and outcome not recorded.

'The liar was the administration' –
(in forbidding ordeals)
admission of guilt; outcome of ordeal not recorded.

'Even if they oust me from the world, I won't be ousted
from the village of the dead' (witches do not go to the village
of the dead) – denial of guilt;
the accused survived.

'My mother, she tricked me into it' –
admission of guilt.

'I will go with my child' –
admission of guilt by the mother of the accused who adopted
the previous name.

Once she has taken her name, the accused abandons her funerary clothing to resume everyday dress. She then goes out into the bush followed by the people. She chooses a place to rest and waits. After a long time, at least some hours (Sheppard 1892: 122, says only ten minutes), one of two things may happen. The accused begins to groan, to totter, to make involuntary movements. The poison has worked and the suspect will die. Word is sent to the officiant who arrives, recites the full motto of the poison once more, and thereby quickens death. As has been seen, Sheppard relates that in fact the officiant suffocated the victim at this stage by jumping on her throat (1892: 2). This did not happen in 1959. In some of the reported cases, however, death does not come easily. The bystanders attribute this to the cunning of the witch, whose life-container cannot be found. They curse her: 'You, you don't want to die now. But it is going to rain, and we will go home. And if you don't die because of your complicated life-container, who will be willing to house you in our village?' In cases such as this a diviner is consulted and tries to discover the life-container. Sometimes the dying person will actually tell someone to bring it, so that she can die. One reported case told of a witch calling for her calabash of water. She started drinking and fell dead. The public concluded that the water was her life-container. In another case, the same day, a woman asked for her personal basket, opened it, and died. Something in the basket or in the opening of it was held to be her life-container.

Once the person is dead, her spouse and closest relatives fetch firewood and palm oil and burn her on the spot, making certain that all the bones are charred. This ensures that the witch will not go to the village of the dead but to the witches' abode, *Bikookatey*, from which there is no return. (Innocent people at death go to *Ilweem*, the village of the dead, and are born after a while.) The relatives who burn the witch seem to be those who normally would make funerary arrangements and participate in an ordinary burial.

The other possible course following the administration of the poison is that the suspect begins to vomit, vomits for several hours, and is saved. This does not mean yet that she is not a witch, for something like black bile should be brought up. Only innocent people have this in their bodies. If the bile is seen by witnesses, the suspect is cleared. Otherwise it will be assumed that the suspect is simply a clever witch, one who carries a miniature canoe in her oesophagus in which the poison is harmlessly collected. In this case anyone may ask that the suspect be tried again. However, even when the black bile is seen, the ritual is not concluded. The next morning at a given time the vindicated suspect and the officiant leave their houses and walk towards each other in the middle of the village square. The former suspect wears her finest dancing clothes and all her jewellery. The officiant holds a hollow iron gong, and the accused throws a cowrie into the gong 'to show the purity of her heart'. The Bushong believe that this is a third ordeal: if the suspect is really guilty she will die when throwing the cowrie into the gong. With this last act the suspect is reintegrated into the community. If she had been brought to trial by an accusation from someone in another lineage, the false accuser would now have to pay compensation of about four times the fee paid to the officiant. Or, alternatively, the lineage of the false accuser could choose to subject someone among themselves to the ordeal, an arrangement which is often made before the first trial even starts.

Finally, even in the pre-colonial past, an accused could refuse to drink the poison, although this would be tantamount to an admission of guilt. She would then not have been forced to take the public ordeal; but *ipweemy* poison would be secretly mixed in her palmwine. The whole ritual was then omitted; but its aim would be achieved if the suspect either died, or vomited her black bile.

As has been seen, the ritual of 1959 seems to have followed very closely what was described in 1892 and 1899. But from this time onward and during most of the colonial period, the ritual was in abeyance. It is thought that the last time that the poison was given with full ceremonial was about 1931. However, the oracular cutting and dropping of the bark was not given up and continued to be practised for another decade. Even the bark-cutting oracle ceased to be consulted in the 1940s. But before it too was suppressed, another punishment of witches convicted by it was practised. The witch was tied to a tree covered with *nkoom* ants, which caused great pain with their stings. By the 1940s the only remaining technique for controlling witches was the anti-witchcraft cult, the first of which arrived in 1933. These were never felt to be satisfactory, however, and it was said: 'The government is unjust. It rears witches, because it banned the ordeal. Since then, good harvests, successful hunting, and fishing have gone too.'

By 1952 a new cult, *Miko mi Yool* (Vansina 1959), coped with the problem as follows. The leaders would prepare a magical powder, one of the components of which was fine sand from a spring, which is a sacred place. The sand was supposed to be lethal. The powder was then slipped quietly into the food or drink of the suspect and, just before this, the formula already cited was used. Before this the dignitaries of the cult would go to the bush with a fowl, a new raphia cloth, and six francs. They 'talked' to the fowl, dug a shallow trench, killed the animal, and let its blood fall into the trench. If the blood flowed freely the culprit would be killed; if it coagulated, she was innocent. The 'talking' represents a prayer or a magical formula. The dead chicken was then brought back to the village and consumed communally by the members of the cult, and most, if not all, villagers, would be members. This particular innovation may have come from the Lulua or the Luba.

But apart from the cults (in which, anyway, not all believed), there remained the old method of slipping *ipweemy* poison into the food or the drink of the suspect. Two cases, dating from 1957, are well attested: in one, the son gave the poison to drink to his own mother; in the other, two brothers were involved. This traditional and more direct way of eliminating suspected witches shows that the anti-witchcraft cults are not the only alternative to the poison ordeal, and implies that they may have other functions than the conviction of witches. On the other hand, the development of various alternatives to the poison ordeal and its immediate revival on the eve of independence are relevant to the argument, relating the apparent spread of witch-craft fears to anomy, resulting from social change (Ward 1956; Goody 1957). It would seem likely that the ordeal acted as a check on witchcraft accusations and that its suppression led to an increase of these. Cultural continuity in these matters has been remarkable, despite the efforts of Europeans to root the customs out. This persistence must be attributed in part to the unceasing flow of gossip about witchcraft, and to accusations which could never be checked. These findings are highly relevant to the discussion of social change.

As a judicial act, it is clear that the ordeal is organized on regular lines. If the accusation comes from the village headman, the village council sitting as a moot decides it. If the accusation concerns only one person in one lineage, the lineage elder decides about it in exactly the same way as he would if a brawl had occurred within his lineage. Cases of murder or bloodshed are not tried at these levels but are normally reserved to the higher courts, which play no role here. This reflects the fact that witchcraft is considered to be a crime by individuals whose actions do not affect the political structure. When they do, they will use sorcery and sorcery will be tried mostly by the centralized courts at the sub-chiefdom or chiefdom level, although the village moot can also take up cases of this kind. Since witchcraft does not really concern the political structure *per se*, it can be handled within the framework of descent groups and residential groups. The following text illustrates the idea that witchcraft, as such, is not a matter for men. The story is told by a woman:

'There was a woman witch who always took her daughter's child with her when she went out to bewitch. As a result the child fell ill, and its mother consulted a diviner, who told her what was happening. Having heard this, the woman looked for a way to convince the men. But there was no way, until the child had died.'

This illustrates that the community run by the *men* will not pay attention to minor squabbles, especially among dependants, as long as public order is not really disturbed by a crime such as murder. Once this happens, though, action can be taken at the next level of the socio-political organization. This point was overlooked in my earlier publication (1965: 114).

The ordeal is primarily judicial, and this comes out in the myth relating to it. This explains that formerly in a mythical past it was invented by a man called 'Justice', and the first stage (the bark test) was used in all trials where no witnesses were available. Later on, it was restricted to cases of witchcraft only and developed into its full form. The elements in the ritual which stress its judicial nature are the behaviour of the suspect towards the officiant and the latter's chiefly regalia. The officiant receives palmwine as if he were a chief, is faced by a kneeling suspect while he himself sits on a large mat, as a chief would, and wears the eagle feathers, the bell, and the leopard-skin of a chief. Moreover, the fact that the suspect answers when called 'witch!' indicates that she is considered guilty until proved otherwise. I also suggest that the crowd which follows the suspect out into the bush is equivalent to the village moot, and that chiefly symbols are worn by the officiant in order to underline that this is no illegal lynching. It must also be stressed that apparently the poison ordeal was but one of several ordeals, since Sheppard (1892: 121) mentions a scalding-water test for thieves, and a red-pepper test for girls accused of misconduct, although the legal contexts in which these are administered are not made clear.

As a *rite de passage*, the symbolism of the ritual is transparently clear, almost every stage representing a step in the passage towards either vindication or death. First, in a series of acts identical with funerary ritual, the person is separated from the living. She enters a new indeterminate status when she is called 'witch'. From that moment on she is really in a social no-man's-land until the end. The ritual concludes with one of two rites ascribing a new status to the person involved. Either she is burned and thereby cut off from normal metempsychosis to be cast into the abode of known witches, or she is reintegrated by the cowrie-rite. This deceptively simple rite involves three of the most powerful Bushong symbols: the cowrie, representing wealth; the finery, representing status display; and the gong, representing political authority. It is difficult to make a definitive interpretation without direct fieldwork, but it may be surmised that here the finery represents the total status of the individual in her community, the status to which she is to be restored. The gong represents not only authority but the whole community. It is significant that the cowrie which shows 'purity of heart' has for its praise-name 'The cowrie of God'. What is clear is that through this act the person proclaims her innocence and is reintegrated into the community (see Vansina 1954: 903 for display and cowries).

Once the legal aspects and the changing status of the person are acknowledged in the ritual, there still remains an important residue, the appeal to the supernatural: both to supernatural beings such as nature spirits and God, and to supernatural forces in the power of the *ipweemy* poison. The poison must be accompanied by a formula, an oath, and a motto, as well as by graphic instruction if it is to work. These words relates its power to that of supernatural beings, as is the case with all Bushong fetishes.

Finally, the question may be raised whether this ritual has not also an element of sacrifice in which a life is given in atonement to be rid of evil. The notion of sacrifice certainly exists among the Bushong. When fetishes are made, fowls are sacrificed and, for specially powerful ones, people used to be killed. In 1892 a sheep or a goat was sacrificed every new moon at the capital, and its blood sprinkled over a wooden statue, as part of a wider ritual to preserve the power of the king and of the moon to renew fertility (Sheppard: 113). Formerly, criminals kept alive for this purpose, *nkukuun*, were sacrificed at the death of kings and of all members of the royal clan, at the enthronement of a king, and at the inauguration of the new capital. Another victim, called the *iyal*, of his own choice went into the tomb and was buried alive at the death of a king. At that moment too, the royal sculptor was also to be buried alive. Nevertheless, there is as far as I can ascertain, no special term in Bushong meaning 'to sacrifice'.

It appears that the Bushong culture recognizes several kinds of voluntary and involuntary deaths, secular and ritual, and it is interesting to consider the extent to which the death of a witch by poison ordeal belongs to the one or the other class. A suicide is a voluntary death. So also is a criminal who is condemned and then required to hang himself. Deaths following illness that have been attributed to natural causes are treated by Bushong as voluntarily accepted, and the funeral ceremonies begin before the person expires (Sheppard 1892: 135). Then there is the voluntary self-sacrifice of *iyal* at the death of a chief. The burial alive of the royal sculptor is more difficult to assess. By contrast, involuntary deaths, apart from victims of ordinary homicide, include two kinds of ritual killing: those who were killed to make a fetish powerful, and the *nkukuun* criminals who were killed at the death of kings.

In one respect, since they finally accept the ordeal and its outcome, witches are like the criminals who hang themselves after conviction. This case also resembles that of the criminals whose lives are sacrificed at the death of a king. There seems to be here a framework for interpreting the witch's ritual death as a parallel form of human sacrifice. A king's death is attributed to sorcery, and criminals are killed. When a lesser political dignitary, a *kôlm* dies, either sorcery or witchcraft may be assigned as cause, and a witch may be tried by ordeal. Thus, in the situation of death, the killing of a witch for a commoner is complementary to the killing of a criminal for the king. The criminal has committed an offence endangering the central political structure, the witch has offended at a lower level of political organization.

The idea of atonement may also be stressed. When a village moot decides on a general trial, it is clear that it wants to get rid of evil and its prayers are directed towards that aim. And the same applies even in cases where one person alone is singled out for trial, since it is then believed that she is the only source of evil in the community at that time. The fact that many suspects seem to be convinced that they are witches, even when we know that they cannot know, seems to indicate a readiness to atone for all. And the notion of atonement is not foreign to the Bushong, since we found it in several dreams of young and old people in 1953. Now, it is true that, in general, atonement has been seen as only one of the characteristics of sacrifice (Evans-Pritchard 1956: 248-86; Hubert & Mauss 1897-8), but is it not possible to have this one aspect dissociated from the others? And is not the essence of piacular sacrifice the substitution of a life to ward off calamities?

The tests used in the ordeal do not refer to the exchange of a life for the riddance of evil, even though this is implied. However, in other clearer sacrificial situations the Bushong do not have a terminology distinguishing between killing, dying, and immolating.

In conclusion, it may be stressed that the poison ordeal is a much more complex ritual than was anticipated before 1959. Perhaps the situation elsewhere in Central Africa is similar, and descriptions of the ordeals might throw comparative light on their special aspects?

The ordeal has many characteristics of the great Bushong rituals, such as those of initiation, death, the passing away of kings and their enthronement, in that it is a typical *rite de passage*, using many of the symbols and acts present in the other rituals. Its distinctive feature is that it is a legal institution. Other ordeals exist, but without much elaborate ritual, as a simple part of a court trial. An analysis of the meaning of the poison oracle symbols shows a quality *sui generis* in its relation to the supernatural. It is not only a dramatic ritual expressing some of the strongest and deepest of Bushong beliefs. Above all, as a grand gesture of atonement, it presents analogies with sacrifice, without being explicitly a sacrificial rite.

NOTES

1. I am very grateful to him for this information. Without it much of this aspect of Bushong life would have remained hidden from me.

2. Unfortunately, without the explanations of the images and symbols typical for mottoes, the stanzas cannot be understood in detail (see Vansina 1965: 104, for an example of a legal motto).

REFERENCES

Courrier d'Afrique 1960. Situation au Kasai: L'affaire d'empoisonnement à Mweka. Wednesday, 6 January, p. 4.

EVANS-PRITCHARD, E. 1965. *Nuer Religion*. Oxford: Clarendon Press.

GOODY, J. 1957. Anomie in Ashanti? *Africa*, 27: 356-63.

HUBERT, H. & MAUSS, M. 1897-8. Essai sur la nature et la fonction du sacrifice. *L'Année sociologique*, 2: 29-108.

JACOBS, J. & VANSINA, J. 1956. Nshoong atoot, het koninklijk epos der Bushoong. *Kongo Overzee*, 22 (1): 1-39.

SHEPPARD, W. H. n.d. *Presbyterian Pioneers in Congo* (the observations date from 1892). Richmond.

VANSINA, J. 1954. Les Valeurs culturelles des Bushong. *Zaïre*, 9: 899-910.

— 1956. Initiation Rituals of the Bushong. *Africa*, 25 (2): 138-53.

— 1959. Miko mi Yool, une association religieuse kuba. *Aequatoria*, 22 (2): 1-10; (3): 81-92.

— 1965. A Traditional Legal System: The Kuba. In Kuper, H. and Kuper, L., *African Law: Adaptation and Development*. Los Angles: pp. 97-119.

WARD, B. 1956. Some Observations on Religious Cults in Ashanti. *Africa*, 26: 47-61.

WHARTON, E. T. 1962. *Led in Triumph*. Nashville. (Diary of W. M. Morrison, 1899, on pp. 48-9).

John Middleton

Oracles and Divination among the Lugbara

In this short paper I wish to describe the oracles and modes of
divination employed by the Lugbara of Uganda.[1] I also discuss
some aspects of Lugbara notions and behaviour to do with sickness and its curing. I have written elsewhere about the roles of
oracle operators, diviners, and prophets among the Lugbara
(Middleton 1960a, 1963a, 1963b, 1965); here I devote most
space to an ethnographic description of these matters, which has
not appeared in print before.[2] A wider, comparative, discussion
must wait for a later opportunity. I call 'oracles' those instruments used by Lugbara to discover the identity of various
mystical powers that are thought to intervene in human affairs;
they consist of an actual physical apparatus of some kind or
other. I use the word 'divination' to refer to the activity of
diviners, persons to whom Lugbara attribute the ability to contact supra-human powers that can affect the living. In a more
conventional usage, divination refers also to the activity of
oracles, but in the analysis of Lugbara divination, in this wider
sense, I find it convenient to make the distinction, which reflects
that made by the Lugbara themselves.

The Lugbara of Uganda and the Congo are Sudanic-speaking
farmers, living in small local settlements at a high density of
population, which in much of the country is as high as two
hundred persons per square mile. Traditionally, they lacked
chiefs, and recognized only the authority of rainmakers, of influential and wise men, and of elders who are the heads of family
clusters. These clusters are the smallest distinct settlements,

and each is based on a three-to-five-generation patrilineage. These lineages are the smallest units in a segmentary system of lineages. They are grouped into what I refer to as minor lineages, each being the core of a territorial grouping, the minor section. These are grouped analogously into major lineages and major sections respectively. These are in turn grouped into sub-clans and sub-tribes, the latter being the jural communities of the Lugbara political system. Clans are dispersed and lack political significance. None of these units above the level of the family cluster have heads with any recognized political or other authority. Since the beginning of the century, chiefs have been appointed by the central governments of Uganda and the Congo, but they play a relatively small role in everyday lineage and neighbourhood affairs. There are also appointed headmen, but they have little judicial authority (Middleton 1958, 1960b).

The observer in Lugbaraland is soon aware that various notions about the mystical causes of good and bad fortune, and especially of sickness, play a large part in everyday life. The dead, witches and sorcerers, and Divine Spirit, which may affect mankind in many ways and in many forms, are important in the Lugbara scheme of things. There is a clear distinction made between the realm of ordered social life and that of unordered Spirit. The former is ideally under the control of men and usually within their knowledge; the latter is not. The Lugbara consider that ideally their realm of social order should not change. In fact, of course, it does change, but men say that this is not directly of their own doing but is the consequence of the actions of mystical powers associated in one way or another with the realm of Spirit (Middleton 1968). Men therefore continually find themselves wanting to contact this spiritual realm, in order to understand the forces from it that affect them. They do this by the consultation of oracles and diviners, and by the observation and analysis of omens and dreams. The consultation of oracles and diviners is the more common and is regarded as the more reliable method.

Before describing the nature of the oracles and diviners themselves, it is convenient to say a little about Lugbara notions of sickness, sin, and good and bad fortune. There is not the space here to list Lugbara sicknesses and their local cures. Both are numerous, and vary from one part of the country to another.

Some are epidemics that affect wide areas (cerebro-spinal meningitis, sleeping sickness, smallpox, and so on); these are dealt with by rainmakers. Others are newly introduced sicknesses such as venereal diseases; sufferers from these either go to a government or mission hospital, or do nothing – they cannot be cured by indigenous means. Others affect individual people in various ways, and these are classified by their believed moral causes and the agents thought to have sent them to the individual sufferers. There are three main categories of sickness of this third kind. One is regarded as the consequence of mystical action of the dead, who send it as a means of showing a person that he has sinned. Sin is regarded by the Lugbara as an action that threatens or destroys the orderly pattern and exercise of authority within a lineage or local group; it is typically part of a process that culminates in sacrifice to the dead. The second type of sickness is thought to be sent by Spirit or manifestations of Spirit to individuals, and lacks the association with sin. The third category also lacks the association with sin, and comprises various sudden and painful sicknesses believed to be caused by witchcraft or sorcery.

Except in the cases of epidemics or 'European' sicknesses, oracles or diviners are consulted to discover the identity of the mystical agents concerned which 'caused' the sickness, and the reparation to be made, either before or after the sick person has recovered. They are also sometimes consulted in order to know the future, but the revelation of the mystical process of sickness and sin is the more usual reason.

II

There are four types of oracle used today throughout Lugbara. I have heard of others, but they are now obsolete, and seem never to have been widely used at any time. It is convenient here to present a straightforward description of these four oracles.

I use the term 'oracle' to refer to various more or less mechanical objects manipulated in order to understand the nature of certain kinds of mystical powers. The generic term for oracle in Lugbara is *andrii*, and the word meaning to operate them is the verb *ndri*. The oracle-operator is *andrii ndripiri* (he who operates oracles). The two words are etymologically connected. The four common oracles are the rubbing-stick oracle (*acife*), the chicken oracle (*buro*), the boiling medicine oracle (*onda*), and the rat oracle (*gbagba* or *kumono*). To consult the rubbing-stick oracle is *ndri* only, but to consult the others is also known as *gba* (put) or *fa* (ask).

The general pattern of consultation is that the ritual guardian of the person who is sick consults the operator of a rubbing-stick. The statement of this oracle may be accepted as it stands, and if the status of the sick person is unimportant this is all that is done, the guardian doing what the operator tells him to bring the sickness to an end – this need not concern us here. But the client may confirm the rubbing-stick by going to another rubbing-stick operator; or he may confirm it by himself operating his own rubbing-stick if he is also himself an operator. Or he may confirm it by consulting some or all of the other oracles in turn, either making them himself or by asking well-known operators elsewhere to do this for him. In the last case he consults first the chicken oracle, then the boiling medicine oracle, and lastly the rat oracle. But he may omit one or even two of these, depending on the importance of the case.

At the consultation, at any oracle except the rat oracle, a number of possible suspected agents, both living and spiritual, is put to the oracle. This is usually done by the client's placing a row of small sticks in front of the operator, or by making certain marks in the ground, one for each suspect.

The rubbing-stick oracle consists of a small stick of sorghum, of the kinds known as *go'do* and *ejio* (the stalks of other millets and maize are not thought strong enough). It is usually about nine inches long. The stalk is held in the operator's left hand. He rubs it with the thumb and forefinger of the right hand, after moistening them with saliva, or he may hold a small twist of grass, moistened in the same way, and rub the stick with that. He interprets the statement of the oracle by the intensity of the squeaking noise so produced and by the way in which the stalk twists and bends in his left hand when his thumb and forefinger stick on the stalk, either by his own pressure or by the saliva becoming dry.

Lugbara say that the power of the rubbing-stick oracle itself (as of all the oracles) comes from Spirit the Creator (*Adroa 'ba o'bapiri*). The skill of the operator does not come specifically from Spirit. It is therefore known as *ondua* (skill) and not as *tali*, which refers specifically to mystical power or skill sent by Spirit to men (Middleton 1960a, ch. V). A man first starts to operate the rubbing-stick oracle after dreaming that he can do so. On awakening he will try, merely taking what seems to him a good piece of sorghum stalk for the purpose, and if after some days he seems to be successful people will consult him. The criterion of success is usually whether or not his stick's statements are consistently confirmed by other oracles. If he is unsuccessful he will soon stop trying. But even if people do not consult him he may still use his stick for his own private confirmation of the statements made by other men's oracles. The skill is often regarded as being hereditary, in a single line of descent only; that is, it passes to eldest sons alone.[3] With the skill may be inherited the actual rubbing-stick, until it becomes unusable through age, when the operator chooses a new one. There is no kind of ritual, initiation, or consecration of the oracle. When not in use, the stick is kept inside the operator's hut, placed with his other small personal possessions in the thatch of the roof.

Almost all operators are men. I have heard of women operators but have never met one. Most operators are also old men, both the elders of family clusters and non-elders. In particular, the younger half-brothers of elders, who cannot acquire prestige through lineage status, may do so by becoming operators. It is these men who tend to dream of operating the oracle; they cannot inherit it.

The chicken oracle consists of a shallow circular depression dug in the ground, usually a little way from the operator's own compound. It is usually about two feet across and six inches deep, and has notches or marks around its circumference to indicate the possible suspects. Small chickens are held down in the centre of the circle and their heads cut off with a knife by the operator. The way in which the bodies flutter about and finally come to rest determines the oracular statement. Sometimes the chickens are first tied to a small stake in the centre of the circle.

The boiling medicine oracle is more elaborate and consists of a number of small clay cups set in a circle in a depression in the ground, over a smouldering fire of sticks of *ali* wood, a species of *Acacia*. In the centre is a large cup with a handle. The operator takes 'medicine' which he has mixed himself, usually from small pieces of *laki* wood (*ziziphus mauritania*) which when put into water produce a foaming brown liquid. He pours this, by means of a snail shell, into the smaller cups, each of which represents a possible suspect. If the medicine in one cup boils over, that particular suspect is thereby shown to be innocent; but if it does not boil over he is shown to be responsible for the sickness in question. It should do this three times, and finally the central cup is used in the same way to confirm the statement.

There is little skill needed to make the chicken oracle, but the Lugbara say that a man needs such skill (*ondua*) to make the cups of boiling medicine oracle. Only a few men can make these cups.[4] A well-known operator told me that it took him at least an hour to make each cup, and that his skill lay solely in this: 'Other people fear this work; they have no skill and they cannot make this oracle.' He operated his own oracle for payment of one or two shillings. This was ostensibly not for his skill in operating it but because 'I stay in the heat of the fire and my body is dried up by the heat'.[5] He also made oracles for other people, for a few shillings, and would lend them his own cups for them to consult for themselves, 'because we are friends'. It is considered that the power of the oracle lies in the cups, but not in the operator or in the 'medicine' used. Some operators of this oracle are elders, some not, but they are always old men.

The rat oracle is simple, merely giving an affirmative or negative reply to a single question. It consists of a rat trap in the form of a board supported at one end by a stick, to which is attached bait, and weighted with stones. If a rat takes the bait the board falls and kills it. The trap is set in the evening: if on the following morning a male rat has been caught, the verdict is affirmative; if a female or no rat, the verdict is negative. Today, modern imported traps bought from Indian shops are often used, but the principle of operation is the same. This oracle stands a little apart from the others. It is in some ways regarded as the 'strongest' of them all. It is used only to confirm the statements of other oracles if they have consistently pointed out that a sickness comes from the patrilineal ghosts and if the sick person is important in status. However, I have known it used if the others have been confused, perhaps by witchcraft: 'If others have mixed their words, the rat oracle will follow the correct words.'

III

Lugbara also believe in the powers of diviners. By this term I refer to people who can communicate with forces outside the immediate world of men, their power to do so being given to them directly by Spirit or by their inheriting it from someone who did receive it directly. Inheritance is by men to their eldest sons, and by women to their eldest daughters. The means of original acquisition is by possession by the immanent aspect of Spirit (*Adro*), who dwells in bushland and near river beds (Middleton 1960a: ch. V; and 1968). Diviners are known as *ojou. Ojou* are also doctors or leeches, whom I describe in the following section.

The principal kind of diviner is the diviner with a divining gourd (*koyo* or *weke*). The diviner is *koyo yapiri* (he/she who shakes the divining gourd) or *weke zapiri* (he/she who shakes the divining gourd). The former term is used in northern Lugbara, the latter in southern Lugbara, and there may be other terms used elsewhere (Crazzolara 1960). There is no difference between the kinds of gourds, nor as far as I know between the methods of divination used. These diviners are usually women, although there are some men who divine and who are often also renowned rubbing-stick operators. Diviners are possessed by Spirit and also undergo a form of initiation before they practise.

Possession is by *Adro*, the immanent aspect of Spirit, or occasionally by the *Adroanzi* (the 'children of *Adro*') (Middleton 1960a: ch. V; and 1968). Poessession takes place in the bushland, where the person concerned 'wanders crazily' (*aciaci azaza*). I have seen this only once, when an adolescent girl ran away for several hours in the empty land away from the settlements. She had thrown away her pubic leaves and was naked; her father and brothers kept near her to see that she came to no harm, but did not approach her and waited for her to return of her own free will.[6] She did so after about five hours. An informant told me on another occasion:

'There is a girl here, and *Adro* can send her to walk in the bushland. If she walks every day in the wild land, then people follow her and watch over her all the time. Then her father thinks and says, "It is like this, indeed, now my daughter is sick", and he goes to a rubbing-stick oracle. The rubbing-stick says, "Take a ram, then call your people, then kill it on the threshold of the compound. When you do this, your brother and yourself, go there to call a diviner." When she is called . . . she begins to divine with her gourd. She says, "Spirit has entered the body of this girl, the girl wishes to become a diviner". When the diviner shakes her gourd, she calls Spirit which chased that girl into the bushland. Spirit is called and says "It was that girl who went to fetch water! I met her there", or perhaps she went near big trees. Spirit says "Well now, now I have returned you to the house of your father. I have left you. Stay, stay well here!" Then she starts the work of diviner and wanders in many places to obtain her wealth, the things she gets by divination.

'Who knows where that Spirit comes from? It cannot be seen if it comes here, it is like the wind. That *Adro yaya* [Spirit the shaker] follows a person in the wind and makes one tremble, it drives one into the bushland. It lives near water in big trees, and if that girl goes and sings or claps her hands it hears her and comes immediately. It catches men and women. It is evil, not a good thing. People fear diviners and Spirit very much.'

Before practising, a diviner must be initiated. This is the only example of formal initiation found in Lugbara. It is known as *'ba ojazu ojouru* (to turn a person diviner-like). Details of the initiation vary from one part to another, and also vary with the sex of the novice. There is no need here to present a long description; but in all cases there is a common pattern.

If the novice is a man, the four[7] elders the most closely related to him in the lineage system act as principals. They call a male diviner, who is paid (traditionally four baskets of millet, but today more usually two or three shillings), otherwise *Adro* will kill him. The elders slaughter a ram at the external lineage shrine of the novice's minimal lineage.[8] If the novice is a girl, only her parents attend and the diviner is also a woman; the rite is held in her compound rather than outside.

The elders bring certain stones and *olugbi* leaves, which are used only in ritual situations. The stones include a tall stone, about a foot in length, which is regarded as male, and a large flat stone, regarded as female and the male stone's 'wife'. There is also a small rounded pebble, about the size of a man's thumb, which represents the novice. The male and female stones may be taken from anywhere, but the novice stone (*lilia*) must come from a stream-bed, the haunt of *Adro*. I was told that the male and female stones represent the fact that Spirit the Creator first created a man and a woman at the beginning of the world from whom are descended all human beings: neither man nor woman can exist independently of the other. The stones are set besides the main stones of the external lineage shrine, with the leaves on top of them. Some of the meat of a sheep is placed over them. A piece of the intestine and some blood are placed in a leaf and rubbed by the diviner on the novice's sternum and insteps, the places where the soul is thought to leave the body. Later, more blood is poured over the threshold of the novice's hut and the sheepskin is placed over it. The novice comes out of the hut, stepping across the skin and returning into the hut four times. If the novice is a girl, she does this three times.

The stones are later placed on the verandah of the new diviner's chief wife, if the diviner is a man; if a woman, she puts them on her own verandah. The stones form a shrine, known as *Adrojo* (*Adro*-house). It consists of the stones covered by a 'house' of thatch set on the top of a small stick, or sometimes of a small inverted basket on the end of a stick.

The new diviner may not divine at all, but she will keep the shrine with her always. Usually a diviner will start to divine some time after her marriage, and especially at times when she is not having intercourse with her husband. But she will not practise much until after the menopause, or unless she proves to be barren. I have heard it said that a diviner who is married and who wishes to divine will refuse intercourse with her husband. In other words, a practising diviner has attributes of non-feminity, represented in terms of asexuality. Male diviners are typically very old men, and I have been told that younger diviners are either impotent or uninterested in women.[9]

Consultation with a diviner is a private, almost secret affair. It is made within the darkness of the diviner's hut or, if the diviner visits the client, in the latter's hut. There are occasions when a diviner practises in the open, but these are when the diviner is in contact with Spirit on behalf of the elders of a lineage, and typically at the external lineage shrines and so outside the compounds and cultivated fields. A similar procedure to that used for the consultation of oracles is followed if the diviner is being asked to divine the causes of sickness: that is, the client puts suggested causes and agents to the diviner, who replies in elliptical terms which the client interprets.

The essential difference between the behaviour of oracle-operators and of diviners is that the latter divine while in a state of possession by Spirit. They are mediums between Spirit and men. They induce possession by means of repetitive shaking of their divining-gourd, which is filled with seeds and used as a rattle; or they may do so by the chewing of *ojo* bulbs or the drinking of crushed bulbs in water or 'medicine'. *Ojo* is the term for several species of plants with bulbs and long fleshy leaves, the most common of which is a type of wild gladiolus which grows in most of the highland areas of Lugbara.[10] When possessed, the diviner utters the purported words of Spirit or other mystical agents, usually in a high falsetto, often interpersing the words with gibberish believed to represent other languages.

IV

There are other types of *ojou* who should rather be considered doctors or leeches. They are of many kinds, with many different names used from one part of the country to another. There is no need here to try to list all the variants. They all have in common that they remove sickness by removing physical objects from the patient's body: the sickness is thought to lie in the object.

They are of two main kinds – those who remove objects by sucking and those who do so by hand. The first kind is known as *ojou ojo nzupi 'ba ruari* (the doctor who sucks *ojo* bulb from people's bodies), *ojou ojo nzupiri* (the doctor who sucks out *ojo* bulb), *ojou ojo nzupi tilesiri* (the doctor who sucks out *ojo* bulb with his mouth), and many similar terms. He or she removes pieces of *ojo* bulb from the patient's body. This is to cure the sorcery sickness caused by the sorcerers known as *elojua*, who are thought to use medicine made from *ojo* bulbs (Middleton 1963a).

The other kind of doctor is the one who removes objects by hand, and is known as *ojou 'ba 'dupiri* (the doctor who draws out (things)), and by other terms. The objects removed are most commonly small pieces of granite and pieces of gristle and bad meat. The stones are said to represent the fireflies (*angarakadio*) that are sent by Spirit the Creator to enter the body of a man who breaks a promise, either one made to other people or merely an intention in one's own mind. The piece of meat or gristle represents the growing piece of placenta that a jealous wife is thought to place in the food of her co-wife's child: it is thought that the placenta grows inside the child's stomach until it kills him (this is a form of sorcery: see Middleton 1963a). Pieces of meat and gristle are also believed to grow inside the stomach of a man affected by the evil-eye, and are also removed by the *ojou 'ba 'dupiri*. Many doctors also practise a speciality in that they tend to produce particular objects such as pieces of wire or metal, small bugs and caterpillars, and so on: these take on the nature of individual trade-marks for particular doctors. But the same distinction is made between inanimate and animate objects.

A point that should be raised here is that of the relationship between diviners and doctors. Lugbara call them both by the same term, *ojou*, so there is an intimate similarity in at least certain essential aspects, despite the apparent differences in the work they perform. Lugbara say that the various skills of an *ojou* are mystical. Those doctors who are also diviners have the greatest mystical skill, *tali*, whereas a doctor who uses one method only is regarded as having merely the most minimal degree of *tali* and indeed is usually considered to have *ondua* a non-mystical skill. What they have in common is that in Lugbara thought both can deal with the consequences of immoral or amoral behaviour, rather than with sickness as such, which is essentially a sign of such behaviour. Doctors cure sicknesses sent by witches and sorcerers, but these are related to Spirit, to a power that lies outside the sphere of the social and the ordered universe (Middleton 1968).

V

As I have mentioned, all oracle-operators – or certainly the majority – are men. Most diviners and doctors are women; and, if men, are typically socially equated in this context with women. Oracle-operators are usually, although by no means invariably, the younger brothers of elders or other important men in lineage seniority. They are also very commonly *'ba rukuza* (men whose names are known). These latter are often themselves elders, but usually only become so after they have acquired the status of *'ba rukuza* and then become elders after lineage segmentation, which they bring about by one means or another so as to give themselves that status. The grounds for being known as *'ba rukuza* are several; but the most important are wisdom, the power to influence others (and especially men of lineages other than their own), and individually acquired wealth. One of the most obvious signs of the first two features is to be a well-known oracle-operator, and such a man can thereby acquire individual wealth. The same skill – in human rather than in spiritual terms – is needed for both statuses: the knowledge of local 'politics' and the ability to help resolve their problems, whether by giving oracular statements or acting as mediators.

In one area of north-central Lugbaraland in which I worked there were sixteen *'ba rukuza*, of whom eleven had been or were oracle-operators. This is an area with much overcrowding on the land, with consequent disputes between fellow lineage members, which are settled by the processes of ghostly and ancestral sickness. Since a man does not consult an oracle-operator closely related to him, we might expect this area to have an unusually high number of operators, and in fact this is so. Elsewhere, there are usually no more than two or three in any single sub-tribal area, and of these only one is likely to have a wide reputation.

The situation with regard to diviners and doctors is rather different. I can find no significance in the difference in distribution of male and female diviners, although female diviners are the more common. However, all diviners who divine with a gourd only and who do not also practise as doctors of one kind or another are women. There are usually about five such diviners in any single sub-tribe. The number of women who have been possessed and therefore have *adrojo* shrines is far larger, but I have no accurate information on this point. Diviners who are also doctors include more women than men, and doctors who do not divine are almost all men. In addition, more men doctors draw out objects by hand than by the mouth, and more women doctors use the mouth rather than the hand. The most significant point here is that possession and trance-like states induced by the consumption of *ojo* bulbs are mainly limited to women. Possession is essentially a feminine phenomenon (Middleton 1969).

VI

Lastly I come to a brief consideration of some of the principal differences in the roles of oracle-operators and diviners.

Oracles are consulted, in general, with regard only to sicknesses which are thought to have been sent by the dead in response to the commission of sin. I have described oracle consultation in the context of sin and sacrifice at length elsewhere (Middleton 1960a). Oracle consultation is essentially a jural process, even though there is no trial, adjudication, or legal sanction in the usual sense of those terms. By it blame for sinful offences, those that disrupt local and lineage authority, is allotted and the former pattern of authority redefined and strengthened. In the western part of Lugbaraland, near the boundary with the Logo, the word *andrii* includes not only the oracles mentioned above but also the poison oracle, known as *e'a*. *E'a* pods (which may include a form of strychnine) are placed on a heated tray, and the ways in which they jump about are interpreted. It is said that in former days the pods might be given to a believed offender to eat: his guilt was established if he died of the poison, but if he vomited he was innocent. This was given to persistently suspected witches and sorcerers, to suspected murderers, and perhaps to others. Details are today not easy to obtain, but it is clear that this was a judicial instrument and related in Lugbara thought to oracles.

Divination, on the other hand, is not part of a judicial process. Diviners do not mediate between human beings (including both living and dead) in the way that oracles do, rather they mediate between human beings and spiritual powers. It might be argued that diviners play a judicial role with respect to the identification of suspected witches and sorcerers. But it should be remembered that they do this only after oracles have shown that witchcraft or sorcery is responsible for a given sickness.

273

Diviners are, however, concerned with lineage segmentation and with the establishment of lineage shrines, as I have mentioned elsewhere (Middleton 1960a). But although the lineage is affected, these situations are concerned mainly with the intervention of Spirit into the affairs of living and dead men. Diviners are also intermediaries in situations in which Spirit more directly enters into the affairs of individual men and women (see Middleton 1968). In brief, diviners deal with the intervention of Spiritual power into the social sphere of authority, whereas oracles are concerned with the maintenance of relations of ordered authority within the lineage and the local community.

Diviners are, in an important sense, thus associated with situations of change in the patterns of lineage and other authority and stability. It is relevant here that Lugbara say that divination with a gourd is a comparatively recent phenomenon and that it was introduced by the famous prophet Rembe. Rembe was the leader of the *Yakan* cult, which flourished between 1895 and 1920. Rembe himself was in Lugbaraland for only a year or so. He induced trance, both in himself and in his followers, by the consumption of *ojo* bulb and by the use of a gourd-rattle He used the gourd when acting as medium between Spirit and men, and was regarded as having feminine characteristics. He may have been homosexual, but he was in any case given the feminine attributes associated with human intermediaries between the earthly and the spiritual world. There is no need to repeat here what I have written elsewhere (Middleton 1963b, 1968, 1969). All that need be said is that prophets are very similar in important ways to diviners.

The distinction between the similarity of oracles throughout Lugbaraland and the variation found in divinatory and curing techniques is striking. There may be other oracles found along the peripheral areas of the country – as the *e'a* oracle in the west – but I have never heard of them.[11] On the other hand, the local differences in forms, techniques, and names for diviners and doctors are very considerable.

It would seem that these differences are related to differences of function. Despite organizational differences from one area to another, the basic lineage structure is similar throughout the country, and all Lugbara hold similar notions as to the proper pattern and exercise of authority within the lineage. But the many and various situations of change that threaten or actually alter this universal pattern vary throughout the country in different areas and at different times. Similarly, the actual incidence and types of sickness and disease vary in space and time. These occurrences are seen by Lugbara as requiring leadership and skills whose power comes from outside the system of lineage authority. The practitioners are regarded as asocial vehicles of spiritual power. They are regarded as uncanny and dangerous, and are feared, and they express their intermediary and liminal status in their eccentric dress, ornament, hairstyles, speech, and so on. They are either women or attributed certainly womanly features. More accurately, since they are typically postmenopausal women, they are female but not women, as the latter are defined by Lugbara, by having the power of procreation.

I have described this notion of liminal sexuality and asexuality elsewhere (Middleton 1968): all that need be mentioned here is that such woman-like persons are regarded by Lugbara as being particularly able to move from the realm of social order to that of spiritual disorder, and back again, and to cope with the confusion between the two spheres in situations of social change.

NOTES

1. Fieldwork among the Lugbara was carried out from 1949 to 1952, with financial assistance from the Worshipful Company of Goldsmiths and the Colonial Social Science Research Council, London. The initial writing up was made possible by grants from the Wenner-Gren Foundation for Anthropological Research, New York, and the Alan Coltart Scholarship Fund, Exeter College, Oxford.

2. There is an account, with illustrations, by Ramponi (1937), but it is somewhat inaccurate.

3. The same is true of the inheritance of the mystical power of rainmaking. A rainmaker who lacks a son is succeeded, at any rate in Lugbara theory, by his sister's son rather than by another and more distant 'son' of his own lineage. But I do not know whether this is true of inheritance of oracular skill.

4. Men make oracle cups and the nozzles for smiths' bellows; but all other pottery objects are made by women.

5. Likewise the blacksmith in Lugbara is paid not for his skill in making spears, knives, and other objects, but rather for the discomfort of staying for so long in great heat.

6. This is the only situation I know in which a girl's father or brother would see her naked after infancy. It would normally give both the men and the girl great 'shame'.

7. Four is the number associated in Lugbara thought with male, three with female.

8. The external lineage shrine is set outside the compounds, in the bushland, and can be visited by elders only (see Middleton 1960a).

9. The one or two male diviners I knew were unmarried, which is rare. Lugbara do not have a specific term for homosexuality, but certainly one of these old men was reputed to commit acts of bestiality.

10. *Ojo* bulbs were used to induce trance-like states among the followers of the prophet Rembe in the *Yakan* cult (see Middleton 1963b, 1969).

11. The prophet Rembe is said to have used a Kakwa oracle in which strips of hide are thrown on the ground, but this is now obsolete in Lugbara. In any case Rembe (himself a Kakwa) was a diviner rather than an oracle-operator and this oracle may never have spread for this reason. It may also be that when he used this oracle he was in fact adjudicating disputes between followers in the *Yakan* cult, but I have no detailed information on this point.

REFERENCES

CRAZZOLARA, J. P. 1960. *A Study of the Logbara (Ma'di) Language: Grammar and Vocabulary.* London: Oxford University Press.

MIDDLETON, J. 1958. The Political System of the Lugbara of the Nile-Congo Divide. In J. Middleton and D. Tait (eds.), *Tribes without Rulers.* London: Routledge and Kegan Paul.

— 1960a. *Lugbara Religion: Ritual and Authority among an East African People.* London: Oxford University Press.

— 1960b. The Lugbara. In A. I. Richards (ed.), *East African Chiefs.* London: Faber.

— 1963a. Witchcraft and Sorcery in Lugbara. In J. Middleton and E. H. Winter (eds.), *Witchcraft and Sorcery in East Africa.* London: Routledge and Kegan Paul.

— 1963b. The Yakan or Allah Water Cult among the Lugbara. *Journal of the Royal Anthropological Institute,* 93 (1): 80-108.

— 1965. *The Lugbara of Uganda.* New York: Holt, Rinehart, and Winston.

— 1968. Some Categories of Dual Classification among the Lugbara of Uganda. *History of Religions,* 7 (3): 187-208.

— 1969. Spirit Possession among the Lugbara. In J. Beattie and J. Middleton (eds.), *Spirit-Mediumship in Africa*. London: Routledge and Kegan Paul.

RAMPONI, E. 1937. Religion and Divination of the Lugbara tribe of North-Uganda. *Anthropos* 32: (3-4) 571-94; (5-6): 849-74.

Michael Onwuejeogwu

The Cult of the *Bori* Spirits among the Hausa

Although, despite the impress of Islam, *Bori* spirits continue to play an important part in Hausa life, modern students of Northern Nigeria have shown less interest in them than earlier writers. This article seeks to bring these neglected spirits the attention they deserve and to shed new light on their relationship to Hausa social structure. It is based both on the existing literature (see References), and on the author's own personal observation of Hausa society, with the additional help of his Hausa friends.

Before we examine how the *Bori* cult operates, we must first outline the ecological and socio-political setting of the Hausa.

Most of Hausaland lies within the high plains of Northern Nigeria. These plains are broken by river valleys. The year is divided into wet and dry seasons. Between April and October the south-west wind blows far inland distributing its moisture northwards in diminishing quantity. This is the farming season, when population movement is least noticeable. Between October to May, the inter-tropical front moves southwards and the north-east wind blows from the Sahara distributing its dusty desiccating effects all over Hausaland. This is a period devoted to trading and creative activities. People move from rural to rural, rural to urban, urban to urban, and urban to rural areas, for various economic, social, political, and ritual reasons.

Violent thunderstorms occur at the beginning and the end of the rains. The annual death toll due to thunder and lightning is considerable. The power of thunder and lightning, storm and wind, features in *Bori* (Buchanan & Pugh, 1955: 14-37; Mary Smith 1954: 74-155; Ahmadu Bello 1962: 5).

279

Hausaland may be divided into the southern savanna and the northern semi-desert. Savanna is the climax vegetation characterized by continuous grass-cover, short and feathery in the north, but tall and coarse in the south. In such a habitat herbivorous and carnivorous animals coexist. Reptiles, birds, and insects of various species are common. This animal life figures prominently in Hausa cosmological beliefs.

The western Sudanic zone of Hausaland is noted for epidemics such as those of cerebro-spinal meningitis, relapsing fever, undulant fever, louse-borne typhus, smallpox. Other common ailments are eye disorders, sleeping sickness, leprosy, mental illness, heat exhaustion, and various skin diseases. An outbreak of cerebro-spinal meningitis in 1950-1 involved 100,000 people, with a record mortality of about 10,000. It is said that this epidemic tends to occur in cycles of from five to six years.

The mode of settlement in both urban and rural areas, the great wave of seasonal movements associated with the dry season, and the open landscape make the spread of epidemic diseases swift. The whole situation was particularly gloomy in the eighteenth and nineteenth centuries, when slave-raiding was rampant and the political and economic conditions of the Western Sudan were unhealthy for the peasantry.

The symptoms of the diseases mentioned have many common features such as sudden onset, rapid rise of temperature, headache, rigor, weakness, giddiness, nausea, vomiting, convulsions, and delirium. In some cases, as with relapsing fever, the patient recovers only to experience another attack after some days. These diseases are commonly attributed to *Bori* spirits, and the *Bori* dancers simulate their symptoms (see *Tables* 1-6, cols. 1 & 2, pp. 293-303).[1]

The Hausa are mostly agriculturalists, having a mixed economy based on both subsistence and cash-cropping. They have specialized craftsmen, and commerce is a highly valued means of acquiring wealth. All Hausa economic activities feature in *Bori*. I shall shortly illustrate how *Bori* is related to the acquisition of wealth and fortune (see *Tables* 1-6, cols. 1 & 2).

Turning from the ecological to the social setting, the Hausa of Northern Nigeria, as is well known, are organized in states. Before the advent of British rule, each state was politically autonomous, cooperating or warring with its neighbours. Each state had a capital surrounded by satellite walled towns and villages. By about the fourteenth century, most of these states had become Islamized, at least nominally. Complete Islamization was achieved after the Holy Wars of 1804–10. Since then, Islam has profoundly influenced their various institutions and style of life. The old pre-Islamic concepts of the world are now neatly interwoven with Muslim concepts, so much so that it is difficult to distinguish their respective strands very clearly.

The territorial organization is not only structurally hierarchical but also pyramidal; thus at the top is the state capital, then the districts and smaller communities, villages, wards, and compounds. The political organization is diversified, having traditionally a bureaucratic establishment of government, military, jural, and police functionaries. The state officials were traditionally arranged hierarchically: the Emir or *Sarki*, the district heads, the village chiefs, the ward heads, and the compound heads. Other subordinate state officials are similarly arranged according to rank and seniority, e.g. using the Habe ranking order: the Madawaki, Galadima, Dallatu Wombai, etc. (M. G. Smith 1960).

Before 1804, Habe kings ruled over Hausaland, but after 1804 the Fulani conquerors took over the control of government in most Hausa states. By the middle of the nineteenth century, Hausa society became highly stratified into three major classes: the hereditary ruling class of the Fulani-gida, the appointive ruling class dominated by Fulani, and the commoners who were mostly Habe. Later I shall show how the *Bori* spirits are similarly grouped into urban and rural dwellers and also arranged in hierarchies, and how each spirit behaves in a way proper to its class.

During the Habe period women were sometimes politically equal to men, for some were rulers and held political offices. They were also often economically independent, owning farms and employing themselves in various economic activities. One of the aftermaths of intensive Islamization was the rapid change in the status of women. According to the school of Islamic law followed, Hausa women must not hold political office; they are legal minors and their proper place is in the home. Thus women on becoming Muslims lost their pre-Islamic political, legal, and economic freedom. They could no longer hold state offices; they became dependent economically and legally on husband or kin. When married, they were secluded inside the compound. I shall show presently how the *Bori* cult is related to such problems of adolescence, marriage, women's aspirations, and male-dominance.

The Hausa live in compounds (*gida*), which are walled or fenced all round. The compound consists of two main parts: the outer and the inner (cf. M. G. Smith 1955: 17-18). Hausa married women are generally totally or partially secluded in the inner compound. Even if they are not, they behave as if they are. Apart from the husband, no person – except children, near kinsmen, and women – is allowed to go beyond the door of the inner compound. But the women have many ways of communicating with the outside world through institutionalized visits, domestic ceremonies and rituals, especially *Bori*, friendship and clientage, and, as a final resort, divorce. The *gida* is thus the centre of marriage and domestic activities. It is an important factor in child education and in *Bori* ritual.

Girls marry between the ages of 12 and 16 years and boys between the ages of 19 and 26. Unmarried Hausa women are looked upon as deviants, for marriage is the normal state of a woman; unmarried men are regarded as socially immature. The Hausa ideal is two wives. About 60 per cent of men are monogamous at any given time, but most will have two wives at one time or another. Divorce is frequent, and it is not uncommon to come across someone who has had a series of marriages (M. Smith 1954).

From the first day of marriage the husband and wife avoid one another in public. The wife is supposed to respect her husband and must not call him by his name. This avoidance relaxes with time. A husband provides his wife with food and labour, involving work outside the compound, if the wife is totally or partially secluded. A husband can chastise his wives if they are disobedient. Despite her seclusion, a woman is never fully incorporated into her husband's kin group. She continues to look to her own kin group for support and protection. And, although her earnings through trading and crafts are her own, she depends on her husband for most needs; this is particularly true if she is an unsuccessful trader or craftswoman.

Whether in seclusion or not, she can leave her husband's compound as a result of a quarrel and seek divorce. She may stay with her parents or report to the village chief or, more frequently, stay with a *Bori* cult leader (*Magajiya*) until a divorce is granted by the court. A girl's first marriage is always arranged for her; this generally ends in divorce and the girl remarries another man of her own choice. I shall show how *Bori* among Hausa teenage girls is connected with this matrimonial system.

The first wife is called the *Uwar-gida* – 'mother of the compound'. The others are called by their own names. The status *Uwar-gida* does not confer any privilege apart from respect, which may only be nominal. Wives cook for and sleep with their husband in strict rotation. Husbands are not expected to interfere in their wives' quarrels, except when these degenerate into actual fighting. The relationship between co-wives may range from non-interference in one another's business to open hostility. Cooperation between them is not uncommon. Co-wives call one another 'my jealous one' – *kiskiyata*. They even employ non-physical means to win the love of their husband or to eliminate the other from the compound. It will be seen later how *Bori*-possessed wives direct their *Bori* against their husband and co-wives.

Hausa kinship and non-kinship behaviour and sentiments embrace avoidance, shame, respect, discipline, obedience, fondness, cooperation and competition, jealousy, aggression, secrecy and open-mindedness. The Hausa child learns from his or her parents and immediate kin how to combine these behaviour patterns and sentiments in dealing with different categories of persons. As the child grows, these patterns and sentiments are ritually integrated and sanctioned. *Bori* spirits here again enter the picture, since they are believed to punish evil-doers by afflicting them with various maladies.

There is a great difference in the way boys and girls are trained. Since this is relevant to explaining the occurrence and frequency of *Bori* possession, I shall briefly examine each pattern.

The Hausa girl is trained from the outset to be highly domesticated. She helps her mother in performing most of the domestic work, sells things for her, and goes on simple errands. When hawking things for her mother, she is in the company of three or more girls of her own age. They attend dances together and go on market expeditions. (M. Smith 1954: 51-6, 61-2). But some upper-class and mallam parents, especially in the cities, keep their daughters in seclusion even before marriage and some send their daughters to Koran schools.

Hausa girls of all classes begin to wear clothes from a very early age. They are taught to exercise restraint in sexual matters and to be modest. But in the case of commoner girls no close check is kept on their activities, with the result that premarital sexual play is condoned. In either category of home, girls love display. Just as they learn to display their wares in the markets and streets and from compound to compound, so also they display their femininity at dances organized in the market and other public places. I shall illustrate later how this love of display on the part of women has influenced the development of *Bori*.

The dilemma of the Hausa girl lies, therefore, in the exercise of restraint and modesty imposed on her and the love of display and sexual freedom permitted by her culture. On marriage, women are abruptly cut off from their life of freedom and display and plunged into the seclusion of the compound. Thus at the climax of the elaborate marriage ceremony, when the bride is crying, her best girl-friend sings to the sound of drums: 'From this year you won't go dancing. . . . You will only dance in the path of the river.' Other girls answer: 'From your compound you'll hear our dancing, but you won't be able to come' (M. Smith 1954: 85-101).

Unlike his clothed sister, the Hausa boy goes about naked until after circumcision at the age of seven. He does no domestic work, but goes to a nearby Koran school. Outside the compound his life is that of a man. At school he learns how to recite and write the Koran; he takes part in ritual begging and all the work prescribed for a Koran scholar. At home he learns his father's trade or he may be apprenticed to a neighbour or relative. At adolescence he makes many friends among girls and competes with other boys in winning the favour of girls. This competition for the favours of the opposite sex continues into the early part of a man's married life. Later I shall illustrate how *Bori* display touches marital relationships.

Although Hausa girls are trained for life in the compound, while the boys are trained for life outside the compound, it seems evident that the boys are better adjusted than the girls. Of these, the upper-class girls and mallams' daughters, who are secluded from childhood, seem to be better adjusted than the commoner girls who have a dilemma to resolve.

This perhaps explains why there seems to be a higher incidence of *Bori* possession among lower-class than among upper-class girls, where seclusion is more stringent; and a higher frequency in females than in males.

THE BORI CULT

Masu Bori (Spirit Owners), or *Yan Bori* (Spirit Children), or *Dowakin Bori* (Horses of Spirits), as those possessed by *Bori* are called, form a loosely organized group. They have a meeting-house where the chief officials of the association live and where other members can rally for the possession rituals and rites.

The officials of the lodge vary, in both number and name, from state to state, but the head of the *Masu Bori* is generally a woman who is called *Magajiya*. In the past her appointment was sanctioned by the *Sarki* or the village chief. The name *Magajiya* is an obsolete political title once held by the *Sarki's* daughter. The *Magajiya* has some other female and male assistants. The male ones are usually messengers and apothecaries of the organization, while the female assistants help in the initiation of neophytes into the secrets and techniques of *Bori*. Details of the function and organization of the lodge are not fully known (see e.g. M. Smith 1954: 224; P. Harris 1930; Tremearne 1913, 1914; Leo Frobenius 1913).

To be possessed means to be mounted by a spirit. Thus the person mounted is regarded as a horse (*doki*) of the spirit, if male; and as a mare (*godiya*), if female. The spirit is believed to mount the head of the person through a miniature object called *tsere* (e.g. a bow), which most *Masu Bori* carry. The spirit rides the person and the person possessed is regarded as the spirit itself. The Hausa will say either that the spirit mounts the person or that the person mounts the spirit. This is because the spirit and the person are identical. In Hausa culture the horse is a noble animal and a symbol of aristocracy. The significance of the horse-complex in *Bori* will soon be apparent.

After the death of a *Bori* cult member, a meeting is held by the *Masu Bori*. The music appropriate to the spirit that mounted the deceased person is continually played to her children until

285

one of them becomes possessed. If this happens consecutively for three days to the same child, it is assumed that the child has inherited the parent's *Bori*.

Alternatively, if a person becomes ill, and, several attempts by the *Masu Bori* to effect a cure having failed, begins to exhibit hysterical tendencies, they will then decide to initiate the person as a *Bori* cult member. This initiation takes about seven days and involves drugging the initiate, teaching him *Bori* music, dancing, going into a trance, foretelling the future, and treating or prescribing remedies for diseases (Tremearne 1913, 1914; P. Harris 1930; M. Smith 1954: 164; Hassan 1962: 64-6).

In the past, before intensified Islamization, sacrifices were made at each stage of the initiation. Nowadays, alms are given as directed by the person possessed or by the *Magajiya*.

For purposes of analysis, two variants of the *Bori* dance must be distinguished. The *Borin jama'u*, i.e. the *Bori* staged in public for the public, and the *Borin gida*, i.e. the *Bori* staged by individuals in the compound for personal purposes. The only difference between them is that the former is more elaborate than the latter.

In the *Borin jama'u* all local *Masu Bori* attend the dance; even married ones may sneak out of the compound to attend. The musicians are males and consist of fiddlers, guitarists, and calabash-rattlers. Each spirit has a praise-song and its own music and special song. The musicians occupy one part of the arena with mats spread in front of them. From behind the musicians, the *Masu Bori* emerge, in turn, to dance.

In order to illustrate its dramatic and expressive character, I shall briefly describe a typical *Bori* dance. The woman puts on the colour appropriate to the spirit and in some cases carries the miniature symbolic object, bow or spear, etc., in her hand. She is now the spirit and acts as the spirit. If, for example, she is possessed by the spirit called Mallam Alhaji, she walks round bent and coughing weakly like an old learned mallam and reads an imaginary Koran. If she is possessed by Dan Galadima, the prince, she acts like a noble man wearing kingly robes. She sits on a mat hearing cases, and people around make obeisance. If she is possessed by Mai-gangaddi, 'the nodding one', who causes sleeping sickness, she dances and suddenly dozes off in the middle of some act and wakes up and sleeps again and wakes, etc. If possessed by Ja-ba-Fari, 'neither red nor white', a spirit that causes people to go mad, she eats filth and simulates copulation (see *Tables* 1-6). In some cases she leaps into the air and lands on her buttocks with feet astride – thrice. She falls exhausted and is covered with a cloth. During this state she may foretell the future. Spectators wishing to obtain a favour from or appease the spirit that has mounted her place their gifts and alms on the mat. Then she sneezes, the spirit quits her, and she becomes normal. During this period she is never referred to as herself but as the spirit.

Bori dances are held in times of national or communal crisis such as epidemics, the abandonment of an old town or the establishment of a new one, crop failure, lack of rain, when opening new and closing old markets, and on market days (M. Smith 1954: 218-22; M. G. Smith 1962).

In the *Borin gida*, staged by female individuals inside the compound, the participants are also members of *Masu Bori* but, because they are married and secluded, they may not take part in the public *Bori* cult or in Muslim public ritual.

A woman starts the event of possession by first screaming loudly. Immediately other *Bori* women living around hear the shrill cry, they proceed to the scene and in a matter of moments the inner compound is converted into a small *Bori* stage.

The women sing and beat calabashes turned upside down, while the originator and some others become possessed, each *Bori* dancing and acting according to the character of the spirit possessing her (*Tables* 1-6; cf. M. Smith 1954: 146-65, 229). *Borin gida* is correlated with the occurrence of crises in the marital life-cycle of the female occupants of the compound – marriage, death, illness, birth, ceremonials, quarrels, and divorce.

THE SPIRIT HIERARCHY

The Hausa believe that spirits live in a spirit world called *Jan gari* located somewhere unknown in the Hausa physical world. The spirits in *Tables* 1-6 are grouped according to Hausa categories and hierarchical arrangement:

(i) The Muslim spirits are called *Yan riga* – those who wear clothes. They are town-dwellers and their king is Mallam Alhaji.

MICHAEL ONWUEJEOGWU

(ii) The pagan spirits called *Babbaku* – black ones – are village-dwellers; some are farmers and others hunters. The chief is Mai-Ja-Ciki.

(iii) The warrior spirits are called *Yan Garki* – children of the shield. Their head is Garki Baba.

(iv) The youths are called *Samari*. Few of them are females. They are Muslims, like their parents (see (i) above). Their leader is Ba Gudu or Mai-Lema.

(v) The children of smallpox (a common epidemic in Hausaland) are called *Yayan zanzanna*. They are spirit children who cause smallpox and other skin diseases. They are divided into *Yam makaranta*, schoolchildren, and *Yan mata*, young girls.

(vi) The bush spirits called *Yan dowa* are spirits of wild-life such as the lion, *Zaki*, and spirits of groves, forests, and waters (cf. Tremearne 1914: chs. 21-8 and appendix 3; 1913: 530-40; M. Smith 1954).

Each community of spirits has its king and hierarchy of officials; even the leper spirit has political authority. The spirits neither die nor grow old. They live in a physical world of eternity subject only to a Higher Being, Allah, in a way not fully understood, except that Allah is the creator of all things. In their timeless world adults remain adults, youths remain youths, and children remain children.

The general attributes of the spirits are invisibility, agility, immortality, omniscience, and omnipotence, but not omnipresence. They are associated with wind and are also called *Iskoki* (the plural of *Iska*, Wind). Some Muslim Hausa identify some of the spirits with Muslim jinns. These spirits are not dead men's spirits and they have nothing to do with witchcraft. (Cf. Tremearne 1914: 19-24, 243-79; Greenberg 1941; M. Smith 1954: 22, 226, 227, 260-1.)

The spirits inflict illness on hidden and unknown evil-doers; they are the fountains of fortune and misfortune, wealth and poverty, happiness and sorrow. The characters of the individual spirits, as shown in their dance movements, are attributes of particular human beings – anger, envy, love, passion, sensuality, nobility, humility, restraint, illhealth, health, violence, etc. The spirits control the moral community by controlling the com-

288

munity's economic activities and its natural environment – epidemics, rainfall, storms, etc.

The *Bori* ritual mirrors Hausa social structure, and the social, moral, and natural orders.

Muslim Hausa and Pagan Hausa have an explicit and strong belief in the power of the spirits, even though some Muslim Hausa exhibit ambivalent attitudes. Ahmadu Bello in his autobiography shows how the belief in spirits influenced his childhood experiences when he writes: 'They believed that the bush, or certain parts of it, was haunted by spirits, most of them evil. We were frightened of them too, but more of the great wind-devils . . .' (Ahmadu Bello 1962: 5). Baba of Karo said: 'All the rulers like the *Bori* . . . all agree with them. So do the malams, secretly' (M. Smith 1954: 222).

Women are more susceptible than men to spirit possession. The spirits are beings of great force and the objects of attitudes of marked submissiveness and subservience on the part of those coming into contact with them. Husbands treat wives who are possessed with a deference and submission that are totally absent in their normal relations. Some men flee from the compound when their wives become possessed and are ready to meet their demands in order to calm them down. When possessed, women defy not only the domestic authority of their menfolk but also the political authorities (cf. M. Smith 1954: 223; Hassan 1962: 64-6). Spectators who are seeking health and prosperity from the spirit put questions about the future to the possessed women. The spirit reassures the supplicants and asks them in return to offer sacrifices or give away goods in alms. The spirit possessing a wife may demand that her husband gives away goods and money; and he, fearing the spirit and in danger of losing face in a society where prestige is based on the ability to give, must obey. By being constantly possessed in her compound, a woman can extort gifts from her husband. This will stir up the jealousy of her co-wives if she has any. If the co-wives are *Bori* themselves, they will react by performing their own *Bori* and making equal claims upon the husband. This is always a big economic embarrassment to husbands. If a wife is not a *Bori* and is unable to cope with this challenge she is likely to seek a divorce, accusing her husband of partiality and negligence. A non-*Bori* junior wife may prefer to stay and meet the challenge

289

by lining up with her husband against the senior *Bori* wife, realizing that the husband will in the long run be forced by circumstances to divorce the *Bori* wife. (I think this is similar to what Baba of Karo did.) Other non-Bori wives may meet the challenge by seeking ritual aid from other *Masu-Bori* or from a Muslim mallam (cf. M. Smith 1954: 164-5, 156, 223).

In the public *Bori* cult (*Borin jama'u*) men compete for the favour of the women attached to the *Bori* dancers or of some of the *Bori* women by giving out goods or money in their honour. Their wives at home, on hearing this, may leave the compound until their erring husbands make good their misbehaviour by giving them twice or more what they have given away to the *Bori* women (M. Smith 1954: 224-6).

The spirits of the *Bori* represent and symbolize Hausa values such as status, authority, political power, prosperity, and the pomp of public life. Since women are, by Hausa marital ideology, excluded from public life and from holding state offices, and since the compound is a physical barrier which helps to shape and intensify their psycho-sociological isolation, it appears that in *Bori* Hausa women experience in fantasy the trappings of officialdom. They experience the world of men, the world of political power, and the world of supposed splendour that society has denied them. *Bori* is therefore a mechanism through which women escape the seclusion of the inner compound and enjoy, at least in fantasy, the public life outside the compound. Thus it is a symbolic way of escape from the role of female to that of male.

Bori is also one of the mechanisms for expressing and suppressing rivalry between co-wives, and the strains and stresses between husband and wife. Wives manipulate *Bori* episodes in such a way as to reduce their husbands to social and economic straits. Hence *Bori* is not only a symbolic way but also a real way of defying the male dominance that pervades Hausa society. In *Bori*, women find an escape from a world dominated by men, and through *Bori* the world of females temporarily subdues and humiliates the world of men.

At present, men play a very significant role in *Bori* ritual and this may be because they take a very active part in Muslim male-dominated rituals. *Bori* is now a more female-dominated ritual so that participant males are regarded as sexual deviants (homosexuals) or as being impotent. But, nevertheless, renowned *Bori* men who are experts in medical and magical practices are respected and frequently consulted.

BORI AND SOCIAL CHANGE

Although we have little secure detailed knowledge of the early development of Hausa cosmological ideas, it seems that the entrenchment of Islam in Hausaland between the nineteenth and twentieth centuries, and especially after the Holy Wars of 1804, considerably affected the *Bori* cult. For if, as some of the evidence suggests, *Bori* formally occupied an important place in the main religious life of the people, the intensification of Islamic belief inevitably thrust it into a subsidiary position. At the same time, some syncretism seems to have occurred, leading to an increase in the actual number of spirits and the inclusion of some Muslim and Fulani elements. At the same time, while women, as we have seen, enjoyed a higher status prior to the Islamic conquest, now they were secluded in their compounds and lost the legal and economic power they had formerly possessed. In pre-Islamic days, divorce was easily obtained by them, but, under Islam, though men could easily divorce their wives, without difficulty, women enjoyed no such privilege. Indeed, the situation now is that, in order to escape from an irksome marriage, a wife has to run away from her husband's compound, taking refuge with a *Magajiya* (*Bori* cult leader). While waiting to gain a legal hearing for her case against her husband, the refugee wife takes advantage of the public displays which *Bori*-dancing affords. And if divorce is thus almost synonymous with *Bori*, these circumstances have stimulated a new pattern of courtly prostitution based on *Bori*. The *Magajiya* thus assumed a double role – at once local leader of the *Masu Bori*, and keeper of a brothel.

In the compound, the old ancestor cult declined and *Bori* spirits were relegated to the women's sphere, where they were manipulated in domestic rivalry. This development must almost certainly have been intensified by the rise in economic prosperity of Hausa men associated with the introduction of cash crops at the beginning of this century. In the period between 1910 and 1950, the heyday of British rule, the prestige and ritual status of *Bori* were further reduced by the ban imposed on it by the

Administration, by the new concepts of disease and cure introduced with modern medicine, by the new dynamism of Islam under British rule, and finally by the growth of a new class of salary-earners in the towns. Although in this process, in reaction to British rule and conquest, some European spirits were added to the *Bori* cosmology, their status in the hierarchy was never properly established. With the operation of these factors, as *Bori jama'u* was driven underground it manifested itself in a new pattern of prostitution in the urban areas while keeping its essential features in the rural areas. In the urban areas brothels increased in number, and *Bori* music and dance were employed for sex display and advertisement.

From 1950 to 1965, with the rise of nationalism, the development of political parties in Hausaland, and the re-definition of the concept of freedom and individualism, *Bori* again took a new trend. The *Magajiya* and her followers became the core organization of the women's wing of political parties and rallies. These women now use *Bori* dance and music not only to win more clients but also to win over members for the political parties they support. These women, under the leadership of the *Magajiya*, are mostly practising prostitutes, new divorcees, those waiting to be granted a divorce, runaway girls, and new girls from the rural areas seeking fortune and excitement in the urban areas. Thus *Borin jama'u*, which formerly had a strong ritual character, has become gradually secularized. In urban areas, the transformation from ritual to secular activity is almost complete, except in rare cases; but the *Bori* ritual continues in rural areas. *Borin gida* remains unaffected, but its frequency is decreasing more rapidly in town than in country.

Today, there is a dance called *goge*. The music and dance is *Bori*-like. Adolescent boys and girls and some older ones enjoy this dance just as Western European adolescents adore pop music, and the behaviour patterns and motives are similar. It is doubtful whether *Bori* spirits have any ritual significance in *goge*, even though dancers still simulate the movements of spirits in modified forms. Musa, a friend and a houseboy, once said to me: 'We go to *goge* to see women and enjoy ourselves'.

BORI SPIRITS

Table 1

MUSLIM SPIRITS

Yan Riga
(Urban Dwellers)

NAME OF SPIRIT	IDENTITY	MAIN MOVEMENTS IN DANCE	AILMENTS, etc.
Mallam Alhaji	King of Muslim spirits, learned	walks round, bends, coughing weakly, sits, counts beads, reading imaginary Koran	gives medicines for any ailments
Kuturu or Uban Dowaki	leper, or keeper of Jan Gari	pretends arms and legs are amputated, brushing away invisible flies from imaginary sores	gives drugs for various diseases; causes leprosy
Mallam Alkali	the learned judge	sits on mat, counting beads, hearing cases	prescribes medicines and charms
Nana Magajiya or Uwar Yara	mother of children	sits on mat, goes round, exhibits paroxysm of passion, etc.	gives children throat trouble and swollen body
Dan Galadima	a prince, son of the king	wears fine robes, walks round, pacing like a nobleman, sits and holds a court	gives fever, etc.
Mallam Dan Sangammi	a mallam	prays, acts as if fencing with sword	gives lumps and deformation
Sarkin Fushi	King of wrath	prays, beats shoulder and chest, rushes at a wall and falls	gives chest troubles
Mallam Duwatsu	mallam of rocks	prays, beats chest with stone	chest trouble and rapid breathing

Table 1 (continued)

NAME OF SPIRIT	IDENTITY	MAIN MOVEMENTS IN DANCE	AILMENTS, etc.
Sarkin Rafi	Chief of rivers, lakes, etc.	yells, jumps, and falls; rushes at a wall and falls; may jump into a well	gives illness caused by damp
Sarkin Makada	Chief of drummers	hops round, playing on his breast with right hand	causes cramps
Wanzami	barber, a judge	hears appeal cases; may shave Dan Galadima	gives baldness and shaving rashes, and causes slow healing after operation
Sarkin Fulani	Chief of Fulani	beats himself with whip, and looks after imaginary herds of cattle	—
Ba-Gobiri	man from Gobir	thrusts spears downwards on both sides, moves round, beats the ground	—
Son-Bawa	enslaver, desirer	pretends to be cutting down opponents with axe	nose-bleeding
Mai-Bulala	one with whip, whips children in school in Jan Gari	flogs his back with whip	makes victim scratch
Sarkin Makafi	Chief of blindness	goes about like a blind person, feeling way with a stick	causes blindness
Ba-Dakwuwa	great warrior, brother of Sarkin Rafi	at dance takes care of himself to attract human mistresses	illness caused by dampness
Mai-Dambace	a boxer, slave of prince	challenges imaginary rivals, goes through action of boxing	gives pains in arms

Table 1 (continued)

NAME OF SPIRIT	IDENTITY	MAIN MOVEMENTS IN DANCE	AILMENTS, etc.
Risana	one of wives of Kuri	moves arms, bites her hands, scratches, yells and jumps thrice	causes itch
Nana Durimi	Nana of Ficus	moves round waving a cloth	listlessness
Nana Tsamiya	Nana of Tamarind divorced wife of Wanzami	—	any illness

Table 2a

Babbaku

(Rural Dwellers)

FARMERS

NAME OF OF SPIRIT	IDENTITY	MAIN MOVEMENTS IN DANCE	AILMENTS, etc.
Mai-Ja-Ciki	crawler-snake	crawls and rolls body along the ground, raises head to look with his evil eyes	general paralysis
Kuri	Fulani, husband of Doguwa and Risana	jumps, hops, beats chest with wooden pestle	gives charm for all sports
Doguwa (with double personality)	the tall one	—	paralysis of limbs; eye sores, etc.
(i) Mai Inna	(i) lives in town, is part-wife of Sambo	(i) as Inna, lies on side, and rocks backwards and forwards	
(ii) Na Daji	(ii) lives in bush, is part-wife of Kuri	(ii) as Na Daji, sits up and pretends to milk	—
Sarkin Noma	Chief of spirit-farmers	walks round, gets drunk	any illness
Ba-Maguje	pagan Hausa	gets drunk and rolls about	causes drunkenness
Mai-gangaddi	nodding one	at dance suddenly dozes off in the middle of some act, wakes, spins, sleeps, wakes, etc.	sleeping sickness
Gajjimare	God of rains and storms – double gender	stands still, falls on back, rolls calling for water	paralysis, and victim cannot sit

296

NAME OF SPIRIT	IDENTITY	MAIN MOVEMENTS IN DANCE	AILMENTS etc.
Samayi	male	stands stiffly, fists clenched	rigors
Wuruwa	sister of Nana Arziki	acts as if settling a baby upon her back	stiff back
Marmarna	—	lies stiffly, calls for water	stiff back
Rako	male	shakes his head and sits down and nods	weakness and loss of power due to old age
Kumo	male	coughs and grunts as if old, sits down, bends over one side	distorts body

Table 2b

Babbaku
(Rural Dwellers)

HUNTERS

NAME OF SPIRIT	IDENTITY	MAIN MOVEMENTS IN DANCE	AILMENTS, etc.
Sarkin Bakka	Chief of the bow	shakes buttocks, jumps up and down, carries miniature bow and arrow looking for game	pricks his victims or drives them mad
Gajere Mai Dowa	dwarf of forest, son of Jigo	names different animals	—
Jigo	father of Gajere	sits and moves like an old man, hunts	shivering fits and fever
Dan Jigo	son of Jigo	breaks calabashes and pottery, etc.	shivering fits and fever
Mahalbiya	markswoman, daughter of Jigo	acts as Jigo	small sores
Jato	fallen mallam, afraid of death	wags buttocks	drives people mad
Ja-ba-fari	half Negro, half Arab; fallen mallam	eats filth, simulates copulation	drives people mad
Ruge	brother of Jato, fallen mallam	wags his buttocks	causes genital diseases
Ba-Toye	never burns	runs fast on ground like flame	burns people
Dundurusu	the blacksmith who works for Jan Gari	kneels and pretends to do iron-work	any illness, stiff and sore arms and hands

NAME OF SPIRIT	IDENTITY	MAIN MOVEMENTS IN DANCE	AILMENTS, etc.
Masaki	weaver	stands, sits; pretends to throw shuttle and weave	any illness, especially those of arms and legs
Sarkin Pawa	Chief of butchers of Jan Gari	pretends to cut throat, cries 'blood!'	—

Table 3

Yan Garki

NAME OF SPIRIT	IDENTITY	MAIN MOVEMENTS IN DANCE	AILMENTS, etc.
Garki Baba	great shield, a Gwari	waves spear with right hand, jumps	any illness
Auta	spirit of the war drums, very fierce	kneels, beats the ground with fists, breaks plates on his head	nervy and shaky
Ba-Absini	Asben spirits and warrior	moves about with spear and pretends to thrust enemies before him	—
Manzo Baba	the great messenger	breaks things	any illness
Manzo Karimi	little messenger, brother of Manzo Baba but they have quarrelled	shakes an imaginary spear in hand, gives alarm, pretends to stab himself	any illness
Mai-cibi	one with navel	places hand on stomach, rocks from side to side	gives large navels and pains
Buzu	slave to Ba-Absini, humble	dances with spear and shields, keeps beat with feet and jumps	—
Kuruma	deaf-mute	makes strange noises, quarrelsome, ridicules all other spirits	dumbness and deafness

Table 4

Samari

NAME OF SPIRIT	IDENTITY	MAIN MOVEMENTS IN DANCE	AILMENTS, etc.
Ba-Gudu	never runs	dances under a canopy, walks around waving spear	—
Zanamma	prevents sleep	walks aimlessly, drives away unfriendly spirits	sleeplessness
Yaura	gambler	walks round, sits down and pretends to gamble	good or bad fortune
Majajin Yauri	heir of Yaura	pulls self all over	makes girls' breasts irritate, and awakens sexual desire
Kaura	midwife	goes on hands and feet	helps pregnant women; incites adultery in men
Saidi	son of Dan Galadima	sits down	unknown ailments of children; seduces females
Ba-Jin-Ciwo	feeling ill	walks around in sickly way, groaning, then falls	sore ribs and internal pains
Ya Biyu and Kuwara	twin sister and brother, children of Dan Galadima by a concubine	both dance together	any illness
Haukaci	mad one	throws clothes roughly, acts like a mad one	lameness

301

Table 5

CHILDREN OF SMALLPOX

Yayan Zanzanna

NAME OF SPIRIT	IDENTITY	MAIN MOVEMENTS IN DANCE	AILMENTS, etc.
		SCHOLARS	
Essiyako	pretends to be warrior	moves round with a spear, sits down and claps his hands	sore eyes and smallpox
Almajiri	disciple	walks round begging, sits down and reads an imaginary Koran	sore eyes
Mai Nasara	the victorious	holds spear, and walks round, mimics some *Bori*	sore eyes, smallpox
Yayan Jidderi		repeats Koran loudly from a board	sore eyes, smallpox
		YOUNG GIRLS	
Meramu	a girl	appears with companions to dance, washes her clothes, spreads them to dry	sore eyes and colds
Nana Hassan	daughter of an Arab spirit	moves round clapping	anaemia and sore eyes
Nana Tsiwa	impertinent daughter of Ba Maguje	rolls on her buttocks side to side, beats stomach, stands and salutes	quarrels among children
Yar Kunama	daughter of scorpion	imitates scorpion movements with hand	pimples and boils
Kaikai	Itch, sister of Dan Galadima	sits down and scratches violently, disliked by boys	itching

Table 6

Yan Dowa

NAME OF SPIRIT	IDENTITY	MAIN MOVEMENTS IN DANCE	AILMENTS, etc.
Zaki	lion	moves on hands and knees, clawing the ground, etc.	invisible scratches
Kura	hyena (male)	moves on hands and knees, rushes at anything red	glandular swellings
Giwa	elephant	moves heavily on all-fours	makes body sore and heavy
Kare	dog	barks in company of Zaki and Kura	cough
Kadda	crocodile	swimming	—
Yan Kurumi	children of grove	walks about, smokes pipe	drunkenness
Yakoba	Chief of Bauchi, a cannibal	biting hands, looks for meat	putrefaction
Nana Arziki	Nana, the Fortune	walks round, claps, lets nose run, cries	paralyses leg
Biri	monkey	squats, climbs	gives lice, destroys crops
Angulu	vulture	squats, flaps arms like wings	causes body odour and makes people smell
Hankaka	white-breasted crow	squats, flaps arm and cries like crow	any illness
Kaguwa	crab		distorts victims' body

303

NOTE

1. *Tables 1-6* are based, with modifications, on material in Tremearne (1912, 1913, and 1914).

REFERENCES

AHMADU BELLO (SIR) 1962. *My Life*. Cambridge University Press.

BANERJEA & BHATTACHARVA, P. B. 1960. *A Hand-book of Tropical Diseases.*

BUCHANAN, K. M. & PUGH, J. C. 1955. *Land and People in Nigeria.* London: English Universities Press.

DRY, D. P. L. 1952. *The Place of Islam in Hausa Society.* (unpublished thesis, Oxford University).

— 1956. Social Development of the Hausa Child. 3rd Int. W. Afr. Conf. 1949.

DURKHEIM, E. 1926. *Elementary Forms of the Religious Life.* London: Allen & Unwin; Glencoe: The Free Press.

FORDE, D. 1934. *Habitat, Economy and Society.* London: Methuen.

— 1946. *Native Economies of Nigeria.* London: Faber.

— (ed.) 1954. *African Worlds.* London: Oxford University Press.

— 1958. The Context of Belief. Liverpool: Liverpool University Press.

FORTES, M. 1959. *Oedipus and Job in West African Religion.* Cambridge: Cambridge University Press.

FROBENIUS, L. 1913. *The Voice of Africa.* 2 vols. London: Hutchinson.

GREENBERG, J. H. 1941. Some Aspects of Negro Mohammedan Culture Contact among the Hausa. *American Anthropologist*, **43**.

— 1947. Islam and Clan Organization among the Hausa. *Southwestern Journal of Anthropology*, **3**.

HARRIS, P. G. 1930. Notes on Yauri (Sokoto Province), Nigeria. *Journal of the Royal Anthropological Institute*, **70**.

HASSAN & NA'IBI (trans.) 1962. *A Chronicle of Abuja.* Lagos.

HOGBEN, S. J. & KIRK-GREENE, A. H. 1966. *The Emirates of Northern Nigeria.* London: Oxford University Press.

MANSON-BAHR, P. H. (ed.) 1954. *Manson's Tropical Diseases.* Philadelphia: Williams & Wilkins; London: Cassell.

MINER, H. 1960. Culture Change under Pressure: A Hausa Case. *Human Organization*, **19** (3): 164-7.

PALMER, H. R. (ed.) 1908. Kano Chronicle. *Journal of the Royal Anthropological Institute,* **38**.
— 1928. *Kano Chronicle: Sudanese Memoirs,* Vol. III.
PROTHERO, R. M. 1958. *Migrant Labour from Sokoto Province.*
SMITH, M. 1954. *Baba of Karo.* London: Faber.
SMITH, M. G. 1955. *The Economy of Hausa Communities of Zaria.* London: H.M.S.O.
— 1960. *Government in Zazzau.* London: Oxford University Press.
— 1961. Kebbi and Hausa Stratification. *British Journal of Sociology,* **12**.
— 1962. Exchange and Marketing among the Hausa. In Bohannan P. and Dalton, G. (eds.), *Markets in Africa.* Evanston, Ill.: Northwestern University Press.
TREMEARNE, A. J. N. 1912. *The Tailed Hunters of Nigeria.* London: Seeley Service.
— 1913. *Hausa Superstitions and Customs.* London: Bale and Danielsson.
— 1914. *Ban of the Bori.*
TRIMINGHAM, J. S. 1959. *Islam in West Africa.* Oxford: Clarendon Press.
— 1962. *A History of Islam in West Africa.* London: Oxford University Press.
YELD, E. R. 1960. Islam and Social Stratification in N. Nigeria. *British Journal of Sociology,* **11**.
— 1961. A Study of the Social Position of Women in Kebbi (unpublished thesis, London University).

Farnham Rehfisch

Death, Dreams, and the Ancestors in Mambila Culture

In this article I outline some Mambila beliefs concerning death
and the afterworld and show how new tenets may be introduced
into the belief system.[1] I begin with a story, supposedly a true
one, told to me by a large number of informants including the
heroine of the tale. The event occurred shortly before my
arrival. However, having myself witnessed several occurrences
of the kind described, it is possible for me to vouch for the
accuracy of the description of some of the events, though of
course not of the 'dream'.

The Mambila, now in Southern Sardauna Province of
Northern Nigeria (then in Adamawa Province of the British
Cameroons), believe that the ancestors, both paternal and
maternal, are very much concerned with the behaviour of their
descendants. Infractions of important rules of conduct are
punished by illness and in some cases death. If a sick person
publicly confesses his or her evil doings, the ancestors are
satisfied and the patient will recover.

When I was in the Mambila village of Warwar in 1953 I
was told about a woman who, in late 1951 or early 1952, was
lying on her bed seriously ill. She was apparently in either a deep
sleep or a coma. In the hut with her was a large number of
persons both male and female. Some of these were her kinsfolk,
some affines, and others neighbours, including influential men.
Outside the house was a larger number of persons anxiously
awaiting the outcome of the sickness. Judging from like events
observed by myself, it is more than probable that some of those
present had come as far as fifteen or twenty miles for this
occasion. Most of the households in the village would be repre-

sented by at least one member. The audience would consist of approximately an equal number of men and women, with perhaps a slight preponderance of males. This is because many of the women residing in the immediate neighbourhood would be busy preparing food for the throng. Those present were not there as idle spectators; many played a role in attempting to cure the sick person.

Both men and women moved in and out of the hut of the sick woman quite freely, except when very secret rituals were being performed. Some of these were carried out by males, and women were prohibited from witnessing them on pain of being made seriously ill. Even the patient, if conscious, was obliged to shut her eyes or turn her back on these performances. A like prohibition was in force when women carried out their own special ritual, since men ran the risk of being made ill should they be witnesses. The aim of these rites was to propitiate the ancestors as well as to combat witchcraft. Attempts were also frequently made to obtain confessions of sins from the patient. People were constantly going up to the sickbed and pleading with her to make efforts to recall forgotten sins. People who had known her well tried hard to remind her of some breach of the rules that she might have forgotten. For example, her sister had accused her many years previously of the theft of an ornament. She now came and pleaded with her to confess. The sick woman insisted that she was not guilty, saying that if she were lying she would surely die. The sister, not entirely reassured, made a public proclamation that even if the woman had perpetrated the theft all was forgiven and the ancestors should not punish her. Other persons with whom the patient had had disputes in the past also came trying to elicit confessions. Should such not be forthcoming they would then publicly proclaim that all was forgiven and, at the same time, take an oath that they were not bewitching the sick person. The oath took the following form: if they were using witchcraft against the woman, they would immediately die and the patient be spared.

In spite of the efforts made, the condition of the woman steadily worsened and virtually all hope was abandoned when she went into either a coma or a very deep sleep. Life appeared to have left her and preparations were being made for her burial, when suddenly she began to stir. She opened her eyes and within

a very few moments she was fully awake and apparently recovered. Shortly afterwards she began to describe her adventures
which I shall call a 'dream', though the Mambila would firmly
resist any such interpretation and would argue that the events
recalled were in fact true.

She said that she had died and come back to life. The ancestors
had come to her and offered a choice morsel of chicken cooked in
palm-oil and highly spiced with red peppers. Who these
ancestors were is not certain, other than its being known that
they must have been her direct ascendants. Having accepted the
food, she died and was taken to the world of the shades. There
she found a village very similar to the one that she had left.
The Mambila believe that the shades live in villages much like
those of the living. Farms surround the settlement as is the case
here on earth. The sick woman, however, found some differences. The shades owned vast quantities of coloured cloth of
European manufacture, a commodity which had only recently
become desirable to the Mambila. There were many chickens to
be seen, far more than would be found in a village of the living
and they had one odd characteristic, namely that all were white.
The houses were all in an excellent state of repair and the
settlement looked extremely prosperous. She began to speak to
some of the ancestors, who asked her about her life on earth.
When she mentioned that she had left two small children
behind, one two years old and the other four, they became very
angry. They scolded her very severely for abandoning her offspring and they said that it was a mistake to have let her die.
The next thing she knew, she awoke on her bed.

The description of this event serves to illustrate a number of
Mambila beliefs and practices. I myself had the opportunity of
witnessing a number of like cases and the scenario was always
similar to the one described above. It is the duty of all kin and
friends of a stricken person to come as soon as they hear of his
or her illness. By so doing they may be able to help to effect a
cure, as indicated above, by reminding the patient of a sin,
which he may then confess. All having knowledge of a curative
ritual are expected to perform it. Those who have had or are
currently having a dispute with the stricken person should make
an appearance in order to swear on oath that it is not their
witchcraft which is causing the illness. In the case of the illness

of one very important man, I saw as many as two hundred people assembled in his compound. These came not only from the sick man's settlement but also from others and included both kin and friends.

The confession of sins, as has been mentioned already, is of the utmost importance. Ancestors punish those who have infringed the rules. Moreover, it is believed that witches are able to attack only those who have misbehaved. A blameless person or one who has confessed is immune from the malevolence of witches.

The purpose, then, of visiting the sick is far more than a matter of courtesy or an expression of solidarity in times of crisis. It is hoped that the act may help to effect a cure. If the ill person is well enough he is bombarded with questions about his past behaviour, with the aim of helping him to recall some infraction of the norms that he may have committed long ago and forgotten, but that none the less may be the cause of his present misfortune. Should his condition not allow of such lengthy questioning, friends and kin discuss the victim's past life among themselves, hoping to bring to mind a possible cause. When one is remembered, they wait until the patient can be approached and then ask him direct questions concerning the suspected cause. A confession may thus be elicited.

The Mambila believe that a person involved in a dispute is a prime target for witches. The assailant may be either the antagonist or a third person, who having heard of the misunderstanding, may utilize his evil powers and hope that he will avoid suspicion, the partner in the quarrel being the prime suspect. It is therefore important that all who have had or have antagonistic relations with the sick person should appear and swear that it is not their witchcraft which is causing the trouble. This oath not only protects them from accusations in the future but also is said to cancel the effect of unconscious witchcraft, if any.[2]

The 'dream' of the woman also illustrates certain commonly held beliefs concerning the afterworld. It is universally asserted that the dead live in villages like those on earth. None of my informants had any idea where these were to be found, though some guessed that they might be on the top of very high hills, others suggested the sky, while some stated that they might be underground. The location of these settlements is of no interest to the people at all, and my questioning did not elicit any curiosity. Some informants were annoyed, because it is said that the shades must be everywhere if they are to observe the behaviour of their descendants; hence an attempt to locate their villages in space might lead to contradictions. There are no fixed ideas as to how the villages of the dead are organized, or of their composition. The problem again is of no concern to the Mambila. This is consistent with the fact that both men and women often live in several settlements during their lifetime and have a wide range of choice available to them when choosing a place to settle (*vide* Rehfisch 1960: 255 ff.).

The life of the dead differs in some respects from that of the living. For example, witchcraft, illness, wickedness, and troubles of all kinds that so often plague the living are unknown among the shades. Food and the all-important beer are always plentiful, the farms yielding bumper crops without having to be cultivated. Access to the shades' village is open to all upon death, as the evil and the good all go to the same place. Death wipes away all evil: even witches, the most wicked of all, join the shades after their demise.

Death is believed to be caused by the ancestors. The process by which it occurs is by the acceptance of a morsel of finely cooked chicken, proffered usually by an ancestor in either line. Yet only those who have been bewitched are bound to accept the fatal food. Hence witchcraft is a contributory factor, and, as the Mambila, say, able to kill.

The heroine of our tale, when questioned, was unable to identify the shade who had offered her the piece of chicken. She insisted that it must be one of her ancestors, this being in conformity with the general view outlined above. It also conforms with the Mambila kinship system, which is multilineal. Within the society are kinship groups with corporate functions. All members trace descent from a common male ancestor or his sibling, but descent may be traced through males or females or both (*vide* Rehfisch 1960: 246 ff.). Ritual performed to propitiate the dead in this society is directed at all a person's ancestors, both known and unknown. No single individual or small group is specially selected, unless divination has shown that one or more specific ancestors are responsible for the particular troubles that the rites are expected to remedy.

When the sick woman reached the village of the shades she was met by a large group of her ancestors. Some she herself thought able to identify, for example, her father, who had died recently, her mother's brother, whom she had known well, having lived for some time in his compound, and finally her father's brother's son. The first two had been long-term residents of Warwar; the third was born there but had lived most of his life elsewhere. Since Mambila say that ancestors are very much concerned with the day-to-day behaviour of their descendants, it is surprising that in this case they were apparently unaware that the woman had left two small children behind. No one remarked on this point, and when I questioned them their only comment was that the ancestors were not doing their job properly. The ancestor's anger upon hearing that the woman had abandoned her offspring is not surprising, since one of the most seriously condemned actions in this society is negligence in respect of one's own children. A parent will himself neither severely punish a child nor beat him, though a neighbour or kinsman may do so. Ancestors are said to punish very severely a parent who beats his own child, whereas they are not concerned if others do so.

This case of a person dying and coming back to earth is not unique. I was told of several instances of this kind. For example, another woman was sent back when the shades discovered that she had left small children on earth. A middle-aged man was revived to look after his adolescent son. Finally, a very old man whose two adult sons were engaged in a very serious quarrel was brought back to life with orders to use his authority to settle the matter in an amicable fashion. I was unable to interview any of these persons but heard the stories in great detail.

The presence of only white chickens in the village of the shades in this case is puzzling. To the best of my knowledge, such a fact had never been previously reported. However, it elicited no surprise on the part of my informants. It might be mentioned here that for one important ceremony performed at the beginning of the New Year it is said to be desirable to sacrifice a pure white cock to the ancestors as a token of thanksgiving. However, on the one occasion when I was able to witness this ritual, a multi-coloured one with a few white spots was used. There were some pure white ones in the village at that time, but I was told that none belonged to the kin group which was responsible that year for providing the chicken. Apparently the colour of the fowl to be sacrificed is of no great importance. In other contexts white fowls are not especially valued. The favourite colour now is that of Rhode Island Reds, a breed imported by some missionaries, and this because of their much larger size than the local breed. The heroine, when asked whether she herself preferred white chickens, said that the colour was irrelevant, only size mattered. She could give no explanation as to why in the village of the shades only white chickens were to be found.

We now come to what is perhaps the most important aspect of the 'dream' inasmuch as it reflects most vividly the changing aspirations and needs among the Mambila. It was reported that the shades had vast stocks of European cloth. Until very recently the Mambila appear not to have desired imported cloth. The women wore no clothes at all, and the men had only loincloths spun and woven by themselves from locally grown cotton. According to my informants, it was only in the late 1940s that local people became interested in purchasing imported textiles. When I arrived in 1953 few had been able to buy cloth, but it was desired by all. Those who had achieved their ambition had for the most part bought only one length of cloth and this was reserved for festive occasions. It is not surprising therefore that it is at this point in time, that is when cloth had become desired by all, that the ancestors are reported to have great quantities of this commodity. All who described the 'dream' to me never failed to mention this part of it, while only a few remembered the white chickens.

The ancestors are said to dislike imported objects. During the performance of important rituals those involved are allowed to wear only cloth of native manufacture. On quite a number of occasions I saw persons stripping down to a loincloth before taking part in such rites. I was allowed to wear a bit more than this on such occasions, since it was said that my ancestors had no aversion to clothing. I asked why, since the ancestors themselves had stocks of imported textiles, did they not want their children to wear it. No answer was forthcoming, though it appears more than likely that sooner or later, as the use of cloth becomes more widespread, this ritual prohibition will disappear and the 'dream' may be used to sanction the change.

The kind of event described above is neither very common nor extremely rare. A number of such instances were reported to me as having occurred in the past. However, no other dreamer, as far as I was able to discover, did more than state what was already known in his description of the village of the shades. Here we had a few innovations, yet they were accepted by all. I heard no scepticism being voiced concerning the veracity of the report by any informant. The tale had been told to persons residing outside the village and was as readily accepted by them. The 'dreamer' gained no long-term prestige from the event. I was told that at the time she was for a very short period a focus of interest, and the subject of her 'dream' was much discussed. By the time that I had arrived many of the details had been forgotten by the majority, but the belief in respect to the textiles remained. It should be added here that this woman had neither previously nor since had any marked psychic experience.

In any society where the ancestors are said to be either the main supernatural beings or the only ones, it seems likely that there will be a conservative ethos. Cultural change may and will occur but slowly, unless a revolutionary change in the belief system such as mass conversion to Islam or Christianity were to take place. Psychic experiences of the type described above may act as catalysts in initiating minor changes. Dream experiences or other contact with the spirits have in other societies introduced more revolutionary changes with great speed as, for example, the Ghost Dance, Cargo Cults in Melanesia, and Prophetic Movements among the Nilotes of the Sudan. The 'dream' described above is of no major sociological significance since it led to no major changes in Mambila social structure or culture, but it may be of importance in the future since it shows the means whereby new ideas, values, and aspirations may be reconciled with the traditional belief system without shaking the foundations of that society.

NOTES

1. The research was carried out under the auspices of the Wenner-Gren Foundation and University College London. The author wishes to express his thanks to both.

2. Witches are usually, if not always, from the same village as the victim. I recorded about fifty cases of witchcraft accusations, and to the best of my recollection none crossed village boundaries.

REFERENCE

REHFISCH, F. 1960. The Dynamics of Multilineality on the Mambila Plateau. *Africa*, **30** (3).

PART V

Enigmas of the Past

Clifford J. Jolly and Peter J. Ucko

The Riddle of the Sphinx-monkey

INTRODUCTION

The identification of species of animals mentioned by classical writers is often hazardous, owing largely to the obscurity and ambiguity of early reports, and to faulty copying. This is particularly true of animals such as the African monkeys, which rarely came to the notice of the classical world. Where the possibility of accurate identification exists, this has generally been made by early scholars, especially the scholar-naturalists of the sixteenth and seventeenth centuries, such as Gesner, Ray, Aldrovandus, Tyson, and Linnaeus.

An apparent exception is the sphinx-monkey, which appears occasionally in the works of Greek and Roman authors, sometimes associated with, although distinct from, the Sphinx of myth and art. The present re-examination of the evidence was prompted by the discovery that the English naturalist Edward Topsel (1607: 14) gives, under the heading of 'sphinga or sphinx', an account which includes features highly characteristic of the gelada baboon, a large distinctive species of Old World monkey. This identification is the more remarkable since this species is generally thought to have been unknown to Western civilization until its disovery in the early nineteenth century (Rüppell 1835: 5-8).

ACCOUNTS OF THE SPHINX-MONKEY

Neither Herodotus (fifth and early fourth century B.C.) nor Aristotle (384–322 B.C.) mentions the sphinx in his work (Godley 1924; Thompson 1910), although both describe other monkeys, including the Barbary ape (*Macaca sylvana*), called

319

'simia', and the common baboon (*Papio* sp.), called 'cyno-cephalos'.

Agatharchides (*c.* 117 B.C.) a Greek who lived and travelled in Egypt and along the coasts of the Red Sea and Indian Ocean, has the following account of the sphinx-monkey (*De Mare Erythraeo* 50, 73; Latin translation by Müller 1882: 159; English translation original):

'Sphinges and baboons [*Papio*] and "garden-monkeys" [*Cepi*, un-identified] are sent to Alexandria from the country of the Troglo-dites and from Aethiopia. Moreover these sphinxes are very similar to those depicted by artists except that they are completely hairy and are mild and gentle in temperament. They are highly intelligent, and on this account may be taught any skill with very little training.'

The author then goes on to describe the baboon, which has the body of a man but the face of a beast, and the female of which carries its womb externally. The latter detail appears also in Aristotle and is clearly a reference to the sexual swelling of the female *Papio*. The cepus is said to have the face of a lion, the body of a leopard, and the stature of a gazelle, and to derive its name from its elegant colouration.

Another Greek traveller, Artemidorus of Ephesus (*c.* 102 B.C.), also mentions the presence of sphinxes in Aethiopia, and is referred to by later authors.

These two authorities are the chief sources on the sphinx-monkey for the geographers Diodorus Siculus (60-30 B.C.) and Strabo (60 B.C.-A.D. 21). The former paraphrases Agatharchides (*Histories* III, 35; Oldfather 1935: 181), adding nothing to the earlier account, while Strabo quotes Artemidorus of Ephesus as his authority on the monkeys of Aethiopia (*Geography* 16, 4, 16; Jones 1930: 337).

Pliny (A.D. 23-79) adds important original information to the earlier sources; much of it derived from the centurions sent by Nero to explore the upper Nile valley (Cary & Warmington 1929: 174-5). The following extracts are taken from the transla-tion by Bostock and Riley (1857) and the references to Pliny's Books are as cited in this translation.

Bk. VI, 34 (Bostock and Riley, p. 95):
'We then come to the town of Suche, the island of Daphnidis and the town of the Adulitae, a place founded by Egyptian runaway

slaves. This is the principal mart for the Trogloditae, as also for the people of Aethiopia: it is distant from Ptolomais five days' sail. To this place they bring ivory in large quantities, horns of rhinoceros, hides of hippopotamus, tortoiseshell, sphingiae and slaves.'

Bk. VI, 35 (Bostock & Riley, p. 100):
'They [the explorers of the Roman expedition] state also that . . . at another island called Articula, the animal known as the sphingion was first discovered by them, and after passing Tergedus, the cynocephalus.'

Bk. VIII, 30 (Bostock & Riley, p. 278):
'Aethiopia produces the lynx in abundance, and the sphinx, which has brown hair and two mammae on the breast, as well as many monstrous kinds of a similar nature;'

Bk. X, 93 (Bostock & Riley, p. 549):
'The sphingion and the satyr stow away food in the pouches of their cheeks, after which they take it out and eat it piece by piece; and thus they do for a day or an hour what the ant usually does for the whole year.'

Pomponius Mela (A.D. 43) probably had the same sources as Pliny and states (III: 9; Frick 1880: 75):

'There are most rapacious, multi-coloured beasts called lycaones [perhaps African hunting dogs, *Lycaon pictus*] and sphinges such as are imported to us.'

Two authors in the second century A.D. mention the sphinx. Artemidorus Daldianus of Ephesus, also a traveller, maintains (*Onirokritikon* II: 12; Pack 1963: 125; English translation original) that:

'Sphinxes, lynxes and cercopitheci (which have tails) and every other similar kind of animal should be classed together.'

Aelian (A.D. 170-235) states of India that (XVI, 15; Scholfield 1959: 277):

'in that land, for example, are the elephant, the parrot, the sphinx-ape and the satyrs, as they are called'.

Later writers of the classical period, such as Solinus (*c.* A.D. 200-300), rely upon Pliny for their information (Mommsen 1864: 128).

An original and most informative source of information on the sphinx-monkey is to be found in the writings of the early

Eastern Christian historian Philostorgius (A.D. 364-425), the more valuable because it is an eye-witness account. He states (*History of the Church* III, 11; Bidez 1913: 72; English translation original):

> 'The sphinx is a certain sort of monkey, I describe it from personal observation. Most of the body is hairy, as in other monkeys, but the chest up to the neck is bare. It has breasts like a woman, and low reddish protrusions, resembling millet-seeds, which surround the naked parts of the body; very prettily fitting in with the human-like flesh-colour in the middle. The face is somewhat round, rather like a woman's. Even the voice is similar to the human, except that it is not articulate, but is like meaningless mutterings uttered rapidly in rage or fear. When the voice becomes sharp it also becomes louder. This beast is extremely savage and wild, and is not easily tamed.'

This text did not come to the notice of the Western Empire until much later, for accounts continued generally to be based on the works of Pliny and his imitators. Thus Isidore of Seville (d. A.D. 640) copies Solinus word for word (XII, 2, 32).

The only medieval account of the sphinx-monkey to come to light appears in the writings of Albertus Magnus (1193-1264). He states (22, 120; Stadler 1920: 1413-14; English translation original):

> 'The mammonetus is a smaller animal than the simia [probably, *Macaca sylvana*] brown on the back and white on the underside, with a long and thickly-haired tail. Its neck is as thick as its head, and therefore it is collared around the hips and not around the neck. Its nose stands out from its face as in man, and is not in line with it as in the simia, and it is called by the Italians spinga. Also it fights with implacable hatred with the simia and, although it is not its equal in strength, it outdoes it in bravery. It comes from the East, but does well in our climate and is frequently seen. It has a round head and a face closer to that of a man than to the simia in appearance.'

In 1551 appeared another account of the sphinx-monkey. Gesner (p. 971) distinguishes carefully between the 'Sphinga fabulosa' and the sphinx-monkey, basing his description of the sphinx-monkey on Pliny, Strabo, Diodorus Siculus, Aelian, and Albertus Magnus, but not referring to the text by Philostorgius.

Another eye-witness account of the sphinx-monkey, by Pierius, was published in 1566 (English translation based on original, Camerarius (1602: 319-20), Molle (1621: 274-5), and Bargagli (1625: 78-9):

> 'Many different authors conclude that Pans, Satyrs, Apes and Cynocephali all belong to the same category of animal, but are nevertheless distinguishable. The *sphinxes* are bred among the Troglodites of Aethiopia, are similar to artistic representations, have black hair, have two teats on their chest and are similar to the mythical animal but somewhat fatter. They are readily tamed and quickly learn many skills and tricks. Albertus Magnus also classes the sphinx among the apes and describes them as noticeable for having two black spots on the jaw and long blackish tail. I myself have seen one of these animals, with smooth white pendulous breasts, when I was in Verona. A certain hawker called Gallus was leading her around. She had recently been brought from islands which were until then unknown. . . . The sphinx had a completely smooth chest, her face and ears were similar to human ones and her back was excessively hairy; dark, long and somewhat thick hair. Her master had his left arm bound with an iron chain to the sphinx and protected by an iron gauntlet. He held a stick in his right hand which he poked into the animal's face time and time again. This made the animal walk on two feet, jump up and down, and every now and then screech. For this the hawker received a good deal of money from the spectators.'

The only account of the sphinx-monkey written originally in English was that of Topsel (1607: 14). This is an interesting account for it is clearly based largely on Gesner's description but, unlike the account in Gesner, it also introduces some of the information recorded much earlier by Philostorgius. It seems likely that Topsel's knowledge of Philostorgius' writings was based on the works of Nicephorus Callistus (1256-1335), for he has a marginal annotation 'calisthius' (*sic*) beside the passage in question. On the other hand, it is clear that Philostorgius' work was already available in Gesner's time for it is referred to by Erasmus (1500-36), and it is therefore unclear why Gesner made no reference to this account of the sphinx-monkey.

Topsel writes as follows:

> 'The sphinx or sphinga is of the kinde of Apes, having his body rough like Apes, but his breast up to his neck, pilde and smooth without hair; the face is very round yet sharp and piked, having the breasts of women, and their favour or visage much like them. In that part of the body that is bare without haire, there is a certain red

thing rising in a round circle like Millet seed, which giveth grace and comliness to their colour, which in the middle part is humaine. Their voice is very like a mans but not articulate, sounding as if one did speak hastily with indignation or sorrows. Their hair brown or swarthy colour. They are bred in India and Ethyopia. In the promontary of farthest Arabia neere Dira, are Sphinges and certain Lyons called Formicae, so likewise they are to be found amongest the Trogladitae. As the Babouns and Cynocephals are more wilde than other Apes, so the Satyres and Sphinges are more meek and gentle, for they are not so wilde that they will not be tamed, nor yet so tame but they will revenge their own harms: as appeared by that which was slayne in a publike spectacle amonge the Thebanes. They carrye their meat in the storehouses of their own chaps or cheeks, taking it forth when they are hungry, and so eat it: not being like the Formicae, for that which is annual in them, is daily and hourly amongest these.'

Topsel is the only author to include a picture of the sphinx-monkey in his account (*Plate* 1). This is an ingenious construction, but is clearly not the work of someone who had himself seen a sphinx-monkey.

Aldrovandus (1645: 244), evidently following Albertus Magnus, included 'spinga' as a synonym of 'cercopithecus'. Tyson (1699: 56-8) reconsidered many of the literary sources which mentioned the sphinx and concluded that it was a real monkey or ape. Linnaeus (1766: 35) used *Sphinx* as a generic term for moth, and as a trivial name for the 'Papio' of Gesner (the mandrill). Zoologists after Topsel excluded the sphinx-monkey from lists of real animals and Topsel's account and illustration of the sphinx-monkey died the immediate death of neglect.

On the other hand, modern classicists have attempted to identify the sphinx-monkey.

Keller (1887: 13-14) concludes that the sphinx-monkey mentioned by several classical authors was a *Cercopithecus*. Annotations both of Strabo and of Diodorus Siculus identify the sphinx-monkey as the large baboon, *Papio sphinx* (Jones 1930: 337; Oldfather 1935: 181). This identification is probably based on Linnaeus, whose use of *Simia sphinx* is, as already noted, based on Gesner's *Papio* and unconnected with the classical sphinx-monkey. Gesner's *Papio*, the mandrill, is a West African species of the equatorial forest and is most unlikely to have been known to the classical world. The same objection rules out

1 The 'sphinx-monkey' featured in an early
seventeenth-century work by Topsel

2 A 'sphingia' on the Palestrina mosaic of the second century A.D.

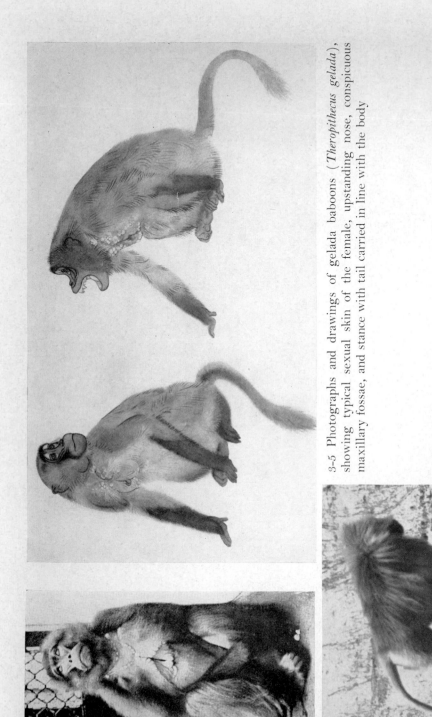

3-5 Photographs and drawings of gelada baboons (*Theropithecus gelada*), showing typical sexual skin of the female, upstanding nose, conspicuous maxillary fossae, and stance with tail carried in line with the body

Stadler's (1887: 1645) identification of Albertus Magnus' spinga as *Cercopithecus diana* Erxleben.

Falconer (1903-12: ch. 4, footnote 1) identifies Strabo's sphinx as the ape *Simia troglodytes*, and Pliny's use of the word sphinx is likewise annotated as the chimpanzee (Bostock, in Bostock & Riley 1855-7: 279). However, not only is the chimpanzee not found in the Nile valley but it has no cheek pouches (which are described by Pliny). Rackham (1940: 52, footnote e) is more cautious and states in his annotation of Pliny (Bk. VIII, 30) that the 'sphingion' is unidentified.

Of the classical dictionaries, only Lewis and Short (1951) venture to identify the animal more closely than 'a kind of ape, living in Ethiopia'; they say that Pliny's sphinx is perhaps the chimpanzee, while the sphingion is 'perhaps the dog-headed ape, *Simia cynocephalus* Linn.', that is *Papio*. As has been seen the first identification cannot be accepted, while the second is most unlikely (see below).

MacDermott (1938: 68) suggests that the sphinx-monkey was a species of guenon (*Cercopithecus*). This identification appears to rest solely on the evidence of the habitat of the species and the possession of cheek pouches but, in fact, the latter are common to all species of the *Cercopithecinae*.

ARCHAEOLOGICAL EVIDENCE FOR THE SPHINX-MONKEY

The single archaeological source of information on the sphinx-monkey is the Palestrina mosaic, which is generally thought to date from the second century A.D. (described and figured by Schmidt 1929; Gullini 1956; Kaibel & Lebegve 1890: 351). This mosaic includes several scenes of hunting on foot and by boat and shows many different birds and mammals, some fanciful and others clearly identifiable. The critical panel of this mosaic shows a hunting-scene in mountainous country. Many of the animals represented are labelled in Greek; next to the word 'sphingia' is shown a medium-sized, maned, brown animal with quadrupedal stance (*Plate 2*; cf. *Plate 5*).

RECONSIDERATION OF THE EVIDENCE

All of the authors cited above distinguish clearly between the sphinx-monkey and the mythical creature of legend and art.

Leaving aside for the present the works of Albertus Magnus, assuming that all the authors from Agatharchides to Topsel were in fact describing the same animal, and accepting that this same animal was the one represented on the Palestrina mosaic, certain of the characteristics of this animal and its provenance become clear.

Aelian states that the home of the sphinx-monkey was India but he mentions no new authority or evidence for this view. Pierius claimed that the sphinx-monkey had been brought from hitherto unknown islands, but Camerarius (IV, 12) who recorded Pierius' statements, himself wondered 'that neither the Portuguese nor the Spaniards nor anyone else that had sailed by so many countries and islands of India and Libya, which had not been known before, had made any mention of the islands of the Satyrs nor of the islands of the Sphinxes'. Camerarius himself favoured the deserts of North Africa (Libya) as the home of the sphinx-monkey, but beyond adage produces no fresh evidence for this view.

All the remaining ancient authors agree that the sphinx-monkey came from Aethiopia. However, this area cannot be directly equated with the modern state of Ethiopia; its original meaning was that part of Africa lying to the south of the Egyptian kingdoms and inhabited by dark-skinned peoples (Lewis & Short 1951). In this sense it would correspond to modern Sudan, Ethiopia, and parts of Somalia. Later usage of the term extended the region to include also other parts of Africa: the Saharan oases and the Atlantic coast. Agatharchides almost certainly meant Aethiopia in its original sense when talking of the habitat of the sphinx-monkey, since the region of the Red Sea and neighbouring parts of the Indian Ocean coast of Africa, as well as Egypt, are known to have been the field of his explorations, and he speaks of the importation of the animal into Alexandria. There is no direct evidence as to the exact part of Africa intended by the first Artemidorus. Strabo places Artemidorus' account of the animals of Aethiopia immediately after a list of place-names evidently derived from the account of the voyage of Hanno the Carthaginian (Müller 1882). Since all these are said to lie beyond the Pillars of Hercules, they are generally considered to be situated on the west coast of Africa (Cary & Warmington 1929). There is no mention of sphinxes in the account of Hanno's voyage, as it has been preserved. Gesner's and Topsel's localities for the sphinx appear to have been derived from the same source, and why they should choose to locate them in Arabia is not clear. Nor does Strabo's arrangement imply that the sphinx came from these particular localities in Aethiopia; he is merely listing all information available about non-Mediterranean Africa. It should also be borne in mind that at this time the circumference of Africa was believed by many to be small, and that the Pillars were therefore situated close to the southern end of the Red Sea; under these circumstances Strabo's arrangement would not appear odd. Pliny mentions that sphinxes were exported from the town of Adulitae; this has been identified as Azull, a town on the Red Sea coast at about 15°35' N. (Bostock & Riley 1855-7: 95) and as a site close to modern Massawa, 15°37' N., 39°29' E. (Cary & Warmington 1929: 167). The fact that the Roman centurions are said to have operated in the Nile valley, perhaps penetrating as far south as the Sudd (Cary & Warmington 1929: 174-5, notes), further supports the thesis that the home of the sphinx-monkey was in this general region.

The black skins of the hunters in the Palestrina mosaic, the species of the identifiable animals represented, and the mountainous nature of the country represented, all indicate that the scene is set in Africa, more specifically in the Ethiopian highlands (Schmidt 1929). Other scenes recorded on the Palestrina mosaic are almost certainly situated on, or near, the Nile.

The evidence for the provenance of the sphinx-monkey is, therefore, fairly consistent and suggests that it was situated somewhere in that part of Africa which is now Sudan and Ethiopia.

The habit, first mentioned by Pliny, of storing food in cheek-pouches, identifies the sphinx-monkey as a member of the sub-family *Cercopithecinae*, since they alone of the primates possess such structures, and rules out immediately all the great apes, the gibbon, and the *Colobus* and langur monkeys.

Five species of *Cercopithecinae* now inhabit the area thought to have contained the home of the sphinx-monkey: two species of *Papio* or common baboon (*Papio anubis* and *P. hamadryas*), the vervet (*Cercopithecus aethiops*), the patas or hussar monkey (*Erythrocebus patas*), and the gelada baboon (*Theropithecus gelada*). The two species of *Papio* are widespread in the region, *P. anubis* inhabiting the forests and savannas of Sudan and western Ethiopia, *P. hamadryas* the drier country to the east. Both extend to about 18°N. in this region. *Cercopithecus aethiops* is confined to open forests and wooded savannas, extending from the south into Abyssinia (Starck & Frick 1958: 64; Dandelot 1959). The patas is an animal of open country and semi-desert, found across the whole of the sub-Saharan zone (Tappen 1960: 102). The gelada baboon is confined to high mountain-tops in Ethiopia (Vram 1923: 210; Tappen 1960: 105).

Both species of *Papio* can be eliminated as the sphinx-monkey on several grounds. First, *Papio* (especially *P. hamadryas*, but also *P. anubis*) was well known to classical writers as a sacred animal of ancient Egypt and was always called 'cynocephalus' Second, the animal shown on the Palestrina mosaic is unlikely to have been a *Papio*, for these baboons carry their tails in a characteristic curve (called the 'riding-whip position') which was accurately represented by ancient artists, while the Palestrina animal has the tail held more or less in a line with the body. Third, *Papio* has no structure which could have been the basis for Philostorgius' account of the breast-patch of the sphinx-monkey. Fourth, Roman explorers are said to have discovered both *Papio*-baboons and the sphinx-monkey, so that these are therefore unlikely to have been the same animal.

Neither *Cercopithecus aethiops* nor *Erythrocebus patas* has a breast-patch; neither animal is maned as shown in the Palestrina mosaic; neither can be accurately described as 'brown' or 'shaggy'.

The gelada baboon, however, is closely similar to the descriptions of the sphinx-monkey. Its habitat is the mountainous part of Ethiopia. Its general colour is brown, its hair is long and shaggy, forming a mane over the foreparts in both the male and the female. It carries its long tail more or less in line with its body. One of its most distinctive features is the patch of naked flesh-coloured skin on the chest which extends in both sexes up to the throat. The female gelada has rows of wartlike excrescences around this patch which vary in prominence according to the stage of its sexual cycle (Matthews 1956). The appearance of this animal (see *Plates* 3, 4, and 5) agrees very closely with the description by Philostorgius and Pierius. Although two pectoral mammae occur in all higher primates, they are especially noticeable on the gelada baboon, for in this species the mammae not only are naked but are thrown into relief by a surrounding patch of light-coloured hair and a median cleft along the line of the sternum. Another distinctive feature of the gelada baboon is the possession, in both sexes, of a pair of deep and conspicuous maxillary fossae, which may well be the origin of Pierius' allusion to black spots on the jaw of the sphinx (see *Plate 3*). Finally, one of the vocalizations of the gelada baboon is a distinctive murmuring, quite unlike the grunts and screeches of other Cercopithecine species, which is excellently described in the accounts of Philostorgius and Topsel.

If the sphinx-monkey of the classical authors was in fact the gelada baboon, then the mammonetus of Albertus Magnus (which he says was called 'spinga' by the Italians) cannot be the same species. It is unlike the gelada baboon in having a white underside, and in being smaller than the Barbary ape (*Macaca sylvana*), and both these features suggest that the description by Albertus referred to a *Cercopithecus* – probably, since its hardiness in captivity is remarked upon, the vervet (*C. aethiops*). However, the description of the animal's nose cannot apply to the *Cercopithecus* – this has the normal flat nose of a monkey. This part of Albertus Magnus' description could fit the gelada baboon, which has a peculiar upstanding nose (see *Plate 4*), for the only other monkeys with such conspicuous noses are the *Nasalis larvatus* and *Rhinopithecus roxellanae*. Both these have far-eastern distributions, are notoriously difficult to keep in captivity, and are extremely unlikely to have reached or survived in classical or medieval Europe. Probably Gesner was correct in suggesting that Albertus Magnus was wrong to equate the mammonetus with the spinga, and it must be presumed that Albertus Magnus drew his information from two sources, one of which described the mammonetus (a *Cercopithicenus*) and the other the sphinx-monkey (gelada baboon). Unfortunately, neither source appears to have survived, although it is known that Albertus Magnus drew upon both Jewish and Arabic writers. Alternatively, Albertus' text may have been edited and rearranged by a copyist who inserted into his account of the mammonetus a sentence describing the sphinx. In any case it is clear from Pierius' reference to Albertus Magnus' description of the sphinx-monkey that his account has not survived intact, for no mention of black spots on the jaw was found in any extant version of Albertus.

THE ANCIENT DISTRIBUTION OF *Theropithecus*

At the present time the monospecific genus *Theropithecus* has a limited and probably relict distribution (see map of NE. Africa).

North-East Africa: Recent Distribution of *Theropithecus gelada*

Various attempts have been made to ally the form with the genera *Macaca* (e.g. Rüppell 1835: 5-8), *Papio* (e.g. Lydekker 1893: 124-5), and *Cercopithecus* (e.g. Garrod 1879: 451), but its discreteness from all of these has been amply demonstrated (e.g. Vram 1923: 169-214; Pocock 1925: 1574; James 1960: 206) and is now generally accepted (e.g. Simpson 1945: 66). Evidence of skull-form, dentition, and limb-anatomy suggests that the animal is a survivor of a group of monkeys highly adapted to life on the ground, widespread in Africa during the Pleistocene (Jolly 1966). None of the sources examined in this article suggest that the gelada baboon has had, within the historic past, a different distribution from the present. Had the gelada occurred widely in lowland Sudan it might have been expected to occur among the imported animals of early Egypt, in the same way as *Papio* baboons. It is possible that the gelada baboon's distribution extended further north-westwards, to the plain of Senaar, for the Roman explorers are said to have seen the sphinx-monkey *before* the cynocephalus on their journey south, and also to have observed it on an island in the Nile (perhaps a promontory), but there is no conclusive evidence that these animals were not captive ones, nor that the Romans were correct in their identification of the sphinx-monkey. Alternatively, it is possible that the explorers did not follow the White Nile as far south as the Sudd but turned eastwards along the Dinder or Blue Nile as far as Lake Tana, and thus were close to the present home of the gelada (see map of NE. Africa).

THE DERIVATION OF THE NAME AND RELATIONSHIP TO THE MYTHICAL SPHINX

Among the Greek-writing authors, the sphinx-monkey is called either sphinx (F) or sphingion (N); these are also used by Latin authors, sometimes Latinized into sphinga (spinga) and sphingium. Of these names, 'sphinx' alone is shared with the mythical monster, for 'sphinga' and 'sphingion' appear to have been reserved for the sphinx-monkey.

Greek and Latin dictionaries derive the name Sphinx from *sphingo*, 'I bind' or 'I squeeze'; hence, 'the Strangler'. No separate derivation is suggested for the name of the monkey which, it is implied, is secondary to and derived directly from the name of the mythical monster. It is a strange fact that the mythical monster, according to the myth, dispatched its victims either by laceration with the claws, or by pushing over a cliff, so that it is unclear why it should ever have been called 'the Strangler'. An alternative, perhaps more likely, explanation of the name of the monkey at least may be suggested, especially if the name was not originally 'sphinx' but 'sphingion'. The latter word, also derived from 'sphingo', appears to have the primary meaning of 'a bracelet or necklace' (Jones & Mackenzie 1940; Sophocles 1888). Thus the animal may simply have been dubbed 'the necklace monkey'; the simile of a pearl necklace is frequently used in modern literature to describe the gelada's pectoral ornamentation (see *Plates* 3 and 4). Similarly, the 'kebos' was called 'the garden monkey' either because it was 'as beautiful as a garden', as most literary commentators have supposed, or, more likely, because it lived in and raided gardens.

The relationship between the iconography of the Egyptian and Greek sphinxes is not the aim of the present paper and has been the subject of numerous studies (e.g. Roscher 1915; Daremberg & Saglio 1919). Moreover, if the Egyptian sphinx was derived from any natural prototype, this derivation must be placed far back in the earliest Dynastic, or even Predynastic, periods of Egyptian history, for the earliest sphinxes appear in Egyptian art of the Early Dynastic period (*c.* 2900 B.C.). At this time the sphinx was already shown as a human-faced lion and, if the imagination is allowed to wander freely, it is tempting to imagine that the gelada baboon, with its tawny, quadrupedal body, its long tufted tail and its mane, as well as its rounded, human-like face and conspicuous mammae, could have been the prototype for this representation.

There is little against assuming that the mythical Greek sphinx was in some way derived from the Egyptian sphinx. It is even possible to imagine that Philostorgius was correct in claiming that the myths associated with the Greek sphinx could have been derived from the riotous career of a gelada baboon which had escaped from captivity. Some of the earliest legends of the Theban sphinx slain by Oedipus mention only that the monster came from Aethiopia, took refuge on Mount Phix, and made forays into the countryside. None of these early attributes of the mythical Greek sphinx are irreconcilable with the evidence derived from the habitat and behaviour of the gelada baboon and it is tempting to speculate, as did also Hesiod, that there may well have been some connection between the Greek name 'sphinx' for the monster, the name of the gelada baboon, 'sphingion', and the name 'Phix' for the mountain on which it is supposed to have taken refuge.

NOTE

Since this article was finished Dr and Mrs Desmond Morris have drawn attention (*Apes and Man*. 1966. London) to the similarity between the spots on the breast of the sphinx illustrated by Topsel (*Plate 1* above) and the pectoral ornamentation of the gelada baboon.

ACKNOWLEDGEMENTS

The authors gratefully acknowledge the assistance of the librarians of University College London, the Warburg Institute, and the Zoological Society of London in finding difficult references. They are indebted to Miss A. Meyer and especially to Dr A. Rosenfeld for looking up many of the remote sources, to Mr C. Haycraft, Mr S. Pembroke, and Dr N. Yalouris for assistance in the translations of the Greek and Latin texts, to Dr L. H. Matthews, Mr M. Wilson, and the Zoological Society of London for permission to reproduce *Plates 3* and *4*, and to Dr J. Crook for *Plate 5*.

REFERENCES

ALDROVANDUS, U. 1645. *De Quadrupeditus digitatis viviparis*. Bonn.

BARGAGLI, M. S. 1625. *I Ieroglifici overo commentaris della occulte significationi de gl'egittii* . . . Venice.

BIDEZ, J. (ed.) 1913. *Philostorgius, Kirchengeschichte*. Leipzig.

BOSTOCK, J. & RILEY, H. T. (eds.) 1855-7. *The Natural History of Pliny*. London.

CAMERARIUS, P. 1602. *Operae horarum subcisivarum, sive meditationes historicae, auctiores, quam antea edita*. Frankfort.

CARY, M. & WARMINGTON, E. H. 1929. *The Ancient Explorers*. London.

DANDELOT, P. 1959. Note sur la classification des Cercopitheques du groupe *aethiops*. *Mammalia*, 23.

DAREMBERG, C. & SAGLIO, E. 1919. *Dictionnaire des antiquités grèques et romaines*. Paris.

FALCONER, W. (ed.) 1903-12. *The Geography of Strabo*. London.

FRICK, C. (ed.) 1880. *Pomponius Mela, De Situ Orbis*. Leipzig.

GARROD, A. H. 1879. Note on the Anatomy of Gelada ruepelli. *Proc. Zool. Soc. London.*

GESNER, K. 1551. *Historiae Animalium. De Quadrupedibus Viviparis.* Vol. I. Frankfort.

GODLEY, A. D. (ed.) 1924. *Herodotus.* London: Heinemann.

GULLINI, E. 1956. *I Mosaici di Palestrina.* Rome. *Archaeologica classica,* supplementary volume 1.

JAMES, W. W. 1960. *The Jaws and Teeth of Primates.* London: Pitman.

JOLLY, C. J. 1966. The Evolution of the Baboons (thesis submitted for a Ph.D., London University).

JONES, H. L. (ed.) 1930. *The Geography of Strabo.* Bk. VII. London: Heinemann.

JONES, H. STUART & MACKENZIE, R. 1940. *A Greek-English Lexicon* (Liddell and Scott). London: Oxford University Press.

KAIBEL, G. & LEBEGVE, A. (eds.) 1890. *Inscriptiones Graecae,* Vol. 14. Berlin.

KELLER, O. 1887. *Thiere des classischen Alterthums in culturgeshicht-licher Beziehung.* Innsbruck.

LEWIS, C. T. & SHORT, C. 1951. *A Latin Dictionary.* Oxford: Clarendon Press.

LINNAEUS, C. 1766. *Systema Naturae.* 12th Edit. Stockholm.

LYDEKKER, R. 1893. *The Royal Natural History.* London.

MACDERMOTT, W. C. 1938. *The Ape in Antiquity.* Baltimore: Johns Hopkins Press.

MATTHEWS, L. H. 1956. The Sexual Skin of the Gelada Baboon. *Trans. Zool. Soc. Lond.,* 28 (7).

MOLLE, J. 1621. *The Walking Librarie, or Meditations and observations historical, natural, political, and poetical.* London.

MOMMSEN, T. (ed.) 1864. *Solinus, Collectionae rerum memorabilium.* Berlin.

MÜLLER, K. (ed.) 1882. *Geographi Graeci minores.* Paris.

OLDFATHER, E. H. (ed.) 1935. *Diodorus of Sicily,* II. London: Heinemann.

PACK, R. A. (ed.) 1963. *Artemidorus Daldianus, Onirocriticon.* Bk. V. Leipzig: Teubner.

PAGE, T. E. (ed.) 1930. *Strabo. Geographies.* London.

PIERIUS, I. V. 1566. *Hieroglyphia, sive de sacris aegyptiorum.* Basle.

POCOCK, R. I. 1925. External Characteristics of the Catarrhine Monkeys and Apes. *Proc. Zool. Soc.,* 2.

RACKHAM, H. (ed.) 1940. *Pliny, Natural History III.* Bk. VIII-IX. London.

The Riddle of the Sphinx-monkey

ROSCHER, W. H. 1909-15. *Ausführliches Lexikon der griechischen und römischen Mythologie. IV.* Leipzig.

RÜPPELL, E. 1835. *Neue Wirbeltiere zu der Fauna von Abyssinien gehörig.* Frankfurt.

SCHMIDT, E. 1929. *Studien zum barberinischen Mosaik in Palestrina.* Zur Kunstgeschichte des Auslandes, Vol. 127. Strassburg.

SCHOLFIELD, A. F. (ed.) 1959. *Aelian. On the characteristics of animals.* Loeb Classical Library. London: Heinemann; Cambridge, Mass.: Harvard University Press.

SIMPSON, G. 1945. The Principles of Classification and a Classification of Mammals. *Bull. Amer. Mus.*, 85.

SOPHOCLES, E. A. 1888. *Greek Lexicon of the Roman and Byzantine Periods.* London.

STADLER, H. (ed.) 1920. *Albertus Magnus. De Animalibus.* Münster.

STARCK, D. & FRICK, H. 1958. Beobachtungen an äthiopischen Primaten. *Zool. Jahrb. Jena.*, 86.

TAPPEN, N. C. 1960. Problems of Distribution and Adaptation of the African Monkeys. *Current Anthropology,* 1 (2).

THOMPSON, D. W. (ed.) 1910. *Works of Aristotle, IV. Historia Animalium.* London: Oxford University Press.

TOPSEL, E. 1607. *Historie of the Foure-footed Beests.* London.

TYSON, E. 1699. *A Philological essay concerning the Pygmies, the Cynocephali, the Satyrs and Sphinges of the Ancients.* London.

VRAM, U. G. 1923. Sul genere Theropythecus. *Arch. Zool. Napoli.*, 10.

Don R. Brothwell

Africa's Contribution to Palaeopathology

From the Past to the Future

It is by a somewhat roundabout logic that one may consider this a suitable topic to include in a book of essays dedicated to Professor Daryll Forde. In his younger days he was associated at University College with the late Sir Grafton Elliot Smith who, although an outstanding anatomist, may well be remembered by future generations more for his contribution to palaeopathology than his other research interests. It is in view of this, and the fact that ancient diseases are once more arousing much interest and human remains from Africa are again of crucial importance in such studies, that I have decided to write about African palaeopathology.[1] It is not, however, my intention to attempt an exhaustive review of the extent or variety of disease evidence in early African populations, but rather to comment more generally on the contributions of African material to this study, and their place in present and even future studies.

For the most part, our knowledge of disease in earlier African populations rests mainly on Egyptian and Nubian mummy and skeletal remains, but gradually more data are becoming available for different parts of Africa. Late Stone Age remains from other regions, particularly South and East African countries, are gradually on the increase.[2] Much of this material has still to be studied in detail for evidence of disease. Similarly, North African late Palaeolithic, Mesolithic, and Neolithic remains (Briggs 1955) are now numerous enough to warrant more exhaustive study for evidence of disease than they have so far received, and indeed the palaeopathology of the Taforalt people has already received attention (Dastugue 1962; Poitrat-Targowla 1962).

THE PAST

Observations on the diseases of past African populations would appear to have been initiated by M. Fouquet (1897); his 'Observations pathologiques' was probably the first substantial study of this nature. Human remains were, of course, being studied prior to this – one may recall Pettigrew's (1834) classic *History of Egyptian Mummies* – but comments on disease were minimal.

Such early work varied considerably in the standard and precision of description and in the amount of data presented. Right from the beginning one or two diseases were destined to be controversial, particularly syphilis. De Morgan (1897) claimed evidence for this disease in early Egyptian remains, and a few years later Lortet and Gaillard (1903-9) described the skull of a young adult female showing vault osteomyelitis, which they considered to be evidence for the disease. However, a little later, after extensive studies of early Egyptian and Nubian remains had been made, Elliot Smith, Wood Jones, and others were to oppose strongly the view that it existed in earlier African populations (Elliot Smith and Dawson 1924).

Other diagnoses came under criticism: for example, the XVIIIth Dynasty skull, considered by Seligman (1912) to be from a cretin, turned out to be that of an achondroplastic dwarf (Keith 1913).

Human remains discovered prior to the beginning of the present century also came under the attention of these early investigators. Thus, the now famous mummy (*Figure 1*) of a priest of Ammon (XXIst Dynasty), which was discovered in 1891, was eventually found on examination to show severe spinal curvature and a large psoas abscess (Elliot Smith & Ruffer 1910). This is perhaps still the only positive case of early African tuberculosis, although there are now quite a number of vertebral specimens known which strongly suggest the presence of the disease even during Predynastic times (Morse, Brothwell, and Ucko 1964).

Strangely, although some techniques of medical biology were called upon to aid in these early palaeopathological investigations, others were not. Histological and biochemical studies were undertaken in some instances. In 1909, Professor Shattock displayed microscopic preparations from the mummy of King Merneptah before the Pathological Section of the Royal Society of Medicine in London. He states that sections of the aorta 'showed the picture of typical senile calcification of the aorta,

FIGURE 1 Lateral and frontal views of part of the mummy of a priest of Ammon. Spinal curvature and psoas abscess are indicated by arrows. *Drawings by Rosemary Powers*

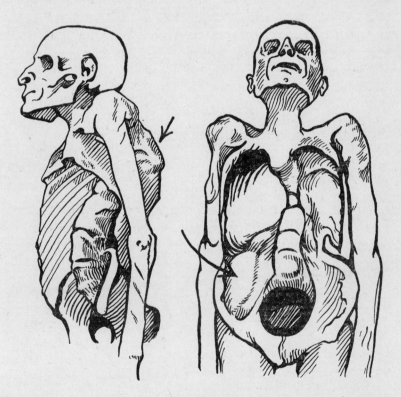

the bony, parallel, elastic lamellae being perfectly preserved, and the interlamellar material thickly strewn with calcium-phosphate'. Further evidence of arterial disease quickly followed (Ruffer 1911), and recent work has confirmed and enlarged on these first studies (Sandison 1962, 1963).

In the search for evidence of early neoplasms, Africa has yielded important contributions. Although tumours – if they leave their mark at all on bone – usually produce well-defined bone growth or areas or erosion, exact diagnosis is by no means an easy matter. By far the earliest possible example of a neoplasm is that in the chin region of the fossil Kanam jaw, considered by Lawrence (1935) to be a 'sub-periosteal ossifying sarcoma'. Although this has been generally accepted, the diagnosis has not gone unchallenged, and there is still some feeling that the extra bone in the symphyseal region may be the result of a long-standing osteitis. Two African cases, originally considered to be osteosarcomas, have also been queried. Ruffer (1914) described a pelvis from the catacombs of Kom el Shougafa in Alexandria which showed enlargement of parts of the ilium and ischium. The nature of the extra bone is, however, by no means typical of an osteosarcoma. Similarly, Elliot Smith and Dawson (1924) mention and illustrate a Vth Dynasty femur showing a large irregular bony mass extending from the distal half of the shaft. Again, it has been attributed to an osteosarcoma, but recently the more likely diagnosis of an osteochondroma has been provided as an alternative (Rowling 1961).

A fairly certain instance of a malignant neoplasm is that noted by Derry (1909) in a pre-Christian (X-group) Nubian. As he says: 'Some erosive process, beginning probably in the man's nose, had completely destroyed the base of the skull, from the cribiform plate of the ethmoid in front to the basi-occipital behind' (41). Fortunately, this specimen (*Plate I*) survived the destructive bombing of the Royal College of Surgeons Museum in London, and now forms part of the palaeopathology collection of the British Museum (Natural History). Although recently re-examined by myself and others, the original diagnosis of a malignancy still obtains.

As I have already stated, it is not my intention to review in breadth the variety of diseases described in earlier African populations. To do so would mean describing such varying evidences as Bilharzia eggs in a XXIst Dynasty mummy, analytic confirmation of uric acid in suspected gouty concretions, and a range of congenital anomalies from the unimportant sacral spina bifida to cleft palate and hydrocephaly. From a single

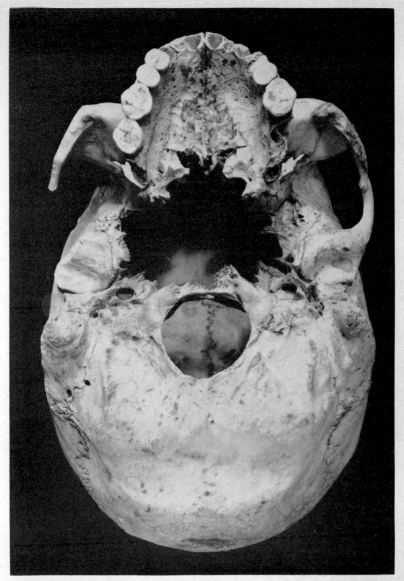

1 Basal view of an early Nubian skull, showing massive bone destruction resulting from a malignant neoplasm. Changes at the bone margin show clearly that the process was certainly *pre-mortem*. British Museum (Natural History)

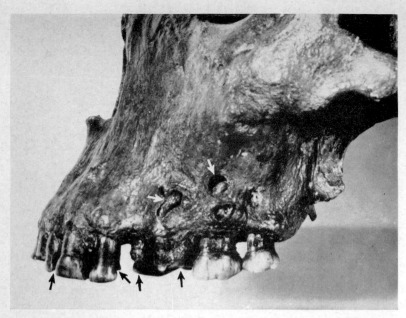

11a Lateral aspect of part of the upper dental arch of the Upper Pleistocene Rhodesian skull. Caries and apical abscesses (arrowed) can be
seen, as well as alveolar recession

11b Part of the jaw of *Telanthropus capensis*, showing a caries cavity on
the mesial surface of the lower right second molar. Photograph by
courtesy of Dr A. J. Clement

possible instance of smallpox one may range through the spectrum of disease to arthritis, described as '*par excellence* the bone disease of the ancient Egyptian and Nubian' (Elliot Smith & Dawson 1924: 159). It is sufficient if I have shown that, from the beginnings of palaeopathological studies, over seven decades ago, human remains from Africa have figured prominently, though not without controversy.

THE PRESENT

During the 1930s, contributions to palaeopathology declined. Judging from the number of publications in this subject during the past five or six years, there is every reason to believe that the study of ancient disease is once again commanding much attention, perhaps even more than in the first three decades of this century.

To some extent, present work is simply adding to previous findings or confirming them; in other ways, new aspects of the study of ancient disease are being explored.

One important difference between earlier and present work is that the statistical treatment of common disease data promises to be more satisfactory. For example, in the case of earlier studies of oral disease – and especially dental caries – earlier studies by Ruffer (1920) and others presented few data of comparative value. If nothing else, however, these earlier studies did help to explode the myth that oral disease was a phenomenon of civilization. The presence of caries (*Plate IIb*) and enamel hypoplasia in australopithecine teeth (Robinson 1952), and caries, tooth-loss, abscesses, pulp exposure, and periodontal infection in Upper Pleistocene (*Plate IIa*) and later prehistoric peoples (Brothwell 1959, 1963) further emphasizes the importance of considering oral health in studies on earlier populations. Moreover, contrary to the statements of some earlier writers, dental decay was not 'exceedingly rare', but affected 7.7 per cent of the teeth of Mesolithic people (Brothwell 1963) and 2.3 per cent of a large sample of Predynastic Egyptian teeth (Brothwell, Wood Robinson, & Carr: unpublished). Bone changes resulting from arthritic processes are similarly being considered with far more precision now, and the work of Stewart (1958) in the United States, Inglemark and colleagues (1959) in

Denmark, and Bourke (1967) in England, shows the variety of data which may be obtained from the careful study of such deformities.

In the field of histological investigations, work has been revived, especially through the efforts of A. T. Sandison of the University of Glasgow. But not all such recent inquiries have been fruitful, and an examination of a mummified hand and foot of a Coptic leper (specimens now in the B.M.N.H. collection) failed to demonstrate the relevant parasite evidence.

Although early human remains were X-rayed soon after the discovery of the technique by Roentgen, only two previous attempts have been made to X-ray series of bodies. (Moodie published his monograph in 1931; the other is an unpublished series of X-rays taken in 1921 and now in the University of California, Lowie Museum of Anthropology.) Recently, Peter K. Gray has started a long-term X-ray study of Egyptian mummies, and has been able to demonstrate pathology in hitherto unstudied bodies. He has also been able to warn against too hasty X-ray diagnosis, and to show that what was previously considered to be alkaptonuric arthritis (calcifications of the intervertebral discs) is in fact an artifact of mummification (Gray 1967).

Micro-radiographic methods are also in an exploratory phase as regards the study of early Nubian series, and members of the University of Utah, at Salt Lake City, are at present studying variations in long bone medulla and cortex by this means. Medical-biological studies have recognized for many years that radiography is an extremely important tool – and indeed X-rays may be critical for diagnosis. It is therefore satisfying that, at long last, it is becoming an essential part of any palaeopathological investigation. In this regard, laboratories undertaking studies of earlier populations should not be seriously deterred by cost, since small X-ray units are not prohibitively expensive and occasionally it is possible to obtain second-hand units in good working order.

Finally, as regards the present, studies on the evolution and ecology of living human parasites, and their vectors, have offered a further road to the consideration of diseases and their significance in past populations. In particular, Lambrecht (1964) has presented convincingly the possible impact of trypanosomiasis on prehistoric African hominid groups. Part of his summary expresses the position well:

'Trypanosomes, two species of which cause African sleeping sickness today, are blood parasites of great antiquity. Their presence in Africa at the time of the first stages of human evolution may have been of great consequence, at first acting as a discriminating agent between resistant and non-resistant types of hominids, and later also in shaping migration routes and settlement patterns. As a possible clue as to why man arose in Africa, the author postulates that trypanosomes may have precluded the development of certain ground-dwelling faunas, allowing certain more resistant primates to fill the empty ecological niches. Some of these primates, thus becoming ground-dwellers, became the precursors of the hominid branch.'

In the same way, Lambrecht usefully considered later human populations, with differences in habitat and economy, and the differential pressure which a disease such as trypanosomiasis might have placed upon them. What Lambrecht did for trypanosomiasis, Bruce-Chwatt (1965) similarly undertook for malaria, and, although these palaeo-epidemiological reconstructions are extremely tentative, they are nevertheless valuable in providing some further perspective to the relationship between earlier populations and disease.

THE FUTURE

I should like to predict that, whereas present work on the spectrum of disease in earlier peoples can be distinguished from past studies by greater caution in diagnosis and more attention to the statistical treatment of some data (including life-expectancy variations), the next few decades may well be remembered as a period of animal observation and even experimentation, and the more determined application of findings on living man to the study of the dead. Finally, it will be, indeed it *must* be, a period of detailed collection of specimens of modern bone pathology. Let me expand on these remarks a little, beginning with my last statement.

One myth, belief in which I shared with others, at least during early acquaintance with palaeopathology, was that the medical museum would be able to produce specimens of bone pathology relevant to a particular inquiry concerning ancient disease. This belief was dispelled when investigating a possible case of mongolism in a Saxon population. Only after a considerable search did I find two modern comparative specimens in Edinburgh. Since then, I have had no better success in considering leprosy, yaws, syphilis, and various other diseases affecting bone; and, even when museum specimens are found, there is often *no detailed catalogue of information available* (and rarely the clinical data desired). The situation in medical museums is unlikely to improve, since modern clinical diagnosis does not demand a knowledge of dry bone pathology. For this reason, palaeopathology must take on the responsibility of collecting specimens of recent bone pathology for comparative use.

Africa, a continent of marked contrasts still as regards regional patterns of disease, nutritional status of different communities, and even inherited anaemias, represents an important collecting centre. Take for example the cranial changes generally known as osteoporosis symmetrica (seen as an extensive pitting of the external surface of the outer table of the vault, often with marked thickening in this region of the skull). It has been discussed by various workers, and suggestions as to cause include thalassaemia, sickle-cell anaemia, and vitamin deficiency. The abnormality, considered in detail recently by Angel (1964), occurs in the Mediterranean area, but can also be found in other African and European material, as well as in the New World. A final solution to this particular abnormality surely rests upon a careful study of such cranial changes in the living and of well-recorded autopsy material. Africa would be an ideal centre for such work.

Because of their evolutionary closeness to Man, non-human primates clearly deserve special consideration. The detail of attention which has been given, for instance, to yellow fever in species of Galago (Haddow and Ellice 1964), and aspects of infection with *Trypanosoma rhodesiense* in monkeys (Woodruff 1959), could similarly be concerned with bone pathology. Recently, Nathan and Haas (1966) have shown that cribra orbitalia, changes to the frontal zone of the orbital interior, can occur in primates other than Man. This offers a new opportunity to study the aetiology of this puzzling condition.

Oral health in non-human primates is another subject that is likely to provide a variety of information pertinent to the study of earlier human populations. Take for instance the baboon, an animal increasingly well known by field and laboratory studies. Like both early and modern primitive communities, baboons may display severe dental attrition, chronic apical infection, periodontal disease, tooth fracturing, and tooth decay. To what extent have similar oral troubles (especially in combination) affected the general 'fitness' of earlier and recent primitive human populations? Direct assessment of these oral conditions in the field is becoming increasingly difficult with the changed economies and ways of life of most primitive peoples, so that the baboon – particularly in his natural habitat – could well provide a suitable 'alternative' for study. There is certainly some field evidence on baboons (Bramblett, personal communication) to suggest that oral ill health in this animal may have effects on its survival similar to those in Man.

I do not suggest that studying animal diseases and extrapolating to Man is an easy matter, but it is certainly a worthwhile and seemingly neglected one and, as I have said, Africa will have its part to play in this field as in the others I have outlined.

NOTES

1. I am using the term broadly, and to include 'palaeo-epidemiology'.
2. For instance the skeletons from Bambandyanalo, reported on by Galloway (1959), and the Gwisho material described by Gabel (1965).

REFERENCES

ANGEL, L. J. 1964. Osteoporosis: Thalassemia? *Amer. J. Phys. Anthropol.*, **22**: 369-74.

BOURKE, J. B. 1967. A Review of the Palaeopathology of the Arthritic Diseases. In D. R. Brothwell and A. T. Sandison, (eds.), *Diseases in Antiquity*. Springfield: Thomas, pp. 352-70.

BRIGGS, L. C. 1955. The Stone Age Races of Northwest Africa. *Bull. Amer. Sch. Prehist. Res.*, **18**: 1-98.

BRUCE-CHWATT, L. J. 1965. Palaeogenesis and Palaeo-epidemiology of Primate Malaria. *Bull. Wld. Hlth. Org.*, **32**: 363-89.

BROTHWELL, D. R. 1959. Teeth in Earlier Human Populations. *Proc. Nutrit. Soc.*, **18**: 59-65.

— 1963. The Macroscopic Dental Pathology of some Earlier Human Populations. In D. R. Brothwell (ed.), *Dental Anthropology.* London: Pergamon, pp. 271-88.

— 1967. The Evidence for Neoplasms. In D. R. Brothwell and A. T. Sandison (eds.), *Diseases in Antiquity.* Springfield: Thomas, pp. 320-45.

DASTUGUE, J. 1962. Pathologie des Hommes de Taforalt (pp. 133-58). In D. Ferembach, *La Necropole Epipaléolithique de Taforalt (Maroc Oriental). Etude des Squelettes Humains.* Centre National de la Recherche Scientifique, Paris.

DE MORGAN, J. 1897. *Recherches sur les Origines de l'Egypte,* 2 vols. Paris.

DERRY, D. E. 1909. Anatomical Report. *Archaeol. Survey of Nubia,* Cairo, *Bull.*, **3**, 29-52.

ELLIOT SMITH, G. & DAWSON, W. R. 1924. *Egyptian Mummies.* London: Allen and Unwin.

— & RUFFER, M. A. 1910. Pott'sche Krankheit an einer ägyptischen Mumie aus der Zeit der 21 Dynastie (um 1000v. Chr.). *Zur Histo. Biol. Krankheitsereger,* **3**: 9-16. Giessen.

FOUQUET, M. 1897. Observations pathologiques, (pp. 350-73). In J. De Morgan, *Recherches sur les Origines de l'Egypte,* 2 vols. Paris.

GABEL, C. 1965. *Stone Age Hunters of the Kafue. The Gwisho A Site.* Boston University Press.

GALLOWAY, A. 1959. *The Skeletal Remains of Bambandyanalo.* Johannesburg: Witwatersrand University Press.

GRAY, P. H. K. 1967. Calcinosis intervertebralis, with special reference to Similar Changes found in Mummies of Ancient Egyptians. In D. R. Brothwell and A. T. Sandison (eds.), *Diseases in Antiquity.* Springfield: Thomas, pp. 20-30.

HADDOW, A. J. & ELLICE, J. M. 1964. Studies on Bush-babies (Galago Spp.) with special reference to the Epidemiology of Yellow Fever. *Trans. Roy. Soc. Trop. Med. Hyg.*, **58**: 521-38.

INGLEMARK, B. E., MØLLER-CHRISTENSEN V. & BRINCH, O. 1959. Spinal Joint Changes and Dental Infections. *Acta Anatomica,* **38**, Suppl. 36.

KEITH, A. 1913. Abnormal Crania – Achondroplastic and Acrocephalic. *J. Anat. Lond.*, **47**: 189-206.

LAMBRECHT, F. L. 1964. Aspects of Evolution and Ecology of Tsetse Flies and Trypanosomiasis in Prehistoric African Environment. *J. Afr. Hist.*, **5**: 1-24.

Africa's Contribution to Palaeopathology

LAWRENCE, J. E. P. 1935. Appendix A (p. 139). In L. S. B. Leakey, *Stone Age Races of Kenya*. London: Oxford University Press.

LORTET, L. C. & GAILLARD, C. 1903-9. La Faune momifiée de l'ancienne Egypte. *Arch. d. Mus. d'Hist. Nat. de Lyon*, 9: 29.

MOODIE, R. L. 1931. Roentgenological Studies of Egyptian and Peruvian Mummies. *Mem. Field Mus. Nat. Hist.*, Chicago, 3: 66 pp.

MORSE, D., BROTHWELL, D. R. & UCKO, P. 1964. Tuberculosis in Ancient Egypt. *Amer. Rev. Resp. Dis.*, 90: 524-41.

NATHAN, H. & HAAS, N. 1966. On the Presence of Cribra Orbitalia in Apes and Monkeys. *Amer. J. Phys. Anthropol.*, 24: 351-9.

PETTIGREW, T. 1834. *History of Egyptian Mummies*. London: Allen and Unwin.

POITRAT-TARGOWLA, M.-J. 1962. Pathologie dentaire et maxillaire de l'homme de Taforalt (pp. 159-71). In D. Ferembach, *La Necropole Epipaléolithique de Taforalt (Maroc Oriental)*. *Etudes des Squelettes Humains*. Centre National de la Recherche Scientifique, Paris.

ROBINSON, J. T. 1952. Some Hominid Features of the Ape-man Dentition. *J. dent. Assoc. S. Afr.*, 7: 102-13.

ROWLING, J. T. 1961. Pathological Changes in Mummies. *Proc. Roy. Soc. Med.*, 54: 409.

RUFFER, M. A. 1911. On Arterial Lesions found in Egyptian Mummies. *J. Path. Bact.*, 15: 453-62.

— 1914. Note on a Tumour of the Pelvis dating from Roman Times (250 A.D.) and found in Egypt. *J. Path. Bact.*, 18: 480-4.

— 1920. Study of Abnormalities and Pathology of Ancient Egyptian Teeth. *Amer. J. phys. Anthropol.*, 3: 355-82.

SANDISON, A. T. 1962. Degenerative Vascular Disease in the Egyptian Mummy. *Med. Hist.*, 6: 77-81.

— 1963. The Study of Mummified and Dried Human Tissues, pp. 413-25. In D. Brothwell and E. Higgs (eds.), *Science in Archaeology*. London: Thames and Hudson.

SCHULTZ, A. H. 1956. The Occurrence and Frequency of Pathological and Teratological Conditions and of Twinning among Non-human Primates. *Primatologia*, 1: 965-1014.

SELIGMAN, C. G. 1912. A Cretinous Skull of the Eighteenth Dynasty, *Man*, 12: 17-18.

SHATTOCK, S. G. 1909. Microscopic Sections of the Aorta of King Merneptheh. *Lancet*, 1: 319.

347

STEWART, T. D. 1958. The Rate of Development of Vertebral Osteo-arthritis in American Whites and its Significance in Skeletal Age Identification. *The Leech*, **28**: 144–51.

WOODRUFF, A. W. 1959. Serum Protein Changes induced by Infection and Treatment of Infection with *Trypanosoma Rhodesiense* in Monkeys. *Trans. Roy. Soc. Trop. Med. Hyg.*, **53**: 327–35.

Bibliography of Professor Daryll Forde

compiled by Katharine Attwood

1925 Values in Human Geography. *The Geographical Teacher* **13**.

1926 *Ancient Mariners.* London: Howe Press.
Megaliths and Metals in Brittany. *Man* **26**, art. 87.

1927 Report on the Excavation of a Bronze Age Tumulus at Dunstable, Bedfordshire. *Man* **27**, art. 12.
The Megalithic Monuments of Southern Finistère. *Antiquities Journal* **7**.

1929 The Megalithic Culture Sequence in Iberia. *Annals of Archaeology and Anthropology* **16**, Nos. 3-4.
The Megalithic Gallery in Brittany. *Man* **29**, art. 80.

1930 On the Use of Greenstone (Jadeite, Callais, etc.) in the Megalithic Culture of Brittany. *Journal of the Royal Anthropological Institute* **60**.
A Creation Myth from Acoma. *Folklore* **41**.
The Early Cultures of Atlantic Europe. *American Anthropologist* **32**: 19-100

1931 *Ethnography of the Yuma Indians.* Berkeley: University of California Publications in American Archaeology and Ethnology. (Bound in **28**, No. 4)
Hopi Agriculture and Land Ownership. *Journal of the Royal Anthropological Institute* **61**.

1931-2 Excavations in two Iron Age Forts at Earn's Heugh, near Coldingham. *Proceedings of the Society of Antiquities of Scotland* **66** (VI, 6th S.)

1932 Ancient Cities of the Indus. *Geography* **17** (3).

1933 The Habitat and Economy of the North Arabian Badawin. *Geography* **18**.

1934 *Habitat, Economy and Society.* London: Methuen. (Paperback edition 1963, University Paperbacks.)

1934-8 Interim Reports on Excavations at Pen Dinas, Cardiganshire. *Bulletin of the Board of Celtic Studies* **7, 8**, and **9**; and *Antiquaries Journal* **15** and **18**.

1936 Land and Labour on the Cross River: The Economic Organization of a Yakö Village, Southern Nigeria. *Man* **36**, art. 123.

1937   Social Change in a West African Village Community. *Man* 37, 8.
Land and Labour in a Cross River Village, Southern Nigeria. *Geographical Journal* 90. (Reprinted in D. Forde, *Yakö Studies*, 1964.)

1938   Dysgwylfa Fawr Barrow, Cardiganshire – a Food Vessel and Dugout Trunk Cremation Burial. *Bulletin of Board of Celtic Studies* 9, 2.
Fission and Accretion in the Patrilineal Clans of a Semi-Bantu Community in Southern Nigeria. *Journal of the Royal Anthropological Institute* 68. (Reprinted in D. Forde, *Yakö Studies*, 1964).

1939   Kinship in Umor. *American Anthropologist* 41 (4).
Africa Surveyed. *Geographical Journal* 93 (5).
Government in Umor. *Africa* 12 (2).
Human Geography, History and Sociology. *Scottish Geographical Magazine* 55.

1941   *Marriage and the Family among the Yakö in South-Eastern Nigeria.* London School of Economics Monographs on Social Anthropology, No. 5. (Second edition: London: Lund Humphries for the International African Institute, 1951.)

1944   Education and the Community in Africa. *Nature* 153.

1945   Social Development in Africa and the Work of the International African Institute. *Journal of the Royal Society of Arts* 93, No. 4682.

1946   (with R. Scott), *The Native Economies of Nigeria.* London: Faber.

1947   The Anthropological Approach in Social Science, (Presidential Address, Section H. British Association). *Advancement of Science* 4, 15.

1948   The Integration of Anthropological Studies. (Presidential Address to the Royal Anthropological Institute, 1948). *Journal of the Royal Anthropological Institute* 78.

1949   Integrative Aspects of Yakö First Fruits Ritual. (Presidential Address to the Royal Anthropological Institute, 1949). *Journal of the Royal Anthropological Institute* 79. (Reprinted in D. Forde, *Yakö Studies*, 1964).

1950   *The Ibo- and Ibibio-speaking Peoples of South-Eastern Nigeria.* Ethnographic Survey of Africa, Western Africa, Part III. London: International African Institute.
Anthropology, Science and History. *Man* 50, art. 254.

(ed. jointly with A. Radcliffe-Brown), *African Systems of Kinship and Marriage*. London: Oxford University Press for the International African Institute.
Double Descent among the Yakö. In A. R. Radcliffe-Brown and D. Forde (eds.), *African Systems of Kinship and Marriage*.
Ward Organisation among the Yakö. *Africa* 20. (Reprinted in D. Forde, *Yakö Studies*, 1964).

1951 *The Yoruba-speaking Peoples of South-Western Nigeria*. Ethnographic Survey of Africa. Western Africa, Part IV. London: International African Institute.

1953 Applied Anthropology in Government: British Africa. In A. Kroeber (ed.), *Anthropology Today*. Chicago: University of Chicago Press.
The Cultural Map of West Africa. *Transactions of the New York Academy of Science*. Ser. 2, **15**.
The Conditions of Social Development in West Africa: Retrospect and Prospect. *Civilisations* **3** (4).
Anthropology in Great Britain and Eire. In Thomas and Pikelis (eds.), *International Directory of Anthropology*.

1954 Foraging, Hunting and Fishing. In C. Singer, E. J. Holmyard and A. R. Hall (eds.), *A History of Technology*, vol. I, Ch. viii, Part 2.
(ed. with Introduction), *African Worlds*. London: Oxford University Press for the International African Institute.

1955 The Human Record. *Diogenes*, No. 9. (Also in translation in French and Spanish editions).
The Nupe. In D. Forde, Paula Brown, R. Armstrong (eds.), *Peoples of the Niger-Benue Confluence*. Ethnographic Survey of Africa, Western Africa, Part X.
The Social Impact of Industrialisation and Urban Conditions in Africa South of the Sahara. *International Social Science Bulletin*. UNESCO, Social Factors in Personality, **7** (1).

1956 Anthropology. *Encyclopaedia Britannica*, U.S.A. 1956 printing. (U.K. 1957 printing.)
Social Aspects of Urbanisation and Industrialisation in Africa: A General Review. In D. Forde (ed.), *Social Implications of Industrialisation and Urbanisation in Africa South of the Sahara*. Paris: UNESCO.
(ed. and Introduction), *Efik Traders of Old Calabar*. Oxford Univesity Press for the International African Institute.
(ed. and contributor), *Select Annotated Bibliography of Tropical Africa* (in 7 sections: Geography, Ethnography and

Sociology, Administration and Government, Economics, Education, Missions, Health). London: International African Institute.

(with M. Douglas), Primitive Economics. In Harry L. Shapiro (ed.), *Man, Culture and Society*, New York: Oxford University Press, ch. XV.

Sozial-und Kulturanthropologie: Anthropologie und Soziologie. *Kölner Zeitschrift für Soziologie und Sozialpsychologie*. 8, Heft 2.

1958 The Context of Belief: A Consideration of Fetishism among the Yakö. (Frazer Lecture: 1957). Liverpool University Press. (Reprinted in D. Forde, *Yakö Studies*, 1964.)

Spirits, Witches, and Sorcerers in the Supernatural Economy of the Yakö. *Journal of the Royal Anthropological Institute* 88, Part II. (Reprinted in D. Forde, *Yakö Studies*, 1964.)

1961 The Governmental Roles of Associations among the Yakö. *Africa* 31, 4. (Reprinted in D. Forde, *Yakö Studies*, 1964.)

1962 Death and Succession: An Analysis of Yakö Mortuary Ceremonial. (Simon Lecture, Manchester University, 1960). In Max Gluckman (ed.), *Essays on the Ritual of Social Relations*. Manchester: Manchester University Press.

1963 On Some Further Unconsidered Aspects of Descent. *Man 63*, art. 9.

Rôle des sociétés dans le cérémonial funéraire des Yakö. *Cahiers d'Etudes Africaines* 3 (3).

Une analyse sociologique des formalités matrimoniales chez les Yakö. *Cahiers d'Etudes Africaines* 3 (4).

Excavations at Pen Dinas, Aberystwyth. *Archaeologia Cambrensis* 112.

Methodology in the Study of African Urbanization: Background and Approaches. In *Urbanization in African Social Change*; Proceedings of the Inaugural Seminar held in the Centre of African Studies, University of Edinburgh, 5-7 January 1963.

Unilineal Fact or Fiction: An Analysis of the Composition of Kin Groups among the Yakö. In I. Schapera (ed.), *Studies in Kinship and Marriage, Dedicated to Brenda Z. Seligman on her 80th Birthday*. London: Royal Anthropological Institute, Occasional Paper No. 16.

1964 *Yakö Studies*. London: Oxford University Press for the International African Institute.

1965 Tropical African Studies: A Report on the Conference Organized by the International African Institute in conjunction with the University of Ibadan, 5-11 April 1964. *Africa* 35 (1).

Social Anthropology in African Studies. (Proceedings of the First Conference of African Studies Association of the United Kingdom, September, 1964). *African Affairs* Spring 1965, Special Issue.

Justice and Judgment among the Southern Ibo under Colonial Rule. In H. and L. Kuper (eds.), *African Law: Adaptation and Development*. California: University of California Press.

1967 Ed. and Introduction (with Phyllis M. Kaberry), *West African Kingdoms in the Nineteenth Century*. Oxford University Press for the International African Institute.

Anthropology and the Development of African Studies (The Tenth Lugard Memorial Lecture). *Africa* 37 (4).

1968 Die Entwicklung der Afrika-Wissenschaften. *Internationaler. Afrika* Forum 4 (2-3): 151-6. Printed in the Report on the Second International Congress of Africanists, Dakar, 11–20 December 1967.

Author Index

Subject Index